Texts in

Philosophy

Volume 4

Computing,

Philosophy

and

Cognition

Volume 1
Knowledge and Belief
Jaakko Hintikka

Volume 2
Probability and Inference: Essays in Honour of Henry E. Kyburg
Bill Harper and Greg Wheeler, eds

Volume 3
Monsters and Philosophy
Charles T. Wolfe, ed.

Volume 4
Computing, Philosophy and Cognition
Lorenzo Magnani and Riccardo Dossena, eds

Texts in Philosophy Series Editors
Vincent F. Hendricks
John Symons

vincent@ruc.dk
jsymons@utep.edu

Computing, Philosophy and Cognition

Proceedings of the European Computing and Philosophy Conference (ECAP 2004)

edited by
Lorenzo Magnani
and
Riccardo Dossena

ISBN 1-904987-24-9
Published by College Publications
Scientific Directors: Dov Gabbay, Vincent F. Hendricks and John Symons
Managing Director: Jane Spurr
Department of Computer Science
King's College London
Strand, London WC2R 2LS, UK

http://www.collegepublications.co.uk

Cover design by Richard Fraser, www.avalonarts.co.uk
Printed by Lightning Source, Milton Keynes, UK

CONTENTS

Cognitive Science, Epistemology, and Metaphysics

Internal and External Representations, Embodiment, Consciousness

Preface

This volume is a collection of papers that explore various areas of common interest between philosophy, computing, and cognition. The book illustrates the rich intrigue of this fascinating recent intellectual story. It begins by providing a new analysis of the ideas related to computer ethics, such as the role in information technology of the so-called moral mediators, the relationship between intelligent machines and warfare, and the new opportunities offered by telepresence, for example in teaching and learning. The book also ties together the concerns of epistemology and logic, showing, for example, the connections between computers, bio-robotics, and scientific research and between computational programs and scientific discovery. Important results coming from recent computational models of deduction, the dynamic nature if meaning, and the role of reasoning and learning in spatial, visual, and exemplar-based computational frameworks are also addressed.

Some stimulating papers carefully study how the interplay between computing and philosophy has also shed new light on the role of rational acceptance in the logic of belief and on the status of old philosophical topics like embodiment and consciousness, the role of information and the problem of realism in the new digital world. Finally, a considerable part of the book addresses the role of internal and external representations in scientific reasoning and creative inferences as well as the place of manipulation of objects and artifacts in human cognition. Taking these topics together this book describes an aspect of an emerging agenda which is likely to carry the interaction between philosophy, cognition, and computing forward into the twenty first century. The volume is based on the papers that were presented at the *International European Conference Computing and Philosophy*, E-CAP2004_ITALY, held at the University of Pavia, Pavia, Italy, in June 2004, chaired by Lorenzo Magnani.

The conference, and thus indirectly this book, was made possible through the generous financial support of the MIUR (Italian Ministry of the University), University of Pavia, CARIPLO (Cassa di Risparmio delle Provincie Lombarde). Their support is gratefully acknowledged. The editors express their appreciation to the members of the Scientific Committee for

their suggestions and assistance: Atocha Aliseda, Instituto de Investiga-
ciones Filosoficas Universidad, Nacional Autonoma de Mexico (UNAM),
Mexico City, Mexico; Diderik Batens, Centre for Logic and Philosophy of
Science, Universiteit Gent, Ghent, Belgium; Robert Cavalier, Department
of Philosophy, Carnegie Mellon, Pittsburgh, PA, USA; Simon Colton, Department of Computing, Imperial College London, London, UK; Roberto
Cordeschi, Department of Communication Sciences, University of Salerno,
Salerno, Italy; Chris Dobbyn, Faculty of Maths and Computing,The Open
University,Walton Hall, Milton Keynes, UK; Roy Dyckhoff, School of Com-
puter Science,University of St Andrews, North Haugh, St Andrews, Scot-
land; Luciano Floridi, Wolfson College, University of Oxford, Oxford, UK
and University of Bari, Italy; Theo Kuypers, Department of Philosophy,
University of Groningen, Groningen, The Netherlands; Nancy J. Nersessian,
College of Computing, Georgia Institute of Technology, Atlanta, GA, USA;
Claudio Pizzi, Department of Philosophy and Social Sciences, University
of Siena, Siena, Italy; Mario Stefanelli, Department of Computer Science,
University of Pavia, Italy; Susan Stuart, Humanities Advanced Technology
and Information Institute, University of Glasgow, Glasgow, UK; Guglielmo
Tamburrini, Department of Philosophy, University of Pisa, Italy; Riccardo
Viale, Fondazione Rosselli, Torino, Italy.

Special thanks to the International Association for Computing and Philosophy (IACAP), to the local organizer Elena Gandini, for her contribution in organizing the conference, and to the copy-editor Linda D'Arrigo.
The preparation of the volume would not have been possible without the
contribution of resources and facilities of the Computational Philosophy
Laboratory and of the Department of Philosophy, University of Pavia.

Other papers, dealing with philosophical, cognitive, didactic, and computational problems, deriving from the presentations given at the Conference
will be published in the book *Computing and Philosophy*, edited by L. Magnani, which will appear in the Philosophy series of Associated International
Academic Publishers, Pavia, Italy. A remaining group of selected papers
will be published in a Special Issue of the Journal *Mind and Society*: Ontology, Meaning. Belief, edited by Lorenzo Magnani.

Lorenzo Magnani, University of Pavia, Italy and Sun Yat-sen University,
Canton, P. R. China

Riccardo Dossena, University of Pavia, Italy

October, 2005

Intelligent Machines and Warfare
Historical Debates and Epistemologically Motivated Concerns

ROBERTO CORDESCHI AND GUGLIELMO TAMBURRINI

ABSTRACT. The early examples of self-directing robots attracted
the interest of both scientific and military communities. Biologists
regarded these devices as material models of animal tropisms. Engineers envisaged the possibility of turning self-directing robots into
new "intelligent" torpedoes during World War I. Starting from World
War II, more extensive interactions developed between theoretical inquiry and applied military research on the subject of adaptive and
intelligent machinery. Pioneers of Cybernetics were involved in the
development of goal-seeking warfare devices. But collaboration occasionally turned into open dissent. Founder of Cybernetics Norbert
Wiener, in the aftermath of World War II, argued against military
applications of learning machines, by drawing on epistemological ap-
praisals of machine learning techniques. This connection between
philosophy of science and techno-ethics is both strengthened and extended here. It is strengthened by an epistemological analysis of
contemporary machine learning from examples; it is extended by a
reflection on *ceteris paribus* conditions for models of adaptive behaviors.

1 Introduction

The so-called "electric dog", the ancestor of phototropic self-directing robots,
designed about 1912 by engineers John Hammond, Jr. and Benjamin Miessner, graphically illustrates the interest of both scientific and military communities for early self-directing robots. In 1918, biologist Jacques Loeb
emphasized the significance of the electric dog as a material model of animal phototropism. He argued that the actual construction of this machine
supported his own theoretical model of animal phototropism, insofar as the
machine was internally organized as prescribed by the theoretical model and
turned out to behave just like heliotropic organisms. Possible applications
of this self-directing device as an "intelligent" weapon were enthusiastically
proposed in 1915, during World War I. Section 2 reports on both motives
of interests for the electric dog.

Lorenzo Magnani and Riccardo Dossena, editors, *Computing, Philosophy, and Cognition*,
pp. 1–19 © 2005, R. Cordeschi and G. Tamburrini

In 1943, psychologist Kenneth Craik named "synthetic method" the process of testing behavioral theories through machine models. The "synthetic method", envisaged by Loeb in his reflections on heliotropic machines, has been enjoying increasing popularity in the modelling and explanation of animal and human behavior from Cybernetics up to the present time. And warfare applications flowing from particular implementations of the synthetic method have flourished too. Pioneers of Cybernetics were often involved in both synthetic modelling and military adaptations of their machine models during World War II. Kenneth Craik is a prominent case in point; Norbert Wiener went as far as claiming that World War II was "the deciding factor" for the development of Cybernetics. But Wiener argued against military applications of cybernetic machines in the aftermath of World War II, especially by drawing on epistemological reflections on machine learning techniques. In 1960, dissenting with AI pioneer Arthur Samuel, Wiener envisaged "disastrous consequences" from the action of automatic machines operating faster than human agents, or the action of learning machines abstracting their own behavioral rules from experience. Wiener tapped from his specialized knowledge to make public opinion aware of dangers connected to military applications of adaptive machines, and to undermine intelligent weaponry rhetoric. Section 3 highlights both collaborative and critical attitudes manifested by pioneers of Cybernetics towards warfare application of their system design principles.

Wiener's arguments vividly illustrate how philosophy of science bears on the implementation of precautionary principles in applied research. This connection between philosophy of science and techno-ethics is strengthened in section 4, on the basis of an epistemological analysis of machine learning from examples. One would like to have a guarantee that a robot will learn to behave as expected most of the time, without bringing about the "disastrous consequences" that Wiener contemplated in awe; but theoretical guarantees of this sort, – it is pointed out by reference to so-called supervised inductive learning, are very hard to come. Finally, Wiener's reflections on the connections between philosophy of science and techno-ethics are extended in section 5 by considering *ceteris paribus* conditions for adaptive machine behaviors.

2   From the "electric dog" to the "dog of war"

It was not unusual to read in American newspapers and popular science magazines from about 1915 the description of a machine that looked like little more than a toy but attracted much attention for its unprecedented features as an "orientation mechanism". This machine, designed in 1912 by two American experts in radio-controlled devices, John Hammond Jr.

and Benjamin Miessner, was actually built by the latter. Two years later, Miessner presented this machine in the *Purdue Engineering Review* under the name of "electric dog," by which it became popularly known.

Miessner described in some detail the behavior of the electric dog in *Radiodynamics: The Wireless Control of Torpedoes and Other Mechanisms* [Miessner, 1916]. The electric dog orientation mechanism included two selenium cells. These cells, when influenced by light, effect the control of two sensitive relays. These relays, in their turn, control two electromagnetic switches: when one cell or both are illuminated, the current is switched onto the driving motor; when one cell alone is illuminated, an electromagnet is energized and effects the turning of the rear steering wheel. In this case, the turning of the machine brings the shaded cell into light. As soon and as long as both cells are equally illuminated with sufficient intensity, the machine moves in a straight line towards the light source. By turning a switch on, which reverses the driving motor's connections, the machine can be made to back away from light. When the illumination intensity is so decreased by the increasing distance from the light source that the resistances of the cells approach their dark resistance, the sensitive relays break their respective circuits, and the machine stops.

The self-directing capacity of the electric dog attracted the attention of Jacques Loeb, described by Miessner as "the famed Rockefeller Institute biologist, who had proposed various theories explaining many kinds of tropism." The explanation of the orientation mechanism, Miessner emphasized, was "very similar to that given by Jacques Loeb, the biologist, of reasons responsible for the flight of moths into a flame". In particular, the electric dog's lenses corresponded to "the two sensitive organs of the moth" (p. 196). Miessner carefully noted that "Hammond had been much taken with the writings of Jacques Loeb" (p. 36)[1].

Loeb reprinted excerpts from Miessner's machine description in *Forced Movements, Tropisms, and Animal Conduct* [Loeb, 1918, pp. 68-69], a book documenting his extensive work on lower organism tropisms. In particular, Loeb carefully documented the ways in which the orientation of bilaterally symmetrical lower animals, like the moth, depends on light. These are in fact "*natural* heliotropic machines". Now, he claimed to have found an instance of "*artificial* heliotropic machine", as he called it, in the orientation mechanism of the electric dog. His surprise was quite justified. Automata of the earlier mechanistic tradition could not simulate the heliotropic behavior

---

[1]See [Cordeschi, 2001, chapter 1] for more details about the working of electric dog and Loeb's theory of tropisms. Arguably, the electric dog is a forerunner of Walter Grey Walter light sensitive "tortoises" and Braitenberg's "vehicles" (see [Walter, 1953; Braitenberg, 1984]).

of biological systems. These automata, based on the concept of clockwork mechanism, were incapable of exchanging information with the environment. In short, what was needed to achieve this kind of simulation was a machine endowed with sense organs, a negative-feedback control device, and motor organs. Hammond and Miessner's automaton was just such a machine, automatically adapting its behavior to the changing conditions of the external environment, and adjusting its movements by means of a negative-feedback control device (the rear steering wheel brought the machine back in the direction of light whenever it went too far off its course). Loeb's keen interest in this machine was motivated on epistemological grounds:

It seems to the writer that the actual construction of a heliotropic machine not only supports the mechanistic conceptions of the volitional and instinctive actions of animals but also the writer's theory of heliotropism, *since this theory served as the basis in the construction of the machine.* We may feel safe in stating that there is no more reason to ascribe the heliotropic reactions of lower animals to any form of sensation, e.g., of brightness or color or pleasure or curiosity, than it is to ascribe the heliotropic reactions of Mr. Hammond's machine to such sensations [Loeb, 1918, pp. 68-69].

This epistemological standpoint was to enjoy increasing popularity in the explanation of animal and human behavior up to our time. According to Loeb, a behavioral theory is supported by the theory-driven construction of a machine that behaves like the living organisms in the domain of the theory. The machine is a material model of biological systems insofar as it *embodies* the assumptions of the behavioral theory serving as a basis for its construction. Loeb regarded Hammond and Miessner's machine as a significant step in the process of eliminating idle hypotheses about purportedly fundamental differences between natural (that is, living or "chemical") machines and artificial (that is, inanimate or "inorganic") machines. In addition, the machine simulation of an organism's heliotropic behavior provided strong evidence that mentalistic language was not needed to predict and explain animal behavior. This simulation showed that the physical principles harnessing the simulating machine suffice to explain the behavior of lower animals in the domain of the biological theory. The elimination of introspective psychology ("speculative" or "metaphysical" psychology, as Loeb called it) from scientific inquiries into animal behaviur is coherent with Loeb's purely automatic (mechanical) account of animal reaction to stimuli, and his concomitant refusal to ascribe sensations to lower animals. The moth does not fly towards the flame out of "curiosity," nor is it "attracted by" or "fond of" light, as earlier animal psychologists put it. It is simply "oriented" by the action of light – just like Hammond and Miessner's machine.

Loeb's interest for Hammond and Miessner's machine was epistemologically motivated, insofar as the electric dog enables one to test the empirical adequacy of some biological theory of behaviour. Different motives of
interest for this machine soon emerged. At the time, Hammond was well-
known for his dirigible torpedoes, - actually remote control radio-directed
boats. Since 1910 he had been running a research laboratory in Gloucester,
Massachusetts, where he was perfecting several radio-controlled torpedoes.
Miessner was one of his main collaborators in the years 1911 and 1912. He
wrote a long description of these devices for *Radiodynamics*, in which he
mentioned earlier related work, in particular the so-called "teleautomata"
or "self-acting automata" built in New York between 1892 and 1897 by
Nikola Tesla, another pioneer of radio-controlled systems.

It was Miessner who explained a chief reason of interest for the orientation mechanism: Hammond's dirigible torpedo "is fitted with apparatus
similar to that of the electric dog, so that if the enemy turns their search
light on it, it will immediately be guided toward that enemy automatically"
(p. 198). In the 1915 volume of the *Electrical Experimenter* one finds an en-
thusiastic description of both Hammond's torpedo and electric dog, jointly
considered as a target-seeking automatic system, and prized for effective
military applicability. This should not come as a surprise, as Europe was
at the time engulfed in World War I.

> [...] The performance of Mr. Hammond's truly marvellous
> radio-mechanical craft [...] seems to inherit superhuman intel-
> ligence [...] It bids fair to revolutionize modern warfare meth-
> ods. The USA Government is seriously considering the purchase
> of the entire rights in this radio control scheme, as worked out
> by young Mr. Hammond and his associate scientist and engi-
> neers. It would be of inestimable value for the protection of
> harbors, [...] and it also could be directed from shore directly
> at or toward any hostile warship it is seen that a very powerful
> weapon is thus placed in the hands of our coast defense corps. It
> has been reported of the late that the Japanese Government has
> been negotiating for the exclusive rights to this invention, but
> undoubtedly the American naval authorities will be wide awake
> to the far-reaching merits and properties of such a system [...]
> Likewise, it has been proved in Mr. Miessner's experiment that
> the deadly naval torpedo or even an automatic bomb-dropping
> aeroplane can be manoeuvred in action from ship or shore by
> the [electric dog]. (*The Electrical Experimenter*, September and
> June 1915, pp. 211 and 43)

Miessner regarded the automatic orientation mechanism that he designed for the electric dog a significant advance over earlier devices, as it made Hammond's torpedo self-directing. He claimed that its self-directing capacity could be further refined on the basis of some experiments in submarine detection and defence. And prophetically concluded:

The electric dog, which now is but an uncanny scientific curiosity, may within the very near future become in truth a real "dog of war", without fear, without heart, without the human element so often susceptible to trickery, with but one purpose: to overtake and slay whatever comes within range of its senses at the will of its master [Miessner, 1916, p. 199].

3   Cybernetics and applied military research: wartime connections

Miessner's forecast was vindicated by the advent, less than thirty years later, of automatic control systems. It was another conflict, the Second World War, as Norbert Wiener pointed out, "the deciding factor" for cybernetic control systems, based on the mathematics of stochastic processes developed by Wiener himself, and the newborn technology of computing machinery [Wiener, 1961, p. 3]. This was particularly evident in anti-aircraft predictors: as Wiener pointed out, it was "the German prestige in aviation and the defensive position of England" (p. 5) which pushed many scientists towards applied research on these automatic devices. Wiener and Julian Bigelow investigated the theory of the curvilinear prediction of flight, and supervised the construction of self-controlling and computing apparatuses based on this theory (several papers Wiener and Bigelow produced on this topic were either secret or restricted). These apparatuses were designed "to usurp" (p. 6) the human functions of computing and forecasting, at least insofar as forecasting the future position of flying targets was concerned.

The epistemological implications of these wartime investigations were worked out later on, once Wiener became acquainted with Arturo Rosenblueth's work on self-regulating mechanisms in biological systems, and were presented in papers outlining scope and heuristic principles of cybernetic research programmes (see [Rosenblueth et al., 1943; Rosenblueth and Wiener, 1945].

Loeb's view of the epistemological and methodological relationship between his tropism theory and Hammond and Miessner's phototropic machine is consistent with Rosenblueth and Wiener's more general analysis of the relationship between theoretical (or formal) models and material models. The latter, in their view, may enable the carrying out of experiments under more favorable conditions than would be available in the original system. This translation presumes that there are reasonable grounds for supposing a similarity between the two situations; it thus presupposes the possession of an adequate formal model, with a structure similar to that of the two material systems. The formal model need not to be thoroughly comprehended; the material model then serves to supplement the formal one [Rosenblueth and Wiener, 1945, p. 317].

A material model taking the form of a machine may enable the carrying out of suitable tests on the theoretical or formal model, because the latter "served as the basis in the construction of the machine", as Loeb put it. This epistemological and methodological standpoint is at the core of the cybernetic programme and motivates much AI and robotics research up to present time[2].

The knowledge flow to and from machine-based investigations into adaptive biological behaviors and applied warfare research is evident in the work of British scientists from the early 1940's. The work of Cambridge psychologist Kenneth Craik is a significant case in point. His investigations on scanning mechanisms and control systems were a major source of inspiration for epistemological claims made in his book *The nature of explanation* [Craik, 1943].

The scientific activity of Craik and other pioneers of automatic computing and control got a shoot in the arm from military research projects carried out during World War II. Grey Walter's recollections graphically convey the interconnection of scientific and defence goals in the control mechanism research community in general, and in Craik's work in particular:

The first notion of constructing a free goal-seeking mechanism goes back to a wartime talk with the psychologist Kenneth Craik, whose untimely death was one of the greatest losses Cambridge has suffered in years [Craik died in 1945 at 31]. When he was engaged on a war job for the Government, he came to get the help of our automatic analyser with some very complicated curves he had obtained, curves relating to the aiming errors of air gunners. Goal-seeking missiles were literally much in the air in those days; so, in our minds, were scanning mechanisms [Walter, 1953, p. 53].

In his 1943 book, Craik stated that thought's function is "prediction" which, in its turn, involves three steps: "translating" processes of the external world, perceived by means of a sensory apparatus, into an internal, simplified or small-scale model; drawing from this model possible inferences

---

[2]For discussion, see [Cordeschi, 2001, chapter 4], and for conceptual connections between cybernetics and contemporary biorobotic modelling, see [Tamburrini and Datteri, forthcoming]. Note however the different conclusions that are drawn from the use of self-regulating machines as models of organisms: for Loeb, this use justifies the *elimination* of mental language in the study of living organisms, for Wiener and co-workers, this use justifies the *introduction* of mental language (under the form of a reinstated "teleological" language) in behavioral inquiries about living organisms [Rosenblueth et al., 1943].

about the world by appropriate machinery; "retranslating" this model into external processes, i.e. acting by means of a motor system (pp. 50-51). According to Craik, both organisms and newly conceived feedback machines are predictive systems, even though the latter are still quite rudimentary in the way of prediction. As an example of such machines, Craik mentioned the anti-aircraft gun with a predictor, so familiar to Wiener and other pioneers of Cybernetics. And he described the human control system as a "chain" that includes a sensory device, a computing and amplifying system, and a response device. This is what Craik called "the engineering statement of man", whose abstract functional organization was a source of inspiration for his military investigations as well. The concept of man as computing and control system (the engineering statement of man) was admittedly a radical simplification, neglecting many dimensions of human psychology that Craik mentioned in *The Nature of Explanation*. But this simplification served to unveil deep connections across academic subjects: psychology, in Craik's words, was to bridge "the gaps between physiology, medicine and engineering", by appeal to the shared functional architecture of computing and control systems.

The development of computer science paved the way to broader functional investigations into adaptive and intelligent behaviors. In particular, the modelling and development of learning systems, capable of improving their performance with experience, became a priority in problem solving, perception, and action planning by machines. Wiener appealed to the early developments of machine learning in order to emphasize the limited control one has, in general, on the outcome of automatic learning procedures, and the "disastrous consequences" that might be expected from this[3]. This epistemological appraisal became a major premise in his arguments against military applications of learning machines. Notably, in a 1960 article he criticized the use of learning machines in decisions concerning "push-button wars":

> It is quite in the cards that learning machines will be used to program the pushing of the button in a new push-button war [...] The programming of such a learning machine would have

---

[3]The association "Computer Professionals for Social Responsibility" established a Norbert Wiener Award in 1987. The motivation for naming this award after Wiener mentions the fact that "Wiener was among the first to examine the social and political consequences of computing technology. He devoted much of his energy to writing articles and books that would make the technology understandable to a wide audience". It is worth recalling, in connection with the techno-ethical issues discussed here, that the Norbert Wiener award was assigned in 2001 to Nira Schwartz and Theodore Postol "For their courageous efforts to disclose misinformation and falsified test results of the proposed National Missile Defense system". See http://www.cpsr.org/cpsr/wiener-award.html

to be based on some sort of war game [...] Here, however, if
the rules for victory in a war game do not correspond to what
we actually wish [...] such a machine may produce a policy
which would win a nominal victory on points at the cost of
every interest we have at hear. [Wiener, 1960, p. 1357]

Arthur Samuel, a pioneer of AI investigations into problem solving and
machine learning, dismissed Wiener's concern on the ground that machine
actions fulfil the intentions of its human programmer or intentions directly
derived from these. In Samuel's words, "the 'intentions' which the machine
seems to manifest are the intentions of the human programmer, as specified
in advance, or they are subsidiary intentions derived from these, following
rules specified by the programmer" [Samuel, 1960, p. 741].

Samuel's sweeping "optimism" is not really supported by theoretical
knowledge of machines. For one thing, the undecidability results, obtained
in the framework of computability theory about 25 years before Samuel's
article was written, suffice to show that machines are, in general, unpre-
dictable. For example, the undecidability of the halting problem shows that
there is no algorithmic procedure enabling one to decide of every given program and input whether that program will eventually halt with a definite
output[4]. Notice that this epistemological limitation concerns the whole class
of algorithmic procedures, independently of whether these are specified by
human programmers or not. Even more significantly bearing on the Wiener-
Samuel controversy is more recent work on machine learning from examples.
This work shows that one has limited control on what a machine actually
learns, at least insofar as major supervised learning techniques are concerned. These epistemological reflections, we submit, strengthen Wiener's
appraisal of limited human understanding and control of automatic learning
procedures, and therefore support the major premise in his arguments for
the implementation of precautionary principles in warfare applications of
learning machines. Let's see.

4   Learning machines and warfare: epistemologically motivated concerns

A central issue in machine learning is whether a machine which learns from
experience and approximates the target function well over a fairly large
set of training examples will also approximate the target function well over
unobserved examples. The connection between this issue and the classical
epistemic problem of induction in both scientific method and practical reasoning was explored by Donald Gillies, who claimed that scepticism towards

---

[4]See [Davis et al., 1994, p. 68].

induction is no longer tenable in the light of recent advances of machine learning in the way of both concept and rule learning [Gillies, 1996]. The epistemic problem of induction is the problem whether and what sorts of constraints can be imposed on inductive patterns of inference, so that their conclusions *be reasonable to believe.* In particular, Gillies appealed to ID3-style learning algorithms to support this claim. If Gillies were right, that is, if the epistemic problem of induction were solved in particular machine learning domains, one would have a guarantee that such learning machines would behave as expected most of the time, thereby defusing Wiener's concerns about the consequences of warfare applications of learning machines. Indeed, Wiener's concerns were motivated just on the ground that one has only limited understanding and control of how learning machines will behave after training.

In contrast with this, we argue that Wiener's concerns are not defused by recent developments of machine learning. More specifically, we argue that a sweeping problem affecting supervised inductive learning in general, and ID3-style learning in particular, jeopardizes the idea that a genuine solution to the epistemic problem of induction is afforded by these learning systems. This is the overfitting of training data, which reminds one that a good approximation to the target concept or rule on training data is not, in itself, diagnostic of a good approximation over the whole instance space of that concept or rule. And the successful performances of machine learning systems are of no avail either in the present context: a familiar regress in epistemological discussions of induction arises as soon as one appeals to past performances of these systems in order to conclude that good showings are to be expected in their future outings as well. Thus, epistemic guarantees about the future behaviors of learning machines are very hard to come. These various problems have to be effectively addressed before one can conclude that Wiener's techno-ethical concerns are put to rest by more recent developments of machine learning.

Let us begin by emphasizing the connection between learning from examples and the epistemic problem of induction. A distinctively inductive assumption is often made about computational systems that learn concepts or rules from examples. Schematically,

(IC) Any hypothesis found to approximate the target function well over a sufficiently large set of training examples will also approximate the target function well over unobserved examples[5].

Clearly, a critical examination of this broad assumption requires an extensive survey of learning systems that goes well beyond the scope of this

---

[5][Mitchell, 1997, p. 23].

paper. Here, we focus on versions of (IC) concerning the inductive decision tree algorithm ID3, for Gillies appealed just to ID3-style learning algorithms to claim that scepticism towards this inductivist claim is no longer tenable [Gillies, 1996].

Let us then consider the following inductive claim:

(IC-ID3) Any hypothesis constructed by ID3 which fits the target function over a sufficiently large set of training examples will approximate the target function well over unobserved examples.

To begin with, let us recall some distinctive features of (the ID3) decision tree learning. Decision trees provide classifications of concept instances in a training set, formed by conjunctions of attribute/value pairs. Each path in the tree represents a classified instance. The terminal node of each path in the tree is labelled with the yes/no classification. The learnt concept description can be read off from the paths which terminate into a "yes" leaf. Such description can be expressed as a disjunction of conjunctions of attribute/value pairs. Concept descriptions that make essential use of relational predicates (such as "ancestor") cannot be learnt within this framework.

ID3 uses a top-down strategy for constructing decision trees. Each non-terminal node in the tree stands for a test on some attribute, and each branch descending from that node stands for one of the possible values assumed by that attribute. An instance in the training set is classified by starting at the top-most, root node of the tree, testing the attribute associated to this node, selecting the descending branch associated to the value assumed by this attribute in the instance under examination, repeating the test on the successor node along this branch, and so on until one reaches a leaf. Each concept instance in the training set is associated to a path in a tree, which is labelled "yes" or "no" at the terminal node. ID3 places closer to the tree root attributes which better classify positive and negative examples in the training set. This is done by associating to each attribute P mentioned in the training set a measure of how well P alone separates the training examples according to their being positive or negative instances of the target concept. Let us call this preference in tree construction the ID3 "*informational* bias".

There is another bias characterizing the ID3 construction strategy. ID3 stops expanding a decision tree as soon as a hypothesis accounting for training data is found. In other words, simpler hypotheses (shorter decision trees) are singled out from the set of hypotheses that are consistent with training data, and more complicated ones (longer decision trees) are discarded. On account of this *simplicity* bias[6], longer decision trees that are compatible with the training set are not even generated, and thus no conflict resolution strategy is needed to choose between competing hypotheses.

We are now in the position to state more precisely inductive claim (IC-ID3), by reference to the main background hypotheses used by ID-3 to reduce its hypothesis space:

(IC-ID3: second version): Any hypothesis constructed by ID3 on the basis of its informational and simplicity biases which fits the target function over a sufficiently large set of training examples will also approximate the target function well over unobserved examples.

Scepticism about this claim is fostered by the overfitting problem. A hypothesis $h \in H$ is said to overfit the training set if another hypothesis $h' \in H$ performs better than h on X, even though h' does not fit the training set better than h. Overfitting in ID3 trees commonly occurs when the training set contains an attribute P unrelated to the target concept, which happens to separate well the training instances. In view of this "informational gain" P is placed close to the tree root.

Overfitting is a significant practical difficulty for decision tree learning and many other learning methods. For example, in one experimental study of ID3 involving five different learning tasks with noisy, nondeterministic data,... overfitting was found to decrease the accuracy of learned decision trees by 10-25% on most problems [Mitchell, 1997, p. 68].

Unprincipled expansions of the original training set may not prevent the generation of overfitting trees, for a larger training set may bring about additional noise and coincidental regularities. Accordingly, claim (IC-ID3) is to be further qualified: the "sufficiently large set of training examples" mentioned there must be "sufficiently representative of the target concept" as well. This means that (implicit) assumptions about the representativeness of concept instance collections play a central role in successful ID3 learning. Consider, in this connection, the post-pruning of overfitting decision trees (Mitchell 1997: 67-72). In post-pruning, one constructs a "validation set", which differs from both training and test sets. The validation set can be used to remove a subtree of the learnt decision tree: this is actually done

---

[6]Simplicity is identified here with the length of decision trees, and the latter is contingent on the choice of primitive attributes. A simplicity bias is introduced in many machine learning algorithms for hypothesis selection [Michalski, 1984, p. 98]: "For any given set of facts, a potentially infinite number of hypotheses can be generated that imply these facts. Background knowledge is therefore necessary to provide the constraints and a preference criterion for reducing the infinite choice to one hypothesis or a few preferable ones. A typical way of defining such a criterion is to specify the preferable properties of the hypothesis, for example, to require that the hypothesis is the shortest or the most economical description consistent with all the facts."

if the pruned tree performs at least as well as the original tree on the validation set. Expectations of a good performance of the pruned tree on as yet unobserved instances rely on the assumption that the validation set is more representative of the target concept than the training set. Thus, the sceptical challenge directed at (IC-ID3) can be iterated after post-pruning, just by noting the conjectural character of this assumption.

In order to counter this sceptical challenge to (IC-ID3), one should look more closely at the criteria used for judging how representative of the target concept are training and validation examples. But additional problems arise here. These criteria may vary over concepts, and are not easily stated in explicit form. In expert systems, for example, the introspective limitations of human experts is a major bottleneck in system development. The process of extracting rules from human experts turns out to be an extremely time consuming and often unrewarding task. These subjects can usually pick out significant examples of rules or concepts, but are often unable to state precisely the criteria underlying these judgments[7]. Accordingly, automatic learning from examples is more likely to be adopted when criteria for selecting significant concept or rule instances are not easily supplied by human experts; and yet an examination of these criteria is just what is needed to support inductive claim (IC-ID3) by appeal to the representativeness of training examples.

Confronted with these various difficulties, which the sceptic consistently interprets as symptoms that inductive claim (IC-ID3) cannot be convincingly argued for, let us try and assume a different perspective on ID3. We have already formed a vague picture of ID3 as a component of a trial and error-elimination cycle: ID3 makes predictions about the classification of concept instances that are not included in the training set, on the basis of assumptions guiding both training set construction and the selection of some concept c. If predictions about unseen instances are satisfactory, then one is provisionally entitled to retain concept c. Otherwise c is discarded, and correction methods (such as post-pruning) come into play, which implicitly modify the original set of assumptions.

To sharpen this description of ID3 processing as a two-layered prediction-test cycle (leading from a falsification of instance classification predictions to a refutation of the conjunction of the various assumptions used to select the falsified hypothesis), one can draw on the above distinction between the *preferences* or biases embedded in ID3 proper (which determine both the language for expressing concepts and the construction of decision trees) on the one hand, and the presuppositions that are used to select training

---

[7]See, for example, the survey of knowledge acquisition methods used in expert system research in [Puppe, 1993].

sets on the other hand. In the end, ID3 learning projections will work as long as both kinds of assumptions will turn out to be adequate in the learning environment. But one has no *a priori* guarantee that this adequacy condition is actually satisfied. In other words, there is no guarantee that such machine, which learns from experience and happens to approximate the target function well over a sufficiently large set of training examples, will also approximate the target function well over unobserved examples[8].

In our opinion, the above epistemological analysis sharpens, in the case of ID3-style learning from examples, the broad motives for Wiener's reservations about warfare applications of learning machines, insofar as the hypotheses underlying successful learning from examples are more precisely identified, and their conjectural character is more clearly brought out. But how significant is this reflection about ID3-style learning for the more general problem Wiener raised about military applications of learning machines? One may reasonably suspect that some of Wiener's concerns can be defused by appeal to some other learning algorithm from examples, for some learning procedures may turn out to be immune from the above sceptical conclusions. In order to effectively address Wiener's concerns, however, one would have to show that the learning procedure in question enables one to accrue reliable information on the approximation or convergence to target functions.

5   Learning machines and normal task environments

The *distribution-free* or *probably approximately correct* learning (pac-learning) [Valiant, 1984] is an approach to machine learning which goes a long way towards meeting the epistemic requirement of reliable control on approximation or convergence to target functions. Pac-learning constraints are meant to ensure that the hypotheses advanced by means of a learning procedure using a reasonable amount of computational resources is most likely correct.

The broad motivations for this approach are informally presented by Valiant in connection with the guarantees one would like to read in the user manual of a newly bought home robot:

... whatever home you take this robot to, after sufficient training on some tasks it will behave as expected most of the time, as long as the general conditions expected there are stable enough. To make this informal statement into a usable criterion, some quantitative constraints are needed in addition. First, the number of training sessions required should be reasonable, as should the amount of computation required of the robot to process each

---

[8]For more extensive discussion of the relationship between AI and the philosophical problem of induction, see [Tamburrini, forthcoming].

input at each such session, Second, the probability that the robot fails to learn because the training instances were atypical should be small. Lastly, the probability that, even when the training instances were typical, an error is made on a new input should be small. Furthermore, in the last two cases the probability of error should be controllable in the sense that any level of confidence and reliability should be achievable by increasing the number of training instances appropriately [Valiant, 1994, p. 102].

In the domain of concept acquisition, for example, pac-learning addresses the problem of characterizing classes of concepts that one can learn with arbitrarily high probability from randomly drawn training examples using bounded computational resources[9]. Conceptually, this is a fairly satisfactory machine learning explicatum of the intuitive idea of an epistemically justified inductive procedure, as long as the "arbitrarily high probability" of a hypothesis is regarded as a meaningful indication that the learning system will behave as expected most of the time. Moreover, as Valiant emphasizes, hypotheses about the representativeness of training examples are not needed here, for the instances can be randomly drawn.

It turns out that the classes of concepts and rules that are known to be pac-learnable are fairly limited[10]. For example, one of the major open problems in pac-learning is the efficient learning of DNF expressions, that is, the kind of learning problems discussed above in connection with ID3 learning. Moreover, the pac-learning approach is not considered as a definitive framework for practical learnability, but rather as a promising starting point [Turàn, 2000]. Accordingly, the relevance of pac-learnable concepts and rules in the military applications that Wiener was concerned with is not immediately obvious. More generally, in order to provide a satisfactory answer to the problem whether any machine learning approach provides a viable strategy to meet Wiener's techno-ethical concerns, one has to address subtle epistemological questions concerning our capability to control and reliably estimate convergence to target functions in practically interesting machine learning applications.

An important proviso in Valiant's vivid illustration of the guarantees one would like to have before buying some home robot has gone unnoticed in our discussion so far: this robot should mostly behave as expected in our homes *as long as the general conditions expected there are stable enough*. This proviso can be reformulated as the requirement that one can expect the robot to manifest a certain behaviour *if the functioning environment is normal*, that is, if no perturbing factors are present in that environment.

---

[9]Computational resources must be polynomially bounded in the parameters expressing the relevant measures of the learning problem.

[10]For discussion, see [Mitchell, 1997, pp. 213–214], and references therein.

The problem of specifying normal functioning conditions for machines is another pervasive epistemological problem, bearing on various techno-ethical issues that arise in AI and robotics, in both learning and non-learning environments. Even assuming that some learning machine has been success-fully trained at some task, the machine may still fail to behave as expected because of abnormal usage context. Specifying these normalcy conditions is akin to the inexhaustible problem of specifying the intended range of va-lidity of any scientific law, given that even so-called universal physical laws hold *ceteris paribus*, that is, when perturbation factors are not present. A complete list of boundary conditions characterizing the range of validity of some scientific law or the environments in which a machine works properly is at best a regulative idea of scientific inquiry: in order to identify *every* causal factor which may disturb the regular behavior of some machine, one should take into account evident constraints (such as, say, "Temperature should not exceed 600° C"), examine conditions that are less readily classi-fied as relevant or irrelevant ("No changes in gravitational force"), and pay some attention even to *prima facie* irrelevant conditions ("No Persian cats under the table"). Thorough examination of potentially relevant boundary conditions is nothing but thorough paralysis of scientific inquiry.

Since one cannot circumscribe precisely the class of normal task environ-ments, for an unlimited number of boundary conditions should be taken into account, a more pragmatic attitude is usually adopted. In user manu-als, one mentions what are deemed the more consequential or more easily overlooked boundary conditions - concerning, say, temperature, voltage, humidity, and so on – relying on a global commonsense judgment by ma-chine users concerning the absence of any other abnormal usage condition. Similarly, for the purpose of testing in a selective manner whether some can-didate boundary condition is actually needed to ensure normalcy, one builds up experimental settings E in which that boundary condition is lifted, and makes the default empirical hypothesis that no other abnormal task condi-tion arises in E. Clearly, when erratic warfare scenarios are substituted for controlled experimental environments E, it is more difficult to support in a responsible way (that is, by severe testing) similar default hypotheses about the absence of disturbing factors, and thus the prediction that the machine will behave as expected in such warfare scenarios, without bringing about the "disastrous consequences" that Wiener contemplated in awe.

6   Concluding remarks

Hammond and Miessner's self-regulating machine was hailed as a signif-icant innovation in apparently distant, but ever since tightly interacting domains of inquiry. According to Loeb, this kind of machines supported his own behavioral theories in biology. And this very machine, insofar as it was endowed with "superhuman intelligence", was seen as revolutionizing modern warfare technologies. Arguably, this is the first time that the potential impact of the newly conceived self-regulating machines on both scientific method and military technology is clearly identified. This potential impact became more evident during the cybernetic age. And the dangers arising from unconstrained military applications of cybernetic machines became more evident too. The connection between philosophy of science and techno-ethics suggested by Wiener's reflections on warfare applications of learning machines has been strengthened here by a reflection on more recent approaches to supervised inductive learning. And possible extensions of Wiener's reflections have been suggested by reference to the *ceteris paribus* problem for scientific laws and machine proper functioning.

Philosophy of science bears on the implementation of precautionary principles about military applications of AI and robotics in ways that have not been discussed in this paper. Notably, current military research on autonomous robotic agents addresses AI problems whose solution paves the way to the solution of any other problem that AI will ever be confronted with. These problems, by analogy to well-known classifications of computational complexity theory, might be appropriately called "AI-complete problems". As an example, consider the problem of recognizing surrender gestures by the enemy, or the capability of telling bystanders apart from hostile forces. Solving these recognition problems involves context-dependent disambiguation of gestures, understanding of emotional expressions, real-time reasoning about deceptive intentions and actions. However, human-level performances in these tasks, especially in uncontrolled warfare scenarios, are a far cry from current AI and robotics research efforts.

Techno-ethical issues arising from warfare applications of robotic and intelligent information systems are prominent items included into a much broader and rapidly growing list of techno-ethical issues emerging in these scientific and technological domains of inquiry. In the near future, robotic and intelligent information systems are expected to interact ever more closely with human beings, and to enhance human mental, physical, and social capabilities in significant ways. Crucial ethical issues in these areas, over and above responsibilities for (possibly unintended) warfare applications, include the preservation of human identity and integrity, applications of precautionary principles with respect to system autonomy, economic and social discrimination deriving from restricted access to robotic and intelligent information resources, system accountability, nature and impact of human-machine cognitive and affective bonds on individuals and society. Epistemological reflections on the scope and limits of our knowledge about

AI and robotic systems are likely to improve our understanding, triaging, monitoring, and overall capability to cope with many of these techno-ethical issues.

Acknowledgements

An earlier version of this paper was presented at the First International Symposium on Roboethics, held at Villa Nobel, Sanremo, Italy, on January 30-31, 2004. We are grateful to the Symposium organizers and to the participants for stimulating comments. Financial support by MIUR (Italian Ministry for Education, University and Research), grant COFIN #2002112548, is gratefully acknowledged.

BIBLIOGRAPHY

[Braitenberg, 1984] V. Braitenberg. *Vehicles. Experiments in Synthetic Psychology.* MIT Press, Cambridge, MA, 1984.

[Cordeschi, 2001] R. Cordeschi. *The Discovery of the Artificial.* Kluwer, Dordrecht, 2001.

[Craik, 1943] K.J.W. Craik. *The Nature of Explanation.* Cambridge University Press, Cambridge, 1943.

[Davis et al., 1994] M. Davis, R. Sigal, and E. Weyuker. *Computability, Complexity, and Languages.* Academic Press, Boston, MA, 1994.

[Gillies, 1996] D. Gillies. *Artificial Intelligence and Scientific Method.* Oxford University Press, Oxford, 1996.

[Loeb, 1918] J. Loeb. *Forced Movements, Tropisms, and Animal Conduct.* Lippincott, Philadelphia and London, 1918.

[Michalski, 1984] R.S. Michalski. A theory of methodology of inductive learning. In R.S. Michalski, J. Carbonell, and T.M. Mitchell, editors, *Machine Learning, An Artificial Intelligence Approach*, pages 83–134, Berlin, 1984. Springer.

[Miessner, 1916] B.F. Miessner. *Radiodynamics: The Wireless Control of Torpedoes and Other Mechanisms.* Van Nostrand, New York, 1916.

[Mitchell, 1997] T.M. Mitchell. *Machine Learning.* McGraw Hill, New York, 1997.

[Puppe, 1993] F. Puppe. *A Systematic Introduction to Expert Systems.* Springer, Berlin, 1993.

[Rosenblueth and Wiener, 1945] A. Rosenblueth and N. Wiener. The role of models in science. *Philosophy of Science*, 12:316–21, 1945.

[Rosenblueth et al., 1943] A. Rosenblueth, N. Wiener, and J. Bigelow. Behavior, purpose, and teleology. *Philosophy of Science*, 10:18–24, 1943.

[Samuel, 1960] A.L. Samuel. Some moral and technical consequences of automation – a refutation. *Science*, 132, September 11:741–42, 1960.

[Tamburrini and Datteri, forthcoming] G. Tamburrini and E. Datteri. Machine experiments and theoretical modelling: from cybernetics to biorobotics. *Minds and Machines*, forthcoming.

[Tamburrini, forthcoming] G. Tamburrini. Ai and popper's solution to the problem of induction. In I. Jarvie, K. Milford, and D. Miller, editors, *Karl Popper: A Centennial Appraisal*, London, forthcoming. Ashgate.

[Turàn, 2000] G. Turàn. Remarks on computational learning theory. *Annals of Mathematics and Artificial Intelligence*, 28:43–45, 2000.

[Valiant, 1984] L.G. Valiant. A theory of the learnable. *Communications of the ACM*, 27:1134–42, 1984.

[Valiant, 1994] L.G. Valiant. *Circuits of the Mind.* Oxford University Press, Oxford, 1994.

[Walter, 1953] W.G. Walter. *The Living Brain.* Duckworth, London, 1953.

[Wiener, 1960] N. Wiener. Some moral and technical consequences of automation. *Science*, 131:1355–58, 1960.

[Wiener, 1961] N. Wiener. *Cybernetics, or Control and Communication in the Animal and the Machine [1948].* MIT Press, Cambridge, MA, 1961.

Roberto Cordeschi
Dipartimento di Scienze della Comunicazione
Università di Salerno, Fisciano (SA), Italy
Email: cordeschi@caspur.it

Guglielmo Tamburrini
Dipartimento di Scienze Fisiche
Università di Napoli Federico II
Compl. Universitario Monte S. Angelo, Napoli, Italy
Email: tamburrini@na.infn.it

Moral Mediators
How Artifacts Make us Moral

LORENZO MAGNANI

ABSTRACT. In recent times, non-human beings, objects, and structures – for example computational tools and devices – have acquired
new moral worth and intrinsic values. Kantian tradition in ethics
teaches that human beings do not have to be treated solely as "means",
or as "things", that is in a merely instrumental way, but also have to
be treated as "ends". I contend that human beings can be treated as
"things" in the sense that they have to be "respected" as things are
sometimes (sections 1-2). People have to reclaim instrumental and
moral values already dedicated to external things and objects. To
the aim of reconfiguring human dignity in our technological world I
introduce the concept of *moral mediator* (section 4.2), which takes
advantage of some suggestions deriving from my previous research
on epistemic mediators and on manipulative abduction. Technology
moves us to a better world. I contend that through technology people can simplify and solve moral tasks when they are in presence
of incomplete information and possess a diminished capacity to act
morally. Many external things, usually inert from the moral point of
view, can be transformed into what we call moral mediators. Hence,
not all of the moral tools are inside the head, many of them are shared
and distributed in "external" objects and structures which function
as ethical devices.

1   Rational acting in a human unsettled world

Morality could be defined, at the very last, as "the effort to guide one's
conduct by reason – that is, to do what there are the best reasons for doing
– while giving equal weight to the interests of each individual who will be
affected by one's conduct: there are not privileged people" [Rachels, 1999].

Moral reasoning could be viewed as a form of "possible worlds" anticipation, a way of getting chances to shape the human world and act in it. It
could be of help to prefigure risks, possibilities, and effects of human acting,
and to promote or prevent a broad variety of guidelines. Hence, we need
1) to possess good and sound principles/reasons applicable to the various
problems, able to give rise to arguments that can be offered for opposite

Lorenzo Magnani and Riccardo Dossena, editors, *Computing, Philosophy, and Cognition*,
pp. 21–36 © 2005, L. Magnani

moral views, and 2) appropriate ways of reasoning which permits us to apply the available reasons in the best way. "Creating ethics" means creating the world and its directions, in front of different (real or abstract) situations and problems. This process requires the adoption of skillful and creative ideas, in order to react in response to new previously unknown cases or in cases of moral conflict. In this way events and situations can be reinvented either as an opportunity or as a risk for new moral directions.

2 Respecting things as people, respecting people as things

In recent times, non-human beings, objects, and structures like technological artifacts and machines have acquired new moral worth and intrinsic values. Kantian tradition in ethics teaches that human beings do not have to be treated solely as "means", or as "things", that is in a merely instrumental way, but also have to be treated as "ends". I contends that human beings can be treated as "things" in the sense that they have to be "respected" as things are sometimes. People have to reclaim instrumental and moral values already enjoyed by external things and objects.

It is well-known that Immanuel Kant's categorical imperative states "*Act only on that maxim through which you can at the same time will that it should become a universal law*" [Kant, 1964, p. 88]. When dealing with "The formula of the end in itself", (pp. 95-98). Kant observes that

> [...] man, and in general every rational being *exists* as an end in himself and not merely as a means for arbitrary use by this or that will: he must in all his actions, whether they are directed to himself or to other rational beings, always be viewed *at the same time as an end* (p. 95).

Kant's considerations lead us to the following practical imperative: "*Act in such a way that you always treat humanity, whether in your own person or in the person of any other, never simply as a means, but always at the same time as an end*" (p. 96). In the "kingdom of ends everything has either a *price* or a *dignity*. If it has a price, something else can be put in its place as an *equivalent*; if it is exalted above all price and so admits of no equivalent, then it has a dignity"(p. 102). Things that human beings need have a "market price"; moreover, items that are merely desired rather than needed have an affective "fancy price" [*Affektionspreis*]. But "[...] that which constitutes the sole condition under which anything can be an end in itself has not merely a relative value – that is, a price – but has an intrinsic value – that is, *dignity*" (*ibid.*)

Kant's wonderful lesson can be inverted: it is possible for things to be treated or respected in ways one usually reserves for human beings. Many things, or means, previously devoid of value, or previously valuable only in terms of their market price or affective price, can also acquire a moral status or intrinsic value. Conversely, just as things can be assigned new kinds of value, so, too can human beings, for there are moral positive aspects of treating people like things, as we shall see[1].

Anthropocentric ideas, like those that inform Kant's imperative, have made it difficult for people to acquire moral values usually associated with things and for things to attain moral worth traditionally reserved for people. We said that, in Kantian terms, people do not have to be "treated as means (and only as means)". I propose upgrading that idea with a new one – respecting people as things in a positive sense. In this scenario, people are respected as "means" in a way that creates a virtuous circle, one in which positive moral aspects enjoyed by things can be used to reshape moral endowments attributed to people.

Perhaps the first "things" to gain new moral rights in western culture were women, a change that was not universally welcomed. Indeed, the ideas propagated in this direction by Mary Wollstonecraft in her 1792 treatise *A Vindication of the Rights of Women* were initially considered absurd [Singer, 1998]. This sort of ideological conflict has been played out again in the last few decades as animal rights advocates and environmental ethicists have waged a struggle similar to the one women faced in the eighteenth century – that of redefining a means as an end. To achieve that goal, some intellectuals and activists have sought to reframe how various plants, animals, ecosystems – even the land itself – are valued so that they are regarded as "ends" and accorded the rights and protection that status entails. As we will see in the following sections also technological artifacts and machines have been redefined as ends and have acquired new moral roles.

A curious example of the importance of my motto "respecting people as thing" is related to the case of the "endangered species wannabes". Many people have complained about disappearing wildlife receiving more moral and legal protection than disappearing cultural traditions. A relatively recent US federal statute, the Visual Artists Rights Act of 1990, appropriates the language of ecological preservation when it establishes "rights of attribution, integrity, and the prevention of destruction of art of recognized stature for the creators of certain paintings, drawings, prints, sculptures, or photographs" [Nagle, 1998]. The importance of this analogy lies in the fact that some people consider themselves endangered because they do not feel

---

[1]To further clarify my concern about the moral relationships between "people" and "things" cf. [Magnani, forthcoming, chapter 1].

as if they are treated as well as things (means).

Let us illustrate some ethical issues just related to the relationship between "beings" and "things".

3   Building ethical chances

Not only researchers in epistemology but also researchers in ethics stress the attention on the role of *imagination* respectively in scientific reasoning and in ethical thinking and deliberations. If we interpret "imagination" just as a process of knowledge gathering and shaping, it can be seen as a process which promotes new cognitive chances leading to see things as we would not otherwise have seen them. To see a "moral world" means to see the world in an original way: ethical understanding involves coming to see some aspects of reality in a particular way that influences human acting in shaping and surviving the future.

Johnson stresses the attention on the cognitive processes which underlie "moral imagination". "Moral principles without moral imagination become trivial, impossible to apply, and even a hindrance to morally constructive action" [Johnson, 1956]. This means that in ethics analogical and metaphorical reasoning is very important, because of its capacity to "reconceptualize" the particular situation at hand. Consequently, model-based tools[2] for ethical deliberations should not be considered negative, as subjective, free flowing, creative processes not governed by any rule or constrained by any rationally defined concepts so that we are led to see imagination as an enemy of morality. The role of a sort of a model-based imaginative activity is clear, for instance, in the *Critique of Pure Reason*, where Kant clarifies the importance of *intermediate* thinking devices able to make human beings capable of linking abstract principles to the real world of experience (cf. the case of the role of imagination in geometrical construction). Relating the discourse to moral rules, Kant develops the idea that a pure moral rule (as a maxim of action) is applied to the concrete experience as a kind of "typification" – a sort of figurative substitute [Kant, 1956]. This typification could be interpreted as a kind of *figurative envisioning* of a non existing world as a means for judging a given moral situation. Kant denies that

---

[2]I introduced the concept of model-based abduction in [Magnani, 2001]. The term "model-based reasoning" is used to indicate the construction and manipulation of various kinds of representations, not mainly sentential and/or formal, but mental and/or related to external mediators. Obvious examples of model-based inferences are constructing and manipulating visual representations, thought experiment, analogical reasoning. In this light also emotional feeling can be interpreted as a kind of model-based cognition. Of course abductive reasoning – which is reasoning to hypotheses – can be performed in a model-based way, internally or with the help of external mediators. In this case I am referring to an activity of producing "moral" hypotheses in an abductive model-based way.

this typification involves imagination, for he maintains moral judgment a matter of pure practical reason, but, as Johnson concludes, "what could be more thoroughly imaginative than this form of figurative envisioning that is based on a metaphoric mapping?" [Johnson, 1956]. It is through this kind of typification that chance production and promotion is enhanced in ethics. How does this occur?

Beyond rules and principles, hence, also prototypes, schemas, frames, and metaphors are vehicles of model-based moral knowledge, sometimes very efficient when facing moral problems. For example, morality as a grammar represents a typical metaphorical "prototype" exploited in ethics: grammatical principles are in analogy to moral principles like in the simple case of "speaking well" and "acting well"; action as a metaphorical "motion" leads to the idea that moral principles would be rules telling us which "action-paths" we may take, which ones we must take, and which we must never take (cit., p. 43). When looking for consequences of our moral actions and deliberations, this envisioning of a non existing world as a means for judging a proposed action can be performed in a model-based way.

In the following sections I will illustrate how these model-based ways of moral behavior are related to what I call "moral mediators".

4   Delegating ethics and the role of moral mediators

In [Magnani, 2001] I have illustrated abductive reasoning (reasoning to explanatory hypotheses) and I have described the role – in science – of what we can call "thinking through doing". This surely suggests that reasoning and inferential processes also have interesting extra-theoretical characteristics. Also moral inferences have a role in the manipulation of various external objects and non-human structures as substitutes of moral "feeling" and "thinking" and supplements to them: there is a morality through doing. In this case the cognitive *delegation* to external objects, artifacts, and machines is constitutively ethical, and relates to the creation of what I call *moral mediators*.

The existence of this kind of extra-theoretical cognitive behavior is also testified by the many everyday situations in which humans are perfectly able to perform very efficacious (and habitual) tasks without the immediate possibility of providing their conceptual explanation. In some cases the conceptual account for doing these things was at one point present in the memory, but now has deteriorated, and it is necessary to reproduce it, in other cases the account has to be constructed for the first time, like in creative settings of manipulative abduction in science.

It is difficult to establish an exhaustive list of invariant behaviors that can be considered ethical manipulative reasoning. Expertly manipulating non-human objects in real or artificial environments requires old and new *templates* of behavior that are repeated at least somewhat regularly. Only exceptionally we are referring here to action that simply follows articulated, previously established plans; at issue are embodied, implicit patterns of behavior that I call tacit templates. This variety of "hidden" moral activity is still conjectural: these templates are embedded moral hypotheses that inform both new and routine behaviors, and, as such, enable a kind of moral "doing". In some situations, templates of action can be *selected* from those already stored in the mind-body system, as when a young boy notices his baby sister crying and, without thinking, automatically tries to comfort the infant by stroking her head or singing a lullaby as he has seen his parents do many times. In other instances, new templates must be *created* in order to achieve certain moral outcomes.

The following tacit templates of moral behavior (cf. Figures 1 and 2) present interesting features[3]:

1. sensitivity to *curious or anomalous aspects* of the moral situation;

2. preliminary sensitivity to *dynamical character* of the moral situation, and not only to entities and their properties;

3. referral to manipulations that exploit *artificial created environments* and *externally induced feelings* to free new possibly stable and repeatable sources of information about hidden moral knowledge and constraints. This template feature is apparent, say, in a discussion of the moral problem of capital punishment when we exploit resources like statistics, scientific research, or information from interviews to gather real rather than faulty information, like the one about the genuine relief the murder victim's relatives feel when the criminal is killed. In this way a new configuration of the social orders of the affected groups of people is achieved[4];

4. various contingent ways of spontaneous moral acting. This case contemplates a cluster of very common moral templates[5] (cf. Figure 1);

5. spontaneous moral action that can be useful in presence of *incomplete or inconsistent information* or a *diminished capacity to act morally*

---

[3] I just list them and describe in some details the templates which are directly related to the construction of moral mediators. For a complete treatment [Magnani, forthcoming].

[4] On the reconfiguration of social orders that is realized in science (laboratories), cf. [Knorr-Cetina, 1999].

[5] Analogues of all these manipulative templates are active in epistemic settings: cf. [Magnani, 2001; Magnani, 2002; Magnani and Dossena, 2005].

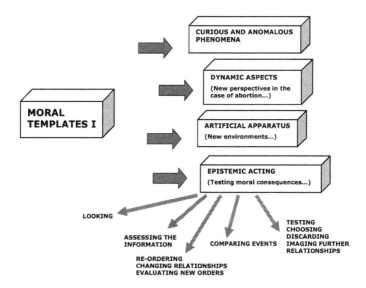

Figure 1. Conjectural moral templates I.

upon the world. Such action works on more than just a "perceptual" level;

6. *action as a control of sense data* illustrates how we can change the position of our bodies (and/or of the external objects) to reconfigure social orders and collective relationships; it also shows how to exploit artificially created events to get various new kinds of stimulation. Action of this kind provides otherwise unavailable tactile, visual, kinesthetic, sentimental, emotional, and bodily information that, for example, helps us take care of other people;

7. action enables us to build new *external artifactual models* of ethical mechanisms and structures (through "institutions," for example) to substitute for the corresponding "real" and "natural" ones. (Keep in mind, of course, that these "real" and "natural" structures are also artificial – our cultural concept of "family" is not a natural institution.) For instance, we can replace the "natural" structure "family" with an environment better suited for an agent's moral needs, which occurs when, say, we remove a child from the care of abusive family members. In such a case we are exploiting the power of a *artificial* "house" to reconfigure relationships. A different setting – a new but

still artificial framework – facilitates the child's recovery and allows him or her to rebuild moral perceptions damaged by the abuse. A similar effect occurs when people with addiction problems move into group homes where they receive treatment and support. An even simpler example might be the external structures we commonly use to facilitate good manners and behavior: fences, the numbers we take while waiting at a bakery, rope-and-stanchion barriers that keep lines of people in order, etc.

Of course many of the actions that are entertained to build the arti-factual models above are not tacit, but explicitly projected and planned. However, imagine the people that first created these artifacts (for instance the founders of the group houses for addicted people), it is not unlikely that they created them simply and mainly "through doing" (creation of new tacit templates of moral actions) and not by following already well-established projects. Many of the actions which are performed to build technological artifacts and machine endowed with moral delegations (moral mediators) are of this type.

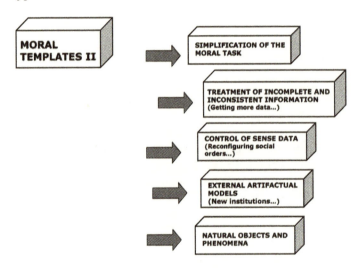

Figure 2. Conjectural moral templates II.

4.1 Moral agents and moral patients

Technological artifacts and machines are designed, produced, distributed, and understood in the human world; they are strictly intertwined with the social interactions of humans: technology affects what people do and how they do it. For example computers possess moral agency because they 1. have a kind of intentionality and 2. can have effects on the so-called "moral patients" that is they can harm or improve the interests of beings capable of having their interests impeded or furthered: "Artifacts are intentional insofar as they are poised to behave in a certain way when given input of a particular kind. The artifact designer has a complex role here for while the designer's intentions are in the artifacts, the functionality of the artifact often goes well beyond what the designer anticipated or envisaged. Both inputs from users and outputs of the artifacts can be unanticipated, unforeseen, and harmful" [Johnson, 2004].

Some ethicists maintain that entities can be framed as moral *patients* and as moral *agents*. Not only human beings but also things can be conceived of as moral patients (as entities that can be acted upon for good and evil) and also as moral agents (as entities that can perform actions and are sources of moral action, again for good or evil).

There are many cases:

1. the two classes are disjoint (no entity qualifies as both an agent and a patient, this is clearly unrealistic);

2. the first class can be a proper subset of the second;

3. the two classes intersect each other; (both cases 2. and 3. are not promising because they both require at least one moral agent that in principle could not qualify as a moral patient (we only have supernatural agents that can fulfil this requirement, for example a God that affects the world but is not affected by the world);

4. all entities that qualify as agents also qualify as patients and vice versa (standard position), and, finally,

5. all entities that qualify as patients also qualify as agents[6].

The fact that animals seem to qualify as moral patients, that are excluded from playing the role of moral agents requires a change in the perspective 5. In short, certainly "things" (and so artificial entities)[7] extend the class

---

[6][Floridi and Sanders, 2004]. Carstein-Stahl [2004] has recently investigated the problem concerning whether computers can be considered autonomous moral agents. Since computers cannot understand the information they store and manage, they lack the basic capacity "to reflect morality in anything". He argues on this point introducing an interesting and curious test called "the moral Turing test".

[7]On the legal extension of personhood to artificial agents (for instance shopping websites) cf. the interesting conclusions of the recent [Chopra and White, 2003]. Very

of entities that can be involved in a moral situation, both as moral agents (for instance Internet) and as moral patients that enjoy intrinsic values (for instance a work of art). Of course the properties enjoyed by "things" of being a moral agent or patient are not the same as that of human beings. To make an example, artifacts can be agents of moral actions, but they are neither responsible nor exhibit free will, full intentionality, and emotions like human beings.

I think this distinction between moral patients and agents, certainly correct and useful, nevertheless obliterates the dynamic aspects instead explained following my perspective in terms of moral delegation and externalization. Indeed moral delegation to external objects and artifacts does not take place because a given thing is supposed to intrinsically possess a given set of properties appraised on their own. For example, the Gioconda has no free will, no proper intentions, and so on. However, the way it dynamically interacts with humans, and how they respond to it, is what gives value to it. In this sense, my conception differs from the one that distinguishes moral patient from moral agent.

According to that view, the Gioconda (or an Internet selling system) would be a moral patient, because it does not possess all those features shared (or supposed to be shared) by human beings (conscious will, an actual free will, proper intentions, etc.). However, this view fails to account for the process by which we continuously delegate and give (moral) value to the things that are around us. For example, how could the patient-agent distinction account for the reason why the first present you received from your girlfriend may acquire such a great (intrinsic) value? It could be an old and haggard t-shirt, but it doesn't matter, indeed.

Moreover, there is an additional reason to prefer my conception about moral delegation described above. The idea that some artifacts and machines should be respected, or should have rights on their own is also based on the claim they perform important cognitive processes, sometimes endowed with instrumental and economical value. They are moral patients and as patients they have to be respected. According to my view, this is a result of a moral mediation. As we delegate to the machines new moral worth, we can use them to depict previously unseen new moral features of cognition, that for human beings acquires a new value and a new extension. Some machines can play the role of moral mediators because they mediate new aspects of human beings' moral lives[8].

The patient-agent distinction specially elicits differences: it is very obvi-

---

up-to-date issues related to the contracts entered into by artificial agents and to their punishment and financial penalties are also discussed.

[8]I will detail this point below in the subsection "Moral Mediators".

ous that the moral agency of computers is not the same as that of human beings, and in this respect it is not different in kind from that of other technologies. It has been argued that computers have a kind of external intentionality (that is expressed in states outside of the body, such as speech acts, written sentences, maps, and other designed artifacts), but they cannot have internal intentionality: their agency can be compared to human "surrogate" agency, such as tax accountants or estate executors [Powers, 2004]. This illustrates the kind of moral character of computer systems by showing that computer systems have a kind of intentionality and have effects on moral patients, hence they are appropriate objects of moral appraisal. In these cases we are faced with a kind of "mind-less morality" [Floridi and Sanders, 2003]. The problem of the moral agency of artifacts also involves the construction of the suitable policies we can (and/or have to) adopt for "punishing" – that is censoring, modifying, re-engineering, removing – them.

I think the more extended concept of "moral mediator" can better encompass and explain the issues above: the moral patients and moral agents are special cases of moral mediators.

4.2   Moral mediators

The considerations in the previous subsection "Distributing Morality" indicate the fact that a significant portion of manipulations is also devoted to building a vast new source of information and knowledge: external *moral mediators*. I have derived this expression from "epistemic mediators," a phrase I introduced in a previous book [Magnani, 2001, ch. 3], which consist of external representations, objects, and artifacts that are relevant in scientific discovery and reasoning processes. As I have already said moral mediators represent a kind of redistribution of the moral effort through managing objects and information in such a way that we can overcome the poverty and the unsatisfactory character of the moral options immediately represented or found internally (for example principles, prototypes, etc.). I also think that the analysis of moral mediators can help accounting for the mechanisms of the "macroscopic and growing phenomenon of global moral actions and collective responsibilities resulting from the 'invisible hand' of systemic interactions among several agents at local level" [Floridi and Sanders, 2003].

More than just a way to move the world toward desirable goals, action also serves a moral role: we have said that when people do not have adequate information or lack the capacity to act morally upon the world, they can restructure their worlds in order to simplify and solve moral tasks. Moral mediators are also used to elicit latent constraints in the human-environment system. The links discovered grant us access to precious new ethical information. For instance, let us imagine a wife whose work requires long hours away from her husband, and her frequent absences cause conflict in their relationship. She then spontaneously begins to spend more quality time with her spouse in an attempt to save their marriage (cf. Figure 3). The mediating effect of her spontaneous action can cause variables affected by "unexpected" and "positive" events in the relationship to covary with informative, sentimental, sexual, emotional, and, generally speaking, bodily variables.

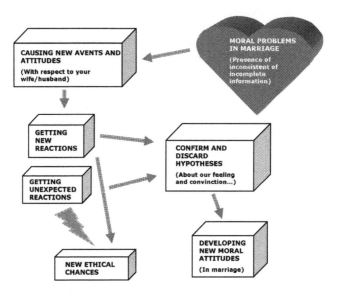

Figure 3. The extra-theoretical dimension of ethical chance in marriage.

There was no discernible connection between these hidden and overt variables before the couple adopted a reconfigured "social" order – that is, increased time together – and uncovering such links reveals important new information, which, in our example, might be renovated and unexpected sexual pleasure, astonishing intellectual agreement, or surprising identical emotional concerns on specific matters.

Natural phenomena can also serve as external artifactual moral mediators: when in previous chapters we considered the problem of "respecting people as things", we were referring to the ability of external "natural" objects to create opportunities for new ethical knowledge, as in the case of endangered species: we have learned something new by seeing how people seek to redefine themselves as "endangered". Many external things that have been traditionally considered morally inert can be transformed into moral mediators. For example, we can use animals to identify previously unrecognized moral features of human beings or other living creatures, as we can do with the earth, or (non natural) cultural entities; we can also use external "tools" like writing, narrative, ritual, and various kinds of pertinent institutions to reconfigure unsatisfactory social orders. Hence, not all moral tools are inside the head – many are shared and distributed in external objects and structures that function as ethical devices.

External moral mediators function as components of a memory system that crosses the boundary between person and environment. For example, they are able to transform the tasks involved in simple manipulations that promote further moral inferences at the level of model-based abduction[9]. When an abused child is moved to a house to reconfigure her social relationships this new moral mediator can help her to experience new model-based inferences – new model-based cognitive hypotheses – (for instance new emotions concerning adults and new imageries about her past abuse).

Moreover, I can alter my bodily experience of pain through action by following the template *control of sense data*, as we previously outlined, that is through shifting – unconsciously – the position of my body and changing its relationships with other humans and non-humans experiencing distress. Mother Theresa's personal moral rich feeling and consideration of pain had been certainly shaped by her closeness to starving and miserable people and by her manipulation of their bodies. In many people, moral training is often related to these kinds of spontaneous (and "lucky") manipulations of their own bodies and sense data so that they build morality immediately and non-reflectively "through doing".

Artifacts of course play the role of moral mediators in many ways. Let us consider some effects on privacy mediated by certain machines. Beyond the supports of paper, telephone, and media, many human interactions are strongly mediated (and potentially recorded) through the Internet. What about the concept of identity, so connected to the concept of freedom? At present identity has to be considered in a broad sense: the externally stored amount of data, information, images, and texts that concern us as individuals is enormous. This storage of information creates for each person a kind of external "data shadow" that, together with the biological body, forms a "cyborg" of both flesh and electronic data that identifies us or potentially identifies us. I contend that this complex new "information being" depicts new ontologies that in turn involve new moral problems. We can no longer apply old moral rules and old-fashioned arguments to

---

[9]Cf. above footnote 2.

beings that are at the same time biological (concrete) and virtual, situated in a three-dimensional local space but potentially "globally omnipresent" as information-packets. For instance, where we are located cybernetically is no longer simple to define, and the increase in telepresence technologies will further affect this point. It becomes clear that external, non biological resources contribute to our variable sense of who and what we are and what we can do. More examples dealing with computational and other artifacts as moral mediators are illustrated in [Magnani, forthcoming].

Throughout history, women have traditionally been thought to place more value on personal relationships than men do, and they have been generally regarded as more adept in situations requiring intimacy and caring. It would seem that women's basic moral orientation emphasizes taking care of both people and external things through personal, particular acts rather than relating to others through an abstract, general concern about humanity. The ethics of care does not consider the abstract "obligation" as essential; moreover, it does not require that we impartially promote the interests of everyone alike. Rather, it focuses on small-scale relationships with people and external objects, so that, for example, it is not important to "think" of helping disadvantaged children all over the world (like men aim at doing) but to "do" so when called to do so, everywhere[10].

Consequently, "taking care" is an important way to look at people and objects and, as a form of morality accomplished "through doing", achieves status as a fundamental kind of moral inference and knowledge. Respecting people as things is a natural extension of the ethics of care; a person who treats "non-human" household objects with solicitude, for example, is more likely to be seen as someone who will treat human beings in a similarly conscientious fashion. Consequently, even a lowly kitchen vase can be considered a moral mediator in the sense I give to this cognitive concept.

When I clean my computer, I am caring for it because of its economical and worth and its value as a tool for other humans. When, on the other hand, I use my computer as an epistemic or cognitive mediator for my research or didactic activities, I am considering its intellectual prosthetic worth. To make a case for respecting people as we respect computers, we can call attention to the values human beings have in common with these machines: 1) humans beings are – biological – "tools" with economic and instrumental value, and as such, can be "used" to teach and inform others

---

[10]Moreover, both feminist skepticism in ethics and the so-called "expressive-collaborative model" of morality look at moral life as "a continuing negotiation *among* people, a socially situated practice of *mutually* allotting, assuming, or deflecting responsibilities of important kinds, and understanding the implications of doing so" [Urban-Walker, 1996, 276]. Of course, this idea is contrasted with the so-called "theoretical-juridical conception of morality".

much the way we use hardware and software, so humans are instrumentally precious for other humans in sharing skills of various kinds; and 2) like computers, people are skillful problem solvers imbued with the moral and intrinsic worth of cognition.

5 Conclusions

The main thesis of this paper is that in recent times, non-human beings, objects, and structures like technological artifacts and machines have acquired new moral worth and intrinsic values. Kantian tradition in ethics teaches that human beings do not have to be treated solely as "means", or as "things", that is in a merely instrumental way, but also have to be treated as "ends". I contend that human beings can be treated as "things" in the sense that they have to be "respected" as things are sometimes. People have to reclaim instrumental and moral values already enjoyed by external things and objects. This is central to the aim of reconfiguring human dignity in our technological world. Aiming at illustrating the intrigue of this ethical struggle between human beings and things I have discussed the role of objects, structures, and technological artifacts by presenting them *moral carriers* and *mediators*. I maintain this perspective can be very fruitful to approach many other problems related to the relationships between machines and ethics.

BIBLIOGRAPHY

[Cartesin-Stahl, 2004] C.B. Cartesin-Stahl. Information, ethics, and computers. the problem of autonomous moral agent. *Minds and Machines*, 14:67–83, 2004.

[Chopra and White, 2003] S. Chopra and L. White. Artificial agents. personhood in law and philosophy. In R. López de Mántaras and L. Saitta, editors, *Proceedings of the 16th European Conference on Artificial Intelligence*, pages 635–639, Amsterdam, 2003.

[Floridi and Sanders, 2003] L. Floridi and J.W. Sanders. The method of abstraction. In M. Negrotti, editor, *Yearbook of the Artificial. Nature, Culture, and Technology. Models in Contemporary Sciences*, Bern, 2003.

[Floridi and Sanders, 2004] L. Floridi and J.W. Sanders. On the morality of artificial agents. *Minds and Machines*, 14:349–379, 2004.

[Johnson, 1956] M. Johnson. *Moral Imagination. Implications of Cognitive Science in Ethics*. The Chicago University Press, Chicago, IL, 1956.

[Johnson, 2004] D.G. Johnson. Integrating ethics and technology. 2004. *European Conference Computing and Philosophy*, E-CAP2004, June 2-5, Pavia, Italy. Abstract.

[Kant, 1956] I. Kant. *Critique of Practical Reason*. Bobbs-Merrill, Indianapolis, IN, 1956. Trans. by L. W. Bleck, originally published 1788.

[Kant, 1964] I. Kant. *Groundwork of the Metaphysics of Morals* (1785) [3d ed.]. Harper & Row, New York, 1964. Reprint of 1956, edited and translated by H.J. Paton, Hutchinson & Co., Ltd., London, third edition.

[Knorr-Cetina, 1999] K. Knorr-Cetina. *Epistemic Cultures. How Sciences Make Knowledge*. Harvard University Press, Cambridge, MA, 1999.

[Magnani and Dossena, 2005] L. Magnani and R. Dossena. Perceiving the infinite and the infinitesimal world: unveiling and optical diagrams and the construction of mathematical concepts, 2005. Forthcoming in *Foundations of Science*.

[Magnani, 2001] L. Magnani. *Abduction, Reason, and Science. Processes of Discovery and Explanation*. Kluwer Academic/Plenum Publishers, New York, 2001.

[Magnani, 2002] L. Magnani. Epistemic mediators and model-based discovery in science. In L. Magnani and N. J. Nersessian, editors, *Model-Based Reasoning: Science, Technology, Values*, pages 305–329, New York, 2002. Kluwer Academic/Plenum Publishers.

[Magnani, forthcoming] L. Magnani. *Knowledge as a Duty. Distributed Morality in a Technological World*. forthcoming.

[Nagle, 1998] J.C. Nagle. Endangered species wannabees. *Seton Hall Law Review*, 29:235–55, 1998.

[Powers, 2004] T.M. Powers. Intentionality and moral agency in computers. 2004. *European Conference Computing and Philosophy*, E-CAP2004, June 2-5, Pavia, Italy. Abstract.

[Rachels, 1999] J. Rachels. *The Elements of Moral Philosophy*. McGraw Hill College, Boston Burr Ridge, IL, 1999.

[Singer, 1998] P. Singer. All animals are equal. *Philosophic Exchange*, 1(5):243–57, 1998. Also in M.E. Zimmerman, J.B. Callicott, G. Sessions, K.J. Warren, and J. Clark, editors, *Environmental Philosophy. From Animal Rights to Radical Ecology*, pages 26-80, Upper Saddle River, NJ. Prentice-Hall.

[Urban-Walker, 1996] M. Urban-Walker. Feminist skepticism, authority and transparency. In W. Sinnott-Armstrong and M. Timmons, editors, *Moral Knowledge? New Readings in Moral Epistemology*, pages 167–292, Oxford, 1996.

Lorenzo Magnani
Department of Philosophy and
Computational Philosophy Laboratory
University of Pavia, Pavia, Italy;
Department of Philosophy, Sun Yat-sen University
Guangzhou (Canton), P.R. China
Email: lmagnani@unipv.it

Telepresence: From Epistemic Failure to Successful Observability

Luciano Floridi

ABSTRACT. The paper introduces a new model of telepresence. First, it criticizes the standard model of presence as *epistemic failure*, showing it to be inadequate. It then replaces it with a new model of presence as *successful observability*. It further provides reasons to distinguish between two types of presence, *backward* and *forward*. The new model is then tested against two ethical issues whose nature has been modified by the development of digital information and communication technologies, namely pornography and privacy, and shown to be effective.

1 Introduction

Telepresence is a philosopher's gold mine. It is such a rich concept and experience, a phenomenon so intuitive and yet so difficult to capture in all its nuances and implications, that its potentialities, as a source of new philosophical questions and insights, seem inexhaustible[1].

Some of the classic issues in philosophy could easily be reconceptualized as problems concerning (tele)presence[2]. Examples include action at distance; the semantics of possible worlds understood as the availability and accessibility of spaces different from the actual; the tension between appearance and reality (where is the agent, really?) and the issuing skeptical challenges; testimony as "knowledge at distance" in time as well as in space; the nature of individual identity in different contexts; the mind/body problem; consciousness as awareness of "there-being". Heidegger without the semantics of presence or *Dasein* would be inconceivable[3]. And Christian

---

[1] [Ijsselsteijn and Harper, 2002] provides a good introduction to presence that prepares the ground for the philosophical debate.

[2] See [Goldberg, 2000] for a collection of essays concerning several philosophical themes related to telepresence.

[3] For a ecological Heideggerian-Gibsonian approach to telepresence see for example [Schuemie *et al.*, 1998].

Lorenzo Magnani and Riccardo Dossena, editors, *Computing, Philosophy, and Cognition*, pp. 37–56 © 2005, L. Floridi

theology has been struggling for centuries with the idea of omnipresence as one of the most significant of God's attributes[4].

As the reader will certainly know, the previous list could easily be expanded. Yet this fascinating survey is not the goal of this paper. Instead, in the following pages we shall explore the conceptual foundation of telepresence theory in order to investigate some of the new ethical implications of telepresence (henceforth simply *presence*, whenever the term causes no confusion). The perspective and methodological tools adopted will be those of the *Information Ethics*, an environmental approach to Computer Ethics developed by the Information Ethics research Group at the University of Oxford (`http://web.comlab.ox.ac.uk/oucl/research/areas/ieg/`).

Here is an overview. The next section provides a critical analysis of the standard approach to the definition of *presence as epistemic failure*. The identification of some of its shortcomings will lead, in section three, to the elaboration of an alternative conception of *presence as successful observability*[5]. Once this analysis is laid down, it will become easier to discuss two important ethical issues related to presence. Section four will introduce the environmental approach to computer ethics and a specific application of the new analysis of presence to forms of pornography enabled by digital information and communications technologies (ICTs). Section five moves towards an assessment of the problem of informational privacy, by discussing a possible objection against the interpretation of presence as successful observability. Privacy itself is analysed in section six. The conclusion briefly summarises the results obtained.

2   The standard approach: presence as epistemic failure

Presence is notoriously a polysemantic concept and a polymorphic phenomenon[6]. However, after almost twenty-five years of research [Minsky, 2001] is usually acknowledged as the beginning of presence studies – some

---

[4]The recent debate on divine presence from a telepresence research perspective is reviewed in [Biocca, 2001], who argues against several conceptual confusions in [Sheridan, 1999] – who builds on earlier work by [Schuemie et al., 1998] and in [Mantovani and Riva, 2001a]. On the same debate see also [Lauria, 2001].

[5]Strictly speaking, as Edward Zalta rightly remarked during the meeting, qualifying ("successful") a dispositional state (observability) raises serious concerns in terms of conceptual analysis. However, the expression here is only meant to remind the reader of the previous model based on epistemic failure. One may speak of "being successful in observing" but the expression is far less catchy. The reader still concerned is invited to replace "successful observability" with any label she or he may find more appealing.

[6][Schuemie et al., 2001] and [Ijsselsteijn et al., 2002] provide recent surveys of several ways in which presence has been interpreted and analyzed, but see also [Lombard and Ditton, 1997].

convergence on a general conceptual map has begun to emerge (see for example [Sacau et al., 2001] and [Ijsselsteijn et al., 2002]). In current studies, presence is often understood as a *type of experience* of "being there", one loosely involving some technological mediation and often depending on virtual environments. An authoritative and influential source like the *International Society for Presence Research* (ISPR), for example, endorses the following analysis (italics added):

> [1] Presence (a shortened version of the term "telepresence") is a *psychological* state or *subjective* perception in which even though part or all of an individual's current experience is generated by and/or filtered through human-made technology, part or all of the individual's perception *fails* to accurately acknowledge the role of the technology in the experience. Except in the most extreme cases, the individual can indicate correctly that s/he is using the technology, but at *some level* and to *some degree*, her/his perceptions *overlook* that knowledge and objects, events, entities, and environments are perceived as if the technology was not involved in the experience. Experience is defined as a person's observation of and/or interaction with objects, entities, and/or events in her/his environment; perception, the result of perceiving, is defined as a meaningful interpretation of experience. (http://www.ispr.info/)

This standard view of presence has been popular at least since the work of [Lombard and Ditton, 1997]. It consists of three fundamental steps:

i) presence is reduced to a type of perception, e.g. visual perception, for example seeing some geographical shapes and colors;

ii) the type of perception in (i) is then specified, cognitively, as a special kind of experience, namely a psychological, subjective, meaningful interpretation of the experienced; for example, experiencing the above-mentioned colors and shapes as a specific type of environment, e.g. a valley on Mars;

iii) the special kind of experience in (ii) is further qualified, semantically, as a perception of contents that *fails*, at least partially, momentarily or occasionally, to be a perception of its machine-mediated nature as well; in our example, this means having the impression of being on Mars, failing to realize that it is actually a computer-mediated environment.

Since these three steps are primarily epistemic, one may refer to (i)-(iii) as a model of presence as *epistemic failure* (the EF model).

The roots of the EF model are (1) *philosophically Cartesian* and (2) *culturally mass-mediatic.* An explanation is in order.

1) The philosophically Cartesian nature of EF can be evinced from the priority assigned to the understanding of presence in terms that are exclusively epistemic. In the quotation above from the *International Society for Presence Research* web site, for example, even the reference to interaction is actually a reference to the *perception* of interaction. A representative case of a Cartesian approach is [Biocca, 2001], who defends an approach based on the philosophy of mind and the classic mind-body dualism of Cartesian origins. Note that, although Biocca seems justified in criticizing some metaphysical approaches, this is not a reason to consider Cartesianism the only available alternative.

When Descartes speculates in the *Meditations* on the possibility of living in a dream or in a Matrix-like reality, somehow artificially generated by a malicious yet omnipotent demon, the stress is precisely on the completely realistic perception of the environment, despite the possibility of an unperceived mediation that makes the perception itself possible yet the environment, and thus our presence within it, entirely fictional. Descartes construes the skeptical challenge in terms of a fundamental tension between the actual experience of something – e.g. Descartes being in his room, in front of the fire, looking at his hands – and the possibility of its (i.e., of the perception) unreliability as a source of access to, or presence in front of, the real nature of the experienced something (Descartes suspects he might be dreaming, or might be misled by a malicious demon).

2) The EF model is eminently modern, strictly related as it is to that priority of epistemology over ontology (the conceptual analysis of the ultimate nature of reality) that characterizes philosophy after the scientific revolution, from Descartes to Kant. The mass-mediatic character of EF (see especially [Lombard and Ditton, 1997]) is a reasonable consequence of this Cartesian root. For modernity – known for the primacy it attributes to knowledge and epistemology – makes increasing room for (one may argue that it was bound to lead to) a culture in which the production (fiction) and representation (communication) of realities become socially and psychologically predominant. Simplifying: having placed knowledge at the center of the stage for some centuries, western thought made almost inevitable the next move, namely the raise of knowledge's products and hence of the infosphere to the key role of primary environment inhabited by the human mind. Correspondingly, the understanding of presence mutates from

a) the mere possibility of an epistemic failure to perceive the difference between what is and what is not real (see Descartes' discussion of the sceptical challenge); to

b) the actual engagement with realities that are known to be artificial or synthetic because demonstrably constructed through the (mass-)mediation of increasingly powerful technologies, which replace Cartesian dreams and demons as the condition of possibility of the experience. In EF, the logical possibility of failure – e.g. one may be dreaming – becomes the failure to perceive the technology that may be making one dream.

To summarize, the EF model promotes an understanding of presence as the Cartesian failure to recognize the technologically (mass-)mediated nature of the experiences enjoyed by the epistemic agent. As a consequence, EF allows to catalogue as presence a variety of radically different phenomena otherwise largely unrelated, from oral and textual representations to immersions in VR scenarios, from radio narratives to online games, from television and cinema to tele-robotics.

It is unclear whether the very wide scope of EF is actually an advantage – providing a conceptual reduction of a broad spectrum of phenomena to a single, unifying frame of interpretation – or arguably the sign of some serious misunderstanding. Several reasons may incline one to take the latter view.

EF embeds an unresolved tension between the subjective, introspective, single-agent understanding of presence – which the model inherits from a Cartesian approach – and the social, public, intra-subjective and multi-agent understanding of presence proper of a mass-mediatic approach. Is telepresence a personal and private experience or is it something made possible only by social interaction? Is solipsistic telepresence an oxymoron? Consider just ordinary presence, not telepresence: was Robinson Crusoe present (did he feel present) on the island before meeting Friday? Of course there is no straightforward answer to this type of questions, because, trivially and boringly, it all depends on what one means by "(tele)presence". However, the fact that similar questions are reasonably prompted by the EF model and yet appear so poorly posed is evidence that there might be something wrong with EF itself. EF starts looking like a position that allows misconceived questions to be asked, the sort of questions that make research go amiss.

The previous suspicion paves the way to another, more substantial criticism. EF manages to be, in different ways, both too exclusive and too inclusive, resulting literally eccentric with respect to its correct focus.

On the one hand, by adopting an anthropocentric perspective – typically Cartesian – the model considers beyond its scope any investigation of cases of presence *of* (not just *through*, or *by means of*) artificial agents. And this because, at least at this stage in the evolution of AI, no machine is capable of subjective experience of any sort, let alone one of a Cartesian nature. Yet telepresent robotics is not just about devices remotely controlled by human operators, it is also and significantly about devices that are able to be present remotely by telecontrolling other devices, while keeping human agents entirely out of the loop, as mere external observers. Along the same line, if more hypothetically, it is hard to see how EF can analyze the concept of presence when the agent involved is a cyborg, that is, an agent who may enjoy some technologically-mediated experiences of presence while at the same time perceiving them precisely as mediated.

On the other hand, the EF model grants full citizenship in the realm of telepresence studies to experiences such as reading a novel or watching a movie, an oddity that causes a loss of specificity and an irrecoverable metaphorization of the concept of "presence at distance".

This metaphorical way of approaching presence can be related to a further difficulty. EF provides a *merely negative understanding* (more on this presently) of presence – as failure to perceive the technologically-mediated nature of the experience – and this is bound to be unsatisfactory. The approach by negation (*per via negativa*) means that one attempts to define or conceptually capture a *definiendum* by saying what the *definiendum* is not. It may work with dichotomies and Boolean concepts: if one understands what "left" means one may also understand the meaning of "right" negatively, as "not-left". It is a standard method in mathematics, where the the method of false position or *regula falsi* helps one to estimate the roots of a nonlinear equation $f(x) = 0$ by an iterative process of "false" approximations. But "failure to perceive" fails itself to be either a Boolean description or a precise concept that can be further refined by iteration. It is comparable to defining a zebra as not quite a horse but close: it includes far too many things (might it be like a centaur? A mule? A camel?) and, although correct, it begs the question, since we might as well speak of a zebra as not a donkey but almost. That we speak of a zebra in terms of not being a horse – that we conceptualize presence as epistemic failure – only shows that we do already possess some fairly detailed idea of what we wish to define – the zebra in front of us or at least in our memory, the actual experience of being telepresent – but that we surrender to the difficulty of providing a tight conceptual analysis. Instead, we opt for what is in fact a merely generic indication, a "you know what I mean", a finger-pointing. This brings us to a further problem.

EF allows odd cases of *nested telepresence*. Consider the *Odyssey*. A large part of Odysseus' adventures are recounted by Odysseus himself after having landed to Scheria, the island of the Phaeacians. One of these adventures is the encounter and blinding of Polyphemus in the Cyclops' island. According to EF, the reader, by being in Homer's narrative space, is also in Scheria where, by listening to Odysseus, she is also in the Cyclops' island. Only a semantic space can allow this nesting. But then only a metaphorical sense of "telepresence" may be at work here. For this nesting has nothing to do with the ordinary set-theoretic sense in which, by being telepresent in a given space S_1, say a hotel room, one is also telepresent in the space S_2 that includes S_1, say in the hotel where the room is. In the latter case, the co-(tele)presence is a logical necessity. In the former case, it can only be a matter of possible mental experience.

We have reached the last problem. EF cannot clearly define *absence*. This is not a philosophical gimmick. Any conceptual analysis of telepresence should also be able to discriminate between, and possibly explain, cases of unachieved telepresence, of failure or interruption of telepresence, of faulty or insufficient telepresence. So here lies another clear sign that the EF model is unsatisfactory. Fortunately, it is also the condition of possibility of a better approach.

Consider a counterfactual analysis: had the agent *not* failed to perceive the technologically-mediated nature of her experience she would not have been telepresent. This is the inevitable logical consequence of EF, but it is also a *reductio ad absurdum*. For surely the doctor teleoperating on a patient is still present, independently of her perception (or lack thereof) of the technological mediation. Surely the soldier is still telepresent on the mine field through a robot, despite all the possible perception of the artificial nature of the experience. The fact is that epistemic failure is not the right criterion to identify cases of telepresence. The good news is that, precisely by focusing on absence, we can gain a better perspective on presence and hence acquire a vantage point to frame some relevant ethical issues.

3   A different approach: presence as successful observability

Concentrating on absence has the immediate advantage of clarifying that speaking of presence in a vacuum of references makes little sense. Something is (tele-)present or (tele-)absent only for an observer and only at a given *level of abstraction*[7].

A level of abstraction (LoA) is a specific set of typed variables. Intuitively, it is representable as an interface, although, strictly speaking, this is inadequate, not least because an interface is usually static, whereas a LoA is dynamic.

---

[7]See [Ijsselsteijn, 2002] for a similar perspective.

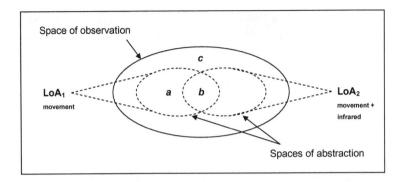

Figure 1. An example of Levels of Abstraction.

Through a LoA the observer accesses the environment, so a LoA could be e.g. the five senses unaided, a microscope, a CCTV or a Geiger counter[8].

Consider a motion detector, for example (cf. Figure 1). In the past, motion detectors caused an alarm whenever a movement was registered within the range of the sensor, including the swinging of a tree branch (object a in Figure 1). The old LoA$_1$ consisted of a single typed variable, which may be labeled MOVEMENT. Nowadays, when a PIR (passive infrared) motion detector registers some movement, it also monitors the presence of an infrared signal, so the entity detected has to be something that also emits infrared radiation – usually perceived as heat – before the sensor activates the alarm. The new LoA$_2$ consists of two typed variables: MOVEMENT and INFRARED RADIATION. Clearly, a cat (object b in Figure 1) walking in the garden is present for both LoAs, but for the new LoA$_2$, which is more finely grained, the branch of the tree swinging is absent. Likewise, a stone in the garden (object c in Figure 1) is absent for both the new and the old LoA, since it satisfies no typed variable of either one.

What the two sensors detect (the word is used here in a purely engineering sense of extracting data from a signal) is movement, a change in the environment, some form of action (e.g. walking) or interaction (e.g. interrupting the flow of a signal) or a transition in the system. More generally, this is one of the two senses in which something is present or absent in a space of observation: as a *dynamic source of action/interaction or change*.

The other sense is as a *static property-bearer*. The immobile branch of the tree is absent both for the old-fashioned sensor and for the new PIR sensor. It is still absent for the latter, even if it moves, because it fails to

---

[8] A full presentation of the LoA methodology is provided in [Floridi and Sanders, 2004].

satisfy another typed variable, the infrared one. The cat, on the contrary, is constantly (i.e., non-intermittently) present for an infrared sensor, even if it does not move, because it is a heat-generator.

The method of LoA is an efficient way of making explicit and managing the ontological commitment of a theory. This is crucial. [Mantovani and Riva, 2001b], for example, acknowledge that "[...] the meaning of presence depends on the concept we have of reality (from the ontology which we more or less explicitly adopt) and that different ontological positions generate different definitions of presence, telepresence and virtual presence." It seems that what is needed is a method of LoA.

The method clarifies that *to be present is to be the value of a typed variable of a LoA* (to paraphrase Quine). To be absent is, of course, to fail to be any such value. This view is consistent with the general thesis, defended in [Mantovani and Riva, 2001b], that presence is an ontology-dependent concept. The social construction of presence, further supported by Mantovani and Riva may be interpreted as a specific case of the broader view articulated in this paper.

As we have just seen, depending on the class of typed variables in question, there might be three ways of being present/absent at a given LoA:

1. as source of action/interaction,

2. as a property-bearer,

3. as both (1) and (2).

Without clause (2) one would be unable to define forms of "passive" presence. Thus, a model according to which *"presence is tantamount to successfully supported action in the environment"* [Schuemie *et al.*, 1998] would fail to acknowledge the fact that x might be present even without any observable (let alone successful) interaction between x and x's environment. Of course, a solution would be to modify our understanding of "interaction" and "environment", but this seems rather *ad hoc*. A more fruitful alternative is to accept that any analysis of presence requires the identification of a space of observation and a level of abstraction. Unperceivable subatomic particles are known to be present from their actions and our interactions. The sofa in the room is present because of its perceivable qualities. The flame of a candle in the room is present because of both. Absence may be equally gradual.

If we now extend the previous analysis to telepresence, the easiest thing is to refer to the new model as being based on *successful observability* (SO), thus:

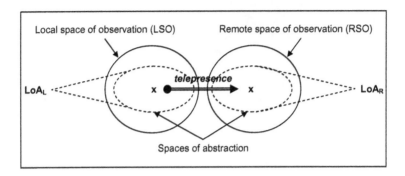

Figure 2. A model of telepresence.

SO) an x observable at a given LoA in a local space of observation LSO is also telepresent in a remote space of observation RSO if and only if x is also observable in RSO at a given LoA.

Note that LSO and RSO need to be different (LSO $\neq$ RSO), whereas the two LoAs may but do not have to be identical (see Figure 2).

The new model shifts the perspective from an internal and subjective assessment of a peculiar experience – presence as epistemic failure – to an external and objective evaluation – presence as successful observability – which requires an explicit definition of the LoAs adopted in the process of analysis. This has at least four major advantages.

The first and most obvious is that, contrary to the EF model, the SO model provides a clear criterion of discrimination between what does and what does not count as telepresence. It thus regiments very clearly the applicability of the concept, which now excludes intentional experiences, which may be technologically-enabled but are in themselves merely psychological – such as reading, listening to the radio or watching a movie – but includes standard cases of presence, such as operating in virtual environments (from immersive virtual realities to text-based virtual worlds such as MUDs, MOOs, IRC, and Chats), remote controlling other artificial agents, being a member of a digital community, playing online. Since there is no presence in a remote space unless the entity in question is observable there at some given LoA, one cannot be telepresent in *War and Peace*, in *Casablanca* or on Scheria.

A further advantage of the new model is that all this is good news for mass-media and literature studies as well. For that peculiar experience of "as if I were there", caused by many forms of communication, will never be properly studied as long as it is catalogued under the wrong heading of telepresence. It requires the development of its own set of conceptual tools. There are, of course, borderline cases, and the new model contributes to explain them. Watching *All My Children*[9] on TV does not make the audience telepresent, either as a property-bearer or as a source of interaction. However, participating by *tele*-phone to a *tele*-vision program does indeed satisfy the criterion laid down by SO, and quite rightly so, for the audience is now capable of some minimal interaction at distance. Indeed, the example shows the need for a deeper understanding of the nature of environments conducive to telepresence. It takes two to interact. Of course, digital ICTs are far more open to the possibility of telepresence than classic mass media, but telepresence is possible even through the latter. The difference lies precisely in the ontological nature of the digital, which not only "augments" the agents' capacities epistemically, but allows the construction of new spaces where the agent can be telepresent interactively. It won't be long before we might be able to experience something like the "wall-to-wall circuit" interactive TV described by Bradbury in *Fahrenheit 451*:

> She [Helen] didn't look up from her script again. "Well, this is a play that comes on the wall-to-wall circuit in ten minutes. They mailed me my part this morning. [...] They write the script with one part missing. It's a new idea. The home-maker, that's me, is the missing part. When it comes time for the missing lines, they all look at me out of the three walls and I say the lines. [...]" "What's the play about?" "I just told you. There are these people named Bob and Ruth and Helen".

A third, important advantage of SO is that it enables one to acknowledge a spectrum of ways of being present, from the *weak presence* of x barely detectable as a mere property-bearer (more on this in section 6) to the *strong presence* of an agent endowed not only with observable properties, but also with the capacity of acting and interacting (the agent can be the receiver of an action and respond to it accordingly) with the environment, both pragmatically (by doing or changing things) and epistemically (e.g. by observing things locally). Presence is no longer a Boolean concept – as in EF – and SO justifies talks of augmented telepresence, or attempts at making telepresence resilient, and so forth.

The last advantage to be stressed finally leads us to the discussion of some ethical issues, in the next section.

---

[9]http://abc.go.com/daytime/allmychildren/.

4   Environmentalism, teleagents and telepatients

Clearly "being there remotely" as a mere property-bearer is far less useful and interesting than being telepresent also as an agent, capable of some successful action and interaction in the remote space. In both cases, however, telepresence, as defined by SO, brings to light the need to analyze ethical problems that, on the one hand, inevitably escape the old EF model (recall the definition of telepresence as a sort of personal experience), and on the other do not seem mere updated versions of the standard problems occurring in everyday life.

The SO model makes explicit that we are confronted by a new ethical context in which teleagents and telepatients interact in technologically-sustained environments. Of course, their actions have moral values and consequences, but our degree of understanding is still low. Needless to say, the slightly sci-fi scenario should not mislead. Million of people already spend an enormous amount of time online, being present in remote spaces in which they both learn and show how to behave. Interestingly, the fact that many of the entities with which human teleagents and telepatients come in contact may be entirely artificial becomes a source of enrichment of our ethical discourse in general. The new scenarios require a sharpening of old conceptual tools and the creation of new ones. For environmentalism acquires a new meaning when one's environment is a remote virtual space and the sort of things one interacts with may have a digital, not a biological nature. A specific example will help to illustrate the point.

According to SO and contrary to EF, classic pornography, in the form of texts, pictures or movies, does not generate any form of presence. In this respect, there is no difference between De Sade's *Justine* and Voltaire's *Candide*: the reader is still left out of the remote space of observation.

It follows that whatever might be morally significant with old-fashioned pornography it cannot be grounded on an analysis of telepresence. The dialectics of exposure seems much more pertinent, for example. This still holds true when the nature of the media change from analogue to digital: a pornographic DVD, even if it provides some choices and options, fails to represent a case of presence, according to the new model.

Things stand rather differently, however, with new forms of ICT-based "pornography" (the quotation marks are required precisely by the novelty), which implement various degrees of interaction without any form of physical intercourse: dedicated telephone services, chatrooms and other multi-user environments, usually employed for role-playing games, or experimental virtual reality scenarios. Here pornography (which is a semantic concept), promiscuity and prostitution (which are pragmatic concepts) merge. In similar cases, the agent is indeed present remotely, at least in the sense supported by SO, in semantic spaces that also allow some degree of inter-action. However, despite the obvious connection with more ordinary form of pornography, one important difference is that the other tele-agents with "whom" the human agent interacts may be entirely synthetic. *S1m0ne*, the film directed by Andrew Niccol about a digitally created actress "who" be-comes a star, offers a great thought experiment. More realistically and less morally, erotic chatterbots nowadays are not science fiction. People have been gallant and tried to date pieces of software. So arguments against pornography based on the crimes, immoralities, degradation, exploitation and health hazards that may affect the people involved – an argument often rehearsed in the context of pornographic videos – may become ineffective. Likewise, any Kantian argument to the effect that no human being should be used as a mere means would be inapplicable. Clearly telepresence in informational environments inhabited by agents of unclear nature is forcing us to rethink our well-entrenched, ethical assumptions.

5   An objection against presence as successful observability

Checking the limits of the old EF model, one may be tempted to raise similar objections against the new SO model. True, SO does provide a definition of presence and a criterion of discrimination between presence and absence. But SO might still be eccentric in a very significant way. For one of the most important types of phenomena, commonly interpreted as presence, refers to the availability of tele-perceptual technologies such as radars, satellites, webcams, sonars, CCTVs. It seems that, without being either a property-bearer or a source of interaction in a RSO, a entity, even an artificial one, might still be present in a RSO remotely, e.g. by means of a monitoring appliance. Yet SO fails to accommodate such types of presence, which might be qualified as telepistemic. It follows that SO needs to be revised, if not abandoned.

The previous objection is correct in drawing the inference, but mistaken in suggesting the need for a solution. What needs to be modified is our understanding of teleepistemics itself. For what looks like telepresence is in fact something slightly different, and understanding the difference casts an interesting light on several issues.

Suppose you are in a room. You are just present in that room. Pull down the wall between that room and the next, and you will not say that you are now telepresent in the next room; you are merely present in a larger room. In chess, when a Pawn reaches the opposite side of the board, it can be promoted to any piece except a King. Suppose the Pawn is promoted to a Queen. Suddenly most of the board becomes a local space, distant only one move. Many telepistemic technologies are "tele-promoting" in this sense. The Queen is not telepresent in a remote space, it is the space of the Pawn that has been enlarged. Take a digital camera. Start monitoring what is happening in your room. Again, you are not telepresent in your room, or at least not according to SO (at least because in this case we have LSO = RSO); the burden of proof that you are is on EF's shoulders. Now imagine making the digital camera one inch longer, and then another inch, and so forth. Or just make your camera increasingly powerful. Gradually, the camera allows you to monitor things that are increasingly further away from your local space. At what point are you telepresent? At ten meters? Fifty? A hundred? When only a cable connects you and the appliance? Or a radio signal? The answer is never, according to the SO model. Making a remote space epistemically available locally is different from being present in that remote space as an entity. It is like pulling down the wall between two rooms. This is why there is no point in using a portable, baby-monitor unit with a range of several miles: the monitor guarantees to the user only telepistemic access to the remote space but no actual interactive presence at distance. If something happens, it is only the more frustrating to know that nothing can be done in time, given the long distance.

The problem with telepistemics consists in a fallacious confusion between

1. the successful observability *of* x not only in LSO but also in RSO; and

2. the successful observation *by* x – which is in LSO – of some y that is present in RSO.

The former is a case of ontic telepresence, the latter is a case of epistemic access at distance. The two phenomena are separate and should not be confused. Compare this to the illusion of movement caused by web-browsing: one feels as if one were being uploaded in different spaces, when in reality one is downloading those spaces into one's own.

Should we then abandon any talk of presence in all those cases of technologically mediated telepistemics? Not so fast. Telepistemics may still be a case of presence, it is just that the previous confusion impedes one to see precisely who or what is telepresent where. It is not the observer x in LSO accessing the entity y in RSO that is present in RSO, but exactly the opposite: by being accessed telepistemically, the y in RSO is now also present in the observer's LSO, typically as a mere property-bearer. Using the previous analogy, once the wall is pulled down, you are not remotely present in the other room; it is the chair that was in the other room that is now locally present in your space. In order to fix the distinction it may be useful to speak of *forward* and *backward presence* (see Figure 3).

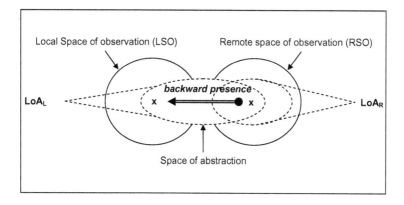

Figure 3. A model of telepistemics as backward presence.

The distinction between *forward* and *backward presence* fits SO perfectly well. Recall that something may be telepresent as a mere property-bearer. The map of a portion of the small crater encircling the Mars Exploration Rover called *Opportunity* shows the location of crystalline hematite. This is a case of *backward presence*. It makes the hematite present in our space, through a stratification of communication and spatial layers. On the other hand, (not we but) the scientists who control *Opportunity* are also *forward present* on Mars, as interactive agents.

Telepistemic technologies have evolved dramatically since Galileo discovered the four satellites of Jupiter with his own telescope. Nevertheless, by looking at pictures on the screen of a computer we (you and I, not the NASA scientists mentioned above) are no more present on Mars now than he was on those satellites.

Mere word playing, one may reply. Forward and backward presence is just like active and passive sentences: there is no substantial difference between "Peter drives the car" and "the car is driven by Peter". You are where I am, I am where you are. The distinction is linguistically possible but conceptually useless.

The impatient complaint is understandable but unjustified. These are different cases, they should not be confused and the distinction between forward and backward presence is no mere hair-splitting. First of all, it helps to clarify that "local" and "remote" are indexical concepts. Like other words and concepts, such as "I", "now", "here", "my" and so forth, they acquire a different meaning depending on the position of the observer. The observer's LSO is not the observed's LSO, obviously. It follows that

SO is correct in stressing the need for an explicit statement of where the observer is before talking of telepresence. There is no obviously privileged space to be defined as *local*. Call this an anti-localist thesis.

Second, presence at its best is usually full, that is, both forward and backward presence. The entity is present in RSO as an interactive agent (full forward presence) and it also observes herself locally as being remotely present (backward presence). It is this feedback function that allows the agent to control her interactions with the remote environment.

Third, but not less importantly, being able to understand the difference between the two types of presence means equipping ourselves with a powerful conceptual tool that can help us to frame some ethical problems far more accurately. Some distinctions can be subtle, but this usually means that they are sharper and cut better. We have seen that interactive pornography is a case of what we can now call *forward presence*. Let us have a look to informational privacy as a case of *backward presence*.

6   Privacy: from intrusion to abduction

The literature in computer ethics on privacy is vast and constantly growing[10], so it is not my intention here even to sketch the current debate. The problem is well known in its outlines. What I wish to point out is the need to acquire the correct overall perspective when approaching it.

Privacy is often discussed topologically, i.e., in terms of spaces. But depending on how one understands presence, two fundamental scenarios become available.

If telepistemics is defined in terms of *remote presence of the observer* – what has been called above as *forward presence* – it is natural to slip into a view that equates the observed's privacy to the protection of her (local or remote) space, whether physical, psychological or informational. One may then be further inclined to apply familiar concepts of space ownership: a right to privacy may be an exclusive right to own and use one's own information or information about oneself, for example. And since information does not need to be removed to be stolen – as it happens with a car, for example – this further reinforces the view that privacy is ownership of an informational space, which is not subtracted to the owner when exploited by someone else. The result is a metaphorical conceptualization of privacy breach as trespassing. Illegal or simply unauthorized access to a web site or a database, or common cases of digital surveillance are portrayed as intrusions in someone else's space or place. It is indicative that the standard line of defence by the intruder – "the gate was open" or "there was no gate"

---

[10]For a recent review and further references see for example chapter 5 in [Tavani, 2003].

– is not rejected as irrelevant, but rather as pertinent yet mistaken, with a "yes, but" kind of rebuttal.

The problem with this approach is that privacy is often exercised in public spaces, that is, in spaces which are not only socially and physically public – a street, a car park, a pub – but also informationally public – anyone can see the newspaper one buys, the bus one takes, the t-shirt one wears, the drink one is ordering. The tension is obvious. There are about 1.5m cameras monitoring public places in Britain. According to one estimate, the average Briton is recorded by CCTV cameras 300 times a day ([The Economist, 2003]). How could the telepresence of an observer through a CCTV system operated by a bank on a street, for example, be a breach of the observed's privacy if the observer is accessing a space which is public in all possible senses anyway? Why the shop records of the customer's purchase of a t-shirt may breach the latter's privacy, if what one wears is visible to all? Attempts at solving these apparent inconsistencies result in strange geometries of overlapping spaces and exercises in conceptual contortionism. The problem is at the origin: an analysis of telepistemics and hence privacy as forward presence is simply not very helpful.

Consider now the conclusion reached in the previous section. Once telepistemics is understood as a way of making the observed locally present – what has been defined above as *backward presence* – a privacy breach is more easily comparable to a case of metaphorical abduction: the observed is moved to an observer's local space (a space which is remote for the observed, recall that LSO ≠ RSO), unwillingly and possibly unknowingly. Of course, what is abducted is only some information; hence no actual removal is in question (recall the example of the car above) bur rather a cloning of the relevant piece of information. And the cloned information is not a space that belongs to the observed and which has been trespassed; it is rather part of the observed herself, or better something that (at least partly) constitutes the observed for what she is. From this perspective, privacy becomes a defence of personal identity and uniqueness. The inconsistency concerning private vs. public spaces does not arise any longer: the observed wishes to preserve her integrity as an informational entity even when she is in an entirely public place. After all, kidnapping is a crime independently of where it is committed, whether in public or not. What one buys, wears or does in public belongs to a sphere that is no one's property in particular, but monitoring and recording it subtracts from this public sphere a portion of the information that constitutes the observed, and makes it part of a space that belongs and is controlled only by the observer, to which the observed herself has no other access, and in a way that may be completely transparent to the observed (the observed is often unaware that part of her information is being abducted).

7 Conclusion

When we hear someone loudly speaking on a mobile phone near us, perhaps in the constrained space of a train, we are often annoyed. We do not wish to listen to her business, but cannot help it. Paradoxically, we know that that person is breaching our privacy, yet the old model of presence would not enable us to say why. We could not stop being present and hence regain our privacy by just becoming fully aware of the technologically mediated nature of the experience. And our privacy is certainly not being breached because she is entering in our informational space: we, after all, are the ones who do the listening. It is because she is abducting us into her informational space, forcing us to be telepresent in her space despite our wills. Our privacy is affected because this is a case of *imposed backward presence*.

The previous is just an example of the kind of approach made possible by the analysis of telepresence developed in this paper, where the old model of presence as epistemic failure has been criticized and an alternative model of presence as successful observability (SO) has been defended as more satisfactory.

The new model SO is based on the general principle that, to be (tele)present is to be the value of a typed variable of a level of abstraction (LoA). SO is no longer Cartesian, for it does not privilege the subjective, internal perception (or lack thereof) of a technologically-mediated displacement. The new model is not even mass-mediatic, for it does not refer to social or shared spaces of communication or fiction. SO is a model developed on principles – anti-psychologism, non-Cartesianism, LoA methodology and minimalism in the ontological assumptions – which are at the roots of the philosophy of information [Floridi, 2002]. According to SO, what matters in the analysis of presence is the occurrence and flow of information. An entity is *forward present* in a remote space if it is successfully observed at a LoA in RSO, either as a property-bearer or as a source of change or action/interaction, that is, as some kind of informational object. An entity is *backward present* in a local space if it is successfully observed at a LoA in LSO at least as a property-bearer, that is, again, as some kind of informational object. Adopting the LoA methodology allows one to specify the ontological commitment in the assessment of presence, while avoiding any (intrinsically unreliable and inevitably opaque) psychologism or qualitative phenomenological description based on the agent's reports of subjective experiences.

We have seen that the SO model provides a new approach to important ethical issues, such as interactive pornography and informational privacy.

Whether the new model can withstand criticism and prove to be fruitful is a question open to further research, but one thing remains unchallenged: the more telepresence becomes an ordinary phenomenon, involving an increasing number of people, the more important it will become to understand its nature and its ethical implications in ways that may be utterly unprecedented and unexpected. ICTs increase the ontic and epistemic power of human agents enormously. With these demiurgic capacities are associated equally vast moral issues. More understanding seems the only key to their proper management. After all, the Queen has responsibilities unknown to the Pawn.

Acknowledgements

I am grateful to Lorenzo Magnani for his kind invitation to E-CAP Italy, and to Rita Lauria, Gianluca Paronitti, Matteo Turilli and Edward Zalta for their comments on previous versions of this paper.

BIBLIOGRAPHY

[Biocca, 2001] F. Biocca. Inserting the presence of mind into a philosophy of presence. *Presence: Teloperators and VCirtual Environments*, 10(5):546–57, 2001.

[Floridi and Sanders, 2004] L. Floridi and J.W. Sanders. The method of abstraction. In M. Negrotti, editor, *Yearbook of the Artificial. Nature, Culture and Technology. Models in Contemporary Sciences*, pages 5–22, Bern, 2004. Peter Lang. Preprint http://www.wolfson.ox.ac.uk/floridi/pdf/tmola.pdf.

[Floridi, 2002] L. Floridi. What is the philosophy of information. *Metaphilosophy*, 33(1–2):123–45, 2002. Preprint http://www.wolfson.ox.ac.uk/floridi/pdf/wipi.pdf.

[Goldberg, 2000] K. Goldberg. *The Robot in the Garden: Telerobotics and Telepistemology in the Age of the Internet*. MIT Press, Cambridge, MA, 2000.

[Ijsselsteijn and Harper, 2002] W.A. Ijsselsteijn and B. Harper. Elements of a multilevel theory of presence: Phenomenology, mental processing and neural correlates. In *Presence-Ist 2000-31014 Ec Public Deliverable (D2)*, 2002. Draft Version 1, December. Text available online.

[Ijsselsteijn *et al.*, 2002] W.A. Ijsselsteijn, H. de Ridder, J. Freeman, and S.E. Avons. Presence: Concept, determinants and measurement. In *Proceedings of the SPIE, Human Vision and Electronic Imaging, V, 39*, pages 59–76, 2002. Paper originally presented at *Photonics West - Human Vision and Electronic Imaging*, San Jose, CA, 23-28 Jan. 2000.

[Ijsselsteijn, 2002] W.A. Ijsselsteijn. Virtually there? A vision on presence research. In *Proceedings of Presence 2002, Oct., 9–11*, pages 245–259, Porto, Portugal, 2002. Universitade Fernando Pessoa.

[Lauria, 2001] R. Lauria. In answer to a quasi-ontological argument: On Sheridan's 'Toward an Eclectic ontology of presence' and Mantovani and Riva's 'Building a bridge between different scientific communities'. *Presence: Teleoperators and Virtual Environments*, 10(5):557–63, 2001.

[Lombard and Ditton, 1997] M. Lombard and T. Ditton. At the heart of it all: The concept of presence. *Journal of Computer-Mediated Communication*, 3(2), 1997. Preprint http://www.ascusc.org/jcmc/vol3/issue2/lombard.html.

[Mantovani and Riva, 2001a] G. Mantovani and G. Riva. Building a bridge between different scientific communities: On Sheridan's Eclectic ontology of presence. *Presence: Teleoperators and Virtual Environments*, 10(5):537–43, 2001.

[Mantovani and Riva, 2001b] G. Mantovani and G. Riva. 'Real' presence: How different ontologies generate different criteria for presence, telepresence, and virtual presence. *Presence: Teleoperators and Virtual Environments*, 8(5):540–50, 2001.

[Minsky, 2001] M. Minsky. Telepresence. *Omni Magazine*, 2(9):45–51, 2001.

[Sacau et al., 2001] A. Sacau, L.B. Gouveia, F.R. Gouveia, and F. Biocca. Presence in computer-mediated environments: A short review of the main concepts, theories, and trends. In *Proceedings of IADIS International Conference e-Society 2003, Lisbon, Portugal, 3–6 June 2003*, 2001. Text available online.

[Schuemie et al., 1998] M.J. Schuemie, P. van der Straaten, M. Krijn, and C.A.P.G. van der Mast. Presence as being-in-the-world. *Presence: Teleoperators and Virtual Environments*, 7(1):78–89, 1998.

[Schuemie et al., 2001] M.J. Schuemie, P. van der Straaten, M. Krijn, and C.A.P.G. van der Mast. Research on presence in virtual reality: A survey. *CyberPsychology & Behavior*, 4(2):183–200, 2001.

[Sheridan, 1999] T. Sheridan. Descartes, Heidegger, Gibson, and God: Toward an eclectic ontology of presence. *Presence: Teleoperators and Virtual Environments*, 8(5):551–59, 1999.

[Tavani, 2003] H.T. Tavani. *Ethics and Technology: Ethical Issues in an Age of Information and Communication Technology*. John Wiley & Sons, New York, 2003.

[The Economist, 2003] The Economist, Jan 23rd 2003.

Luciano Floridi
Dipartimento di Scienze Filosofiche
Università degli Studi di Bari, Italy;
Faculty of Philosophy and Sub-Faculty of Computation
Information Ethics Group, Oxford University
Email: `luciano.floridi@philosophy.oxford.ac.uk`

A Model of Lakatos's Philosophy of Mathematics

ALISON PEASE, SIMON COLTON, ALAN SMAILL, AND JOHN LEE

ABSTRACT. Lakatos outlined various methods by which mathematical discovery and justification can occur. These methods suggest ways in which concepts, conjectures and proofs gradually evolve via interaction between mathematicians. Different mathematicians may have different interpretations of a conjecture, examples or counterexamples of it, and beliefs regarding its value. Through discussion, concepts are refined and conjectures and proofs modified.

We have implemented some of Lakatos's methods in a multi-agent dialogue system. Each agent has a copy of Colton's theory formation system HR, which can form concepts and make conjectures which empirically hold for the objects of interest supplied. Distributing the objects of interest between agents means that they form different theories, which they communicate to each other. Agents then find counterexamples and use Lakatos's methods to suggest modifications to conjectures and concept definitions.

We describe our implementation and discuss the questions which have arisen and our answers, including extensions to Lakatos's theory and a more fine-grained approach to some of the methods which he identifies. We argue that the questions are important as they coincide with questions philosophers such as Feferman have asked about Lakatos's work, and that our answers improve Lakatos's theory according to Thagard's criteria of consilience and simplicity.

1   Introduction

Lakatos attacked the view that mathematical knowledge is timeless, certain and *a priori* [Lakatos, 1976]. Lakatos's work in the philosophy of mathematics is a controversial mathematical analogy of Hume's problem of induction combined with Popper's theory of falsification. That is, Lakatos both identified the problem of the impossibility of mathematical knowledge, and suggested a solution. His solution consisted of heuristic methods which guide the development of mathematical conjectures, concepts and proofs. These

Lorenzo Magnani and Riccardo Dossena, editors, *Computing, Philosophy, and Cognition*, pp. 57–85 © 2005, A. Pease, S. Colton, A. Smaill, and J. Lee

evolve through dialectic and analysis sparked by counterexamples. Counterexamples therefore, play a vital role in [Lakatos, 1976], though they are a starting, rather than finishing point: criticism has to be constructive if it is to be valuable.

This work has been described as a "masterpiece" [Kadvany, 2001, p. 1]; "the first major bridge between historical philosophy and serious mathematics" [Kadvany, 2001, p. 14]; a "brilliantly sustained tour de force" [Feferman, 1978, p. 311]; and "a philosophical and literary achievement of the stature of Hume on natural religion or Berkeley's Hylas and Philonous" [Hacking, 1981, p. 135]. Lakatos himself has been described as "one of the most original philosophers of science of the twentieth century" [Kadvany, 2001, p. 1].

We have implemented aspects of Lakatos's theory as a computer model. We believe that doing so helps us to raise questions and identify ambiguities and gaps in the theory. The computational approach also allows us to propose and evaluate answers to these questions.

2   Lakatos's logic of discovery

Lakatos's work on philosophy of mathematics had three major influences. Firstly Hegel's dialectic, in which the *thesis* corresponds to a naive mathematical conjecture and proof; the *antithesis* to a mathematical counterexample; and the *synthesis* to a refined theorem and proof (described in these terms on [Lakatos, 1976, pp. 144-145]). Lakatos emphasises the dialectical aspect in the style of his book, which takes the form of a dialogue in a classroom. Thus he is able to represent different mathematical and philosophical positions by using the voices of different students. The role of the teacher in the book is to ensure that the discussion keeps moving and they do not get caught up in petty asides or dead end avenues. Secondly, Lakatos used Popper's ideas on the impossibility of certainty in science and the importance of finding anomalies. Lakatos argued that Hegel and Popper "represent the only fallibilist traditions in modern philosophy, but even they both made the mistake of preserving a privileged infallible status for mathematics" [Lakatos, 1976, p. 139]. Thirdly, Polya [Polya, 1954] and his work on mathematical heuristic – the study of the methods and rules of discovery and invention – was also a major influence; in particular his work on defining an initial problem and finding a conjecture to develop. Lakatos claims that his own work starts where Polya's leaves off.

Rather than being concerned with whether mathematical knowledge is possible (the argument between dogmatists – who claim that we can know – and sceptics – who claim that we cannot know, or at least that we cannot know that we know), or what type of knowledge it might be, Lakatos emphasised the importance of guessing. In [Lakatos, 1978], he argued that the important question is not *how do we know?*, but rather *how can we improve our guesses?* He presented a fallibilist approach to mathematics, in which proofs, conjectures and concepts are fluid and open to negotiation. Lakatos strongly criticised the deductivist approach in mathematics, in which definitions, axioms and theorem statements are presented with no explanation about their development, and considered to be eternal, immutable truths. Instead, Lakatos saw mathematics as an adventure in which – via patterns of analysis – conjectures and proofs are gradually refined but never certain. He warned that hiding this process makes the subject impenetrable to students and prevents experts from developing concepts or conjectures which may arise out of earlier versions of a theorem statement. Lakatos demonstrated his argument by presenting case studies of the development of Euler's conjecture that for any polyhedron, the number of vertices (V) minus the number of edges (E) plus the number of faces (F) is equal to two; and Cauchy's proof of the conjecture that the limit of any convergent series of continuous functions is itself continuous. [Lakatos, 1976] is a rational reconstruction of the history of philosophy of mathematics as well as these two mathematical conjectures, tracing psychologism, intuitionism, rationalism, historicism, pragmatism, dogmatism, Kant's idea of infallible mathematics, refutationism, inductivism and deductivism. As one of the characters puts it [Lakatos, 1976, p. 55], they discuss the packaging – the philosophical framework, as well as what's in the packet – the mathematical content.

Lakatos held an essentially optimistic view of mathematics, in which the process of mathematics traditionally thought of as impenetrable and inexplicable by rational laws – those which come down to lucky guess work or intuition, are seen in a rationalist light, thereby opening up new arenas of rational thought. He challenged Popper's view [Popper, 1972] that philosophers can form theories about how to evaluate conjectures, but not how to generate them, which should be left to psychologists and sociologists. He did this in two ways - arguing that *(i)* there *is* a logic of discovery, the process of generating conjectures and proof ideas *is* subject to rational laws; and *(ii)* the distinction between discovery and justification is misleading as each affects the other; *i.e.*, the way in which we discover a conjecture affects our proof (justification) of it, and proof ideas affect what it is that we are trying to prove (see [Larvor, 1998]). This happens to such an extent that the boundaries of each are blurred.

The first chapter of [Lakatos, 1976] was published as [Lakatos, 1963–64]; however the second chapter and the appendices of [Lakatos, 1976] were not published during Lakatos's lifetime, as he saw this work as an unfinished project (perhaps analogous to his view of mathematics). One drawback of this failure to publish is that he could not answer criticisms of the book. The fact that Lakatos never pronounced himself completely happy with his theory does, however, strengthen our argument that this work is worth implementing, as it implies that there may be gaps in the theory which we can hopefully identify and fill.

3   Why implement Lakatos's ideas?

Sloman [Sloman, 1978] argues that the computational paradigm provides new tools for understanding the processes which philosophers study, including the philosophy of mathematics. Thagard [Thagard, 1993] also emphasises that philosophy of science and artificial intelligence have much to learn from each other. In particular, we believe that since [Lakatos, 1976] was the first attempt to characterise informal mathematics (see [Corfield, 1997] and [Feferman, 1978]), it is likely to be incomplete, and hence be open to criticism and extension. We argue that, in accordance with the computational philosophy paradigm, implementing Lakatos's theory has enabled us to improve upon it. This dialogue format enables us to model social processes, and hence our implementation contrasts programmes such as BACON [Langley et al., 1987] and PI [Thagard, 1993] which model the thought processes of an individual. A further benefit of implementing Lakatos's ideas is that they suggest ways of improving the fields of automated theory formation and theorem proving (see section 8).

4   Lakatos's three main methods

Lakatos [Lakatos, 1976] explicitly outlines six methods for modifying mathematical ideas and guiding communication: surrender, monster-barring, exception-barring, monster-adjusting, lemma-incorporation and proofs and refutations. Of these, the three main methods of theorem formation are monster-barring, exception-barring, and the method of proofs and refutations [Lakatos, 1976, p. 83]. Crudely speaking, monster-barring is concerned with concept development, exception-barring with conjecture development, and the method of proofs and refutations with proof development. However, these are not independent processes; much of Lakatos's work stressed the interdependence of these three aspects of theory formation.

We are currently implementing all three main methods but for the purposes of this paper concentrate on the first two only, namely monster-barring and exception-barring.

4.1   The method of monster-barring

Monster-barring is a way of excluding an unwanted counterexample. This method starts with the argument that a "counterexample" can be ignored because it is *not* a counterexample, because it is not within the claimed concept definition. Rather, the object is seen as a monster which should not be allowed to disrupt a harmonious theorem. For instance, one of the students suggests that the hollow cube (a cube with a cube-shaped hole in it) is a counterexample to Euler's conjecture, since $V - E + F = 16 - 24 + 12 = 4$. Another student uses monster-barring to argue that the hollow cube does not threaten the conjecture as it is not in fact a polyhedron. The concept polyhedron then becomes the focus of the discussion, with the definition being formulated explicitly for the first time; as "a solid whose surface consists of polygonal faces" (according to which, the hollow cube *is* a polyhedron), and "a surface consisting of a system of polygons" (according to which, the hollow cube is *not* a polyhedron) [Lakatos, 1976, p. 14]. Using this method, the original conjecture is unchanged, but the meaning of the terms in it may change.

4.2   The method of exception-barring

Lakatos's treatment of exceptions is noteworthy for two reasons. Firstly, he highlights their role in mathematics – traditionally thought of as an exact subject in which the occurrence of exceptions would force a mathematician to abandon a conjecture. Secondly, Lakatos showed how exceptions, rather than simply being annoying problem cases, which we may be able to dismiss as monsters, can be used to further knowledge. *Piecemeal exclusion* is one way to deal with exceptions. It does this by excluding a type of polyhedron from the conjecture, in order to exclude a whole class of counterexamples. This is done by generalising from a counterexample to a class of counterexamples which have certain properties. For instance, the students generalize from the hollow cube to *polyhedra with cavities*, and then modify Euler's conjecture to "for any polyhedra without cavities, $V - E + F = 2$". Thus exceptions are seen as objects which are valid (as opposed to monsters) and force us to modify a faulty conjecture by changing the domain to which it refers. *Strategic withdrawal* is the only one of the methods which does not directly use counterexamples. Instead, it uses positive examples of a conjecture and generalizes from these to a class of object, and then limits the domain of the conjecture to this class. For instance, the students generalize from the regular polyhedra to *convex polyhedra*, and then modify Euler's conjecture to "for any convex polyhedra, $V - E + F = 2$".

4.3   The method of proofs and refutations

As the title of the book suggests, this is the most important method, to the extent that the rest of the book is often seen by commentators and critics as a lead up to this method, for instance [Feferman, 1978]. It starts off as the method of *lemma incorporation*, and is developed via the dialectic into the method of *proofs and refutations*.

Lemma incorporation works by distinguishing global and local counterexamples. The former is one which is a counterexample to the main conjecture, and the latter is a counterexample to one of the proof steps (or lemmas). A counterexample may be both global and local, or one and not the other. When faced with a counterexample, the first step is to determine which type it is. If it is both global and local, *i.e.* there is a problem both with the argument and the conclusion, then one should modify the conjecture by incorporating the guilty proof step as a condition. If it is local but not global, *i.e.* the conclusion may still be correct but the reasons for believing it are flawed, then one should modify the guilty proof step but leave the conjecture unchanged. If it is global but not local, *i.e.* there is a problem with the conclusion but no obvious flaw in the reasoning which led to the conclusion, then one should look for a hidden assumption in the proof step, then modify the proof and the conjecture by making the assumption an explicit condition.

Proofs and refutations consists of using the proof steps to suggest counterexamples (by looking for objects which would violate them). For any counterexamples found, it is determined whether they are local or global counterexamples, and then lemma incorporation is performed.

5   Implementing a model of Lakatos's theory

It is not our purpose here to give a detailed description of our system, which is a work in progress. Rather, we hope to use a brief description of the system to highlight questions about Lakatos's theory which our system has helped us to raise and to answer. Modelling Lakatos's theory has two benefits:

• the process of having to write an algorithm for the methods forces us to identify areas in which Lakatos was vague, and aspects he omitted; and

• running the model allows us to test hypotheses about the methods, for instance that they apply to scientific thinking, or that one method is more useful than another. These hypotheses may be claims that Lakatos or other commentators have made, or new ones.

In sections 5.2 and 5.3 we discuss questions and answers which have arisen during our implementation of the methods of monster-barring and piecemeal-exclusion, *i.e.*, of type*(i)*; and in section 6 we consider more general questions, of type *(ii)*.

5.1   System details

Our system is an extended version of the theory formation program HR [Colton, 2002]. HR starts with objects of interest (*e.g.*, integers) and initial concepts (*e.g.*, divisors, multiplication and addition) and uses production rules to transform either one or two existing concepts into new ones. For example the production rule *size*, would take the concept "divisors of an integer" and produce the Tau function "number of divisors of an integer". HR could then use the *split* production rule to produce the concept "number of divisors of an integer = 2", *i.e.*, the concept of a prime number. The production rules are usually applied automatically, according to search strategies which the user inputs at the start of the run, but the user can also force the application of a production rule at any given time, in order to produce a desired concept. This is done by selecting one (or two) concepts in the theory, the production rule and the parameters which determine how the rule applies, and putting this step to be carried out at the top of the agenda. Forcing is a way of fast tracking: finding concepts which would eventually have been found automatically, to be found sooner.

All concepts are represented by a definition, data-table (giving the values of every object of interest in the theory for the given concept), and categorisation (in which all objects of interest with the same value are categorised together). For instance the concept *prime number*, with objects of interest 1-5 would be represented as the **definition:** a is an integer $\& |\{b : b$ is an integer $\wedge b|a\}| = 2$; **data-table:** $1 = false; 2 = true; 3 = true; 4 = false; 5 = true$; and **categorisation:** $[[2, 3, 5], [1, 4]]$. Conjectures, such as concept X implies concept Y, are made empirically by comparing the example sets of different concepts. For instance, HR has made the conjecture that if the sum of the divisors of n is prime, then the number of divisors of n is prime, by noticing that the data-table of the first concept is a sub-table of the second [Colton, 2002]. HR also uses third party automated reasoning software in order to prove or disprove its conjectures. HR evaluates its conjectures and concepts using various ways of measuring interestingness [Colton *et al.*, 2000], and this drives the heuristic search.

Our extended version is implemented in an agent architecture consisting of a number of students and a teacher, in keeping with the dialectical aspect of [Lakatos, 1976]. Each agent has a copy of HR, and starts with a different database of objects of interest to work with, and different interestingness measures. Making the evaluation subjective agrees with Larvor's point[1] that Lakatos considered mathematics to be a matter of taste: "Why not have mathematical critics just as you have literary critics, to develop mathematical taste by public criticism?" *Gamma* – [Lakatos, 1976, p. 98]. Students

---

[1] Personal communication.

send conjectures, concepts, counterexamples, or requests such as barring a specific object of interest from the theory, to the teacher. The teacher sends requests to the students such as "work independently", "send a concept to cover counterexamples $[x, y, z]$", or "modify faulty conjecture C". The students use the methods prescribed by Lakatos to modify a faulty conjecture. Below we describe Lakatos's monster-barring and exception-barring methods.

5.2   Implementing and extending monster-barring

In [Lakatos, 1976], a series of definitions of polyhedron are suggested and negotiated. Students who want to defend the conjecture argue for definitions which *exclude* a proposed counterexample, or monster. Students who want to attack the conjecture argue for definitions which *include* a given counterexample, *i.e.* which would mean that the conjecture is false. The teacher resolves each such discussion by asking the class to accept the strictest definition, *i.e.* that which excludes the monster, leaving the conjecture open.

Which mathematical objects can be ambiguous?

In order to implement monster-barring we have to introduce ambiguity into our model, which forces us to answer questions about what sort of thing can be ambiguous. In mathematical theories, at least two types of component may be ambiguous – objects of interest and concepts. For instance, it may be ambiguous whether the object of interest $\aleph_0$ (the size of the set of all integers – the first transfinite number) is really a number or not; and it may be ambiguous whether the definition of the concept of prime number is "any number with exactly two divisors", or "a number which is only divisible by itself and one" (the difference being whether we consider the number 1 to be prime or not). The type of ambiguity can also take different forms. For instance, an object of interest could be ambiguous in two ways. Firstly, there may be two different objects with the same name, such as one object with six faces, eight vertices and twelve straight edges, and another object with six faces, eight vertices and twelve curved edges both being referred to as a cube and represented by the number of faces, vertices and edges. Secondly, there may be a single object which is represented in multiple ways, such the object star polyhedron being represented as having twelve vertices, thirty edges and twelve faces (where a single face is seen as a star polygon), as well as having sixty triangular faces, forming thirty two vertices and ninety edges. The second case is described in Lakatos's method of monster-adjusting, which is where a counterexample is reinterpreted so that it no longer violates a conjecture – in this method subconcepts such as the concept *face* are shown to be ambiguous.

In our implementation objects of interest and core concepts can be am-

Object A has
6 faces, 8 vertices
and 12 edges

Object B has
6 faces, 8 vertices
and 12 edges

Object C has
12 faces, 12 vertices, and 30 edges, ·
60 faces, 32 vertices and 90 edges

Figure 1. If we represent polyhedra in terms of the number of faces, vertices and edges, then objects A and B have the same representation, even though they are different objects, and object C has two different interpretations.

biguous. Students can question whether the definition of a core concept includes a specific object or not, for instance whether the concept of number should include zero, or whether a platypus is really an animal.

When should monster-barring be performed?

Implicit in the method of monster-barring is the fact that each party has a reason for wanting to define a concept in a certain way. This is a common phenomenon in everyday reasoning; for instance, politicians will define "unemployment" or "violent crime" differently, depending on whether they wish to argue that the figures have risen or fallen. In [Lakatos, 1976] the students discuss what was their original, unexpressed, intended definition and whether it corresponds to the explicit definition they are currently defending. Very little time is spent on why an alternative definition is first proposed, or why it may eventually be accepted or rejected; in [Lakatos, 1976] the teacher always instructs the class to accept the monster-barring definition, *i.e.* that which excludes the monster. This is a gap in the theory; always accepting the strictest definition is an unrealistic way of settling the dispute. As Corfield says; "Mathematicians have an intuitive feeling of the behavior of objects they try to define – the process of discovery involves the struggle to find a good or 'right' definition" [Corfield, 1997, p. 113]. We have addressed this gap in our algorithm for the way in which students decide: *(i)* whether they want propose an alternative definition or not, and *(ii)* given a proposed new definition, whether they want to accept it or not. There are a range of motives which mathematicians have behind a decision to reject or accept a concept definition. In the context which Lakatos presents, the most obvious is to defend or attack a given conjecture (*i.e.*, Euler's conjecture). Another factor (which Lakatos does not consider) is the effect that choosing one of two competing definitions will have on the rest of a mathematician's theories or beliefs (this is known as the degree of *entrenchment* in belief revision [Gärdenfors, 1992]). In our implementation we have extended Lakatos's theory to reflect this.

Suppose that a student is sent an object of interest which is a counterexample to a conjecture that the group is currently discussing, and the object is new to the student. If this object is presented as an example of a concept C which the student is familiar with, then it is clear that there is some ambiguity over the definition of C. For instance, suppose a student receives the "number" 0 when it has only previously seen positive examples of number (1,2, etc.). In this case the concept "number" is ambiguous. The student then has two ways to decide whether it wants to bar the object (where the user decides which of the two ways should be used, at the start of the run). The first way is to test whether the counterexample breaks more than a (user-defined) percentage of all the conjectures in the student's theory, and if so, it proposes to monster-bar the counterexample. The second way is to test to see whether the new object is a "culprit breaker". This means that not only is the object a counterexample to the conjecture under discussion, but if it is allowed into the student's theory then it forces other objects in the theory which previously supported the conjecture, to become counterexamples to the conjecture. For instance, suppose that the conjecture under discussion is the conjecture that there do not exist integers a, b, c such that $a + b = c$ and $c|a$. A student which has the integers $1 - 10$ in its theory may make this conjecture, as it is true of all of its objects. However if the number 0 is proposed as a counterexample by another student, the first student will find that if it allows 0 into its theory, it does not just have a single counterexample – 0 – to this conjecture, but that the existence of 0 has forced all of the other objects to become counterexamples as well. For instance, if we take $b = 0$ and $a = c$, then 1 is a counterexample since $1 + 0 = 1$ and $1|1$, and similarly 2 is also a counterexample since $2 + 0 = 2$ and $2|2$, etc. So allowing 0 into the theory means that there are now 11 sets of counterexamples a, b and c. In our algorithm, if the object in question forces other objects into being counterexamples for a higher number of conjectures than a minimum, user set proportion, then the object is called a "culprit breaker", and monster-barred.

Rather than the teacher instructing the students to use the narrowest definition, once a concept has been raised as being ambiguous and two definitions suggested, each student decides which definition they prefer and votes accordingly. The definition is then decided democratically, based on these votes. If the votes are equal, then we follow Lakatos's principle of taking the narrowest definition. The students make the decision based on the proportion of conjectures in their theories which still hold under each of the rival definitions. Clearly this way of determining a definition means that we have to be able to accept the "monster". In our algorithm, if the consensus between the students is to extend a definition, then the teacher asks them all to perform monster-*accepting* by agreeing on the new, wider definition. [Lakatos, 1976, p. 83–99] does raise this issue, calling it concept stretching: however the discussion in this part of the book principally concerns the semantics and methodology of monster-barring rather than reasons for proposing and accepting a rival definition.

What sorts of definitions are proposed?

In [Lakatos, 1976], there are two types of concept definitions: an initial vague concept, which is not explicitly defined but some positives are known; and an explicit definition, for which the extension of the concept should be easier to determine. The two ways in which HR [Colton, 2002] can represent concepts corresponds to these – a core concept has no explicit definition, and a concept which HR has generated does.

The process of monster-barring in [Lakatos, 1976] might start with a vague definition and become more specific, or start with a specifically defined concept and by discussion reach agreement to define it in a different, yet still specific way. We have extended this by implementing the case which starts and finishes with a vague concept, *i.e.* a specific definition is not reached, but agreement is reached about whether a concept includes a given object or not. This is useful as explicit and precise definitions cannot always be reached nor agreed upon – even so called specific definitions are really just removing the level of vagueness. For instance defining a polyhedron as "a solid whose surface consists of polygonal faces" [Lakatos, 1976, p. 14] *is* being more explicit about what is meant by the concept polyhedron, but there is still ambiguity in the subconcepts solid, surface, polygon and face. We have implemented the process of generating a specific definition from a vague concept C, by finding all of the concepts which are conjectured to be equivalent to C, and then selecting the most interesting of these.

Our monster-handling algorithm

Students send each other objects of interest if they arise as counterexamples to a conjecture which the group is discussing. If a student is sent an object of interest which it has not seen before, as an example of a concept C, then it will first check to see whether its user-given flag to monster-bar is set. If it is not set, then the student simply adds the new object to its theory. If it is set, then the student:

1) decides whether to perform monster-barring;

It does this by performing one of the two tests above: if the new object is either a counterexample to more than a user-defined percentage of the student's total conjectures, or if it is a culprit breaker, then the student performs monster-barring. Otherwise it adds the new object to its theory and reject the conjecture under discussion as being false.

2) generates a new definition of the concept;

It can either generate a new, explicit definition of C, which excludes the monster; or it can generate a new, vague definition of C which excludes the monster from the list of objects which C covers.

When a student receives a proposal to bar a monster, it:

3) evaluates whether it agrees or disagrees with the proposal.

It does this by calculating the percentage of its own conjectures that the proposed "monster" breaks, and voting on whether to bar the object or not.

When the teacher receives votes on barring or accepting an object, it waits until it has received a vote from each of the students, and then counts them. If the votes to bar the object outweigh those to accept it, then the teacher tells the students to downgrade the "monster" from object of interest to "pseudo object" in their theories. Pseudo objects do not count as counterexamples so cannot threaten conjectures, but are around in the theory and can be upgraded to object at a future stage. If an explicit definition is given, then the students have to replace their old concept definition with the new one. Alternatively, if the votes to accept the object outweigh those to bar it, the teacher will tell the students to *add* the object to their theories.

Illustrative examples

As we have developed our system in number theory, we looked for instances of ambiguity in this domain, which we could model. The most ambiguous concept was that of number itself, with plentiful examples of monster-barring and eventual monster-accepting. For instance, the number 1 was initially barred by the Pythagoreans as it challenged their belief that all numbers increase other numbers by multiplication; $\sqrt{2}$ violated the Greek belief that all numbers describe a collection of objects; and $x = \sqrt{-1}$ violated the law that you cannot multiply two numbers together to give a negative number. Now of course 0, 1, irrational and imaginary numbers are accepted as numbers, and the concept of number has been generalized to complex numbers and beyond (quarternions). Another example is Cantor's introduction of transfinite numbers, which were not considered to be valid numbers by most mathematicians in Cantor's time, such as Kronecker. The "number" $\aleph_0$, for instance, is a counterexample to the conjecture that if you add a non-zero number to another number, then the result is bigger than the second number, since $\aleph_0 + \aleph_0 = \aleph_0$. Similarly it violates the conjecture that any positive number multiplied by integer $n > 1$ is bigger than the number, as $\aleph_0.n = \aleph_0$. The law of monotonicity, that for all numbers a, b and c, if $b < c$, then $a + b < a + c$ fails if $a = \aleph_0$ (for any finite b and c). For these and other reasons, initial reaction to Cantor's work was hostile, and $\aleph_0$ was branded a monster, and barred from the concept of number. To-day, however, these objects are accepted as numbers, and laws of arithmetic previously thought to hold for all numbers are now limited to a specified subset of number, such as the natural numbers or the reals. Clearly number theory, and other areas of mathematics, have been greatly enhanced by all of these additions.

Example to demonstrate the culprit breaker

The students debate whether the object 0 is a number or not.

Input information:

We ran the agency with two students and a teacher. The first student started with the integers $0-10$ and the other student started with the integers $1-10$ (i.e., they did not know the number 0). Both students started with the background concepts of integers, divisors, and multiplication. The teacher requested non-existence conjectures, i.e. conjectures about a concept which has no known examples. The students were set to work individually for 20 steps and then enter into discussion. The students were both set to use monster-barring, and specifically to testing to see whether an entity was a culprit breaker when deciding whether to propose monster-barring or not. The monster-barring minimum was set to 15%, i.e. if a proposal to monster-bar an entity was made, a student would evaluate it by testing to see whether the entity was a counterexample to more than 15% of its conjectures (in which case the student would agree to bar it).

Results of run:

The second student made the conjecture that there do not exist integers a, b such that $b+a = a$ and $a+b = a$, and sent it to the teacher, who put it in the agenda for discussion. The teacher then asked for counterexamples to the conjecture, and the first student sent back all its integers, since having 0 in its theory meant that *every* number is a counterexample, e.g. 1 is a counterexample since $1 + 0 = 1$, similarly 2 is also a counterexample since $2+0 = 2$, etc. The teacher then asked for responses to the counterexamples, and the student with 0 tested to see whether there was a single "culprit" entity which was forcing all of its objects of interest to be counterexamples, and concluded that 0 was a culprit entity. As a consequence it then sent the request to the teacher to monster-bar 0. The teacher put this request into the agenda, and sent it to the second student, who tested to see how many of its conjectures the number 0 broke. It found that 0 broke 63% of its conjectures, and as that was more than 15%, voted to monster-bar 0. The teacher counted the votes and told both of the students to down-grade

0 to a pseudo-entity. Both students then added 0 to their pseudo-objects of interest list, which meant that it was now in both of their theories but did not count as a valid integer.

Example to demonstrate the generation of an explicit concept definition

The students debate whether the object $A1 = < P(\{a,b\}) \setminus \phi, \cup >$ is a group or not. That is, $A1$ is an algebra consisting of the set of subsets of $\{a,b\}$ except the empty set, and the operation set union. Since the empty set is not included, this object has no identity and therefore no inverse.

Input information:

We ran the agency with three students and a teacher. The first student started with 14 examples of groups, up to size 8, and the other two students started with two algebras, $A1$, which is of size 3 and has no identity and no inverse for any of the elements, and $A2$, which is of size 4 and has an identity but no inverse element for two of the elements in it. All students start with the core concepts being an element of a group, the operator function, identity and inverse. In order to get the illustrative example, we forced the concept the existence of an identity element in a group, in the first student's theory. If we did not do this, it would find the concept automatically within 40 theory formation steps; we do it for the purposes of this example only. The monster-barring minimum is set to 15%, and the students are set to suggest an explicit definition if they perform monster-barring. The teacher asked the students to work individually for 40 steps and then send in their best conjectures.

Results of run:

The first student sent the conjecture that something is a group if and only if it has an identity element. The second and third students both sent the first algebra in their theories, $A1$ as a counterexample. As this is a new object for the first student, it checks how many of its conjectures it breaks and finds that it breaks 19%. Since this is greater than the minimum set, the student proposes to bar $A1$ as a monster and sends the statement that $A1$ is not a group, as a group must have an inverse element for every element in the group. The other two students check whether $A1$ is a counterexample to any of their conjectures, find that it is not, and reject the proposal to bar it, saying that it *is* a group, as a group is any set of objects with an element in it. As the first student is out-voted, the teacher tells it to add $A1$ to its theory.

It is in the method of monster-barring that the dialectic is most at play, where concepts develop from simple, often poorly understood, vague and ambiguous ideas to rich and sophisticated notions – analogous, as Larvor points out, to the dialectical pattern in Plato's Republic where they discuss and develop the concept of justice. This concept development is done by discussing propositions or conjectures in which the concept features – for instance that the *just* man is a happy man, or that for all *polyhedra*, $V - E + F = 2$ ([Larvor, 1998, p. 10]).

Lakatos thought that monster-barring was not a productive reaction to a counterexample; he calls it a "usually barren Euclidean defence mechanism" [Lakatos, 1978, p. 15], associated with dogmatists who defend or protect a conjecture at all costs. He criticises it because as well as specializing (hence reducing the domain – and therefore the value – of a conjecture), rather than generalizing a conjecture, it results in long and complex definitions, whose history mathematicians have no idea about; this is especially unhelpful for students. (Lakatos gives the example of the definition of ordinary polyhedron which takes up 45 lines in the 1962 edition of the *Encyclopaedia Britannica* [Lakatos, 1976, p.53, footnote 3].) One advantage of this method of course, is that by excluding objects on the concept level rather than at the conjecture level, all conjecture statements involving this concept can be concisely expressed.

5.3 Implementing the method of exception-barring

Introducing a further distinction

Piecemeal exclusion in [Lakatos, 1976] always consists of barring a class of object. However, in our implementation we introduce a further distinction. We differentiate between concept-barring, where a concept is excluded, and counterexample-barring, where counterexamples are listed separately in the conjecture as exceptions. Using counterexample-barring, therefore, no overall concept is found which covers the counterexample(s). Introducing this distinction raises the question of *when* we should use concept-barring and when we should use counterexample-barring. We have resolved this by looking to see whether a student already has a concept in its theory which exactly covers the counterexamples, in which case it uses concept-barring. If unsuccessful, and there are few counterexamples, say $[x, y, z]$, it makes the concept X of being x, y or z and then uses counterexample-barring.

Other types of conjecture

Piecemeal exclusion in [Lakatos, 1976] is applied only to one conjecture, in particular that one concept (polyhedra) almost implies another (shapes which satisfy the Euler equation). We represent this as $poly(x) \leadsto euler(x)$. Clearly there are other types of conjecture than implication in mathematics. Equivalence conjectures are another type, in which the definitions of two concepts are logically equivalent $(P \leftrightarrow Q)$. This raises the question of how to apply piecemeal exclusion to other types of conjecture such as equivalences, and what sort of conjectures would result. We answer these questions below.

As described above (section 5), one way concepts are represented in the HR system [Colton, 2002] is as a data-table, *i.e.*, examples with corresponding values (eg $prime(5) = true$, or $\tau(5) = 2$). We can represent an equivalence or implication conjecture as two sets of examples (corresponding to the two concepts) where the intersection contains those examples which share the same values. The example in [Lakatos, 1976] is represented as such in the left hand diagram in Figure 2:

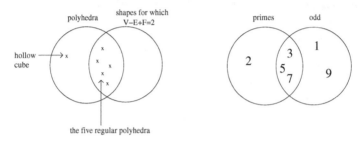

Figure 2. In the left hand diagram, we represent Euler's conjecture as overlapping sets. In the right hand diagram, we see represent the conjecture that primes ⟿ odds as overlapping sets.

As this example is an implication we only have counterexamples on one side, *i.e.*, in one set. However, for equivalences, we may get counterexamples on both sides, as in the example on the right hand side of Figure 2. In this case we might want to apply piecemeal exclusion *twice*. This would result in two implication conjectures. For instance, from the faulty conjecture "$\forall x.prime(x) \leftrightarrow odd(x)$", (using integers 1-10) suppose the system used counterexample-barring to produce the concepts *primes except 2* and concept-barring to produce the concept of *odd non-square numbers*. This would result in the generation of two conjectures: "all primes except 2 are odd" (which is true) and "all odd non-square numbers are prime" (which is false – the first counterexample is 15).

In addition to implication and equivalence conjectures, [Colton, 2002, ch. 7] suggests two further types: *non-exists*, where no examples satisfy the definition of a given concept ($\nexists x$ such that $P(x)$), and *applicability*, where examples satisfying a definition are restricted to a particular finite set (concept $P(x)$ is only applicable to examples in set S). We are currently considering the application of piecemeal exclusion to faulty conjectures in these formats.

Our piecemeal exclusion algorithm

Given a near equivalence $P \rightsquigarrow Q$, a student agent will get the list of counterexamples and determine whether each counterexample satisfies the definition of P or Q (using the set analogy, we say that a counterexample is *in* P or Q). There are three cases:

Case 1: all counterexamples are in P
(i) look for a concept X in the theory which exactly covers the counters. If unsuccessful, and there are few counterexamples, say $[x, y, z]$, then make the concept X of being x, y or z.
(ii) form the new concept $P \wedge \neg X$
(iii) add the new concept to the theory, which will force the formation of this conjecture: $P \wedge \neg X \leftrightarrow Q$

Case 2: all counterexamples are in Q
As for case 1, instead forming the concept $Q \wedge \neg X$ and the conjecture $P \leftrightarrow Q \wedge \neg X$

Case 3: there are counterexamples in both P and Q
(i) find a concept X in the theory which exactly covers the counters in P. If unsuccessful, and there are few counterexamples, say $[x, y, z]$, then make the concept X of being x, y or z.
(ii) form the new concept $P \wedge \neg X$
(ii) form the concept $P \wedge \neg X$
(iii) add this new concept to the theory, which will force the formation of this conjecture: $P \wedge \neg X \rightarrow Q$
(iv) repeat steps *(i)* to *(iii)*, swapping P and Q.

If a student gets a near implication then there can only be counterexamples on one side, *i.e.* either in concept P or in Q (but not both), and so the steps in either case 1 or case 2 are performed.

Illustrative examples

Example to demonstrate concept-barring on a near-equivalence conjecture

Using three student agents and a teacher, we get the conjecture that an integer is non-square if and only if it has an even number of divisors.

Initial information

Student 1 starts with objects of interest $1 - 10$, and core concepts integer, divisor and multiplication. It is set to make implications from subsumptions, and to use piecemeal exclusion. Before running it independently we force the concepts square and integers which have an even number of divisors. Student 2 starts with the same input as Student 1, except with integers

11 − 50. Student 3 starts with integers 51 − 60, core concepts integer, divisor and multiplication, and the forced concept of integers which have an even number of divisors.

The run

The teacher sends a request to work independently for 20 steps, and then send back their best implication conjecture. Student 3 forms the conjecture that all integers have an even number of divisors, and sends it to the teacher, who puts it on the group agenda for modifications. The other two students then find counterexamples [1,4,9] and [16, 25, 36, 49] respectively, then find the concept of squares and form the new concept of non-squares. They then use this new concept to form the conjecture that all non-squares have an even number of divisors.

Example to demonstrate counterexample-barring on a near-implication conjecture

Using two students and a teacher, we get the conjecture that *all even numbers except 2 are the sum of two primes* (Goldbach's conjecture).

Initial information

Student 1 starts with the integers 1 − 10 and core concepts integers and divisors. It is set to make implications from subsumptions and to use piecemeal exclusion. We force the concepts even numbers and integers which are the sum of two primes. Student 2 starts with the same information except integers 11 − 20.

The run

The teacher sends a request to work independently for 20 steps, and then send back their best implication conjecture. Student 2 forms the conjecture that all even numbers can be expressed as the sum of two primes. The teacher sends a request for modifications, and Student 1 finds the counterexample 2, and makes the concept even numbers except 2 and the conjecture that all even numbers except 2 are the sum of two primes.

6   Answers suggested by the computational approach

Having a computational model enables us to test hypotheses about Lakatos's theory. These may arise during implementation or have been suggested by Lakatos or his critics. In this section we outline questions and criticisms of the theory, and ways in which our model has allowed – or might allow us – to answer them. In particular we refer to Feferman's ten criticisms of [Lakatos, 1976], in [Feferman, 1978, pp. 316–320] (we note the criticism number in italics).

6.1   The scope of the methods

Although Lakatos is praised for the extremely detailed and in-depth analysis of his case studies – in particular of Euler's conjecture, he has been criticized (see, for instance, [Feferman, 1978]) for only considering two examples. Certainly it is difficult to claim to have found patterns general to mathematical and even other types of discovery from such a small sample. We see determining the scope of the methods as one of the major contributions of our work, and suggest an alternative to [Larvor, 1998, p. 11] who claims that "this type of dispute [whether Lakatos's methods are typical or atypical of mathematical reasoning] can only be resolved by extensive historical research". Producing a computer model gives us an obvious way of testing the variety of domains to which the methods can be usefully applied.

It is worth noting that while Lakatos did claim that his methods are general enough to apply to other domains, both mathematical and non-mathematical, he did not believe them to be the sole explanation of mathematical discovery. Indeed, as Larvor argues, Lakatos did not believe that there is a unique logic of mathematical discovery, much less that he had found it. (Larvor points out that it was the editors, rather than Lakatos, who gave the book the subtitle *the* logic of mathematical discovery.) Instead – in his original thesis at least – he states the more modest aim of pointing out "some tentative rules which may help us to avoid some deeply entrenched wrong heuristic habits" (Thesis, p. 75; quoted in [Larvor, 1998, p. 12]). This view, that there are many ways of practicing mathematics is echoed in philosophy of science – for instance Bird [Bird, 1998, ch. 8] and Feyerabend [Feyerabend, 1975] argue that there is no such thing as *the* scientific method.

Applying the methods to other areas of mathematics

Feferman [Feferman, 1978] argues that the methods only explain a small fraction of mathematical reasoning. For instance, he argues that the main method – proofs and refutations – fails to account for foundational changes before 1847 *(i)*. He also questions Lakatos's claim that the method of proofs and refutations is most appropriate to young, growing theories *(ii)* – arguing that *(a)* Lakatos's main example of the method – Euler's conjecture – was not a young, growing theory, and *(b)* there are examples of young, growing theories - such as continuous probability measures – which progressed without recourse to counterexamples and therefore without recourse to Lakatos's method. Hacking [Hacking, 1981] argues that since Lakatos's reasoning assumes the hypothetico-deductive model, its relevance is restricted to this type of knowledge – and there are other styles of knowledge such as Crombie's six styles of reasoning (see [Crombie, 1994]). He warns us not to let "the eternal verities depend on a mere episode in the history of human knowledge" [Hacking, 1981, p. 143].

Our implementation strategy has been to develop the methods in other mathematical domains, mainly number theory, but also group, ring and field theory, and to use the domain of algebraic topology as a test domain. In this way, we can ensure that we implement them in a general way. This also lets us investigate whether the methods are sufficiently general to produce interesting mathematics in areas other than topology, vector algebra and real analysis.

Applying the methods to empirical sciences

[Lakatos, 1976] is often seen as Lakatos's attempt to apply Popper's philosophy of science to mathematics. There are both methodological and epistemological parallels: the view that mathematics advances by studying refutations and therefore practitioners should focus on finding counterexamples and anomalies, and the belief that there is no certain knowledge – both mathematics and science are fallibilist. We have already noted one key difference between Popper and Lakatos – the discovery/justification distinction; another (pointed out by Larvor [Larvor, 1998]) is what we should do with the refutations once we have found them – Popper's naive falsificationism tells us to reject the hypothesis, whereas this reaction is the first and most naive method in [Lakatos, 1976] – the method of surrender – to which Lakatos devotes only one out of the total 120 pages in the book. More sophisticated methods use the counterexample to refine the conjecture and concepts in it.

Lakatos partially addresses this problem by inheriting Kuhn's ideas on demarcation. Kuhn argued [Kuhn, 1970] that the boundaries between scientific and non-scientific knowledge are not sharp; and Lakatos thought that the degree to which mathematics and science are the same type of (empirical) knowledge, corresponds to the degree to which his methods apply to science as well as mathematics. Lakatos claimed that "mathematical heuristic is very like scientific knowledge – not because both are inductive, but because both are characterised by conjectures, proofs, and refutations. The – important – difference lies in the nature of the respective conjectures, proofs (or, in science, explanations), and counterexamples" [Lakatos, 1976, p. 74]. He credits Polya's stress on the similarities between scientific and mathematical heuristic as one of the most important contributions of his work (see [Lakatos, 1976, p. 74], footnote 1).

Feferman [Feferman, 1978] also asks *(x) what is distinctive about mathematics?* He argues that Lakatos's methods do generalize to other domains, that his logic of mathematical discovery is really a logic of *rational* discovery. However, Feferman sees this as a shortcoming, claiming that they would then be overly general and "could account only for a few gross features of the actual growth of mathematics"[Feferman, 1978, p. 320].

In order to see whether our model could effectively be applied to non-mathematical domains, we tested it on a machine learning data-set. This consisted of 18 animals, with information on whether they were covered by hair, scales or feathers; the number of legs they have; whether they are homeothermic; whether they produce milk/lay eggs/ have gills; what sort of habitat they live in; and what class of animal they are – mammal, fish, reptile or bird. We ran our agency with two students, where the first was given the platypus as an example and the second student was not. The platypus arose instantly as a counterexample to a conjecture which the first student proposed, and the second student found that it violated many of its conjectures, and requested that it be monster-barred. Upon examining its own conjectures, the first student agreed and narrowed its definition of animal to exclude this problem case. This is a nice example of how monster-barring works in non-mathematical domains. It mirrors the situation in the 19th century when the platypus was first brought from Australia to Britain, and was initially thought to be a hoax played by taxidermists. It was described by Darwin as a "funny sort" [Mozley Moyal, 2001], and Burrell claims that "No animal has given rise to so much controversy among both layman and professed zoologists" [Burrell, 1927, p. 1]. This example shows how we can extend Lakatos's work by testing his claims, for instance, that his methods do extend to empirical science.

6.2 Applying Lakatos's methods to other types of conjecture

Feferman [Feferman, 1978] points out *(vii)* that all the examples of conjectures given by Lakatos are of the form $\forall x[A(x) \rightarrow B(x)]$ and gives examples of other types of conjecture found in mathematics and the form their refinement might take. As we discussed in section 5.3, this is an aspect which has arisen in our implementation and we have suggested and implemented ways of applying the methods of other types of conjecture.

A related criticism is that, with the exception of strategic withdrawal, they are only applicable to the type of conjecture which could be falsified by counterexample [Feferman, 1978]; *(ii)* and *(iii)*. This corresponds to the criticism of Popper's falsificationism (e.g., see [Bird, 1998]), that it only applies to scientific hypotheses which are generalizations. This excludes, for instance statistical hypotheses (nothing can falsify a probabilistic hypothesis). While we cannot avoid this criticism, we can investigate how limiting this is, by running the model on a wide variety of domains, and testing to see how many of the theorems and conjectures which are considered interesting in the field it generates.

6.3   How should we apply the methods?

How do the methods compare?

In both Lakatos's and commentators' writings, *e.g.* [Corfield, 1997], there is a clear hierarchy of methods, where they are presented as being increasingly sophisticated. Therefore much work focuses purely on the final method to be described – proofs and refutations. Indeed the first method, of surrendering a conjecture as false when faced with a counterexample, is not mentioned in any book on Lakatos that we have seen, and Lakatos wrote that "Mere "falsification" (in Popper's sense) must not imply rejection" [Lakatos, 1981, p. 116]. He called exception-barring, monster-barring and monster-adjusting "conventionalist strategems" [Lakatos, 1981, p. 117], and thought that they are *ad hoc* in the sense that once applied, the new conjecture has no excess empirical content than the old one. Therefore they cannot form part of a progressive research programme (*i.e.* one which successfully predicts novel facts). Commentators usually make scant reference to these methods, with the assumption often being made that [Lakatos, 1976] is solely about the final method.

By running our system on different combinations of the methods and evaluating the resulting mathematical theories, we are able to investigate these views. For instance, we hold that surrender is useful in preventing resources from being wasted on dead end conjectures. The challenge is to find ways of knowing when to use a counterexample to surrender a conjecture, and when to use it as a catalyst for refining the conjecture. Similarly we hold that the method of exception-barring has enabled us to generate interesting conjectures (see section 5.3); and by allowing us to explore concepts more fully, monster-barring can generate interesting discussion.

Our agency currently operates at three levels of increasing autonomy:
- the user sets flags which instruct student agents to use a given method;
- the teacher agent can request that the students use a given method, and
- students can choose themselves by deciding whether to defend or attack a given conjecture, based on how many counterexamples they have in their own theories.

We are investigating which method works best in a given situation by empirical testing.

When should we stop applying them?

Feferman claims that guesswork in mathematics finishes with the mathematician's successful struggle to solve a problem, as opposed to the picture which Lakatos paints of endless guessing *(iv)*. Certainly there needs to be some limit on our system as to when it can apply each method. Conjectures which have been over-modified will become dull or too specific (for instance after repeated application of piecemeal exclusion). This will also prevent the system from investigating more interesting paths. The question of what exactly over-modified means now arises. Our system currently stops modifying a theorem either when no more counterexamples can be found, or when the theorem prover Otter [McCune, 1990] (to which it has recourse) has proved a conjecture. Additionally, the student agents are not allowed to attempt to bar an object if a vote has been agreed to accept it, *i.e.*, monster-barring is only allowed once per object. Each agent keeps track of the history of a modified conjecture, *i.e.*, which methods have been applied to it. We plan to use this history to put further checks on the number of times a student can perform a given method on the same conjecture. The best frequency for these checks will be determined by empirical testing.

7 Evaluating theories within the philosophy of science

In the philosophy of science, ideas on evaluating a theory or hypothesis came before ideas on how the hypothesis is discovered. In computational philosophy of science it appears to be the other way around. That is, ideas on how to generate, or discover programs which model scientific progress have come before ideas on how we should evaluate these programs. Clearly much work in the philosophy of science examines what makes a scientific theory good, for example [Popper, 1972]. Yet, although much of philosophy concerns evaluating different arguments, there seems to have been little explicitly written about how to evaluate meta-theories, *i.e.*, philosophical theories about scientific theories. If the field of computational philosophy of science is to progress, there has to be discussion and agreement on the criteria by which we judge computational theories (philosophical theories which are at least partially derived using computational techniques). Additionally, these criteria must be formal enough that comparative claims can be supported and progress measured. Unsurprisingly, this mirrors the situation in the machine creativity field, in which attempts are being made to find a framework which is both practically useful and theoretically feasible, *i.e.*, formal but not oversimplified (for example [Pease *et al.*, 2001], [Ritchie, 2001]).

We have not seen criteria set out purely for this purpose. For instance, Thagard [Thagard, 1993] suggests criteria for evaluating explanatory theories. These are intended for evaluating scientific, rather than philosophical theories, and have been extracted from studying examples of scientific theories. However, Thagard also claims that they can be used to determine the best explanation in metaphysical theories [Thagard, 1993, p. 99]. The criteria are consilience, simplicity and analogy. Consilience is a measure of how many observables a theory explains, and the variety and importance of the facts explained. The notion of simplicity is a way of constraining consilience by ensuring that the theory is not *ad hoc*. This means that the theory explains more than just the data which it was introduced to explain, *i.e.*, it is not fine-tuned. Hence the first and second criteria need to be taken in conjunction with each other. Lakatos does briefly use analogical reasoning in [Lakatos, 1976, p. 70]. This is where one of the students tries to find a conjecture which differs from Euler's conjecture to discuss, having decided that more discussion about the same conjecture will be fruitless. He recalls that the original conjecture was found by considering the theorem that for all polygons, the number of edges is equal to the number of vertices; and looking for an analogous relation in the polyhedra domain. However, as this idea is not central to the book, and HR already has the functionality to generate initial conjectures in other ways, we have not implemented this aspect yet. Hence Thagard's third criterion is not relevant to the evaluation of our extended theory.

Since we are extending Lakatos's work, our computational theory should explain everything his does and more. This makes the comparison easier as we do not have to show that our theory explains a wider variety or more important facts than those which Lakatos's explains. Rather, we need to show that it explains aspects of mathematical development which are omitted in Lakatos's theory.

Evaluating our computational model of monster-barring

Our addition of monster-accepting clearly explains aspects of theory formation which Lakatos did not address. This satisfies Thagard's criteria of consilience. In order to evaluate whether we have increased simplicity, *i.e.*, whether it explains more than the specific data in the domain of algebraic topology, we look to another mathematical domain which has arisen during our discussion, number theory, to see whether it applies there. Burton [Burton, 1985] asserts that the number zero, first appeared in the Western number system as a place holder in around 150 *A.D.* (in Babylonian positional notation, the number 1, for instance, would have been ambiguous as it could equally represent 10, 100, etc.). However, he states, it was not held to be a valid counting number for centuries, only being commonly used in practical calculations in the 1500s. This was partially due to the Greek reluctance to accept it – they branded it a monster for various reasons, including its violation of the conjecture that if you add a number to another number, then the second number always changes. (When zero was eventually accepted as a number, this conjecture was modified to exclude zero, *i.e.* if you add a *non-zero* number to another number, then the second number always changes.) In section 5.2 we saw a similar story with the introduction, initial hostility towards, ambiguous status and eventual acceptance of: the number 1, irrational and imaginary numbers, and $\aleph_0$. Thus it is clear that concepts within mathematics sometimes widen to include an object, rather than always narrowing to exclude it, and therefore our addition of monster-accepting not only satisfies Thagard's criteria of consilience but also his principle of simplicity.

Evaluating our computational model of piecemeal-exclusion

Implementing piecemeal-exclusion has led to a more fine-grained approach which differentiates between excluding counterexamples and excluding concepts. Further examples of conjectures in which counterexamples are explicitly excepted, as opposed to finding a concept which covers them and excepting that, include: all even numbers except 2 are expressible as the sum of two primes (this is Goldbach's famous conjecture); and all primes except 2 are odd. The first is an open conjecture (although discovered in 1742, it is still unproved), and the second is a theorem. Additionally we have seen examples in which applying the method to an equivalence, as opposed to an implication conjecture, suggests further conjectures of interest. Thus we argue that our extension has improved on Lakatos's original work.

We also hold that our implementation has enabled us to answer general questions about Lakatos's work. For instance, the question arose in section 6.1 of whether his ideas translate to non-mathematical domains.

8 Other benefits of the computational approach

There are other benefits to implementing Lakatos's work (and other theories within the philosophy of science). For instance, we can use his ideas to help us to develop new techniques which aid scientists in their work [Langley, 2002]. As with much work in the automated reasoning field, HR [Colton, 2002] was originally developed for this purpose, *i.e.*, to help mathematicians discover new results, and we consider that our extended version of automated theory formation contributes to this purpose. Research – for instance [Fielder, 2001] and [Langley, 2002] – has shown that scientists prefer to know the background of a claim made by a computer program - rather than take it on trust. This fits perfectly with Lakatos's philosophy of presenting the history of a result rather than isolated results with no explanation as to the thinking behind them.

A final motivation behind computational philosophy of science is to develop new techniques which are useful in finding new knowledge of interest to experts [Langley, 1999]. Lakatos's ideas have provided us with this inspiration: we have developed a system – Theorem Modifier, or TM – which uses Lakatos-style methods to modify faulty conjectures into true ones. Given a conjecture, the system uses the Otter theorem prover [McCune, 1990] to first try and prove the conjecture. If it fails, the system uses the Mace model generator [McCune, 2001] to produce examples which support the conjecture, and examples which falsify the conjecture. We then use concept barring and strategic withdrawal methods implemented within the HR system to find concepts covering a subset of the falsifying examples and/or concepts covering a subset of the supporting examples. The system uses piecemeal exclusion on the first type of concept to withdraw into a more specialized conjecture, and strategic withdrawal on the second type of concept, again to specialize the conjecture. A set of modified conjectures is generated this way, and each is tested for theorem-hood by Otter. The user is shown only those modified theorems which Otter has proved.

Full details and results are reported in [Colton and Pease, 2004]; here we give two illustrative examples to give a flavor of our results. In the TPTP library of first order theorems [Sutcliffe and Suttner, 1998], the first non-theorem in group theory states that, given the definition of the commutator operator on two elements x and y being $comm(x, y) = x * y * x^{-1} * y^{-1}$, then this operator is associative if and only if the product of the commutator is always in the center of the group (defined to be the set of elements which commute with all others). Hence this theorem states that: $\forall x, y, z \ (comm(comm(x, y)), z) = comm(x, comm(y, x)) \Leftrightarrow \forall u, v, w \ (comm(u, v)*w = w*comm(u, v)))$. Mace could not find any counterexamples to this, but it did find four groups for which the conjecture is true. As strategic withdrawal does not need any counterexamples, TM could continue. It found that, with the extra axiom that the groups are self inverse (*i.e.*, $\forall x \ (x = x^{-1})$), the conjecture actually holds. As an example in ring theory, one non-theorem in [Sutcliffe and Suttner, 1998] states that the following property, P, holds for all rings: $\forall w, x \ ((((w*w)*x)*(w*w)) = id)$ where id is the additive identity element. Mace found 7 supporting examples for this, and 6 falsifying examples. HR produced a single specialization concept which was true of 3 supporting examples: $\nexists b, c \ (b*b = c \wedge b + b \neq c)$. Otter then proved that P holds in rings for which HR's invented property holds. Hence, while TM could not prove the original theorem, it did prove that, in rings for which $\forall x \ (x * x = x + x)$, property P holds. The specialization here has an appealing symmetry.

9 Conclusion

Lakatos's philosophy of mathematics provides us with a rich source of ideas on how mathematical theories can evolve. We have argued that the process of implementing his philosophy of mathematics has forced us to ask searching questions, such as: what types of object can be ambiguous; how ambiguity arises and how it is resolved; how we can decide between rival definitions, and how to widen a definition; what sorts of things can usefully be barred in a conjecture statement, and how we might apply the methods to types of conjecture other than implications; and to suggest answers. This process has led to an extended computational theory of mathematical development. Running the model has enabled us to answer questions about the applicability of the methods to other mathematical, and non-mathematical domains.

This project is a work in progress and we hope to implement further methods, increase the sophistication of the agents, and test more hypotheses. Our goals include testing to see whether the age of the theory affects the efficiency of the methods[2]. For instance, a new concept which is suggested in monster-accepting may break the current conjecture but show the promise of exciting new theories. HR records the number of steps is has been running for, so the age of its theories is easily determined. We are also currently completing our implementation of the method of proofs and refutations.

Given that Lakatos emphasized the informal nature of mathematics, our attempt to implement and therefore formalize it could be seen as being as objectionable as the editors addition of the "final" chapter (chapter 2) in the history of Euler's conjecture – thus presenting his work as a finished philosophy rather than a step on the path of Hegel's dialectic. Our justification for this is that we by no means finalize the work, we investigate which parts can be formalized and whether and how that adds to Lakatos's work. We do not see modeling informal mathematics as paradoxical, rather as a contribution both to philosophy in terms in investigating what can be formalized and how that affects a theory, and to automated theory formation and mathematical reasoning by modeling mathematics as it is actually done by humans.

Lakatos's is an essentially optimistic doctrine: he believed that knowledge does grow, and the growth of knowledge provides a demarcation between rational and irrational thought. His Hegelian influences, that any methodological precept is open to revision, suggest that we can apply his philosophy to his own philosophy, as well as to mathematics and science. We believe that developing his theory by implementing it as a computer model provides a new and exciting perspective on his work.

Acknowledgements

Thanks to everyone at the ECAP conference for interesting and helpful discussion, in particular to Brendon Larvor.

---

[2]Thanks to Brendon Larvor for this suggestion.

BIBLIOGRAPHY

[Bird, 1998] A. Bird. *Philosophy of Science*. Routledge, London, 1998.

[Boden, 1990] M.A. Boden. *The Creative Mind: Myths and Mechanisms*. Weidenfield and Nicholson, London, 1990.

[Burrell, 1927] H. Burrell. *The Platypus*. Angus and Robertson Ltd., Sydney, 1927.

[Burton, 1985] D. Burton. *The History of Mathematics*. Allyn and Bacon, Inc, Boston, USA, 1985.

[Colton and Pease, 2004] S. Colton and A. Pease. The TM system for repairing non-theorems. In *Workshop on Disproving, Proceedings of IJCAR'04*, pages 13–26, 2004.

[Colton et al., 2000] S. Colton, A. Bundy, and T. Walsh. On the notion of interestingness in automated mathematical discovery. *International Journal of Human Computer Studies*, 53(3):351–375, 2000.

[Colton, 2002] S. Colton. *Automated Theory Formation in Pure Mathematics*. Springer-Verlag, 2002.

[Corfield, 1997] D. Corfield. Assaying Lakatos's philosophy of mathematics. *Studies in History and Philosophy of Science*, 28(1):99–121, 1997.

[Crawshay-Williams, 1957] R. Crawshay-Williams. *Methods of Criteria of reasoning: An Inquiry into the Structure of Controversy*. Routledge and Kegan Paul, London, 1957.

[Crombie, 1994] A. C. Crombie. *Styles of Scientific Thinking in the European Tradition: The History of Argument and Explanation especially in the Mathematical and Biomedical Sciences and Arts*. Gerald Duckworth & Co, Ltd, 1994.

[Feferman, 1978] S. Feferman. The logic of mathematical discovery vs. the logical structure of mathematics. In P.D. Asquith and I. Hacking, editors, *Proceedings of the 1978 Biennial Meeting of the Philosophy of Science Association*, volume 2, pages 309–327. Philosophy of Science Association, East Lansing, Michigan, 1978.

[Feyerabend, 1975] P. Feyerabend. *Against Method*. Verso, London, 1975.

[Fielder, 2001] A. Fielder. Dialog-driven adaptation of explanations of proofs. In Bernhard Nebel, editor, *Proceedings of the 17th International Joint Conference on Artificial Intelligence*, pages 1296–1300, Seattle, WA, 2001. Morgan Kaufmann.

[Gärdenfors, 1992] Gärdenfors. *Belief revision*. Cambridge University Press, Cambridge, 1992.

[Hacking, 1981] I. Hacking. Lakatos's philosophy of science. In I. Hacking, editor, *Scientific Revolutions*, pages 128–1443. Oxford University Press, Oxford, 1981.

[Houk et al., 1995] J.C. Houk, J.L. Davis, and D.G. Beiser. *Models of Information Processing in the Basal Ganglia*. A Bradford Book. MIT Press, 1995.

[Kadvany, 2001] J. Kadvany. *Imre Lakatos and the Guises of Reason*. Duke University Press, Durham and London, 2001.

[Kuhn, 1970] T. Kuhn. *The Structure of Scientific Revolutions*. The University of Chicago Press, Chicago, USA, 1970.

[Lakatos, 1963–64] I. Lakatos. Proofs and refutations. *The British Journal for the Philosophy of Science*, 14(53–56), 1963–64.

[Lakatos, 1976] I. Lakatos. *Proofs and Refutations*. CUP, Cambridge, UK, 1976.

[Lakatos, 1978] I. Lakatos. Infinite regress and foundations of mathematics. In J. Worral and G. Currie, editors, *Mathematics, Science and Epistemology*, pages 3–23. Cambridge University Press, Cambridge, 1978.

[Lakatos, 1981] I. Lakatos. History of science and its rational reconstructions. In I. Hacking, editor, *Scientific Revolutions*, pages 107–127. Oxford University Press, Oxford, 1981.

[Langley et al., 1987] P. Langley, H. Simon, G. Bradshaw, and J. Żytkow. *Scientific Discovery*. MIT Press/Bradford Books, Cambridge, MA, 1987.

[Langley, 1999] P. Langley. The computer-aided discovery of scientific knowledge. In *Proceedings of the First International Conference on Discovery Science*, Fukuoka, Japan, 1999. Springer.

[Langley, 2002] P. Langley. Lessons for the computational discovery of scientific knowl-
    edge. In *Proceedings of First International Workshop on Data Mining Lessons
    Learned*, pages 9–12, Sydney, 2002.
[Larvor, 1998] B. Larvor. *Lakatos: An Introduction*. Routledge, London, 1998.
[McCune, 1990] W. McCune. The OTTER user's guide. Technical Report ANL/90/9,
    Argonne National Laboratories, 1990.
[McCune, 2001] W. McCune. Mace 2 reference manual. Technical Report ANL/MCS-
    TM-249, Argonne National Laboratories, 2001.
[Mozley Moyal, 2001] A. Mozley Moyal. *Platypus: The Extraordinary Story of How a
    Curious Creature Baffled the World*. Smithsonian Institution Press, 2001.
[Pease et al., 2001] A. Pease, D. Winterstein, and S. Colton. Evaluating machine cre-
    ativity. In R. Weber and C. G. von Wangenheim, editors, *Case-Based Reasoning:
    Papers from the Workshop Programme at ICCBR'01*, pages 129–137, Washington,
    DC, 2001. Naval Research Laboratory, Navy Centre for Applied Research in Artificial
    Intelligence.
[Polya, 1954] G. Polya. *Mathematics and plausible reasoning*, volume 1, Induction and
    analogy in mathematics. Princeton University Press, 1954.
[Popper, 1972] K. R. Popper. *Objective Knowledge*. OUP, Ely House, London, 1972.
[Ritchie, 2001] G. Ritchie. Assessing creativity. In G. Wiggins, editor, *Proceedings of the
    AISB'01 Symposium on AI and Creativity in Arts and Science*, pages 3–11. SSAISB,
    2001.
[Sloman, 1978] A. Sloman. *The Computer Revolution in Philosophy*. The Harvester
    Press, Ltd., 1978.
[Sutcliffe and Suttner, 1998] G. Sutcliffe and C. Suttner. The TPTP problem library:
    CNF release v1.2.1. *Journal of Automated Reasoning*, 2(21):177–203, 1998.
[Thagard, 1993] P. Thagard. *Computational Philosophy of Science*. MIT Press, Cam-
    bridge, Mass, 1993.

Alison Pease
Centre for Intelligent Systems and their Applications
School of Informatics
University of Edinburgh, Edinburgh, UK
Email: alisonp@dai.ed.ac.uk

Simon Colton
Department of Computing
Imperial College, London, UK
Email: sgc@doc.ic.ac.uk

Alan Smaill
Centre for Intelligent Systems and their Applications
School of Informatics
University of Edinburgh, Edinburgh, UK
Email: A.Smaill@ed.ac.uk

John Lee
Human Communication Research Centre
University of Edinburgh, Edinburgh, UK
Email: J.Lee@ed.ac.uk

The Role of Computers in Scientific Research: A Cognitive Approach

Roberto Feltrero

ABSTRACT. It is this paper's intended aim to make use of the distributed cognition perspective to offer a better account of the new role of computers in scientific cognition and of the methodological and epistemological consequences of this process. An extension of the conceptual tools provided by this framework is proposed. We claim that computers extend our capabilities by providing us with new cognitive methodologies that were not available for us with the cognitive tools used so far. A case study in evolutionary simulation models is offered to illustrate these assertions. The use of these computational tools – which cannot be assimilated to the classical methods of algorithmic computation – can provide scientists with new methodologies for modeling whose epistemic relevance, however, can be better understood regarding these models as cognitive tools.

1 Introduction

Computers have, in a direct or indirect way, become indispensable tools for scientific research. This is a widely recognized fact. But such recognition does not apply to their epistemological consequences. For most scientific tasks, computers are merely used as fast calculation machines. In these cases, deep epistemological considerations seem wholly unnecessary. However, nowadays there is an increasing interest on computational modeling tools. When computational models are being used to obtain new hypothesis, to explore variations of a theory and, even, to produce emergent computational "experiments", it seems that epistemological issues can be regarded as deep enough philosophical questions.

The main cognitive and philosophical issue for us to be addressed would be: "do computers extend the scientists' cognitive capabilities?" Our answer will be affirmative, both for computational tools and computational models. The specific aim of this essay is, in fact, within the range of the more general question about the role of computers as tools for cognitive activities. Whether computers extend, enhance, increase, accelerate, empower or transform our cognitive activities are questions that belong to

Lorenzo Magnani and Riccardo Dossena, editors, *Computing, Philosophy, and Cognition*, pp. 87–98 © 2005, R. Feltrero

the shared field of epistemological and sociological studies of computational technology. By addressing these questions from the point of view of scientific cognition, the most demanding of cognitive activities and the one that is most restricted by methodological concerns, we will be able to explore in a thorough way the epistemological dimensions of that assumed extension and to provide appropriate criteria for the identification of what is epistemologically new in the realm of scientific languages and tools, that is, the realm of cognitive implements for scientific cognition.

By trying to demonstrate the epistemological and methodological relevance of simulations as cognitive tools, we support the claim that evolutionary simulation models (ESM) can extend scientific cognition in epistemically relevant ways . We make use of the cognitive conception of distributed cognition – and hopefully make a contribution to develop it – in order to understand the cognitive role of such computational methodologies in scientific activities.

2 Scientific distributed cognition

Every philosophical approach to scientific methodology have always reflected a specific conception of human cognition [Churchman, 1971]. This essay is written according to the idea – let us say "set of ideas" – of human cognition as an embodied, situated and distributed cognition [Beer, 2000; Clark, 1997; Clark, 1998]. The idea of distributed cognition [Hutchins, 1995a] seems particularly appropriate for a correct analysis of the role of computers in scientific research, taking the latter as a particular specimen of a human cognitive activity and the former as tools for cognitive activities.

Within the field of cognitive studies of science [Carruthers *et al.*, 2002], little work has been done so far using the distributed cognition framework, and most of it belongs to Ronald Giere [Giere, 2002b]. Therefore, Giere's work will be an unavoidable guideline for the arguments here deployed. His studies are focused on the distributed character of scientific cognition, claiming that scientific knowledge is an impersonal product of the whole scientific community that includes human agents as well as several types of artefacts. Instruments, experimental apparatuses, material models and, of course, computers, are considered cognitive implements for scientific research. The substantial role attributed to artefacts, already present in Hutchins' definition of distributed cognition, leads us to consider them at a same level with human agents for the purposes of cognitive analysis. Both are vehicles of representational information in such a way that a cognitive unit is made up of both human agents and artefacts within a flow of representationalstates [Hutchins, 1995b].

Giere's work particularly emphasizes the cognitive role of material resources. And this is where his proposal differs from the mere idea of collective or social cognition. Cognitive activities as calculation or data interpretation are not just distributed among scientists but also directly implemented by material resources as, for example, high-speed computers. Therefore, as Giere claims [Giere, 2003, p. 2] "Nor would such a project [the Hubble telescope] be possible without high-speed computers to acquire and process gigabytes of data. This reflection takes us beyond simple collective cognition to a more general notion of distributed cognition".

Analyzing scientific cognitive practice a an example of complex cognitive systems involving artefacts leads us to study the cognitive role of such artefacts. As cognitive tools, artefacts affect the way scientific procedures are implemented and, even, the whole culture of science. In the case of computers, Giere claims "It must be granted that straightforward computation is a large component in modern scientific cognition. Indeed, it is astounding the extent to which, since the 1950s, the computer has changed the way science is done". [Giere, 2003, p. 4]

The above mentioned cognitive analysis can be done in two ways, either by focusing on what the computer revolution amounts to in terms of making tough algebraic and arithmetic operations easy, or by taking into account the new perspectives in computational modeling tools. Giere's analysis seems to embrace the first possibility. He describes "calculators and computers [are] designed so as to be easily operated by a human with a pattern matching brain". [Giere, 2002a, p. 2]

So far, this is a vision where computers are considered as cognitive tools providing fundamental assistance to human cognition in the sense remarked by Hutchins: "rather than amplify the cognitive abilities of the task performer or act as intelligent agents in interaction with them, these tools *transform* the task the person has to do by representing it in a domain where the answer or the path to the solution is apparent. [...] the existence of such a wide variety of specialized tools and techniques is evidence of a good deal of cultural elaboration directed toward avoiding algebraic reasoning and arithmetic". [Hutchins, 1995a, pp. 154–155]

Within this vision, the *computational turn* is inevitably restricted. It is true that many of the computational resources available in, for instance, personal computers' graphical interfaces, help to produce cognitive outcomes. But instead of enhancing the cognitive capabilities of their users, they just transform complex cognitive tasks into perceptual ones. This is a good deal in terms of offloading computational effort and is it enough to state, as Giere does that "[...] a person plus a computer constitutes a powerful cognitive system that can carry out cognitive tasks far beyond the capabilities of an unaided human"? [Giere, 2002a, p. 2]. But maybe, considering computers as powerful tools that help to solve complex calculations is not enough to explain the epistemological revolution deployed by computers in science. The following analysis will be focused on the methodological and epistemological revolution provided by computational modeling and, more precisely, by a new type of computer simulations: Evolutionary Simulation Models (ESM). In order to make such an analysis, we need first to make some conceptual distinctions to clarify the cognitive and epistemological role of computational tools.

3   Extending cognitive analysis

Adopting a distributed cognition approach can shed some light on the epistemological problems involved in the use of computational modeling techniques and reveal some technical, methodological and moral problems related to the role of computers as tools for cognitive activities. But in order to do so, we need first to add some conceptual tools to those provided by the distributed cognition approach so as to have a more general cognitive picture. The core idea here is to establish some distinctions between the epistemic function of several computational aids for scientific cognition.

The cognitive framework of embodied, situated and distributed cognition is not, for sure, the best framework to provide analytical distinctions. The dynamical and interrelated character of the real-time adaptive cognition as stated by this framework accounts for the fact that in it every ontological or conceptual distinction tends to be blurred by the relationships among the different variables and elements involved. Anyway, and just for the sake of the argument, it would useful here to introduce a distinction between the most common concepts used to emphasize the cognitive aid of computers – augmentation, enhancement, etc. – and the more philosophical concept of extended mind.

There are three main philosophical approaches that stress the fundamental role of environment on helping and driving cognitive activities. They are the situated mind approach [Suchman, 1987], the distributed cognition proposal [Hutchins, 1995a] and the theory of activity based on Lev Vytgosky psychology [Vytgotsky, 1986]. The concept of *extended mind* [Clark and Chalmers, 1998] is related to those theories – and is related to the concepts of situated, distributed or scaffolded mind – as it emphasizes the role of context in cognitive processes. The thesis supporting this concept corroborates the role of environment manipulation in shaping and transforming cognitive problems. The authors claim, "[...] it is not implausible to suppose that the biological brain has in fact evolved and matured in ways which directly factor in the reliable presence of a manipulable external environment. It certainly seems that evolution has favored onboard capacities which are especially geared to parasitizing the local environment so as to reduce memory load, and even to transform the nature of the computational problems themselves." [Clark and Chalmers, 1998, p. 7]

The previous quotation seems to support the augmentative role of external environment for cognitive activities. But the definition provided by Clark and Chalmers goes beyond simple augmentation and points to a more committed idea of extension when they advocate an "[...] active externalism, based on the active role of the environment in driving cognitive processes".

It is clear, then, that in these arguments defending the concept of an extended mind we find both senses, augmentation and extension, according to the distinction we will make below. However, to say that a cognitive process is being driven by the environment is a stronger claim than saying that we use the environment to offload computational resources, and to say that an external resource substitutes a part of a cognitive process implies assessing that "that part of the world is (so we claim) part of the cognitive process" (ibid.). But if a part of the cognitive process is implemented by an external resource in a way that it drives the cognitive process – by means of actively selecting relevant variables or representational media – then distribution is a soft concept for characterizing the active role of the external tool.

Clark and Chalmers do not develop the strongest sense of mind extension that their definition implies because they prefer to stress the idea of the distribution of cognition through the environment. The very point here is to address this strongest sense by means of introducing new concepts and widening the cognitive approach used so far. This expansion of cognitive analysis here advocated aims at developing the strongest idea of extended mind on behalf of its ethical and epistemological concerns. In order to do so, it is necessary to grasp the idea of resources that are not available to a cognitive agent by means of a further distinction: transparent and opaque cognitive tools. A *transparent cognitive tool* is an external device implementing a cognitive task by using a methodology that is clearly understandable and transformable by the human user. An *opaque cognitive tool* is an external device achieving a cognitive task with a methodology not obviously understandable to the human user.

The above given definition consciously and deliberately opposes the one proposed by Norman [Norman, 1999]. Transparent technologies for Norman are those that allow us to achieve, in the easiest possible way, a certain task, without noticing the technological methodology involved. There is no need to understand how it works. Here we advocate the full understanding of the transparent technological resource; we can only consider a tool transparent if we can fully understand and manipulate it. Norman defines opacity not as "hard to understand" but as visible in use, that is to say, we must be aware of the technological structure to achieve our task. We need technological skills for dealing with an opaque tool. Here we will try to show how some technologies can be opaque precisely because their main driving features are not obvious to the user's cognition but can, nevertheless, be truly driving her cognitive processes; that is to say, they can extend her cognitive capabilities in a relevant way.

The very point of this distinction is to address the issues of the cognitive and epistemological relevance of cognitive tools, but it can also be useful to tackle with other questions. This distinction seems to fit better with ethical and sociological claims about control and design in technology. If the task of computer technologies is to automate cognitive functions and those functions are emergent outcomes of the triad brain, task and technology, the more transparent technologies are, the more possibilities to achieve new emergent functions regarding each user and her task. Transparent tools, in the sense proposed by Norman, are easy to use in order to achieve one's particular task, but are usually closed to the possibility of relevant modifications made by the user, precisely to adapt them to her particular task.

All this considered, we propose the following distinction regarding computational technologies. By increased, enhanced, improved, accelerated or empowered cognition, we here refer to the result of applying cognitively transparent computational technologies to cognitive activities. What we try to ensure by this is that those activities are enhanced by computational technologies in such a way that the global cognitive process is being controlled by human agents. In this case, technological developments are subject to inspection and control, precisely because the relevant algorithms used to accomplish the relevant tasks are the product of cognitively transparent design.

On the other hand *extending cognitive technologies* here refer to those computational technologies whose outcomes are not obviously understandable for the user. The use of these outcomes, or the deep analysis of how the computational tool can reach them, can drive user's cognitive processes in new directions previously not available to her cognitive resources or abilities.

The distinction here proposed may be problematic while dealing with everyday cognition. Most of our computational technologies solve problems which are not available to our personal cognitive capabilities. Therefore, they truly extend most users' cognitive capabilities. Moreover, non self-evident cognitive outcomes can be understood just as the result of augmentation devices and even the synergy provided by the connectivity and responsiveness of such technologies can drive to unexpected, and therefore extending, results. In these cases, the discussion regarding the cognitive transparency of these tools has an ethical and sociological interest, when control problems and democratic design of those technologies are involved.

There are also some ethical and methodological concerns to justify our distinction in the scientific use of computational technologies. If availability is useful for the effective and accurate use of tools for everyday activities, within scientific research this availability is mandatory. In order to open up the results to peer-to-peer inspection, re-construction and evaluation, every methodological tool, internal or external must be fully understandable. Therefore, computational methodologies have to be transparent (in the sense here proposed) to scientific evaluation.

But more interestingly, when dealing with scientific cognition, the distinction proposed becomes an epistemological one. Being science – as traditionally conceived – an open and common box of epistemological resources available to every scientist, an opaque computational technology is one whose outcomes cannot be neither understood nor reproduced without the help of computers. They become external constitutive cognitive technologies [Dascal, 2002]. That is to say, they become a new epistemological resource which is not possibly available with traditional tools. In this regard, fast calculation computers are not extending tools because the equations and processes being implemented are well understood by scientists and programmers. There is no epistemological novelty. Even though it would be almost impossible to achieve the same scientific task without such computational resources, it could be claimed that these can be replaced by human agents solving equations in a finite (though long) period of time.

Some opaque computational tools can, alternatively, extend scientists' cognitive and epistemological resources. It is the main claim of this essay that computational modeling can drive scientists cognitive processes. In this way, computational models can extend scientific cognition. They become, thus, extending cognitive technologies. If the outcome of the computational model has been produced by an opaque methodology, this extension is an epistemic extension, – that is to say, can drive to new knowledge not available with traditional epistemic tools. It is time now to analyze a case study in support of these claims: Evolutionary Simulation Models.

4 ESM and extended scientific cognition

There is nowadays an increasing tendency to use computational simulation and modeling in many sciences, from biology to economics [Grim, 2004]. As it has already been pointed out, such computational models can provide us with new methodologies for scientific reasoning and even, for understanding scientific cognition [Thagard, 1988; Thagard, 1992]. But many of these models, clearly rely on the self-explanatory nature of algorithms to account for the function and justification of their scientific outcomes. This kind of models are, according to our terminology, augmenting models since the knowledge involved in the design of the algorithms belongs to the scientist' mind.

The most radical characterization of extending cognitive tools that we want to survey in relation to ESM requires, first of all, that we understand how these models can drive scientific enquiry. But in order to do so, we have to conceive them not as classical computational – algorithmically transparent and self-explanatory – models, but as models whose structure can provide us with new insights, precisely because it is independent of the evolutionary learning algorithm that has generated it. As it happens, complex models produce emergent outcomes whose structure is not obvious to the scientist [Bedau, 1997; Bedau, 1998]. In addition to this complexity, in ESM, the processes of learning and evolution of the artificial agent in a particular environment leads to that artificial agent accomplishing tasks by using strategies that are unexpected and opaque at first glance for the very designer. In this sense, ESM can be considered opaque and, therefore, extending cognitive tools.

This is the very feature that makes of ESM extending cognitive tools: its *opacity* [Di Paolo *et al.*, 2000]. The evolved model provides a structure – typically the evolved neuronal activation patterns – that can be analyzed in detail by scientists. From that analysis, scientists can elaborate new hypothesis about the complex mechanisms responsible for outcome behavior. This is accomplished in this way because that structure is difficult to anticipate or describe by a human agent calculating differential equations. The complexity of relationships and recursive influence between the system's variables make such calculations a very difficult task for human agents, as it is evident in the mentioned case of the computers working in the Hubble project. But, what is important here is that, while the calculus strategy in the Hubble computers is transparent and related to the task description, in the case of ESM the differential equations designed for the learning algorithm, and even the low level variables that we introduce to modify the outcome behavior of the system, do not show a transparent relationship to the behavioral level of description. Unlike what happens with calculators or conventional computers, in this case there are no arithmetical models of the behavioral level built, either as hardware or as software, by human agents into the machine. These are real material models with their own cognitive structure to be studied.

Hypothesis in such a study would have to account for complex phenomena involving many variables and interacting components whose underlying variables' relationships are, moreover, non-linear and recursive. We would even need to hypothesize with a down-top methodology to understand the role of the most simple variables in the overall behavior of the whole system (for example, how neuronal features affect the agent behavior or learning). So ESM seem to be an appropriate cognitive resource to find hypothesis and to provide conceptual explanations for such complex issue. In addition, ESM allow us to reproduce/simulate system behavior with numerical methods, providing us with a quantified analysis of complex dynamical systems. As, nowadays, there are not any other available methodologies that can deal, so accurately, with this kind of phenomena, we can conclude that ESM extend scientific cognition.

Considering some computerized tools as extending cognitive tools does not support the claim for any kind of cognitive human-like agency, consciousness or attribution of folk psychology concepts to computers. But if we are to study the epistemological role of such tools, it becomes necessary to emphasize that distinct feature. Because in the mentioned cases, computational tools do really extend our cognitive abilities. Some epistemological and methodological restrictions should, nevertheless, be taken into account in order to understand in a proper way the scientific role of these modeling tools. Again, understanding them as cognitive tools will help.

The non-predictable character of the evolved structures produced by the simulation has driven many authors to consider the models as empirical objects, as "real" instances of a particular phenomena [Kitano et al., 1997]. We agree with R. Giere that evolutionary simulation models have to be considered cognitive tools for modeling (whose most relevant feature in contrast with other kind of models is that everything about the model is explicitly represented) [Giere et al., 2001, p.27]. It is in this way that their epistemological relevance has to be carefully considered, and it should not be possible to analyze their evolved outcomes in the same way as we would do with empirical objects. The evolved structures can be considered as a computational implementation of our hypothesis about a particular domain. This means that ESM are a special kind of conceptual tool. Unlike traditional conceptual analysis, where the conclusion follows logically and clearly from the premises, an evolutionary simulation model may have a hidden explanatory structure that requires further analysis to explain results. Moreover, these results have to be related to the empirical data and the theoretical knowledge already available to be understood. It is in this step where the evolved structures can drive scientific inquiry into new directions not even imagined before.

Here we find a good example of the cognitive extension provided by ESM. Traditional "cognitive" activities of a single scientist (hypothesis search, abductive reasoning, etc.) have, so far, depended upon the scientist's own "brilliant ideas". ESM models can provide us with these very ideas when analyzing their opaque evolved structures. The simulation extends the scientist's mind driving scientific inquiry into paths suggested by the evolved patterns that achieve the task.

5   Conclusion

Evolutionary simulation models are capable of extending our cognitive resources to establish causal relations between different levels of description [Barandiaran and Feltrero, 2003]. They show their scientific value on hypothesis generation by discovering intermediate explanatory patterns in the evolved agent. Their epistemic relevance has to be understood within the framework of theoretical inquiry at a same level of analysis with other theoretical tools. They are also active tools capable of extending our cognitive abilities and methodologies because their outcomes are not obvious to human agents.

The well-known passive computers and new information technologies are changing the way science is done, simplifying computationally complex tasks, improving scientific communication and providing new computational tools for new kinds of distributed research. But this alone is not enough to state that individual cognitive abilities are being extended by computers. However, when new computational based methodologies as ESM provide epistemically revolutionary cognitive methodologies, we can, then, consider these as extending cognitive technologies and, therefore, capable of amplifying scientists' cognitive capabilities in relevant ways.

Acknowledgements

This work was funded by: research project from the Spanish Department of Science and Technology (I+D BFF2002-03656), UNED research project 2001V/PROYT/03-HUMANÍSTICA Y SOCIAL and the UNED research fellowship that I hold. The development of this paper has benefited from my discussions with Xabier Barandiaran about the role of simulated and robotic models in scientific explanation.

BIBLIOGRAPHY

[Barandiaran and Feltrero, 2003] X. Barandiaran and R. Feltrero.   Conceptual and
     methodological blending in cognitive science: The role of simulated and robotic models in scientific explanation. Presented at the 12th International Congress of Logic Methodology and Philosophy of Science. Oviedo, Spain, 2003, 2003.

[Bedau, 1997] M.A. Bedau. Emergent models of supple dynamics in life and mind. *Brain and Cognition*, 34(5–27), 1997.

[Bedau, 1998] M.A. Bedau. Philosophical content and method of artificial life. In T.W. Bynam and J.H. Moor, editors, *The Digital Phoenix: How Computers are Changing Philosophy*, pages 135–152, Portland, 1998. Basil Blackwell.

[Beer, 2000] R. Beer. Dynamical approaches to cognitive science. *Trends in Cognitive Sciences*, 4(3):91–99, 2000. http://vorlon.cwru.edu/~beer/Papers/TICS.pdf.

[Carruthers *et al.*, 2002] P. Carruthers, S. Stich, and M. Siegal, editors. *The Cognitive Basis of Science*. Cambridge University Press, London, 2002.

[Churchman, 1971] C.W. Churchman. *The Design of Inquiring Systems*. Basic Books, 1971.

[Clark and Chalmers, 1998] A. Clark and D. Chalmers. The extended mind. *Analysis*, 58(1):7–19, 1998.

[Clark, 1997] A. Clark. *Being There: Putting Brain, Body, and World Together Again*. MIT Press, Cambridge, Mass., 1997.

[Clark, 1998] A. Clark. Embodied, situated and distributed cognition. In W. Bechtel and G. Graham, editors, *A Companion to Cognitive Science*, Malden, MA, 1998. Blackwell Publishers.

[Dascal, 2002] M. Dascal. Language as a cognitive technology. *International Journal of Cognition and Technology*, 1(1):35–89, 2002. http://www.tau.ac.il/humanities/philos/dascal/papers/ijct-rv.htm.

[Di Paolo *et al.*, 2000] E.A. Di Paolo, J. Noble, and S. Bullock. Simulation models as opaque thought experiments. In M.A. Bedau, J.S. McCaskill, N.H. Packard, and S. Rasmussen, editors, *Artificial Life VII: Proceedings of the Seventh International Conference on Artificial Life*, pages 497–506, Cambridge, MA, 2000. MIT Press.

[Giere *et al.*, 2001] R. Giere, L. Steels, S. Franklin, and J. Pickering. Comments on Barbara Webb's article: "Can robots make good models of biological behaviour?". *Behavioral and Brain Sciences*, 24(6):1051–1094, 2001.

[Giere, 2002a] R. Giere. Models as parts of distributed cognitive systems, 2002a. http://www.tc.umn.edu/~giere/ [Last Access: 30/08/2003].

[Giere, 2002b] R. Giere. Scientific cognition as distributed cognition. In P. Carruthers, S. Stich, and M. Siegal, editors, *The Cognitive Basis of Science*. Cambridge University Press, 2002b.

[Giere, 2003] R. Giere. Computation and agency in scientific cognition, 2003. http://www.tc.umn.edu/~giere/ [Last Access: 30/08/03].

[Grim, 2004] P. Grim. Computational modeling as a philosophical methodology. In L. Floridi, editor, *Philosophy of Computing and Information*, pages 337–349, Oxford, 2004. Blackwell.

[Hutchins, 1995a] E. Hutchins. *Cognition in the Wild*. MIT Press, Cambridge, Ma, 1995a.

[Hutchins, 1995b] E. Hutchins. How a cockpit remembers its speeds. *Cognitive Science*, 19:265–288, 1995b.

[Kitano *et al.*, 1997] H. Kitano, S. Hamahashi, J. Kitazawa, and K. Takao. The virtual biology laboratories: A new approach to computational biology. In P. Husbands and I. Harvey, editors, *Proceedings of the Fourth European Conference on Artificial Life (ECAL'97)*, pages 274–283, Cambridge, MA, 1997. MIT Press/Bradford Books.

[Norman, 1999] D.A. Norman. *The Invisible Computer*. MIT Press, Cambridge, MA, 1999.

[Suchman, 1987] L. Suchman. *Plans and Situated Actions*. Cambridge University Press, Cambridge, UK, 1987.

[Thagard, 1988] P. Thagard. *Computational Philosophy of Science*. MIT Press, Cambridge, MA, 1988.

[Thagard, 1992] P. Thagard. *Conceptual Revolutions*. Princeton University Press, Princeton, 1992.

[Vytgotsky, 1986] L. Vytgotsky. *Thought and Language*. MIT Press, Cambridge, MA, 1986. (1962, trans.).

Roberto Feltrero
Department of Logic, History and Philosophy of Science
UNED, Madrid, Spain
Email: rfeltrero@bec.uned.es
URL: http://www.uned.es/dpto_log/rfeltrero

Problems with Simplicity and Analogy in ECHO and TEC

MARCELLO GUARINI AND PIERRE BOULOS

ABSTRACT.   Paul Thagard has proposed the Theory of Explanatory Coherence (TEC) to explain scientific reasoning. It integrates considerations of analogy, explanatory breadth, higher-order explanation, simplicity, and unity into one theory. In an attempt to gather evidence for this theory, Thagard constructed the computer program ECHO (Explanatory Coherence by Harmony Optimization). We will argue that (a) the presentation of the role played by simplicity and analogy in TEC is ambiguous, and (b) once disambiguation takes place, underdetermination problems threaten the purported evidential link between ECHO and the different ways of interpreting TEC. TEC is biscriptive - it provides an adequate descriptive account of how scientists reason when they reason at their best. Thagard has claimed that TEC can provide us with prescriptive guidance. By using underdetermination arguments to question the strength of the support that ECHO can provide for TEC, our main aim is to question the extent to which ECHO and TEC (in their current forms) can provide prescriptive guidance with respect to matters of simplicity and analogy in scientific reasoning. Also, we sketch out some alternative ways of understanding the role of simplicity and analogy in scientific reasoning.

1   Introduction

For a number of years, Paul Thagard has not only been making contributions to cognitive modeling, he has been applying those contributions to philosophical problems. For example, he has put forward a theory of coherence as constraint satisfaction, and he has applied that theory to a number of different philosophical and scientific problems. The purpose of this paper will be to point out concerns with some applications of his connectionist coherence theory to scientific reasoning.

Part two of this paper contains a general account of Thagard's Theory of Explanatory Coherence (TEC) and the computer program that implements TEC. The program is called ECHO (Explanatory Coherence by Harmony

Lorenzo Magnani and Riccardo Dossena, editors, *Computing, Philosophy, and Cognition*, pp. 99–111 © 2005, M. Guarini and P. Boulos

Optimization). One of the uses of ECHO is to gather support for TEC. The idea is to run simulations of theory conflicts taken from the history of science to see if ECHO can select the theory that, as a matter of historical fact, actually won out. Thagard and others have used ECHO to model theory conflicts, and the ability of ECHO to select the appropriate theory in a variety of conflicts is said to provide support for TEC. The arguments in part three are designed to show that (a) Thagard's use of simplicity and analogy in TEC is in need of clarification, and (b) once this clarification has taken place, the evidential link between ECHO and TEC can be shown to be weak, at least with respect to the support ECHO is said to provide for the role of analogy and simplicity in TEC. The paper concludes with a quick discussion of the prospective growth of knowledge and how it might influence the account of the role played by simplicity and analogy in scientific reasoning.

2   Thagard on TEC and ECHO

TEC is a special case of a more general coherence theory of constraint satisfaction. The more general theory of constraint satisfaction was developed by Paul Thagard and Karsten Verbeurgt [Thagard and Verbeurgt, 1998, pp. 2–3], and it is committed to the following seven principles.

1. Elements are representations such as concepts, propositions, parts of images, goals, actions, and so on.

2. Elements can cohere (fit together) or incohere (resist fitting together). Coherence relations include explanation, deduction, facilitation, association, and so on. Incoherence relations include inconsistency, incompatibility, and negative association.

3. If two elements cohere, there is a positive constraint between them. If two elements incohere, there is a negative constraint between them.

4. Elements are to be divided into ones that are accepted and ones that are rejected.

5. A positive constraint between two elements can be satisfied either by accepting both of the elements or by rejecting both of the elements.

6. A negative constraint between two elements can be satisfied only by accepting one element and rejecting the other.

7. The coherence problem consists of dividing a set of elements into accepted and rejected sets in a way that satisfies the most constraints.

One possible application of this theory is to scientific reasoning, where the elements in question are propositions expressing hypotheses or evidence. Each proposition can be represented using a neuron. Connections between the neurons can be used to represent the links between propositions. For example, if hypothesis H_1 explains evidence E_1, then there will be an excitatory link between the neurons representing H_1 and E_1. If H_2 competes with H_1 for acceptance, then there will be an inhibitory link between H_1 and H_2. This approach allows us to conceive of theory selection from among existing competitors as a coherence problem. Roughly, theory conflicts are represented using propositional and evidential elements, and the problem becomes one of trying to decide how to partition these elements into two sets – accepted or rejected. To do this, principles need to be laid down that capture what goes on in scientific reasoning. The following principles summarize Thagard's (adapted from [Thagard, 1992b, pp. 65–66]) Theory of Explanatory Coherence:

1. *Symmetry*: Both local coherence between two propositions and local incoherence are symmetric relations.

2. *Explanation*: (a) if P explains Q, then P coheres with Q; (b) if P and Q jointly explain R, then P and Q cohere; and (c) as the number of hypotheses required for explanation of E increases, the degree of coherence between each of those hypotheses and E decreases.

3. *Analogy*: If P and Q are similar and explain similar propositions, then P and Q cohere.

4. *Data Priority*: Observation descriptions have independent (but defeasible) priority.

5. *Contradiction*: Propositions that contradict one another incohere..

6. *Competition*: P and Q are competitors and incohere if these conditions are satisfied: P and Q independently explain E; P is not involved in explaining Q; Q is not involved in explaining P, and there is no R such that P and Q jointly contribute to explaining R.

7. *Acceptability*: The acceptability of a proposition depends on the contribution it makes to global coherence.

The versions of TEC and ECHO discussed in this paper are the second versions; a discussion of the slightly different earlier versions can be found in Thagard's 1989. ECHO implements TEC by establishing excitatory and inhibitory links between the neurons representing the propositions involved in a theory conflict. The links are established in accordance with the principles of TEC. All the evidence units are linked to a special evidence unit whose value is clamped at 1. All other units start at a preset default value. All units then send their output to all the units they are connected to. The values of all units are synchronously updated. The units send out their new values, and then they update again. This process continues until little or no change is detected. If this happens, then the network is said to have settled. The units that have a value over zero are said to be accepted; those less than zero are said to be rejected. Data priority is implemented by linking all evidence units to a special evidence unit that always fires with force 1, but that does not guarantee that the evidence units will all be accepted. Depending on the links that exist between the evidence units and the explaining hypotheses, it is possible for evidence units to be rejected. The special evidence units add a kind of defeasible "umph" to the evidence. In the updating process, it is possible for the units not to settle. This is not surprising since there is no guarantee that there is one solution that is better than all the rest, and in looking for the optimal solution, ECHO may end up oscillating between different but equally strong solutions. It is also worth noting that when two complex theories are compared, ECHO need not select all of one over all of the other. It may settle on some hypotheses from one theory and some from another.

3   Simplicity and analogy

ECHO has been applied to a variety of scientific revolutions, and each time it selected the appropriate theory - Copernicus over Ptolemy, Newton's theory of motion over Descartes', Lavoisier's chemistry over phlogiston theory, Darwin's theory over Creationism, Wegener over his opponents, and the Hylicobacter theory of Peptic ulcers over the acid theory ([Thagard, 1989; Thagard, 1992b; Thagard, 1999]; see also [Nowak and Thagard, 1992a; Nowak and Thagard, 1992b]). There are a variety of parameters that need to be set in ECHO. Excitation is the parameter for a positive or excitatory link between two neurons, the weight by which inputs are multiplied; inhibition is the parameter for a negative or inhibitory link between two neurons, the weight by which inputs to those neurons are multiplied. There are simplicity impact and analogy impact parameters. These control the extent to which simplicity and analogy influence outcomes. More will be said about these below. While there are other parameters – decay and data impact – these will not figure in our arguments below. Changing the parameters may (depending on the problem at hand and the extent to which the parameters were changed) lead ECHO to change the results it generates. We will use the notation $ECHO(x, y)$ to indicate ECHO being run with excitation of x

and inhibition of y. ECHO$(0.04, -0.06)$ is the implementation of that Thagard used to generate the correct results for all the cases mentioned above. Moreover, Thagard has claimed (and we have confirmed) that many other possible combinations of parameter values can be used to generate the correct answer for all those cases. However, not all of those parameter will lead ECHO to behave as one might expect when it comes problems pertaining to simplicity and analogy. To see this, simplicity and analogy need to be discussed in more detail.

Our concern begins with the fact that there are different ways to interpret TEC. For example, Thagard gives the following detailed account of the second principle of TEC:

If $P_1 \ldots P_m$ explain Q, then:

(a) For each P_i in $P_1 \ldots P_m$, P_i and Q cohere.

(b) For each P_i and P_j in $P_1 \ldots P_m$, P_i and P_j cohere.

(c) In (a) and (b) the degree of coherence is inversely proportional to the number of propositions $P_1 \ldots P_m$. [Thagard, 1992b, p. 66]

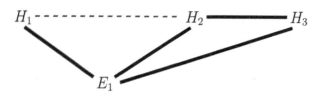

Figure 1. An example of simplicity. Solid lines indicate excitatory links due to explanation. The dashed line indicates an inhibitory link due to competition. H_2 and H_3 jointly explain E_1 (evidence); H_1 explains the evidence by itself.

He points out that (c) is an attempt to capture the role played by simplicity. Consider the example in Figure 1. H_1 (all on its own) explains E_1. H_2 and H_3 jointly explain E_1. H_1 contradicts H_2. Call this the paradigm case of simplicity. ECHO will give the strongest significance to simplicity when the simplicity impact parameter is set at 1 (and no significance when it is set at 0). Our argument assumes that simplicity impact is set at 1. What this means is that if two propositions are required to explain a piece of evidence, then the weight of the excitatory connections between the evidence and each of those propositions is $x/2$, where x is value of the excitation parameter. If it takes three propositions to explain one piece of evidence, then the weight of the excitatory connections between the evidence and each of those propositions is $x/3$. And so on. In the paradigm case of simplicity, ECHO$(0.04, -0.06)$ will accept H_1 and E_2, and reject H_2 and H_3. Strictly speaking, every implementation of ECHO with a non-zero value for the simplicity impact parameter implements the conditions of principle two of TEC. However, Thagard [Thagard, 1992b, p. 78] suggests that, other things being equal, theories that employ auxiliary hypotheses will be rejected in favor of those that do not. Call this view the *strong view of simplicity*. "Other things being equal" means that both theories explain the available evidence; no other high order hypotheses are explaining low order hypotheses; analogy is not an issue, and so on. We will show that the *strong view of simplicity* goes beyond what is stated in (c), and that not all implementations of TEC and ECHO realize the *strong view of simplicity*.

In the paradigm case of simplicity, ECHO$(0.02, -0.02)$ accepts H_1, H_3, and E_1, but it rejects H_1. In other words, even though

(i) the link between H_2 and E_1 is weaker than the link between H_1 and E_1;

(ii) the link between H_3 and E_1 also is weaker than the link between H_1 and E_1, and

(iii) (i) and (ii) are in agreement with condition (c) of TEC's second principle,

ECHO selects the theory of H_1 conjoined with H_3 over the simpler theory H_1 when the value for excitation is set to 0.02 and inhibition to -0.02. In still other words, according to how ECHO implements TEC, it is not true that if other things are equal, theories that employ auxiliary hypotheses will be rejected in favor of those that employ fewer or no auxiliary hypotheses. Whether this result obtains depends on the parameter values specified. In spite of the fact that the excitatory links in the more elaborate theory are weakened in accordance with condition (c), the more elaborate theory is selected. Simplicity is still in effect, but when 0.02 and -0.02 are selected as values for inhibition and excitation respectively, they mitigate the effect of the simplicity preference to the point where it does not get Thagard's preferred answer (H_1 over H_2 and H_3) for the paradigm case of simplicity.

The above is significant since Thagard attaches a fair bit of importance to simplicity. On a strict interpretation of TEC, both ECHO$(0.04, -0.06)$ and ECHO$(0.02, -0.02)$ are implementations of TEC. However, Thagard sometimes writes as if rejecting H_2 and H_3 while accepting H_1 in the paradigm case of simplicity is part of the understanding of simplicity that is meant to be covered by the second principle of TEC. Strictly speaking, TEC can be implemented in a way that is committed to the strong view of simplicity or to its rejection, but Thagard appears to favor the strong view. Let us call a rewritten version of TEC that includes all of TEC but goes on to endorse the strong view of simplicity TEC_2. Let us call a rewritten version of TEC that endorses all of TEC but goes on to reject the strong view of simplicity TEC_3. $ECHO(0.04, -0.06)$ implements TEC_2 (which subscribes to the strong view of simplicity), and $ECHO(0.02, -0.02)$ implements TEC_3 (which subscribes to the weak view of simplicity). The point of ECHO is to show that TEC can be computationally implemented, and that when it is implemented, it can appropriately model (under certain kinds of idealization) many episodes in the history of scientific reasoning. If $ECHO(0.04, -0.06)$ gets the correct answers when presented with problems from the history of science, then that is evidence in favor of TEC_2. However, when presented with *the same* problems from the history of science, $ECHO(0.02, -0.02)$ also gets all the right answers, which provides evidence for TEC_3. Evidence from the history of science underdetermines the choice between TEC_2 and TEC_3. In other words, given the simulations run thus far, there is no way to use ECHO to choose between the strong and week conceptions of simplicity. Moreover, given the simulations run thus far, there is no way to use ECHO to choose either TEC_2 or TEC_3 over the original TEC since all are equally supported by ECHO simulations.

At this point, it might be tempting to object, "So what? If the simulations run on ECHO cannot support the strong view of simplicity over the weak view, then maybe we should not care about the distinction. Simply abandon the preference for a strong view of simplicity, and all is fine. The only problem here is the preference for the strong view of simplicity." Well, we think that is not the only problem. The weak view of simplicity implemented in $ECHO(0.02, -0.02)$ has a very counterintuitive consequence. In the paradigm case of simplicity H_1 and H_3 are both accepted even though (i) H_1 is individually sufficient for explaining E_1, and (ii) H_3 was part of a *competitor* theory! $ECHO(0.02, -0.02)$ implements such a weak view of simplicity that it goes out of its way to blend hypotheses from two different theories together when one of those hypotheses would have worked just fine all on its own. This is not to say that the simplicity constraint plays no role. For example, when the simplicity impact parameter is set to 0 (eliminating the effect of simplicity), it turns out that neither $ECHO(0.02, -0.02)$ nor $ECHO(0.04, -0.06)$ will uniformly accept Copernican hypotheses over Ptolemaic hypotheses, but they will prefer Copernicus if simplicity impact is set to 1 (full force). Consequently, in spite of fact that $ECHO(0.02, -0.02)$ fails radically in the paradigm case of simplicity, it does not follow that simplicity plays no role whatsoever. Other simulations can be used to establish that it has *some* role. Our point is that the role simplicity plays in some implementations of TEC and ECHO can lead to problematic results in the paradigm case, and existing simulations cannot be used as evidence against those implementations.

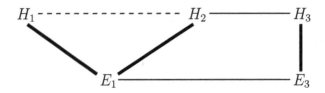

Figure 2. An example of analogy. Thick solid lines indicate excitatory links due to explanation; thin solid lines indicate excitatory links due to analogy, and the dashed line indicates an inhibitory link due to competition.

An argument similar to the above could be run on the third principle of TEC, which deals with analogy. (Our argument assumes that the analogy impact parameter is set at 1.) Thagard [Thagard, 1992b, pp. 78–79] explains the third principle as follows: "If P_1 explains Q_1, P_2 explains Q_2, P_1 is analogous to P_2, and Q_1 is analogous to Q_2, then P_1 and P_2 cohere, and Q_1 and Q_2 cohere" [Thagard, 1992b, p. 66]. He uses a simple example to illustrate this point, from which Figure 2 is derived. Say H_1 explains E_1, H_2 explains E_1, and H_3 explains E_3. Also, say H_2 is analogous to H_3, and E_1 is analogous to E_3, and H_1 contradicts H_2. Call this the paradigm case of analogy. If we assume other things are equal, then ECHO(0.04, −0.06) will reject H_2 and accept H_1, E_1, H_3, and E_3, and this appears to be Thagard's preferred answer. However, it is possible to adhere to the above principle without selecting H_2 over H_1. All that the above principle requires is that an excitatory link be established between H_2 and H_3 and between E_1 and E_3. Depending on how we select parameter values for excitation and inhibition, it is possible to establish the requisite excitatory links without rejecting H_1. For example, ECHO(0.02, −0.02) accepts H_1, H_2, and H_3 (as well as both evidence statements). Let us call the view that H_1 should be rejected in favor of H_2 in examples like the above the *strong view of analogy* (the view Thagard appears to endorse). Strictly interpreted, TEC does not contain the strong view of analogy as a necessary component. Say we rewrite TEC to include all its existing principles and expand it so that the strong view of analogy is a necessary component; call this TEC$_4$. Say we rewrite TEC to include all its existing principles and expand it so that the strong view of analogy is rejected; call this TEC_5. It turns out that (so far) the evidence from the history of science cannot be used to choose between TEC_4 and TEC_5. ECHO(0.02, −0.02) implements TEC_5 but not TEC_4, and ECHO(0.04, −0.06) implements TEC_4 but not TEC_5. As was mentioned above, ECHO(0.02, −0.02) and ECHO(0.04, −0.06) get qualitatively equivalent answers on problems from the history science, so the ECHO simulations of those problems appear to give no reason to prefer ECHO(0.02, −0.02) over ECHO(0.04, −0.06). But that appears to mean that ECHO (so far) gives us no reason to prefer TEC_5 over TEC_4, no reason to prefer the strong conception of analogy over the weak conception.

Call a version of TEC that accepts *both* the strong view of simplicity and the strong view of analogy TEC_6. Call a version of TEC that rejects *both* the strong view of simplicity and the strong view of analogy TEC_7. ECHO(0.02, −0.02) will model TEC_7 but not TEC_6 and get all the correct answers when given examples from the history of science. ECHO(0.04, −0.06) will model TEC_6 but not TEC_7 and get all the correct answers when given examples from the history of science. Appeal to the historical examples given is insufficient for selecting TEC_6 over TEC_7.

4   Theory evaluation and the growth of knowledge

The purpose of this paper is not to suggest that there is no role for considerations such as simplicity and analogy in theory evaluation. Nor is it our goal to suggest computational modeling (connectionist or otherwise) is not useful in doing epistemology and philosophy of science. However, we think that there is a dimension to theory evaluation that TEC does not engage, and which it needs to engage if it is to adequately account for the role of analogy and simplicity. This dimension pertains to the growth of scientific knowledge. Let us take the case of analogy. There are examples where analogies appear to support a theory, and examples where they do not. A crucial difference, at least in some cases, may be the ability of the analogy to suggest directions for future research and the prospect for greater development of the theory. For example, consider the competition between Copenhagen and Bohmian interpretations of quantum mechanics. The explanations of Bohmian mechanics appear to have more analogies with those of classical mechanics than Copenhagen approaches do. In spite of the fact that both approaches are predictively equivalent, the Copenhagen approaches appear to be dominant. Why aren't the analogies working in favor of the Bohmian approaches? Here is one possibility. Three of the four forces of nature are well accounted for by quantum mechanics; the fourth force – gravity – is accounted for using space-time theory (general relativity). If one is inclined to believe that a quantum theory of gravity would lead to a better account

of the interaction of the four forces, and one conceives of such a theory as
one more step away from classical physics, and one infers that the way to
make progress in physics is to continue moving away from classical physics,
then analogies with classical physics would be perceived as having little
or no weight since they are not perceived as leading to progress. We are
not endorsing the view that analogies with classical physics cannot lead to
progress. Rather, we are claiming that *if* an analogy is judged as not being
progressive or at least potentially progressive, then it will carry little or no
weight. What this suggests is that the evaluation of a theory depends, at
least in part, on the prospects the theory has for growth, for generating new
results. The role of analogy may best be understood in that context.

With respect to simplicity, it might be possible to motivate it in ways that
are not considered in TEC. A first motivation for simplicity might look like
this: it is obvious that we have finite cognitive resources, so if we are going
to put our resources to the best possible use, we should avoid unnecessarily
committing them since that will free up more resources for the pursuit of
various goals such as truth seeking, error avoidance, understanding, practical wisdom, or anything else that might be specified as an appropriate goal
of reasoning. Consequently, some role must be given to simplicity in the
theory of reasoning. The preceding motivation for simplicity is concerned
with efficiency. A second motivation for simplicity might look like this:
since we have finite cognitive resources, the size of a theory that we can
survey, contemplate, and evaluate is finite; assuming that the demands of a
theory of reasoning (scientific or otherwise) will not exceed what is humanly
possible, some sort of simplicity constraint *might* work as a way of ruling
out or contributing to the ruling out of theories that are just too large for
us to manage. This second motivation for simplicity is concerned with the
limits of human cognition. A few things need to be noticed about these
motivations. First, it is not obvious that either of them will favor strong
simplicity over weak simplicity (or *vice versa*). The nature of their motivation is very general, and much more needs to be said if we are to select
one version of simplicity over the other. Second, the efficiency motivation
is concerned with conserving cognitive resources so that *we may have more
resources left over to grow our knowledge*. So an appropriate account of the
role of simplicity may require reference to the growth of knowledge. Finally,
while simplicity may place different kinds of constraints on a theory of reasoning, at least some of them would have to be defeasible. For example, if
theory T_1 is simpler than T_2, and the two are empirically equivalent at a
given moment in time, but T_2 is judged as having greater prospects for theoretical and empirical growth than T_1, then T_2 will generally be preferred,
ceteris paribus, of course.

Alvin Goldman [Goldman, 1987; Goldman, 2002] has discussed five epistemic virtues: reliability, power, fecundity, speed, and efficiency. We think that these, or some variant on them, will help us to better understand the epistemological role of analogy and simplicity. Power is measured by the ability of a practice or process to solve problems we are interested in. Speed is the rate at which some practice or process generates results, and efficiency takes into consideration the cost (cognitive or otherwise) of generating results. Fecundity has to do with the ability of a practice to generate results for many people (not just a very small group of elite scientists). Clearly, analogies that are powerful and generate results quickly will be well regarded. If analogies can generate interesting hypotheses while using fewer resources than some other method of generating hypotheses, that would count in favor of analogies as well. Finally, a theory having analogies may be easier to teach than one that does not, making it accessible, available, and useful to a wider audience (i.e. more fecund). With respect to simplicity, things may be a little different, but some of these virtues may still be an issue. For example, while it is not clear that simpler theories are more powerful than less simple theories, simpler theories (as already argued) may be more efficient to use (require less time and cognitive resources) than more complex theories. Simpler theories may also be more fecund. Thagard [Thagard, 1993; Thagard, 1994; Thagard, 1995; Thagard, 1999; Thagard, 2000] is clearly interested in the social dimension of theory appraisal in science, so the suggestions being made herein may not be at odds with the spirit of his thought.

In short, we do not deny that some sort of simplicity and some sort of analogy have a role to play in scientific reasoning. Moreover, we think that this role can be understood in an epistemological manner; we are *not* saying that simplicity and analogy are to be relegated to the role of mere psychological aids. Of course, there is much more that needs to be said about the role of simplicity and analogy both at the level of the individual thinker and at the social level. We sketched out the direction in which we think this work should go, and we have argued that, in its current form, TEC does not capture the concerns that motivated our brief sketch of the significance of simplicity and analogy.

Appendix

Thagard's published code, COHERE, was downloaded from the website `cogsci.uwaterloo.ca`. For this paper, it was loaded and compiled on a Macintosh G3 processor using Macintosh Common Lisp – MCL 4.3 on Mac OS 9.2 and MCL 5.0 on Mac OS X (10.3). COHERE was also ported to a Pentium III machine running Microsoft Windows 2000 and compiled on

Digitool's Xanalys LispWorks 4.2 and 4.3 (Personal and Enterprise Editions). In Lisp, the parameter defaults for ECHO are listed in the following way:

```
(defun defaults ()
(setq *asymptote* .0001)
(decay .05)
(excit .04)
(inhib -.06)
(output -0.99)
)
```

Our simulations vary the data excitations (up or down) and the inhibitions (always negative and up or down). So by our stipulations in the paper, ECHO(0.02, −0.02) means data excitation is 0.02 and inhibition is −0.02. Coding this meant making the appropriate changes in the code above:

```
(defun defaults ()
(setq *asymptote* .0001)
(decay .05)
(excit .02)
(inhib -.02)
(output -0.99)
)
```

Differences pertaining to how platforms handle floating point calculations may affect exact numerical values of the output (however our results differed negligibly from one platform to another), and qualitative results appear robust. For example, while we could not always replicate Thagards numerical results, our simulations generally produced the same list of accepted and rejected propositions as Thagard's.

Acknowledgment

Marcello Guarini wishes to thank the Humanities Research Group at the University of Windsor for an internal fellowship that supported the research presented in this paper.

BIBLIOGRAPHY

[Goldman, 1987] A. Goldman. Foundations of social epistemics. *Synthese*, 73:109–144, 1987.
[Goldman, 2002] A. Goldman. *Pathways to Knowledge: Private and Public*. Oxford University Press, Oxford, 2002.

[Nowak and Thagard, 1992a] G. Nowak and P. Thagard. Copernicus, ptolemy, and explanatory coherence. In R.N. Giere, editor, *Minnesota Studies in the Philosophy of Science Volume 15: Cognitive Models of Science*, pages 271–309, Minneapolis, 1992a. University of Minnesota Press.

[Nowak and Thagard, 1992b] G. Nowak and P. Thagard. Newton, descartes, and explanatory coherence. In R.A. Duschl and R.J. Hamilton, editors, *Philosophy of Science, Cognitive Science, and Educational Theory and Practice*, 1992b.

[Thagard and Verbeurgt, 1998] P. Thagard and K. Verbeurgt. Coherence as constraint satisfaction. *Cognitive Science*, 22, 1998.

[Thagard, 1989] P. Thagard. Explanatory coherence. *Behavioral and Brain Sciences*, 12:435–467, 1989.

[Thagard, 1992a] P. Thagard. Computing coherence. In R.N. Giere, editor, *Minnesota Studies in the Philosophy of Science Volume 15: Cognitive Models of Science*, pages 485–488, Minneapolis, 1992a. University of Minnesota Press.

[Thagard, 1992b] P. Thagard. *Conceptual Revolutions*. Princeton University Press, Princeton, 1992b.

[Thagard, 1993] P. Thagard. Societies of minds: Science as distributed computing. *Studies in History and Philosophy of Science*, 24:49–67, 1993.

[Thagard, 1994] P. Thagard. Mind, society, and the growth of knowledge. *Philosophy of Science*, 61:629–645, 1994.

[Thagard, 1995] P. Thagard. Explaining scientific change: integrating the cognitive and the social. In D. Hull, M. Forbes, and R. Burian, editors, *PSA 1994*, volume 2, pages 298–303, East Lansing MI, 1995. Philosophy of Science Association.

[Thagard, 1999] P. Thagard. *How Scientists Explain Disease*. Princeton University Press, Princeton, 1999.

[Thagard, 2000] P. Thagard. *Coherence in Thought and Action*. MIT Press, Cambridge MA, 2000.

Marcello Guarini
Department of Philosophy
University of Windsor
Windsor, Ontario, Canada.
Email: mguarini@uwindsor.ca

Pierre Boulos
School of Computer Science
University of Windsor
Windsor, Ontario, Canada.
Email: boulos@uwindsor.ca

Computer Science as a Subject Matter for Philosophy of Science

PETER KÜHNLEIN

ABSTRACT. I argue that the long-lasting lack of consciousness of philosophy of science with regard to computer science is owing to the impression that significant empirical content of the latter is missing. The investigation of computer science has been delegated to philosophical logic for reasons of its special structure that was recognised. There are, however, subfields of computer science that in fact are strongly influenced by empirical sciences. Consequently, these areas have to be considered as good candidates for investigations by philosophers of science. I will introduce Embodied Conversational Agents and, more general, Human Computer Interfaces as sample areas for which this holds. I will conclude with some brief remarks about modern versions of Turing-type tests.

Introduction

Newell and Simon (1976) claim that Computer Science is an empirical science. They make this claim in the following way [Newell and Simons, 1976, p. 115]:

> Computer science is an empirical discipline. We would have called it an experimental science, but like astronomy, economics, and geology, some of its unique forms of observation and experience do not fit a narrow stereotype of the experimental method. None the less, they are experiments. Each new machine that is built is an experiment. Actually constructing the machine poses a question to nature; and we listen for the answer by observing the machine in operation and analyzing it by all analytical and measurement means available. Each new program that is built is an experiment. It poses a question to nature, and its behavior offers clues to an answer.

Note that the distinction they make is between that of an empirical discipline and an experimental science. They argue that the distinction is on the

Lorenzo Magnani and Riccardo Dossena, editors, *Computing, Philosophy, and Cognition*, pp. 113–129 © 2005, P. Kühnlein

basis of whether true experimental methods are available in the respective
discipline. Their negative examples comprise – along with economy – parts
of physics. The reason for excluding these fields from the experimental sciences, they argue, is that they lack appropriate forms of observation and
experience. This is a little surprising, as one would have expected the claim
that astrology, economy and geology to be excluded due to the fact that
repetition of observations under reproducible conditions is not easily possible. Nagel [Nagel, 1979] discusses this particular problem for the case of
social sciences, of which economics is a part. He observes that "experiments
in [a certain] strict sense can apparently be performed at best only rarely in
the social sciences, and perhaps never in connection with any phenomenon
which involves the participation of several generations and large numbers of
men" [Nagel, 1979, p. 451]. Economy seems to qualify as a candidate for a
science that fulfils the conditions Nagel has in mind, so in this sense it would
not count as an experimental science. But if impossibility of repetition of
experimental conditions is the reason that these fields are excluded, it is not
clear why computer science should be excluded from the experimental studies on the same grounds: if anything is possible with computers, then it is
reproducing the same conditions for observing their behavior over and over
again. Longo [to appear] in fact argues that it is this property that limits
the use of computers in modeling reality if complex dynamical systems are
at issue – and hence for modeling some really interesting physical claims.

Newell and Simon [Newell and Simons, 1976], continue the quotation
given above thus:

> Neither machines nor programs are black boxes; they are ar-
> tifacts that have been designed, both hardware and software,
> and we can open them up and look inside. We can relate their
> structure to their behavior and draw many lessons from a single
> experiment. We don't have to build 100 copies of, say, a theorem
> prover, to demonstrate statistically that it has not overcome the
> combinatorial explosion of search in the way hoped for. Inspec-
> tion of the program in the light of a few runs reveals the flaw
> and lets us proceed to the next attempt.

Obviously Newell and Simon consider the fact that it is not necessary,
though possible, to run a machine again and again in order to answer the
question why a certain software/hardware configuration shows a specific behavior as sufficient to exclude computer science from the experimental sciences; but at the same time they count it as an empirical one. The implicit
claim seems to be that the former depend on insights being gained from
multiple instantiations of similar experimental settings for empirical knowl-

edge. Probably they have statistical laws in mind with this claim. Clearly, if absence of the necessity (as opposed to possibility) to repeat observations is the relevant criterion to disqualify a discipline from the experimental sciences, then computer science can be excluded along with geology and the rest.

For the rest of this paper I will accept this definition of computer science as an example of a non-experimental empirical science. I will in the following section 1 have a look at the Turing Test as a special case of empirical investigation in computer science. In section 2, I will introduce the notion of Embodied Conversational Agents (ECAs) and show how experimentally derived knowledge sneaks into computer science from a source very different from that envisaged by Newell and Simon. In section 3, I will briefly present ECAs as a modern variant of Turing Tests.

At the root of the exposition is a question in the face of Newell's and Simon's claim: if computer science is an empirical science, why has philosophy of science not responded to it with much interest yet? I will argue that Newell and Simon's claim simply is too general and the type of empirical knowledge they have in mind too simple. The fact that computer runs sometimes – and hopefully most of the time – are successful and that the decision whether they are is an empirical question does not thrill philosophers of science enough to wake their interest in computer science as an empirical science. Coffee machines mostly are successful in the task they are designed for; this does not wake philosophers' interest in coffee machine design as an empirical task, although the question whether the coffee machine did well is an empirical (and important) question, too.

I will try to show, by referring to ECAs, that computer science has more to offer than successful runs of machines to make philosophers of science interested.

1   The Turing test

Let me start with an interesting case of – although imagined – computer run which in fact has attracted the attention of philosophers, though not philosophers of science. Turing, in 1950, proposed a certain procedure that, according to him, should help decide whether or not intelligence should be ascribed to a computer. He introduces this procedure by describing the following game:

> The new form of the problem can be described in terms of a game which we call the "imitation game". It is played with three people, a man (A), a woman (B), and an interrogator (C) who may be of either sex. The interrogator stays in a room apart

front the other two. The object of the game for the interrogator
is to determine which of the other two is the man and which is
the woman. He knows them by labels X and Y, and at the end
of the game he says either "X is A and Y is B" or "X is B and
Y is A".

It is generally understood that the game, if Turing is right, can be used
to decide whether a computer is intelligent, cf. [Clark, 2001, p. 21]. Let
the computer be substituted for either A or B, then, following some standard interpretation of the Turing Test, e.g. [Copeland, 1993], it counts as
intelligent just in case an interrogator can not decide whether X or Y is
human.

The Turing Test, with its presupposition that there really is a sense in
which it is possible for a machine to possess intelligence, gave rise to many
philosophical debates. As Akman and Blackburn [Akman and Blackburn,
2000] have it:

> For some the relevance of the Turing test to AI is unproblematic:
> in fact, Ginsberg [Ginsberg, 1993] defines AI as follows: "Artifi-
> cial Intelligence is the enterprise of constructing a physical sym-
> bol system that can reliably pass the Turing test". Others find
> the link problematic. [...Still others] have raised fundamen-
> tal objections to the test (the best known of these is Searle's
> [Searle, 1984] Chinese Room Argument) and concluded that the
> AI enterprise is ill-founded.

I will not argue for or against the plausibility of the Turing test, but my
concern is with the way the test is set up. The first point to remark is
that according to the description given by Turing, the interrogator and A
as well as B have to be situated in different rooms. Of course, a number
of additional accompanying precautions have to be taken beside this, owing
to limited technical possibilities.

> In order that tones of voice may not help the interrogator the
> answers should be written, or better still, typewritten. The ideal
> arrangement is to have a teleprinter communicating between the
> two rooms.

Then (and the situation did not improve very much in this respect) there
simply didn't exist speech synthesizers that could produce acoustic output.
Hence it is clear that the initial plausibility of the Turing Test as a strategy to answer the question whether it is possible to ascribe intelligence to
machines depended crucially on the latter restriction.

It is probably because of the simplicity of the strategy to use a typewriter that philosophers never cared about this aspect of the Turing test. But for sure today computer scientists might pursue a completely different strategy than restricting the human communicative abilities for purposes of the test: they might as well use speech synthesis and virtual reality (VR), thus improving the interaction abilities of the computer. I will introduce the idea behind a very modern human-computer interface in the following section, demonstrating where the empirical content that should thrill philosophers of science sneaks into computer science.

2   Machines and user interfaces

For a long time people have been fascinated by the idea to construct human-like machines. The following paragraphs are dedicated to some of the developments that are related to modern computers. I will not try to give a comprehensive historical overview of this development; such enterprises can be found in a number of articles, e.g. [Smith, 1970].

One of the most famous examples of machinery that simulates human behavior (though by far not the earliest) is von Kempelen's fake chess "robot" known as "the Turk", cf. [Standage, 2002] for an extensive historical excursion on the Turk. Standage reports that at these times designers of robots strived to use empirical knowledge for the design of their machinery. Thus Vaucanson seems to have built a mechanic flutist that contained artificial lung and lips in the 1730s, as well as a couple of other interesting machines. Behind this use of simulation techniques Standage identifies solid interest in the insights of medical science and biology. So people were disappointed when they found that the behavior of some machine that resembles human behavior to some degree but was caused by a mechanism that corresponded in no detail of construction to a biological organism. This was the case with a predecessor of Vaucanson's flutist. Cases of deception concerning the biological realism of the construction were one of the reasons why the public was skeptic with regard to the possibility of genuine simulation of life.

The fascination of the idea to use knowledge obtained from empirical science to approximate human behavior, and finally life itself, ever closer is very obvious in Shelley's [Shelley, 1998] *Frankenstein* novel. The monster that is described in the novel exhibits behavior that is close enough to human behavior to be both threatening and ridiculous for its environment. And the strategy Shelley ascribes to Frankenstein in his pursuit of building the monster is quite similar to that of Vaucanson and his contemporaries when they built their machines. The difference lies in the material, which, in Shelley's fantasy, was organic material, and, in the design reality of the 18th century, was anorganic. The (fictitious) choice of parts of corpses as

Figure 1. Konrad Zuse and the Z3.

the basis for the construction of a living organism had – as one of its effects
– the result that trickery in the process was precluded.

Yet in the digital age with its dawn in the early 20th century, design questions related to appearance had to step back behind technical necessities.
The primary input devices for computers initially have been switches and
buttons, the output side consisted of lamps and meters. (Although what I
have in mind primarily are digital computers, there have been attempts at
developing analog computers as well. The meters were their primary output
device, while the lamp was that of the early digital machines, like the Zuse
Z3.) The interpretation of the output signals (let alone the correct coding
of the input) was not intended to be intuitively understandable. Rather,
operators programming and using these machines were experts with an explicit training. This fact will be immediately agreed on by anyone who has
personally tried to program a computer with an early generation of input
device such as punch cards or punch tapes.

Things started to become different with the appearance of more human
readable output devices (CRTs, Teletypes) and the use of keyboards as
the main input devices. Still the use of computers was very restricted to
scientific, engineering and business tasks. But the interaction with them was
now closer to what people knew from human-human communication. (By
the way, this was approximately the stage of technical development Turing
might have envisaged as a prerequisite for his test.) This is interesting,
because the development that took place was one that was not necessitated
by requirements of some task. Rather, ease of use of the machinery was the
guiding principle.

This principle can be witnessed even more clearly when the development of human-computer interfaces (HCI), as they are called today, is considered. The so-called desktop metaphor for HCI was the next major step towards ECA. It was suggested by a group of developers at the Stanford Research Institute (latter known as SRI). The interaction shifted from the sole use of the keyboard as the input device and, for the first time, a computer mouse was employed for that purpose. (The mouse was invented by Douglas Englebart in 1967 and patented in November 1970.) In the development of this style of interaction psychological, sociological etc. knowledge was taken into account to optimize handling. Specialists from outside computer science contributed their skills to the design of the "windows, icons, menus and pointers" that make up the appearance of the graphical user interfaces (GUIs). The desktop metaphor makes interaction with the computer easier than it was before. Nevertheless, there are diverse implementations of the desktop concerning both functionality and appearance. Especially the latter fact shows that there is still a residue of specialist knowledge that has to be acquired by computer users in order to be able to handle the machine correctly and efficiently. Only on this assumption the existence of manuals, on-line help and lists of frequently asked questions (FAQ) can be explained: if the use of machines with GUIs were completely intuitive, there would be no use for explanations for their handling. There would be no FAQs.

3   Embodied conversational agents (ECAs)

Apart from the usual military applications, the search for learning-free styles of interaction with computers is the main motivation behind the development of Embodied Conversational Agents (ECAs). The idea is spelled out in [Cassell *et al.*, 1999a] as follows:

> In the current paper we argue that while [the conversation] metaphor has been useful to HCI, its use to date has been just that: a metaphor. We believe that interfaces that are truly conversational have the promise of being more intuitive to learn, more resistant to communication breakdown, and more functional in high *noise* environments. Therefore, we propose to leverage the full breadth and power of human conversational competency by imbuing the computer with all of the conversational skills that humans have: to whit, the ability to use the face, hands, and melody of the voice to regulate the process of conversation, as well as the ability to use verbal and nonverbal means to contribute content to the ongoing conversation.

The proposal that Cassell et al put forth suggests that software developers not only use notions borrowed from communication studies in order to
describe human-computer communication. Rather they should try simulating actual human-human communication using an artificial communicator
as one conversational participant. A considerable number of AI labs have
since taken up this proposal and established groups that design ECAs that
imitate humans in conversational interaction. As Stronks et al [Stronks *et
al.*, 2002, p. 89] have it, a

> lot of effort is put into research to make ECAs more lifelike
> and believable and to make communication with ECAs more
> effective, efficient, and more fun.

I will not discuss the problematic use of "lifelikeness" or "believability"
in the context of communication with machines. Much less even will I discuss the question whether it should be considered as a goal that is worth
pursuing to have machines that can simulate human behavior. (This would
inter alia mean raising questions that are relevant for Frankenstein-cases.)
Rather, I want to turn to a special case of research like this, and show
which kind of empirical (and experimental) knowledge is absorbed by ECA
developers and turned into algorithms. The case I have in mind is that of
Multimodal Communication (often called MMC or M^2C). There have been
a number of conferences and workshops on MMC recently where the connection between multimodality and lifelikeness or believability of ECAs was
highlighted. What can be concluded from a comparison of the main bulk of
papers that were delivered at these conferences is that AI researchers consider as one of the basic cases of MMC the combination of spoken language
and gestural information. So, here is the plan for the rest of this section: in
subsection 3.1 I, will go into some detail with respect to currently relevant
accounts of spoken communication, with clear focus on psycholinguistic theory as perceived by computer scientists. Subsection 3.2 will be devoted to
the dominant view on gestural expressiveness; I will explain how gestures
are seen to be syntactically partitioned and grouped. Subsection 3.3 will,
finally, give an impression of how the integration of speech and gesture is
implemented in an artificial communicator.

3.1   Speaking and listening

One of the contemporary standard views on language production is put
forward by Levelt [Levelt, 1989]: on this account, the human production
system is strongly modular, reminiscent of the picture Fodor [Fodor, 1983]
has of the human mind as a whole. For Levelt, then, the production of
speech takes its departure from the formation of a thought, what he calls

Figure 2. Stefan Kopp from the Knowledge Based Systems Group at Biele-feld interacting with the ECA Max in an "imitation game".

message generation, in a module called the conceptualizer. This module is fed by general memory and perception and in turn feeds into the formulator module. Here, grammatical, i.e., semantic and syntactic properties of the spoken item to-be are determined and delivered to the phonological encoding. As an output, the formulator sends a phonetic plan, or internal speech, to the articulator and to the speaker's speech comprehension system. It thus enables the speaker to get an internal feedback via the unspoken message plus an external feedback via audition. The speech comprehension system parses the spoken output and feeds back into a monitoring loop that is part of the conceptualizer module. The comprehension system shares a lexicon with the formulator. This guarantees the possibility for the speaker to rec-ognize all the words and word forms that the speaker herself/himself can produce.

The process that is involved in the production of speech has several in-teresting features; first, it is incremental. That means that a subsequent module can start working while the preceding is still producing its output. Such a construction secures swift and quick production and explains why there need not be a huge delay between the reception of one piece of text and a corresponding response. According to Levelt [Levelt, 1989, p. 24], a "processing component will be triggered by any *fragment* of characteristic input". Second, the process is serial. This means that a module can not start producing output without its corresponding input from the preceding module, and it uses to a high degree the sequencing of the input to produce its own output. There are, however exceptions where "lookaheads" [Levelt, 1989, p. 25] are allowed that are needed to avoid, e.g., mispronunciation.

Despite the superficial plausibility of Levelt's model (it forms the basis for the Interactive Alignment Model by Pickering and Garrod [Pickering and Garrod, 2003], one of the most advanced frameworks for research in psycholinguistics) it has been attacked on various reasons. Some of these reasons were of a theoretical nature, e.g., because the modularity of the production system was attacked. This line of attack clearly was pursued by researchers who preferred a radical pdp connectionist model in the spirit of Rumelhart and McClelland [Rumelhart and McClelland, 1987] to a modular one. A different line of attacks used the empirical predictions that can be derived from Levelt's model. Strong claims are made in Levelt's theory with regard to slip of the tongue phenomena. Some of its opponents exploited these empirical consequences of the setting to try to refute the theory.

Nevertheless, both among psycholinguistic and computer scientists' models Levelt's theory plays an important role. For the ECA case, this can be demonstrated by the example of Padilha and Carletta [Padilha and Carletta, 2002]. They describe experimental work they conducted by means of ECAs to simulate group conversations in small working groups. After reporting a number of results they obtained, they consider what would happen if they improved an implementation they had by adopting "a model of the speaker [...], such as the one proposed by Levelt". They ponder that this would result in the influence of a broader range of discourse phenomena. But the crucial thing is that Levelt's model is demonstrably of impact within computer science, especially within ECA design.

I don't go into details concerning the different possibilities to model theories. What is a fact for any of the modeling styles is that the empirical content of the theories, the predictions and assumptions they make, will be inherited by the algorithms computer scientists turn them into.

3.2 Gestures: pointing out the relevant things

Gesture research is – as compared to linguistics – a rather new field in the humanities. There has been some work in this field in the 1930s, but systematic and experimental studies were scarcely conducted until around 1980. One of the reasons for this offset surely is the comparably high degree of complexity in transcription and the fact that recording gestural movement was connected with some expenditure.

I will not go through the history of gesture research here; instead, I will exemplarily discuss the account of the most relevant proponent to date, David McNeill, and point out the connection to speech production in his work.

In [McNeill, 1992], the author proposes a functional classification of gestures. He divides them into deictics (used for pointing), iconics (expressing properties of objects), emblematic gestures (being encoded in a rigid vocabulary, e.g. the "Italian" gestures) and so forth. On the other hand, he describes structures that can be identified underlying the execution of gestures. A gesture, according to him, consists of five parts: rest position, preparation, stroke, retraction and rest position again. Of these, only the stroke (which is the most expressive part of the gesture) is obligatory, while the others are optional. Stroke as well as preparation can be followed by "holds", i.e. short pauses in the movement. McNeill thus gives both a classification and a description of the dynamics of gestures.

The stroke of the gesture carries the central information that is encoded by it. E.g. in the case of a simple pointing gesture with the index finger as the body part that is used for pointing, this would be the moment or duration of time where the finger is actually directed at the object that is the target of the pointing. (With a "definition" like that, things can become a little complicated in cases of deferred reference or deferred ostension, as discussed by Quine [Quine, 1960] or Nunberg [Nunberg, 1979]. But I assume simple cases here to avoid complications.) The information that is encoded is formed at the growth point, as it is called in McNeill's terms. Interestingly, McNeill [McNeill, 1992, p. 232] refers to Levelt's theory of speaking when he introduces this notion. He states that the

> growth point is the first chunk of information to be handed over from the conceptualizer (Levelt doesn't use the term "growth point", but the concept is the same). This growth point is the theme of the utterance, viz., the reference (real or fictional) about which the utterance provides further information and tends to be the first word to be uttered.

The total set up of McNeill's conception of the articulation apparatus is more complicated than that of Levelt's, which, given that the former, but not the latter, is intended to account for the production of multimodal utterances, is not surprising.

Again, just like in the case of Levelt's theory, McNeill's theory predicts certain empirical phenomena. One of the predictions is that in the case of co-verbal gesture, the gesture precedes its semantically related verbal expression by a small interval, typically in the order of 250 ms. And again, there have been doubts cast upon these predictions and, consequently, the theory. Kranstedt et al. [Kranstedt *et al.*, 2004] report findings which indicate that in a certain class of dialogs there is a surprising number of gestures that do not precede, but follow the "affiliate", as they call the verbal counterpart of the gesture.

Thus, McNeill's theory is as vulnerable for empirical attacks as Levelt's – which does not surprise, given that they are theories from psychology, i.e. empirical theories. But once again, the interesting fact is that the empirical content is infused into the algorithms that control the behavior of ECAs that are designed to be able to recognize or produce gestures. This will become clear in the following subsection.

3.3   Integration

The goal of ECA design, as was explained before, is to adopt as many characteristics of human-human communication for human-machine communication, and thus making the latter more "natural" or "believable". To achieve this goal, the AI researchers must develop a strategy to combine the information that is distributed over the different modalities into a single piece. (The counterpart of McNeill's "growth point".)

In fact, computer scientists are well aware of some of the problems that are tied up with the use of temporal relations as a means of constructing the complex semantic information. Latoschik [Latoschik, 2001] notes that the usual procedure to interpret both gesture and speech independently (my translation)

> presupposes an independent analysis of each modality. On this basis, a correspondence between the information from each channel has to be determined – a task that is usually called *correspondence problem*.

The problem Latoschik has in mind is the question on the basis of which properties the corresponding pieces of information can be identified. This, of course, is a version of a problem that by the name "binding problem" well-known from neurosciences and psychology. Dennett [Dennett, 1991] has forcefully argued that in both contexts pure temporal correlation is not sufficient for establishing a correspondence. Nevertheless, computer scientists – in the absence of a more appropriate criterion – wrote their algorithms using exactly the temporal relations as a basis for both generation of multimodal utterances and integration in the case of interpretation. I first give an example from multimodal integration; the communicative "partner" in this case is not an Embodied Conversational Agent. I quote from the field of robotics here that is quite close to ECA design in some respects, about which I will not say anything here. The example consists of the following quotation from [Lemon *et al.*, 2003, p. 237]:

When the system receives an utterance from the user, candidate referential phrases (X) can be retrieved via parsing. In order to generate dialogue moves correctly and interpret such phrases in an [Information State], the following sorts of rules are employed (here noun phrases refer to physical objects with locations):

[...]

Resolve-deixis(X): when X is "here", look at the modality buffer for the last resolved gestural expression (mouse click) and bind to that. If none exists, give up. If the referential term is "there" look at the salience list for the last resolved referential expression (gesture or spoken) and bind to it. If the expression is "that Y" or "this Y" and the user has gestured, match the points. If the user has not made a gesture then move into the resolve-ambiguity state – i.e. put *resolve-ambiguity*(Y) on top of the system agenda.

[...]

Here, quite obviously the temporal relations between the parts of multimodal utterances are used to establish semantic correspondences: when the dialogue module receives as input an utterance of a deictic expression, it looks for a preceding occurrence of a gesture. The value of the deictic expression (the denotation) is then calculated from the value of the gesture, simulated by a mouse action.

Lemon et al are silent about the reason why the dialog manager is supposed to look backward for a preceding gesture, instead of, say wait for the next occurrence. It might be the case that they just intuitively chose to pursue this strategy. But there is a very clear example from ECA literature that shows that at least some of the researchers design their algorithms based on psycholinguistic or psychological theories. The example is [Tepper *et al.*, 2004]; the authors describe how gestures can be simulated by an ECA they developed in the NUMACK project without use of pre-designed video clips that are combined or similar "of the shelf" solutions. Rather, they want to have a system that can calculate, i.e., has an algorithm for, the ECA "movements". Here is the quotation that can be used as evidence:

We tackled that problem in the previous MAX system [...], which uses a generation model that creates all verbal and gestural behaviors from formal specifications of their overt form. In particular, this system comprises a hierarchical model for calculating and controlling upper-limb movements of the avatar's skeleton in real time, which allows for flexibility with respect

> to the producible forms of gesture, and a fine adaption to tem-
> poral constraints as imposed by cross-modal synchrony. [...]
> Following McNeill [McNeill, 1992], we assume that the stroke
> corresponds to the words with which it temporally co-occurs.

Although Tepper et al do not explicitly state that the constraints on timing their system obeys are the constraints that are proposed by McNeill [McNeill, 1992], the last sentence in the above quotation gives reason to believe that this piece of empirical content ultimately comes from McNeill's studies. Besides this textual evidence, there is even more reason to assume so, given the interrelations between the research groups that are involved in the NUMACK project: there is a close relation between the McNeill-Lab, the AI group at Bielefeld and Cassell's MIT group. There even exist common publications e.g. by Cassell, one of her co-workers and McNeill [Cassell et al., 1999b] on timing phenomena.

Given the dependence of the parameters of ECAs algorithms on psychological and psycholinguistic theories and observational results, it is clear that the success of the implementations (lifelikeness etc.) co-varies with the correctness of the theories and empirical observations in this direction: incorrect theories, if faithfully implemented, lead to unsuccessful programs, and wrong parameters hamper the believability of the ECAs. It is in this sense that the algorithms and implementations are empirically rich, and it is at this point where experimental results in the sense defined by Newell and Simon as quoted at the beginning of this paper sneak into computer science. Although, of course, the machines themselves don't have to be tested statistically for correct runs, the parameters that determine their behavior are experimentally derived.

4   ECAs as 21st century Turing tests

A last, and probably quite obvious, point to mention is the sense in which ECAs can be considered successors for the Turing test. The first thing to observe is that the notion of intelligence doesn't play any role in ECA design as I set it out. The properties that are tested for, rather, are those of believability and lifelikeness. Of course one could try to give those notions interpretations that come close to what Turing wanted to test initially with his imitation game. But computer scientists typically avoid using mentalistic notions in this context and confine themselves to a behavioural vocabulary.

As Cassell et al [Torres et al., 1997] have it, the

> Turing test has always been conceived of as a test of the content
> of a computer's contribution to a conversation. That is, from
> typed output, we are supposed to try to tell whether the text

was generated by a human or a computer. [...] What about a face-to-face Turing test? What kind of behaviours would a computer have to exhibit to convince us that it is not a grey box but a living, breathing body?

The latter is, of course, way off the intention of what should be tested by the Turing test. The test is not intended to give a proof of a things being a living, breathing body. (I take it that Cassell equates this metaphor with "believability" or "lifelikeness" instead.) Rather, it is intended to test for intelligence. What Cassell proposes is to perform a test that is a Turing-type test, with the criterion of indistinguishability (with respect to a certain property or set of properties) of one "subject" from a reference candidate. The general form of a test-recipe for Turing-type tests would look like this:

"A machine is X if it is indistinguishable from a human with respect to Y"

If "intelligent" is substituted for X, and "verbal behaviour" for Y, the resulting recipe is the one for the classical Turing test. For Cassell's purposes, X needs to be substituted by "lifelike" (or "believable") and Y by "multimodal behavior": The difference is that the criteria are stronger (multimodal behavior in the sense intended includes verbal behavior), but the property that is ascribed on the basis of passing the test is much weaker (to my mind) or at any rate different.

5 Conclusion

The specialist area of ECA development within computer science is in fact a field of research in a science that is massively laden by empirical knowledge. By contrast, computer science as a whole is empirically poor in the sense that no relevant experimental results have to be derived from runs of machines. While it is understandable that philosophy of science did not show much interest in computer science, things are different with ECA or HCI design. Here, a close exchange with empirical sciences, and especially a strong dependence on findings thereof, can be observed. These contaminations of pure logic (in the form of algorithms) by empirical findings (in the form of psychological results) should thrill philosophers of science.

BIBLIOGRAPHY

[Akman and Blackburn, 2000] V. Akman and P. Blackburn. Editorial: Alan turing and artificial intelligence. *Journal of Logic, Language, and Information*, 9(4):391–395, 2000.

[Cassell *et al.*, 1998] J. Cassell, O.E. Torres, and S. Prevost. Turn taking vs. discourse structure: How best to model multimodal conversation, 1998.

[Cassell *et al.*, 1999a] J. Cassell, T. Bickmore, M. Billinghurst, L. Campbell, K. Chang, Vilhjálmsson H., and H. Yan. Embodiment in conversational interfaces: Rea. In *Proceedings of the CHI conference '99*, 1999a.

[Cassell et al., 1999b] J. Cassell, D. McNeill, and K.E. McCullough. Speech-gesture mis-matches: Evidence for one underlying representation of linguistic and non-linguistic information. *Pragmatics and Cognition*, 7(1):1–33, 1999b.

[Clark, 2001] A. Clark. *Mindware – An Introduction to the Philosophy of Cognitive Science*. Oxford UP, 2001.

[Copeland, 1993] B.J. Copeland. *Artificial Intelligence: A Philosophical Introduction*. Blackwell, 1993.

[Dennett, 1991] D. Dennett. *Consciousness Explained*. Penguin Books, 1991.

[Fodor, 1983] J. Fodor. *The Modularity of Mind*. MIT Press, 1983.

[Ginsberg, 1993] M. Ginsberg. *Essentials of Artificial Intelligence*. Morgan Kaufmann, San Mateo, CA, 1993.

[Kranstedt et al., 2004] A. Kranstedt, P. Kühnlein, and I. Wachsmuth. Deixis in mul-timodal human-computer interaction: An interdisciplinary approach. In A. Camurri and G. Volpe, editors, *Gesture-Based Communication in Human-Computer Interac-tion*. LNAI 2915, Springer Verlag, 2004.

[Latoschik, 2001] M.E. Latoschik. *Multimodale Interaktion in Virtueller Realität am Beispiel der virtuellen Konstruktion*. infix diski volume 251, akademische verlagsge-sellschaft aka gmbh, Faculty of Technology, University of Bielefeld, Berlin, 2001. PhD thesis.

[Lemon et al., 2003] O. Lemon, A. Bracy, A. Gruenstein, and S. Peters. An information state approach in a multi-modal dialogue system. In P. Kühnlein, H. Rieser, and H. Zeevat, editors, *Perspectives on Dialogue in the New Millennium*. Benjamins, 2003.

[Levelt, 1989] W.J.M. Levelt. *Speaking*. MIT Press, 1989.

[Longo,] G. Longo. Computer imitation and mathematical understanding. To appear.

[McNeill, 1992] D. McNeill. *Hand and Mind - What Gestures Reveal about Thought*. MIT Press, 1992.

[Nagel, 1979] E. Nagel. *The Structure of Science – Problems in the Logic of Scientific Explanation*. Hackett, 1979.

[Newell and Simons, 1976] A. Newell and H.A. Simons. Computer science as empirical enquiry: Symbols and search. *Communications of the ACM*, 19(3):113–126, 1976.

[Nunberg, 1979] G. Nunberg. The non-uniqueness of semantic solutions. *Linguistics and Philosophy*, 3, 1979.

[Oviatt, 1999] S. Oviatt. Ten myths of multimodal interaction. *Communications of the ACM*, 42(11):74–81, 1999.

[Padilha and Carletta, 2002] E.G. Padilha and J. Carletta. A simulation of small group discussion. In J. Bos, M.E. Foster, and C. Matheson, editors, *Proceedings of Edilog 2002*, 2002.

[Pickering and Garrod, 2003] M. Pickering and S. Garrod. Toward a mechanistic psy-chology of dialog: The interactive alignment model. *Behavioral and Brain Sciences*, 2003.

[Quine, 1960] W.V.O. Quine. *Word and Object*. MIT Press, 1960.

[Rumelhart and McClelland, 1987] D.E. Rumelhart and J.L. McClelland. *Parallel Dis-tributed Processing – Explorations in the Microstructure of Cognition*. MIT Press, 1987.

[Searle, 1984] J.R. Searle. *Minds, Brains and Science*. Harvard University Press, Cam-bridge, MA, 1984.

[Shelley, 1998] M. Shelley. *Frankenstein: 1818 Text: The modern Prometheus*. Oxford Paperbacks, 1998. ed.: Butler, Marilyn.

[Smith, 1970] Th. Smith. Some perspectives on the early history of computers. In Z. Pylyshyn, editor, *Perspectives on the Computer Revolution*. Prentice-Hall, 1970.

[Standage, 2002] T. Standage. *The Turk*. Walker and Company, 2002.

[Stronks *et al.*, 2002] B. Stronks, A. Nijholt, P. van der Vet, and D. Heylen. Designing for friendship: Becoming friends with your eca. In A. Marriott, C. Pelachaud, T. Rist, Z. Ruttkay, and H. Vilhjalmson, editors, *Proceedings of the Workshop Embodied Conversational Agents: Let's Specify and Compare Them!*, Bologna, 2002. On occasion of the AAMAS Conference.
[Tepper *et al.*, 2004] P. Tepper, S. Kopp, and J. Cassell. Content in context: Generating language and iconic gesture without a gestionary. In *Proceedings of the Workshop on Embodied Conversational Agents*. AAMAS 2004, 2004.
[Torres *et al.*, 1997] O. Torres, J. Cassell, and S. Prevost. Modeling gaze behavior as a function of discourse structure. In *First International Workshop on Human-Computer Conversations*, Bellagio, Italy, 1997.
[Turing, 1950] A.M. Turing. Computing machinery and intelligence. *Mind*, 49:433–460, 1950.

Peter Kühnlein
Collaborative Research Center SFB 360
University of Bielefeld
Bielefeld, Germany
Email: p@uni-bielefeld.de

Designing Human Interfaces. The Role of Abduction

LORENZO MAGNANI AND EMANUELE BARDONE

ABSTRACT. In this article we claim that interface plays a key role in understanding human-computer interaction. Interface is considered a kind of mediating structure that we can illustrate in terms of an epistemological model able to depict various features of the mediation involved. We also show how human-computer interaction can be better understood as an inferential process where the interface provides clues from which the user can correctly infer how to cope with a product. Hence, we refer to this inferential process as genuinely abductive. In the last section some kinds of inferential abductions that can be employed in designing and evaluating web interfaces are described.

1 Introduction

C.P. Snow pointed out that technology is a queer thing since its ambivalence. It can be a great gift on one hand, but it can turn out to be irritating on the other. Computer programs, computational tools, cell phones, and all kind of technological stuff, enable us to accomplish a great array of things: calculating, organizing, drawing, writing, playing some instrument, etc.. All that is the great gift Snow talked about. However, carrying out all these activities is not costless. The computer (or our mobile) is not an oracle, that is "just ask, and you'll get back the answer"; we cannot tell a computer, "please, I need to send en email to a friend of mine" and it immediately opens our mail client and it chooses the most suitable layout for the email you are going to write. All these activities involve being able to cope with technologies. Indeed, a tool or a computer program enhances our cognitive abilities, but that implies being able to know how to exploit their functionalities. Hence, the problem is concerned about how to design technologies so that humans can easily exploit their potentialities. How can we design products that can easily help humans to accomplish different tasks?

The question is not trivial and it is not related only to *Human Computer Interaction* (HCI). We know that external objects can be valuable aids to

Lorenzo Magnani and Riccardo Dossena, editors, *Computing, Philosophy, and Cognition*,
pp. 131–146 © 2005, L. Magnani and E. Bardone

cognition. Several cognitive scientists have shown how external artefacts shape our cognitive abilities. However, very few words have been spent about how to design those artefacts that can effectively overcome human limitations and extend human cognitive abilities. What are those principles we can fruitfully employ to create cognitive artefacts?

2   Interfaces as mediating structures

The first point we want to make is about the notion of interface. According to Raskin [Raskin, 2000], the way we interact with a product, what we do and how it responds is what defines an interface. This is a good starting definition in one important respect: an interface is not something given or an entirely predefined property, but it is the *dynamic* interaction that actually takes place when a product meets the users. More precisely an interface is that interaction that mediates the relation between the user and a tool explaining the approach we need to exploit its functions. Hence, an interface can be considered as a *mediating structure.* According to [Hutchins, 1995], a mediating structure is a kind of *representation,* both internal and external, that changes the way a certain task can be carried out. Consider, for instance, the following two medical prescriptions [Norman, 1993]:

Now, suppose we should answer to the question "how many pills should I take at lunch time?". Here we have two different ways of representing the problem. The first is a traditional medical prescription that simply tells us what kind of pills we should take, whereas the second is a matrix.

If we consider the two representations we immediately come up with the conclusion that the way the second represent the task is much easier than the first; the matrix representation makes the solution *more transparent.* The medical prescription in figure X is far more complex. Just at the first line we need to think about what "1 tablet 3 times a day" means. Once we came up with the number of pills we should take, we have to write it down. Then pass to the second line, and so forth. In contrast, the second representation is much simpler: answering to the question simply means scanning down the lunch column "L" and counting the colored squares. We may even say that one gets the answer *at a glance.*

As the example shows, we may say that the environment physically encodes and stores the change made upon it so as every change becomes a *clue* (spatial or visual, in the example above) that affects a certain reaction from it. Analogously we might claim that an interface mediates the relation between the user and a tool *affording* her or him to use it a certain way.[1]

---

[1]The concept of *affordance* is relevant; we might say the change stored within the environment *affords* a certain reaction rather than others. For more information about the concept of affordance, see [Gibson, 1979].

Understanding the kind of mediation involved can be fruitfully investigated from a cognitive and epistemological point of view. More precisely we claim the process of mediating can be better understood when considered to be an inferential one (cf. below).

In the real world there are many things that human beings use without thinking about or without explicit instructions. For instance, we immediately come up with the idea that a chair is more suitable for sitting than a narrow column or a table. We do not need a manual to know how to cope with a chair: that is clear *on the face of it*. Several researchers [Hollan *et al.*, 2000; Kirsh, 2004] have recently pointed out that designing interface deals with displaying as many clues as possible from which the user can correctly and quickly *infer* what to do next. [Shneiderman, 2002] has recently suggested that the value of an interface should be measured in terms of its consistency, predictability and its controllability. These are all to some extent epistemological values. But in which sense could an interaction be predictable or consistent? Even if the inferential nature of such interactions is acknowledged, as of yet no model has been designed which takes it into account. How can understanding the inferential nature of human-computer interaction shed light on the activity of designing good interfaces? Here the cognitive task required is twofold: first, investigating what kind of inference is involved in such an interaction. Second, explaining how the analysis of the nature of computer interaction as inferential can provide useful hints about how to design and evaluate inferences.

In both cases we will consider the concept of abduction as a keystone of a broad cognitive model.

3 Abduction in designing interfaces

3.1 Abduction as sign activity

Charles Sanders Peirce [Peirce, 1923], more than one hundred years ago, pointed out that human performances are inferential and mediated by signs: here signs can be icons, indexes, but also conceptions, images and feelings. We have signs or clues, that can be icons, but also symbols, written words, from which certain conclusions are inferred.

According to Peirce all those performances that involve sign activities are abductions [Peirce, 1972]. Abduction is the process of *inferring* certain facts and/or laws and hypotheses that render some sentences plausible, that *explain* or *discover* some (eventually new) phenomenon or observation; it is the process of reasoning in which explanatory hypotheses are formed and evaluated. There are two main epistemological meanings of the word abduction: 1) abduction that only generates "plausible" hypotheses ("selective" or "creative") and 2) abduction considered as inference "to the best explanation", which also evaluates hypotheses [Magnani, 2001]. Consider for example the method of inquiring employed by detectives [Eco and Sebeok, 1991]: in this case we do not have direct experience of what we are taking about. Say, we did not see the murderer killing the victim. But we infer that *given* certain signs or clues, a *given* fact must have happened. More generally, we guess a hypothesis that imposes order on data. Analogously, we argue the mediation activity brought about by an interface is the same as that employed by detectives. Designers that want to make their interface more comprehensible must uncover evidence and clues from which the user is prompted to correctly infer the way detective does; this kind of inference, still explanatory, could be called *inference to the best interaction*.

We can conclude that how good an interface is depends on how easily we can draw the *correct* inference. A detective can easily discover the murderer, if the murderer has left evidence (clues) from which the detective can infer that *person and only that person* could be guilty. According to the definition stated above the interaction is not simply the possible ones, but it is supposed to be *the best*. Thus, how *quickly* the user can infer what to do next is a central point. Sometimes finding the murderer is very difficult. It may require a great effort. More precisely, we may argue that how quick the process is depends on whether it is performed without an excessive amount of processing. If clues are clear and well displayed, the inference is promptly drawn. As [Krug, 2000] put it, it does not have to *make us think*.

3.2   Sentential and manipulative abduction

In order to clarify this point even more, let us introduce the important distinction between theoretical and manipulative abduction [Magnani, 2001]. The distinction provides an interesting account to explain how inferences that exploit the environment visually and spatially for instance provide a quicker and more efficient response. Theoretical and manipulative abduction mainly differ regarding whether the exploitation of the environment is or is not crucial to carry out reasoning. Theoretical *abduction* (sentential and model-based) mostly refers to an internal (mental) dimension of abductive inference. In the case of sentential abduction signs and clues are expressed in sentences or in *explicit* statements. This kind of abduction has been extensively applied in logic programming [Flach and Kakas, 2000] and in artificial intelligence in general [Thagard, 1988]. An example of theoretical model-based abduction is creative reasoning performed through imageries or the so-called thought experiments.

In contrast *manipulative abduction* occurs when the process of inferring mostly leans on and is driven by the environment, included our how bodies. Here signs are diagrams, kinesthetic schemas, decorated texts, images, spatial representations, and even feelings. In all those examples the environment embodies clues that trigger an abductive process helping to unearth information that otherwise would have remained invisible and to guess hypotheses. Frequently the exploitation of the environment comes about quickly because it is performed almost tacitly and implicitly. Many examples have demonstrated that problem solving activities that use external visual and spatial representations are quicker and more efficient than sentential ones. We can conclude that in devising interfaces designers have to deal mostly with the latter type of abduction. Interfaces that lean on the environment are tacit and implicit and for this reason much quicker than sentential ones. The following is a clear example. When people have to cope with a software, they very seldom pick the 300 pages manual and read it: they just *try it* and look at what happens [Larkin and Simon, 1987]. That is to say, the 300 pages manual mainly involves a *sentential* interaction that is often time-consuming. We could eventually know that a document can be formatted typing "ALT+C+L", but we do not get any visual, spatial, even manipulative feedback, that could be more useful to learn how to cope with it.

4   How to mimic the physical world within a digital one

Investigating the activity of designing interfaces from the "abductive" perspective described above helps designers in another important respect: how to mimic the physical world within a digital one to enhance understanding.

As we have previously seen, the environment enables us to trigger inferential processes: it can do it if and only if it can embody and encode those signs through which one can infer what to do next. For example, if you are working in your office and you would appreciate a visit from one of your colleagues, you can just keep the door open. Otherwise you can keep it closed. In both cases the environment encodes the clue (the door kept open or closed) from which your colleagues can infer whether you do or don't want to be disturbed. Here the questions we immediately come up with is: how can we encode those signs in a digital world? How can we enrich it so as to render it capable of embodying and encoding clues?

The question of how to enrich the digital world mainly concerns on how to mimic some important features of the physical world in the digital one. Often common people refer to an interface as easy-to-use, because it is more intuitive. Therefore, we do not need to learn how the product actually works. We just analogically infer the actions we have to perform from ordinary ones. More generally, metaphors are important in interface design, because they relate digital objects to the objects in the physical world which the user is more familiar with[2].

In the history of computer interface many attempts have been brought about to replace some physical features in the digital one. For instance, replacing command-driven modes with windows was one of the most important insights in the history of technology and human-computer interaction [Johnson, 1997]. It enabled users to think spatially, say, in terms of *"where is what I am looking for?"* and not in terms of "what sequence of letters do I type to call up this document?".

Enriching the digital world deals to some extent with "faking", transforming those features embedded in the physical world into illusions. For example, consider the rule of projection first invented by Filippo Brunelleschi and then developed by great painters like Leon Battista Alberti and Leonardo da Vinci. In Peircean terms, what these great painters did was to scatter those signs to create the illusion of three dimensional representations. It was a trick that exploited the inferential nature of visual construction [Hoffman, 1998][3]. In his *On Painting*, Leon Battista Alberti [Alberti, 1991] devised a method to *simulate* a three-dimensional space.

Figure 1.

Hence, the question is: how could we exploit inferential visual dimensions to enhance the interaction in the digital world? In the window metaphor we do not have rooms, edges, folders, such as in the physical world. They are, so to say, illusions, they are all produced by an inferential (abductive) activity of human perception analogously to what happens in smashing three

---

[2]There are several problems related to metaphors in interface design. For further information on this topic, see [Collins, 1995].

[3]About the inferential role of perception, see [Rock, 1982] and [Thagard and Shelley, 1997].

Figure 2.

to two dimensions. Here, we aim at showing how visual, but also spatial, temporal, and even emotional abductive dimensions can be fruitfully implemented in an interface. Roughly speaking, we argue that *enriching digital world* precisely means scattering clues and signs that in some extension *fake* spatial, visual, temporal, and other dimensions, even if that just happens within a flat environment.

As we have already said, many researchers have pointed out that good interfaces are those that display as many clues as possible from which the user can correctly and quickly *infer* what to do next. Acknowledging this inferential dimension is also important to suggest possible future trends and fruitful guidelines for web interfaces design. In the following section we will provide a row of example taken from web design as possible future developments.

5   Abduction and web interfaces

Peirce stated that all thinking is in signs, and signs can be icons, indices, or symbols. Moreover, all *inference* is a form of sign activity, where the word sign includes "feeling, image, conception, and other representation" [Peirce, 1923]. Following this point of view we may argue that the kind of signs involved, whether visual, spatial, temporal, and so on, contribute to enhance a certain kind of understanding. In web sign activity we can recognize four abductive (or inferential) dimensions: visual, spatial, temporal, and emotional[4]. We will discuss in detail these four aspects by providing examples taken from the field of web design.

5.1 Visual abduction

Visual dimension is certainly one of the most ubiquitous features in web interaction. Users mainly interact with web pages *visually* [Kirsh, 2004; van Schaik and Ling, 2001]. Here signs and clues are colors, text size, dotted line, text format (bold, underline, italics): they convey visual representations and can assign weight and importance to some specific part. Consider for example the navigation menu in the figure below:

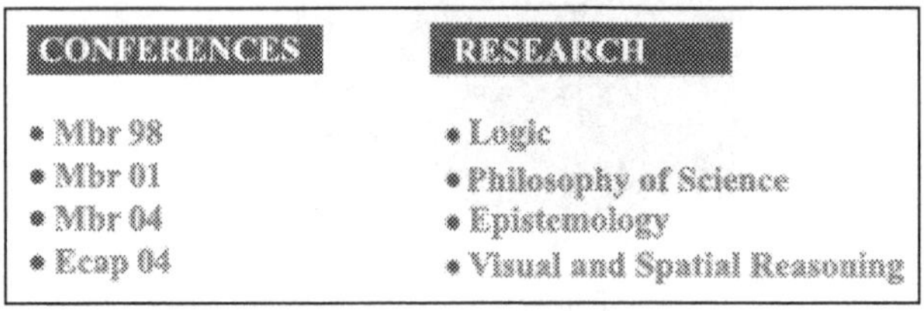

Figure 3. Visual abduction

Here, colors, capital letters and text size provide visual clues capable of enhancing the processing of information. The attention is immediately drawn by the menu header that represents its content (conference and research); capital letters and the colors serve this function.

Then, the dotted list of the same color of the menu header informs the user about the number of the items. Hence, the fact that items are not visibly marked as menu headers gives a useful overview (Figure 4). Once the user has chosen what to see (conference or research), she can proceed to check each item according to her preference (Figure 5).

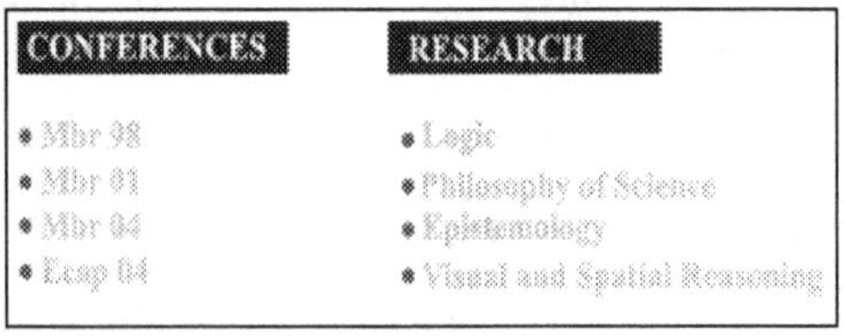

Figure 4.

---

[4]For further details about visual, spatial and temporal abduction, see [Magnani, 2001]. About emotion as an abductive inference, see [Peirce, 1972].

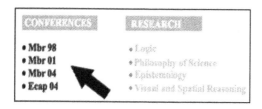

Figure 5.

In this example the user is guided to draw the correct inference: it enables her to *understand* what she could consult.

In contrast, consider for example the same content represented as in Figure 6.

Conference, Mbr98, Mbr01, Mbr04, Ecap 04, Research,
Logic, PhilosophyEpistemology, Visual and Spatial Reasoining

Figure 6.

In this case, even if the content is identical the user does not have any visual clue to understand what she is going to consult. She should read all the items to infer and, hence, understand that she could know something about past and future conferences and about the research topics. If one stopped her reading after the third item (MBR04), she couldn't infer that this page also deals with philosophy of science, with epistemology, and so on. She does not have enough clues to infer that. In contrast, in the first example the user is immediately informed that this website contains information about conferences and research.

5.2   Spatial abduction

As mentioned above, the windows metaphor is certainly one of the most important insights in the history of interface technology. This is due to the fact that, as Johnson maintains, it enables the user to think in terms of *"where is what I am looking for?"* and not in terms of "what sequence of letters do I type to call up this document?", as in a command line system [Johnson, 1997]. The computer becomes a space where one can move through just double-clicking on folders or icons, or dragging them. The difference is well described in Figure 5 and Figure 6.

In the first figure (Figure 7), the file named "note.txt" is deleted by *dragging* it to the bin: say, the task of deleting is accomplished by a movement analogous to that used in the physical setting. Whereas, in the second figure (Figure 8) the task is carried out by *typing* a command line composed by the command itself ("rm", that stands for remove") and the file to be deleted ("note.txt").

Figure 7.

Figure 8.

In designing web pages, spatial dimension can be mimicked in other ways. One of the most well known examples is represented by the so called *tab*. Tabs are usually employed in the real world to keep trace of something important, to divide whatever they stick out of into a section, or to make it easy to open [Krug, 2000]. In a web site, tabs turn out to be very important navigation clues. Browsing a web site Users often find themselves lost. This happens especially when the web pages they are consulting do not provide spatial clues from which the user can easily infer where she is. For instance, several websites changes their layout almost in every page: even if provided by a navigation menu, they are not helpful at all. In contrast, tabs enhance spatial inference in one important respect.

Consider the navigation bar represented in Figure 9. In this example, when the user is visiting a certain page, for example, the homepage (Figure 9.A), the correspondent tab in the navigation bar becomes the same color of the body page. As Krug noted, this creates the illusion the active tab actually moves to the front [Krug, 2000] Therefore, the user can immediately infer where she is by exploiting spatial relations in terms of background-foreground.

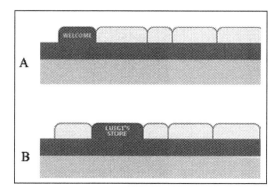

Figure 9. The tabs.

5.3 Temporal abduction

The idea of time is closely connected with representing things or events in a chronological order. Any interaction takes place in time, say, it has got a past, a present and a future. And knowing how a certain interaction has evolved or is evolving is fundamental to coordinate it. But how could we infer the history and, most of all, the history of interaction? Here the concept of temporal abduction can turn out to be useful.[5] In web designing, the question to be addressed in this case is: how could it be possible to keep track of the history of user's visited pages?

Now, what kind of sign should we employ in order to implement the history of an interaction? A well known example is represented by the so called *visited link*. Shortly, every time we turn back to a page containing a link previously visited, that link appears marked by another color. Consider the example in Figure 10 and 11. Figure 10 shows a Google®search result page *before* visiting the first document matched; Figure 11 shows a Google®search result page *after* visiting the first document matched; the visited link has been marked with another color (purple) so that the user can easily infer that it has already visited.

This example clearly shows how the link marked is a sign from which the user can infer the history of her interaction. Often search engines keep track of past interactions by adding a list. For instance, www.ingenta.com

---

[5]The term *temporal abduction* was first introduced by [Magnani, 2001].

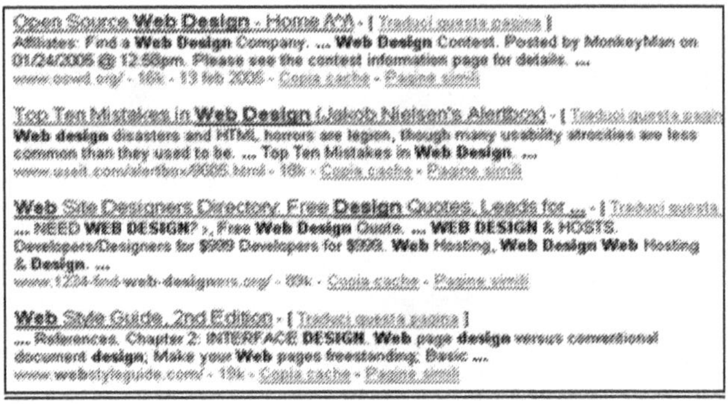

Figure 10.

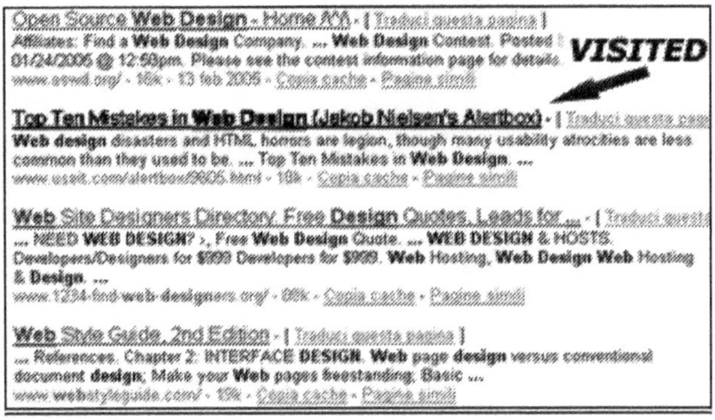

Figure 11.

provides a "current history search" list that contains all keywords inserted (see Figure 12).

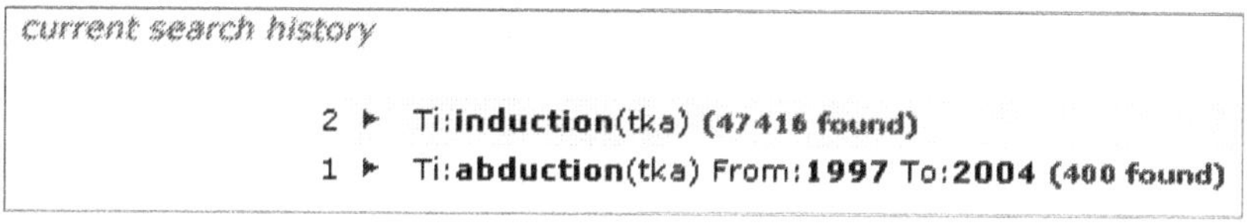

current search history

2 ▶ Ti:**induction**(tka) **(47416 found)**

1 ▶ Ti:**abduction**(tka) From:**1997** To:**2004** **(400 found)**

Figure 12.

This method is certainly very useful to the aim of recalling past queries and their results. However, in this last example the computational resources requested both of the system and of the user are much more complex than in the case of the Google example. In the latter case, the fact that the history is visually encoded renders easier to cope with. In the former one, processing the information is less quick, because it is sententially encoded, and, most of all, the amount of information to be processed is increased.

In conclusion, referring to temporal abductive inferences is interesting because it shows how the temporal dimension mainly concerns on detecting those clues from which the user can infer what he has done[6].

5.4 Emotional abductive inference

Recently several researchers have argued that emotion could be very important to improve *usability* [Norman, 2004]; [van Schaik and Ling, 2001]; [Lavie and Tractinsky, 2004]. The main issue in the debate is: how could emotionally evocative pages help the user to enhance understanding? Abduction may once again provide a useful framework to tackle this kind of question. As Peirce put it, emotion is the same thing as a hypothetic inference [Peirce, 1923]. For instance, when we look at a painting, the organization of the elements in colors, symmetries, and also the content, are all clues which trigger a certain reaction.

Consider, for example, the way a computer program responds to the user when a forbidden operation is trying to be performed. An alert message suddenly appears often coupled with an unpleasant sound. In this case, the response of the system provides clues (sounds, vivid colors such as red or yellow) from which we can attribute a certain state to the computer (*being upset*) and hence *quickly* react to it. Moreover, engaging an emotional response renders that reaction instantaneous: before reading the message the user already knows that the operation requested cannot proceed. Thus, a more careful path should be devised. Exploiting emotional reactions can

---

[6]Cf. [Hollan *et al.*, 2000].

be fruitful also in another respect. It conveys a larger amount of information. For instance, university web sites usually place a picture of some students engaged in social activity in their homepage. This does not provide direct information about the courses. However, this triggers a positive reaction in connection with the university whose site is being visited. Either way icons are drawn aims at emotionally affecting the user. Even if they do not strictly resemble the physical feature, they can prompt a reaction. Let us consider now the Figure 13.

Figure 13.

The image in the Figure 13 is taken by NOAA's Cessna Citation Jet on Sept. 23, 2001 from an altitude of 3,300 feet. It is how ground zero looks like after terrorist attack on September 11th. Now, let us turn to the Figure 14.

The image represents ground zero as well. Indeed, there is something different with respect to the previous image. The image represented in the first case is just a computer-like simulation. The *details level* cannot give us a *realistic* impression of what happened. It lacks colors, for instance: it is *cold-hearted*. On the contrary, the second image conveys a number of details the first figure lacks. For instance, we can have an idea on how huge ground zero is comparing its size with the size of other buildings all around. In this sense, colors, buildings, and even the windows of them, are all signs from which an emotional reaction is carried out.

6   Conclusion

In this article we have claimed that interfaces play a key role in under-standing the human-computer interaction. Referring to it as a mediating

Figure 14.

structure, we have also shown how human-computer interactions can be better understood using an inferential model. The interface provides clues from which the user can correctly infer how to cope with a product. Hence, we have referred to that inferential process as genuinely abductive. In the last section we have suggested possible future trends relying on some examples from web interfaces design.

BIBLIOGRAPHY

[Alberti, 1991] L.B. Alberti. *On Painting.* Penguin, London, 1991.

[Collins, 1995] D. Collins. *Designing Object-Oriented Interfaces.* Addison-Wisely, New York, 1995.

[Eco and Sebeok, 1991] U. Eco and T. Sebeok. *The Sign of Three: Dupin, Holmes, Pierce.* Indiana University Press, Indianapolis, 1991.

[Flach and Kakas, 2000] P. Flach and A. Kakas. *Abductive and Inductive Reasoning: Essays on Their Relation and Integration.* Kluwer Academic., Dordrecht, 2000.

[Gibson, 1979] J.J. Gibson. *The Echological Approach to Visual Perception.* Erlbaum., New Jersey, 1979.

[Hoffman, 1998] D. D. Hoffman. *Visual Intelligence.* W.W. Norton., New York, 1998.

[Hollan et al., 2000] J. Hollan, E. Hutchins, and D. Kirsh. Distributed cognition: Toward a new foundation for human-computer interaction research, 2000.

[Hutchins, 1995] E. Hutchins. *Cognition in the Wild.* The MIT Press., Cambridge (Mass.), 1995.

[Johnson, 1997] S. Johnson. *Culture Interface.* Perseus Books Group, New York, 1997.

[Kirsh and Maglio, 1994] D. Kirsh and P. Maglio. On distinguishing epistemic from pragmatic action. *Cognitive Science*, 18:513–549, 1994.

[Kirsh, 2004] D. Kirsh. Metacognition, distributed cognition and visual design, 2004.

[Krug, 2000] S. Krug. *Don't Make Me Think*. New Riders Publishing, New York, 2000.

[Larkin and Simon, 1987] J.H. Larkin and H.A. Simon. Why diagram is sometimes worth ten thousand words. *Cognitive Science*, 11:65–99, 1987.

[Lavie and Tractinsky, 2004] T. Lavie and N. Tractinsky. Assessing dimensions of perceived visual aesthetics of web sites. *International Journal Human-Computer Studies*, 60:269–298, 2004.

[Magnani, 2001] L. Magnani. *Abduction, Reason and Science. Processes of Discovery and Explanation*. Kluwer Academic/ Plenum Publishers, New York, 2001.

[Norman, 1993] D. Norman. *Things that Make us Smart*. Basic Books, New York, 1993.

[Norman, 2004] D. Norman. *Emotional Design: Why We Love (Or Hate) Everyday Things*. Basic Books, New York, 2004.

[Peirce, 1923] C.S. Peirce. *Chance, Love and Logic. Philosophical Essays*. Harcourt, New York, 1923.

[Peirce, 1972] C.S. Peirce. *Peirce, C.S. (1972). Charles S. Peirce: the Essential Writings*. Harper and Row, New York, 1972.

[Perry, 2004] M. Perry. Distributed cognition. In J.M. Carrol, editor, *HCI Models, Theories, and Frameworks*. Morgan Kaufman, 2004.

[Raskin, 2000] J. Raskin. *The Humane Interface*. Addison-Wesley, New York, 2000.

[Rock, 1982] I. Rock. Inference in perception. In *PSA: Proceedings of the Biennial Meeting of the Philosophy of Science Association*, pages 525–540, 1982.

[Shneiderman, 2002] B. Shneiderman. *Leonardo's Laptop. Human Needs and the New Computing Technologies*. The MIT Press., Cambridge (Mass.), 2002.

[Susi and Ziemke, 2001] T. Susi and T. Ziemke. Social cognition, artefacts, and stigmergy. *Journal of Cognitive Systems Research*, 2:273–290, 2001.

[Thagard and Shelley, 1997] P. Thagard and C.P. Shelley. Abductive reasoning: Logic. visual thinking, and coherence. In M.L. Dalla Chiara, D. Mundici K. Doests, and J. van Benthem, editors, *Logic and Scientific Method*, pages 413–427. Kluwer, 1997.

[Thagard, 1988] P. Thagard. *Computational Philosophy of Science*. The MIT Press., Cambridge (Mass.), 1988.

[van Schaik and Ling, 2001] P. van Schaik and J. Ling. The effects of frame layout and differential background contrast on visual search performance in web pages. *Interacting with Computers*, 13(5):513–525, 2001.

[Zhang, 1997] J. Zhang. The nature of external representations in problem solving. *Cognitive Science*, 21(2):179–217, 1997.

Lorenzo Magnani
Department of Philosophy and
Computational Philosophy Laboratory
University of Pavia, Pavia, Italy;
Department of Philosophy, Sun Yat-sen University
Guangzhou (Canton), P.R. China
Email: lmagnani@unipv.it

Emanuele Bardone
Department of Philosophy and
Computational Philosophy Laboratory
University of Pavia, Pavia, Italy
Email: bardone@unipv.it

Music to Our Ears: A Required Paradigm Shift for Computer Science

DAVE BILLINGE AND TOM ADDIS

ABSTRACT. We previously studied the way people communicate musical experience. We concluded that discussions do lead to some appreciation of others' internal experience. However, nobody can have direct access to others' internal experience so we suggest that the only way in which it can be understood is through *inference*. In order to create a computer model of this process we have to rely on formal languages, which are all *referential*, that is, they utilise denotational semantics. We adopt Wittgenstein's *Tractatus,* which is a theory of description based upon referential semantics, to provide a model of computer languages. This model highlights the problem that computer languages have an untenable dual semantic. This dual-semantic creates insurmountable demands on computer representations of the world and by implication on computer models of the human cognitive process. However, this tension could be resolved if computers-as-agents, and people, constructed models of the world that were merely *sufficient* to meet the needs of surviving in a social world. This process requires a notion of *inferential* semantics as opposed to referential semantics. We propose a formal computer model of inferential discourse based on a belief system and we detail experiments to detect the discourse features of this inferential process.

1 Introduction

A brief note about our title: Wittgenstein perceived the process by which he manipulated his ideas as analogous to a composer creating a symphony. Since the focus of our experiments is music discourse, and since we use Wittgenstein's major works and expose an essential difficulty in human computer interaction that we hope may be resolved, this title seemed most apposite.

We previously studied the way people communicate musical experience on the assumption that descriptive words in isolation can convey a stable meaning. This assumption was considered reasonable at the time from a denotational or referential semantic view of language. Computer scientists

Lorenzo Magnani and Riccardo Dossena, editors, *Computing, Philosophy, and Cognition,*
pp. 147–162 © 2005, D. Billinge and T. Addis

tend to assume this view. The assumption proved false in this aesthetic context in that there was no consistency in the way people assigned descriptive words to musical experience. Conventionally assigned words could be used neither to identify music to which they had been assigned nor were they consistently chosen to describe music that was heard. As a means of communication, language in this form fails [Billinge, 2001]. The consequence of this is that the use of experiential keywords or their logical combination (e.g. in an internet search engine) cannot be used to retrieve items of music exemplifying that experience; yet that experiential dimension may be considered to be the essential purpose of music.

Despite these disappointing and remarkable results, we know that people do talk and discuss their musical experience and we presume that such discussions lead to an appreciation of each other's views. It has been suggested to us (a private communication) that these discussions are primarily phatic; yet there is persuasive evidence for some sort of link between music and language at the level of semantic processing (for example [Koelsch *et al.*, 2004]), which lends support to there being information content. Additional to the above social reasons for getting together in groups, we also see a value for the individuals in such discussions, in that they provide those who participate with an enhancement of their own experiences through those of others. This means that better choices can be made, such as which concert to attend, by finding out who responds to music as you do and who does not and what reports on potential concerts these others make. The optimal moment for setting up this process of experiential correspondence is when the group has just had a common experience.

2   Inferring internal experience

Since nobody can have direct access to another's internal experience of music (or anything else for that matter), then the only way in which such experience can be understood is indirectly through inference. We can infer each other's experience because we share the state of being a person, within a culture, using a common language and the above-mentioned recent experience (perhaps of a musical performance). It is hence possible through conversation to build an internal model of another person's view of the world. The only practical requirement for this model is to make accurate predictions about one's own future experiences where those experiences are a result of another's guidance. In essence to test whether they are indeed a useful guide.

If the non-technical music literature for audiences, such as record reviews, concert reports, descriptive, as opposed to analytical, music histories and biographies, are examined, it becomes evident that the common experience does not have to be music itself in order for one person to describe an experience to another. The rich and extensive use of metaphor in music description suggests that emotional resonance and association to a commonly understood situation can be employed to trigger what, to the author of the description, is his "accurate" emotional response to a piece of music. This suggests that language's semiotic component has a central role in these descriptions. However, semiotic associations are variable and uncertain between individuals because they depend primarily upon individual experiences. We suggest that conventional tropes, constantly reinforced by a group, may provide a more stable base for conversation. Communication, in this case, will depend mostly upon our shared humanity, sometimes upon our personal experiences and little upon any referential semantic.

3   A philosophical paradigm and computing

The implications of such observations on the communication of internal experience are radical. They have led us to take Wittgenstein's *Tractatus* [Wittgenstein, 1921] as a paradigmatic description of the current state of computer science. This early work (T) encapsulated a formal and logical representational schema into a descriptive form that was based upon denotational (or referential) semantics. In this case, the referents (the objects) have some logically strange properties. They must be:

- *independent* in that they can freely combine to form "states of affairs" that can be described (T2.01, T2.0272, T2.0122, T2.0124)

- *atomic* in that there are no smaller constituents (T2.02, T2.021)

- *in all possible worlds* (T2.022, T2.023)

- *immaterial* (T2.0231, T2.0233)

- *indescribable* except by their behavior (form) (T2.021, T2.0121, T3.0271)

- *self governed* in that they have their own internal rules of behavior (T2.0141, T2.033, T2.012, T2.0121, T2.0123, T2.01231, T2,03)

These referents (objects) are intended to be more than just elements of description; they form the real world (T2.04, T2.06). From these referents, the full force of logic, predicate and propositional calculus retains stability of meaning and sense. Such a stance results in the position that everything is potentially unambiguously describable (T2.225, T2.224, T7).

The *Tractatus* provides an extensive model of languages. Wittgenstein stated as much in a letter to Bertrand Russell dated 19th August 1919 (in

[Monk, 1991]). "The main point is the theory of what can be expressed by propositions – i.e. by language – (and, which comes to the same, what can be thought)..." The argument is that names (in practice signs; the visible part of an expression or name) in propositions do not always refer to primitive objects but are themselves referencing propositions (T3.14, T3.31, T4.03, T4.22, T4.221, T5.135 and further discussed in the Philosophical Investigations [Wittgenstein, 1953, pp. 43–60]). These, in turn, are complexes that finally end up as compound statements whose ultimate referent is the bit. For example, in computer languages we have seven bits of the ASCII code identifying 1000001 as the character A and 1000010 as the character B etc. There are also special characters such as "delete" 1111111 and "start" 0000001. Here the bit is the mechanical equivalent of Wittgenstein's referent objects and it is the bit viewed as *any* distinction that endows it with all the properties (*independent, atomic*, etc. see above) of such an object. Thus it is at the bit that the program links to the world and has meaning. It is this meaning that allows the program to have "sense" with respect to the computer. This formal semantics and the ability for programmers to create procedures and sub-routines (sub-propositions or expressions) is the primary characteristic of all recent high level and assembler programming languages.

Let us further illustrate this link to the bit. Computer engineers, in error correcting codes, use tautology, for example the 8th bit used to check parity. Since a tautology (or contradiction) is independent of the model (assignment of truths) it expresses no information about the world (reality) (T4.461, T4.4661). So if a tautology suddenly is no longer valid and ceases to be a tautology, by appearing False, (or if a contradiction, by appearing True) then the sense of one part of the proposition has changed. This can only mean that the meaning of a primitive object (a bit) or name (a sign) is no longer correctly assigned; the computational engine has changed.

4   A paradigm shift

The problem here is that computer languages have a dual semantic in that the program signs (e.g. the names/labels given to data items, procedures and sub-routines) at the highest level also have referents in the world. This is the analysis of the user domain in terms of records (as in database and program structures), relations (as in normalized data structures) and objects (as in object-orientation). It is this analysis that identifies constructs in the world that are meant to be stable and unchanging (as per *Tractatus* referents) to which names can be given and meaning assigned.

Now it is acceptable that propositions can represent material properties (T2.0231), relationships (T2.031), and any complex model of the world

(T3.1, T3.11, T3.32, T4.01, T4.021) but a proposition can have one and only one complete analysis (T3.25). Such an analysis is dependent upon only the essential features of the proposition (program) that link it to the referent objects (which is the bit in our case). A computer program, as we have seen already, has such an analysis with respect to the computational engine, so the "alternative" interpretation of a program depends upon its accidental features (T3.34). This develops a peculiar tension in program design that is hard to keep stable, particularly with respect to the informal, and often undefined, mechanism which links the program names with the user's domain.

The *Tractatus* is a magnificent piece of work and, as we have noted, can be viewed as an effective description of how programming languages should be linked to a computer through sense assignment. There is no problem with the engineering necessity of this approach to sense and meaning. On a broader scale it sidesteps many of the paradoxes of the linguistic philosophy of the day. However, it has one fatal flaw when applied to the human use of language and its author eventually exposed this flaw. He noted that it is not possible to unambiguously describe everything within the propositional paradigm. He found that the normal use of language is riddled with example concepts that could not be bounded by logical statements that depended upon a pure notion of referential objects. One of his illustrations is an attempt to define a game (P69 – P71). Such a definition cannot be achieved that will either exclude all examples that are not games or include all examples that are. We refer to such a set of games as an irrational set since membership can never be determined with a finite set of rules [Stepney *et al.*, 2004]. It is through such considerations that Wittgenstein proposed a new linguistic philosophy that was based upon what we (the authors) are calling inferential semantics.

5   Inferential semantics

From an engineering point of view the only information that can be experienced by an individual is the result of the interaction of the individual's sense organs with the world. This is not a passive view since these organs are also controlled by an inference engine; namely the human mind. It is only through inference and the senses that we experience the world and relate to other people. So like the computer we might be able to trace the sense of our understanding of the world through the tracing of internal constructs to our senses. However, this would not be of any great help to other people since it is unlikely that we are identical in the same way as two computers, constructed according to a defined engineering plan, are identical. If we were to be different by as little as one bit we could not ever be sure that a "program" would mean the same if "run" in different heads or that it would even "run" at all. So tracing and knowing the "program" (or our internal constructions) is not very useful.

What could work, from a purely pragmatic point of view, is if individuals could construct models of the world, and other people, that were sufficient to meet the needs of surviving in the world and with others. This model does not have to be exact, just sufficient. However, to do this we have to extend our semantic model to have another definition of meaning; a definition that does not depend upon the direct referencing of objects. For Wittgenstein, the *meaning* of a word was also defined as its *use in language* (P43).

We can interpret this extended definition of meaning to imply a *process* of inference. During conversation, both observed and participating actively, a process is going on where a model of the meaning of words is being constructed through inference. This is a group activity and one designed to construct something common in the way language and the world may be perceived; a way that allows communication to occur. However, these models are only understood by their effectiveness, their ability to make predictions and their coherence within a group-dynamic situation. They can never have been "seen" directly since they only exist within an individual. It is the hidden dimensions of the model that express concepts and since these dimensions are likely to be different for different people we have the effect of distinctions having no proper boundaries that can be logically defined. This is the family resemblance effect detected by Wittgenstein and illustrated by his example (P67). It is an effect that fuzzy sets, in some cases probability and belief networks were intended to overcome (see also P71) without losing the power of referential assignment. Very recently a research team in Mexico, in conjunction with Salford University, involved in machine learning have started to explore the use of family resemblance with a learning system in order to approach human performance in categorization [Vadera et al., 2003]. The tension between the essential and accidental meaning is no longer a problem since the internal model works through the common interface of the senses that give the primary meaning and the inference process that gives a fluid and dynamic construct for making decisions about action. [We would also note ongoing work in dynamic meaning negotiation by Roberta Ferrario at Trento Italy, Claudia Arrighi and also H.H. Clark at Stanford, Bob Brandom at Pittsburgh and by Michael Dummett.]

6   Modeling inferential semantics

In our model of an individual's mechanism for modeling a group's, or another individual's, view of an experience (e.g. of music) we will assume for the moment that this consists of a single unspecified dimension. Along each dimension (which we will divide into sections for computational simplicity) will be a "belief" in a particular value. "Belief" is defined as a probability that a particular value is correct and it is from this probability distribution that an action may be chosen. The mechanism of choice is described in [Addis and Gooding, 1999].

In order to get the model started we will also make the initial assumption that the experiences others have will be the same as one's own personal experiences of an event or set of events. Since an individual's experience is certain to that individual we can assign a belief of "one" to an experience-value (intensity) along a single dimension for each of his experiences. We treat each value as though it were a hypothesis. This initial model is based upon the observation that we are all human. However, we will use language and observations to modify this initial belief-model of others' perceptions by making it consistent with our interactions with them. We will also allow each individual to be able to ask questions of another individual by way of experimental tests on their personal belief-models. These questions will be comparative questions such as "Do you like music A better than music B?" or more generally "Does music A have more emotional effect than B?" Using a similar updating mechanism as in [Addis and Gooding, 1999] we can modify the initial model for each individual depending upon the answer they give for the questions.

We can now produce a set of changes that depend upon the kind of answer received by the individual from a member of the group. We use an a priori distribution associated with the question "Is A more than B along this dimension?" These a priori distributions are governed by the answers, by the current belief distribution of each event (piece of music) and the total range of beliefs.

We start with the proviso that person X can have no doubt about his own beliefs. We, the authors, also make the initial assumption that person X assumes person Y holds the same beliefs as him, and holds those beliefs with equal certainty. Figure 1 shows that Person X rates Music A as 3 on his scale and Music B as 8. He has absolute certainty that this is his opinion, so the belief is 100% for both ratings. Note that the nature of the scale does not matter, but let us say it is a measure of emotional impact.

Person X assumes that Person Y has identical opinions. Thus Figure 2

X questions Y on his ratings. In effect he is asking Y if he believes the same as him. X asks: "Is Music B more than Music A?" Y can only respond with "Yes", or "No". If Y responds, "Yes" then X has some limited evidence on which to adjust his internal model of Y. X knows that Y has the same sequence, $A < B$, but he has no evidence as to where either of these items is on the scale. Music B could lie anywhere from 2 to 9, providing

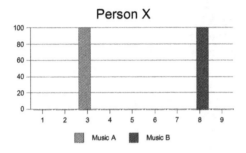

Figure 1.

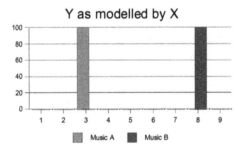

Figure 2.

$A < B$, thus A could lie anywhere from 1 to 8. The result is that X's new model of Y is moderated from his initial position to something like Figure 3

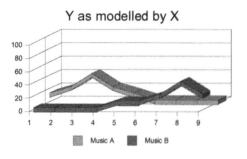

Figure 3.

The effect of X's prior assumptions, his beliefs, is now clear. Though he has no evidence for Y's actual opinion, as noted he only knows that for Y, $A < B$, his internal model distributes Y's scores unevenly with peaks at the points he, X, believes himself. X's model of Y is explicitly influenced by X's prior belief. We will pursue the issue of how he can resolve this below.

Next we must consider the situation if Y's reply to the question, "Is Music B more than Music A?" is "No". X's model of Y must now reflect a wider range of possibilities predicated upon $B \leq A$. Thus, logically (Figure 4)

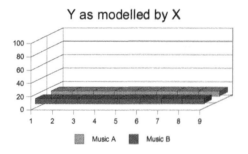

Figure 4.

But we are not dealing with a machine; we are dealing with a person influenced by belief. If Y says "No", does X then think to himself, "Oh, so Y has a completely equal opinion of both pieces"? Of course not, he asks, rhetorically, "Really? Is this likely?" and models Y as Figure 5

He has not relinquished his belief in $A < B$, even though this directly contradicts Y's answer, but he has both moderated his scaling and moved the two peaks closer together. We note that Figure 5 and Figure 3 are

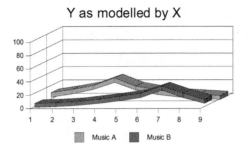

Figure 5.

similar despite being the result of two contradictory replies. Y cannot ask for the precise distribution of X's ratings. He can only ask whether they are *More*, *Most* or *Least*. This restriction allows our modeling tool to be a computer, which as we note is restricted to rational sets in which the world is all encompassed in *Either $A < B$ or $B \leq A$.*

Y wants to ask "Really?", but he cannot, so he asks the nearest possible question. He either asks the same question again to be sure he heard correctly despite his belief, or he asks a question that will help him better isolate Music A from Music B. He can choose to go along with his own belief that $A < B$ and ask "Is A least?", or its opposite, "Is B most?" For Y this will seem illogical, which it is, but it is a consequence of X having beliefs which he is not willing to relinquish without some resistance, without some further checking of the evidence: an example of Thomas Kuhn's resistance to paradigm change [Kuhn, 1970]. Y must answer "No" to either question, which could result in X restructuring his internal model by cautiously reversing the peaks thus.

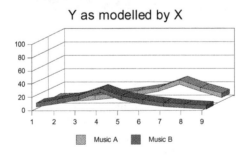

Figure 6.

His model still shows an unwillingness to believe that Y disagrees completely and he will go on to ask one of the reverse pair of his previous questions, viz: "Is B least?", or its opposite, "Is A most?" The answer to either must be "Yes" and this must result in X's model of Y moving closer to the "truth".

We can now return to the situation above [Figure 3] and note that the same question pairing, "Is B least?", or its opposite, "Is A most?" will have the same effect of moving X's model of Y closer to the "truth".

The issue, illustrated by this, admittedly long-winded, explanation, is that we can enable a logical model in a computer, which is based on rational sets, to usefully model a human situation based on irrational sets.

7   Experiments to detect the process of inferential semantics

We have carried out a series of experiments to detect the process of infer-ence. Small groups of participants are placed in a conventional listening environment and played a sequence of four items of classical music. This music provides the trigger for the subsequent discussion. Whilst listening, the participants are asked to make brief notes about their reactions. These notes serve as an aid during discussion. When the listening is over they are asked to rank the pieces according to how much they enjoyed them. They are then asked to justify their ranking to the others in the group. Because the pieces have been ranked there is an intentional inbuilt bias to-wards discussion in terms of "more-than" and "less-than". The model we are developing has, as its analogue of humans changing their opinions, an algorithm that increases or decreases a value between 0 and 1. This aids the process of belief probability distribution noted above. Participants are observed to make comparisons. Any comparison can be interpreted as the raising or lowering of a belief value.

The nature of the "enjoyment" can be any possible dimension of musical reaction. For example, "enjoyment" might be of an open ended set of emo-tional states like "tragedy", "happiness" or "solemnity", It might also be a member of the set of what one might call "dispassionate" reactions, for example "rhythmicality", "liveliness" or "tunefulness". The essence of our model is that the label given to the chosen dimension of experience does not require to be understood by anyone except the perceiver, whose internal semantic is not open to inspection. The statements of comparison are all we can model. For this reason we need to trigger as much comparative talk as possible.

In the sessions such phrases as "A is 'more powerful than' B" are heard to occur with high frequency. Because each participant is required to justify their chosen ranking, each is obliged to listen to explanations that might change their minds on their own rankings. Even two quite different dimensions might interact to generate change. For example a participant arguing for their ranking on a dimension of "tunefulness" will have to use whatever linguistic skills they have to explain why the rankings were given. Because no defined technical vocabulary exists to express such distinctions, the participant rapidly resorts to tropes of various kinds, for example metaphors and similes. Whatever lexical items emerge, the participants know that they are attempting to describe a common experience, namely the music they have just heard. Lacking a defined vocabulary they are therefore forced to understand one another by means of inference. That inference, in turn, focuses on the use of comparison. All this is in line with our current theoretical stance.

The final task is to write down the names of the other group members in the order in which the participant rates them as reliable guides on concert going or record buying. This is an explicit guide to us as to whose internal model of musical reaction is perceived as most in sympathy with the participant's own.

A series of eight discussions have resulted in a total of approximately 8 to 10 hours of recorded conversation and over 30 sheets of participant notes. The process of transcription and analysis is giving us evidence of how these people carry out the process of understanding by inference. Factor analysis is being particularly emphasized to see if there is evidence of the common dimensions we seek.

We have not modeled the whole experiment, only the process described above of how an individual models another individual's internal view.

This model is based on the Belief System [Addis and Gooding, 1999] and it provides the following:

i. the mechanism of choosing experiments (here it is a query) based on a range of belief

ii. a way to update the belief based on query results, thus modeling other's experience by inference.

iii. a demonstration that for the same internal experience, different models can be built for different actors

Compared to the actual experimental situation, the model is limited as to queries used, but it does provide a base for the process of query and inference to be carried.

The model set up is the same as the actual experiment in that there are 4 actors and 4 pieces of music. Each actor has a scale (0 to 9) for each piece of music in his view. Each actor has a separate scale of belief for each piece of music for each other actor. For example Actor 1 has 3 belief models for the other 3 actors. Each model consists of 3 ranges of belief for 4 pieces of music. So each actor has a total of 12 ranges of belief on the scale [0...9].

The differences from the actual experiment are a limited range of queries, namely "More?", "Least?" and "Most?" The actors ask questions in turn and can only ask one question per turn. Only the actor asking the question can update his belief, so there is no allowance for other actors overhearing the conversational exchange.

We also make two assumptions for this illustration: that at the initial stage, each actor assumes that other actors have his ratings; that each modeling actor tends to ask the other actor about the music of which he, the questioner, has the most uncertain model. We again assert that the modeler can have no doubt of his *own* experience. This is unquestionable.

Here, as an example of the model in action, are the results of three actors 1, 3 and 4 creating an internal model of Actor 2, (Figures 8, 9 and 10) through conversation with Actor 2. The internal experiences for each actor are shown in Figure 7 and in particular Actor 2 is shown shaded:

	Actor1	Actor2	Actor3	Actor4
Music1 (A)	1	5	4	9
Music2 (B)	3	0	3	7
Music3 (C)	6	3	5	5
Music4 (D)	9	8	7	2

Figure 7.

Since the distribution of the beliefs in values is likely to be spread out what is plotted is the average of that distribution or expected belief value for each piece of music. As can be seen from Figures 8 to 10 (below) all the final orderings of the music are the same no matter what starting point the original ordering might have been. The amount of discussion about a piece of music between the modeling actor and the modeled actor (2 in the example below) is illustrated by the density of points on a line. The final orderings reflect the correct orderings for the actor being modeled (2) but the absolute values are not identified. That is, no one gets to 5, 0, 3 and 8 (see Figure 7), but they do get the correct sequence and they all arrive at quite similar absolute values, circa 5, 2, $3^1/2$ and 6. This is not too surprising since the only metaphors that have been used to assess the model are concerned with order. For the purpose of assessing others to be suitable scouts on your behalf that is all that is needed.

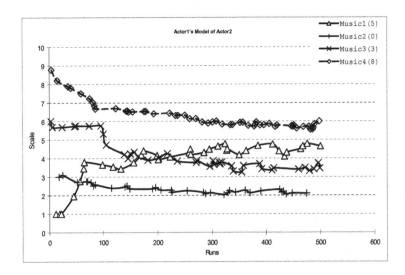

Figure 8. Actor 1's Model of Actor 2.

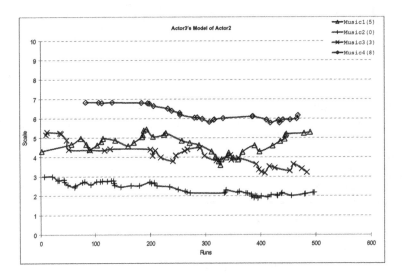

Figure 9. Actor 3's Model of Actor 2.

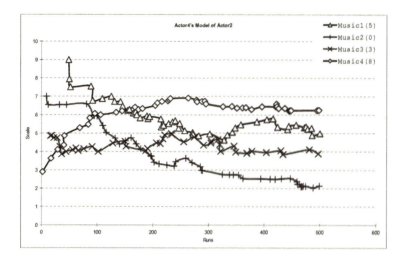

Figure 10. Actor 4's Model of Actor 2.

8   Concluding remarks

These are the results of a model run before we have fully examined the experimental results. We intend to use the actual numbers given by the participants in our sessions and plug these into the model. We will then compare the predicted outcomes of the model with the actual outcomes of session conversations as recorded. We will try to compare the patterns of questioning of the model, shown above as the frequency of symbols per unit of line-length per piece of music, with those of the experimental sessions. We expect to change the model to fit in with observations. Our model should thus become more able to predict conversational behavior within this scenario. From this in turn we hope to arrive at a more general theory of inferential conversation.

9   Acknowledgement

We would like to thank our research student Fei Wang for his work on the programming of the model. We would also like to thank those who continue to participate so enthusiastically in our experiments.

BIBLIOGRAPHY

[Addis and Gooding, 1999] T. Addis and D. Gooding. Learning as collective belief-revision: simulating reasoning about disparate phenomena. In *Proceedings of the AISB'99 Symposium on Scientific Creativity*, 1999.

[Billinge, 2001] D. Billinge. *An Analysis of the Communicability of Musical Predication.* PhD thesis, University of Portsmouth, England, 2001. PhD thesis.

[Koelsch *et al.*, 2004] S. Koelsch, E. Kasper, D. Sammler, K. Schulze, T. Gunter, and
    A. Friederici. Music, language and meaning: Brain signatures of semantic processing.
    Nature Neuroscience, 7(3), 2004. Nature Publishing Group.
[Kuhn, 1970] T. Kuhn. *The Structure of Scientific Revolutions*. University of Chicago
    Press, 2nd edition, 1970.
[Monk, 1991] R. Monk. *Ludwig Wittgenstein: The Duty of Genius*. Vintage Books,
    London, 1991.
[Stepney *et al.*, 2004] S. Stepney, S. Braunstein, J. Clark, A. Tyrrel, A. Adamatzky,
    R. Smith, T. Addis, C. Johnson, J. Timmis, P. Welch, R. Milner, and D. Partridge.
    Journey: Non-classical philosophy - socially sensitive computing in journeys. In *Non-
    Classical Computation: A Grand Challenge for Computing Research, 18 May*, 2004.
    http://www.cs.york.ac.uk/nature/gc7/newcastle.htm.
[Vadera *et al.*, 2003] S. Vadera, A. Rodriquez, and E. Succar. Family resemblance,
    bayesian networks and exemplars. *AISB Quarterly*, 114:1–11, 2003.
[Wittgenstein, 1921] L. Wittgenstein. *Tractatus Logico-Philosophicus*. Routledge and
    Kegan Paul, London, 1961 edition, 1921.
[Wittgenstein, 1953] L. Wittgenstein. *Philosophical Investigations*. Blackwells, Oxford,
    1953.

Dave Billinge
Department of Creative Technology
University of Portsmouth
Portsmouth, UK
Email: dave.billinge@port.ac.uk

Tom Addis
School of Computer Science and Mathematics
University of Portsmouth
Portsmouth, UK
Visiting Research Fellow Science Studies Centre
Department of Psychology, University of Bath
Email: tom.addis@port.ac.uk

Philosophy of Information
a New Renaissance and the Discreet Charm of the Computational Paradigm

GORDANA DODIG-CRNKOVIC

ABSTRACT.   The ontology of each theory is always embedded in natural language with all of its ambiguity. Attempts to automate the communication between different ontologies face the problem of compatibility of concepts with different semantic origins. Coming from different Universes, terms with the same spelling may have a continuum of meanings. The formalization problem met in the semantic web or ontology engineering is thus closely related to the natural language semantic continuum.

The emergence of a common context necessary to assure the minimum "common language" is a natural consequence of this process of intense communication that develops in parallel with computationalization of almost every conceivable field of human activity. The necessity of conceptualization of this new global space calls for understanding across the borders of previously relatively independent, locally defined Universes. In that way a need and potential for a new Renaissance, in which sciences and humanities, arts and engineering can reach a new synthesis, has emerged.

1   Computing/informatics and a new Renaissance

Computing/Informatics are characterizing our epoch in the most profound ways, in everything from the ubiquity of computers in our everyday life to the computational tools for simulation and testing of scientific and philosophical theories [Floridi, 2003]. There is a significant shift relative to the previous industrial-technological era when the ideal was the perfect machine and "objective knowledge" reduced at best to an algorithm for constructing a complete theory according to a set of derivation rules, starting from a limited number of axioms (Hilbert's program). The problem is that every theory is inevitably coupled to its context. This implies that no scientific method can be completely disconnected from the rest of the world. There are always subtle connections established through the use of the semantic continuum of natural language that are impossible to avoid even in the most formal theories.

Lorenzo Magnani and Riccardo Dossena, editors, *Computing, Philosophy, and Cognition*, pp. 163–176 © 2005, G. Dodig-Crnkovic

Contrary to the preceding mechanistic ideal, Computing/Informatics has successively developed into a very much human-centered discipline. Insight into the limitations of the formalization/mechanisation project has led to a new awareness of the eminently human character of knowledge and its connection to value systems and the totality of the cultural context. This indicates that there is a potential for a new Renaissance, in which science and humanities, arts and engineering can reach a new synthesis, enriching and inspiring each other via modern computing and communication tools [Dodig-Crnkovic, 2003].

In spite of the insufficiency of formal systems to construct a complete world-view, their appeal nowadays seems to be stronger than ever, see e.g. ontology engineering [Gruber, 1995; Smith and Welty, 2001].

2   The discreet charm of the computational paradigm and philosophy of information

Everyone knows that computational and information *technology* has spread like wildfire throughout academic and intellectual life. But the spread of computational *ideas* has been just as impressive.

Biologists not only model life forms on computers; they treat the gene, and even whole organisms, as *information systems.* Philosophy, artificial intelligence, and cognitive science don't just construct computational models of mind; they take cognition *to be computation*, at the deepest levels.

Physicists don't just talk about the information carried by a subatomic particle; they propose to unify the foundations of quantum mechanics *with notions of information*. Similarly for linguists, artists, anthropologists, critics, etc. [Cantwell Smith, 2003]

One problem of Philosophy of Information and even other theories building on the idea of information is the inadequacy of our understanding of information and its complementary term computation. Cantwell Smith finds the relation between meaning and mechanism the most fundamental question of interest in that context.

The German, French and Italian languages use the respective terms "Informatik", "Informatique" and "Informatica" (Informatics in English) to denote Computing. It is interesting that the English term "Computing" has an empirical orientation, while the corresponding German, French and Italian term "Informatics" has an abstract orientation. This difference may be traced back to the tradition of nineteenth-century British empiricism and continental abstraction respectively.

The question of nomenclature (Philosophy of Computing or Philosophy of Information?) can be seen in the light of the following common dichotomies: information - computation; data structure - algorithm; particle - field. The analogy from physics is particularly instructive: particles are considered as the primary principle, while fields/interactions are defined in terms of particles as particle exchange.

Information as the central idea of Computing/Informatics is both scientifically and sociologically indicative. Scientifically, it suggests a view of Informatics as a generalization of information theory that is concerned not only with the transmission/communication of information but also with its transformation and interpretation. Sociologically, it suggests a parallel between the industrial revolution, which is concerned with the utilization of energy, and the information revolution, which is concerned with the utilization of information [Dodig-Crnkovic, 2003].

According to [Floridi, 2002]

> The Philosophy of Information is a new philosophical discipline, concerned with
>
> a. the critical investigation of the conceptual nature and basic principles of information, including its dynamics (especially computation and flow), utilization and Sciences; and
>
> b. the elaboration and application of information-theoretic and computational methodologies to philosophical problems.

At present we can witness a vivid development of all abovementioned research fields within the Philosophy of Information [Floridi, 2003]. One can see the realization of Leibniz's dream of a universal encyclopedia as a practical utilization of Informatics. We perceive its revival in the form of ontology engineering. Business, medicine, World Wide Web, sciences, administration... all is to be formalized, systematized, so that they hopefully can start to communicate in an automatic way. Automated discovery is but one aspect of the formalization project of Informatics.

The attempt to automate the communication between different ontologies meets the problem of compatibility of concepts with different semantic origins. Coming from different universes, words with the same spelling may have a continuum of meanings – a problem that has to be dealt with. The formalization complex is closely related to the natural language semantic continuum.

3 Universes in the universe

> Metaphysics only recently has undergone a revolution so deep
> that nobody has noticed it: indeed ontology has gone mathemat-
> ical and is being cultivated by engineers and computer scientists.
> As a matter of fact a number of technologies have been devel-
> oped... certain exact theories concerning the most basic traits
> of entities or systems of various genera. Switching theory, net-
> work theory, automata theory, linear systems theory, control
> theory, mathematical machine theory, and information theory
> are among the youngest metaphysical offspring of contemporary
> technology. [Bunge, 1977]

The Universe is an idea different in different epochs. At some time it
was a living organism, at yet another time, mechanical machinery - the
Cartesian-Newtonian clockwork. Today's metaphor of the Universe is more
and more explicitly becoming a computer. What exists is what is in the
computer according to Fredkin and Wolfram [Weinberg, 2002; Wolfram,
2002; Wright, 1988].

The Universe Computer metaphor may be read in two ways. Firstly, the
Universe in its existence at some level of abstraction may be understood
as an enormous informational and computational system. In a Computer
Universe every physical process can be seen as computation.

The computer is a symbol manipulating machine - given a symbolic input,
it manipulates the symbols to produce an output (Haugeland). Taking
a broad definition of a symbol, one can claim that any physical object
may be seen an implementation of arbitrary function. Some philosophers
hold that the above notion of computer is so general that it is vacuous
(Searle, Putnam). Actually saying that the universe is well represented
by a computational model is not more radical than saying that universe is
made of matter/energy. The claim that the computational stance is highly
expressive and philosophically fruitful does not necessarily mean that the
Universe has no other meaning but that of a computational mechanism.

Secondly, our own computers, conceived as earthly images of the Universe-
computer show a tendency to contain the totality of ideas of the world as it
appears to humanity of today. In that sense what is saved in the computers
and communicable via computers becomes gradually all that there is.

Historically there was a transition between the world of traditional philosophical and scientific models whose knowledge filtered and crystallized
through millennia and the new computerized world where the facts were
collected and organized in an ad-hoc and pragmatic manner, during the
recent decades. Computers were originally used to process and save infor-

mation for certain specific, often practical and short-term purposes. The focus was on calculation, data collection and storage. The idea of using computers as a means of communication emerged later. In the calculation era, different databases containing a huge amount of useful data were created. The next step was to recognize that enormous volumes of work could be saved if the data already existing could be re-used and its communication to others made possible. That is where ontologies come in.

The idea of ontology is more than two thousand years old and comes from the philosophy of the time which encompassed all the known sciences. Ontology in its original sense might be defined as "What may be known about what may exist." Epistemology searches for the nature of knowledge and defines what knowledge is. Taxonomy provides a means of developing classification schemes for elements of ontology in its representational form. Semantics establishes the relation between taxonomy as an ideal scheme, and reality. In that way it makes possible the resolution of the ambiguities of meaning resulting from less than perfect representations.

> If all databases and the data residing in unstructured text corpora could be made compatible in the way described, then the prospect would arise of merging all of the separately existing digital resources in such a way as to create a single knowledge base of a scale hitherto unimagined, thus fulfilling the ancient dream of a Great Encyclopedia comprehending the entirety of human knowledge. [...] Unfortunately, however, as experience has shown, the construction of such single benchmark ontology proved to be a much more complex task than was originally envisaged. [Smith and Ceusters, 2003]

The crucial issue here seems to be the relation between what philosophers originally meant by ontology and what the ontologies [Gruber, 1995; Smith and Welty, 2001] of today's information systems are, the relation between the whole and the parts, a classical philosophical problem.

The primary meaning of ontology is the totality of all that exists and may exist. At the moment we focus on a part of the totality and treat it as our new totality of everything that matters, we lose the sense of the rest of the world as it is present in its entirety. Think of emergent properties. They are based on simple elements/parts having simple relations as e.g. cell automata (see e.g. [Wolfram, 2002]. Focusing on particular cells may never reveal the potential complexity of the composite system built of simple cells. Taking our particular world for the totality of the universe, "pars pro toto" (the part for the whole), we perform a logical somersault. It might work at times in some cases and in specific con-texts, but certainly not in general.

4 Search for a common language

In addition to the question of the relation part-whole when dealing with the unification of semantically heterogeneous ontologies, another problem on a basic level is the problem of the common (universal) language that is necessarily embedded in the natural language.

4.1 A quest for absolute truth in language and formalization problems

All around us are facts that are related to one another. Of course, they can be regarded as separate entities and learned that way. But what a difference it makes when we see them as part of a pattern! Many facts then become more than just items to be memorized – their relationships permit us to use a compressed description, a kind of theory, a schema, to apprehend and remember them. They begin to make some sense. [Gell-Mann, 1994, p. 89]

The dream of a universal formal system that can be used to produce all truths and only truths within some area of knowledge is very old. Descartes' philosophy demanded that words in the scientific language should possess precise and unambiguous meanings. Leibniz developed an idea of universal symbolic and logical calculus (calculus ratiocinator). The idea was to produce a completely rigorous and unambiguous language.

Later on even logical positivists (Carnap, Wittgenstein, early Russell) aimed at the total reconstruction of science and its formalization. Central for logical positivism was the creation of a universal language. Closely related is the idea of logical atomism of Frege, Russell and Wittgenstein which is the belief that language is divisible in elementary particles of sense.

Davidson's approach to the problem of the theory of meaning adequate to natural language (see [Davidson, 1984] leads to his proposal that meaning is best understood via the concept of truth, and, more particularly, that the basic structure for any adequate theory of meaning is that given in a formal theory of truth. The meanings of sentences are seen to depend upon the meanings of their parts, that is, upon the meanings of the words that form the finite base of the language and out of which sentences are composed.

Compositionality does not compromise holism, since not only does it follow from it, but, in Davidson's approach, it is only as they play a role in whole sentences that individual words can be viewed as meaningful. It is sentences, and not words, that are thus the primary focus for Davidson's theory of meaning. Here the question may be posed: Why not to take into consideration that even sentences change their meaning depending on the context? Choosing sentences as basic building blocks of meaning, one should keep in mind that those elements are parts of a complex structure of language, and their meaning is defined among others by their function as parts of the whole. Davidson summarizes the problem of language translation in his Principle of Charity:

> So again, the word charity is a misnomer because it's not a matter of being kind to people; it's the condition for understanding them at all. Thus, charity has two features: one is that you can't understand people if you don't see them as sharing a world with you; the other is that you can't understand people if you don't see them as logical in the way that you are – up to a point, of course.

This view is complemented by Quine's (see [Quine, 1964]) thesis of indeterminacy of translation. The thesis is that divergent translation manuals can be set up between natural languages such that they all are compatible with empirical facts but nevertheless diverge radically from each other in what sentences they prescribe as translations of sentences in the foreign language. Each manual works individually, but they cannot be used in alternation: the fusion of two of these manuals does not in general constitute a manual that is compatible with all empirical facts.

Davidson's Principle of Charity gives us the necessary conditions for a translation to be possible at all. This problem can be generalized to any sort of communication of meaning from one ontology to the other. Quine tells us that in relation to the real world many languages can be equivalent. The same reality can be described in different terms. The question of communication between different universes leads to the problem of defining the common context necessary for the translation. Applying this general problem to the communication between computers/databases can be very instructive. Computers use formal languages today, but the general lines of reasoning about the language apply.

Leibniz hoped that the formal language will save us from the unnecessary ambiguity of the natural language. In the early 1920s, Hilbert's program for mathematics aimed at a formalization of all of mathematics in axiomatic form, together with a proof that this axiomatization is consistent. Whitehead and Russell's Principia Mathematica, the most famous work on the foundations of mathematics intended to deduce all the fundamental propositions of mathematics from a small number of logical premises, establishing mathematics as applied logic. However, Gödel, inspired by Hilbert's program, proved in 1931 that any such formalization is doomed to incompleteness. Gödel's theorems [Gödel, 1992] show that in any sufficiently powerful logical system, statements can be formulated which can neither be proved nor disproved within the system, unless the system itself is inconsistent. That is "one of the keenest insights in the history of mathematics" according to Hofstadter, [Hofstadter, 2000]. Gödel's results are interpreted as the proof that there are limitations to the powers of any particular formal system or equivalently of every (discrete state) machine. Gödel's argument is often used to claim that strong artificial intelligence is impossible. Yet it has only been stated without any sort of proof that no such limitations apply to the human intellect [Dodig-Crnkovic, 2001]. In what way is then Gödel's limit overcome in natural intelligence (natural language)? It's rather simple - natural language is both inconsistent and incomplete but – remarkably enough – it works!

Das Glasperlenspiel (The Glass Bead Game), a novel by Herman Hesse, contains a beautiful example of the ideal of a universal language implemented in a form of language-game. The language of the Game, as distinct from the natural language was supposed to be hard-structured and closed: new symbols and rules were introduced only in very exceptional cases. We recognize there the echoes of Hilbert's program for constructing perfect language computing machinery.

The world of omnipotent formal systems that could be used to reconstruct the Universe in its entirety proved to be yet another paradise from which we were expelled. Nevertheless, Leibniz's grand project of creating a universal encyclopedia by collecting all existing knowledge based on universal language has still a very strong appeal. The approach nowadays, however, is more pragmatic. We are not searching for absolute truth or absolute certainty. We are searching for reasonable approximations to the real world in an attempt to manage its complexity.

4.2   Lexical ambiguity and vagueness of language

There are a number of different languages such as natural languages, the symbolic formal languages of logic and mathematics, languages of physical processes, including molecular interactions, the language of DNA and similar. Some are relatively hard and closed (Aristotelian logic), while others, natural languages, for example, are soft and open. Reading a very old book in your own language can convince you that language is dynamic, it is continually changing. New words are constantly created; words which have become old are forgotten or replaced by synonyms used more frequently. Fields of great interest are finely resolved and generate a multitude of words. The opposite is true when a certain activity loses its interest – related words are soon forgotten.

It is interesting to analyze the functioning of natural language since it can reveal a great deal about how we conceptualize and handle our Universe.

In natural language, not only separate words are facts of language, but also words in their combinations, in relations to sentences, whole texts and the totality of context. An isolated word has a spectrum of meanings that is so wide that it sometimes includes even antonyms. The place of the word in the network of meanings of other words and sentences helps pinpoint the meaning of the word in a text.

In Humboldt's opinion every language is a kind of Weltanschauung. This is especially manifest in the languages of science which are very different in different fields. The language of physics (which is different from the language of e.g. chemistry) has its own fine structure: the language of classical mechanics, the language of thermodynamics, the language of optics, the language of quantum mechanics etc. As a consequence we can see each language as a Universe defining the meaning of its constituent parts, and the structures built upon them through their mutual relations.

The minimum common structure in all languages appears to be logic. However, classical Aristotelian logic proves inadequate for the description of the entire real world. A simple logical structure is not even sufficient to describe the complexity of the world of science; hence the well-known paradoxes of physics such as the dual (particle-wave) nature of light. Not to mention the process of scientific discovery.

In physics there are interfaces between different levels of abstraction (levels of common modeling language) in which separate adjacent Universes of different scales must be connected by a type of translation mechanism, resembling a system of locks used to lift or lower boats from a certain water level to the next (different) one. There is no formalism yet devised to derive a theory of a human cell from the first principles (axioms) with rules of inference. The similar is true for the mathematics.

> You see, you have all of mathematical truth, this ocean of math-
> ematical truth. And this ocean has islands. An island here,
> algebraic truths. An island there, arithmetic truths. An island
> here, the calculus. And these are different fields of mathemat-
> ics where all the ideas are interconnected in ways that mathe-
> maticians love; they fall into nice, interconnected patterns. But
> what I've discovered is all this sea around the islands. [Gregory
> Chaitin, an interview, September 2003]

After long experience with formalization of the most rigorous field of human knowledge, mathematics, Russell declared: "All thinking is vague to some extent and complete accuracy is a theoretical ideal not practically attainable". [Russell, 1921]

4.3 Problem of synonymy

No morphemes are *identical* with respect to the meaning they contain. This is illustrated by Frege's Puzzle about identity statements given in Begriffsschrift [Geach and Black, 1960]. "Mark Twain is Samuel Clemens" is true if and only if "Mark Twain" and "Samuel Clemens" denote the same person. So the truth of "$a = b$" requires that the expressions on both sides of the identity sign denote the same object. The problem is that the cognitive significance (or meaning) of the two sentences differ. We can learn that "Mark Twain = Mark Twain" is true simply by inspecting it; but we can not learn the truth of "Mark Twain = Samuel Clemens" in the same way – it contains additional information.

Synonymous means *interchangeable*. In principle one word can be interchanged with its synonym while the meaning of the whole (to a reasonable degree) is retained. But as mentioned, there are no two different words with exactly the same meaning. Each time we exchange a word for its synonym, we change slightly its semantics. We can represent a word with its synonyms in a very schematic way by a frequency distribution diagram of Figure 1. The longest staple in the diagram is that representing the synonym most frequently used in a certain Universe of discourse. The notion of a distribution function of the word meanings is implicitly present in dictionaries. (Webpages, 6)

It is clear that the frequency distribution of its synonums varies when the same word is used within different Universes. (Take e.g. the word "ring" and its synonyms in fashion and mathematics). This is a consequence of the fact that the meaning is defined by the way of use/measuring/observing the phenomenon. Just by replacing a word with its synonyms, and, in a next step, with the synonyms of the synonyms etc, can make us cover the whole of the cobweb of language in which everything is connected to everything else and influenced by everything else.

4.4 The probabilistic nature of language

How is the function of a sign (such as word) in the semantics of a sign system (language) to be described? How is the meaning of a word created? An interesting, Bayesian model is proposed by Nalimov [Nalimov, 1981; Nalimov, 1982].

Every sign is connected in a probabilistic way with a variety of meanings, so the receptor has a prior distribution function of sign (word) meanings which is in general different from that of the transmitter and depends on the previous context that both of them have. Bayes theorem states that the most probable interpretation of the word is that which maximizes the product of the *a priori* probability $P(\mu)$, and the *a posteriori* probability

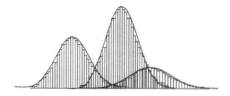

Figure 1. Meaning shift as a consequence of replacing a word by its synonym. Each curve represents the frequency distribution of its synonyms.

$P(\mu|Y)$.

(1) $P(\mu|Y) = P(Y|\mu)P(\mu)/P(Y)$

If *a priori* nothing is known about the distribution $P(\mu)$ all values of μ are equally distributed on a straight line. For a continuously changing random variable, the probability of hitting a strictly fixed point in measuring equals zero, which in our case is interpreted as the exact meaning of the word.

We can relate the features of language (software) with its corresponding hardware. In the human brain all the pathways are massively interconnected, not just hierarchically as levels of integration, but also horizontally. The combination of highly organized, highly complex processing systems and subsystems, with this massive interconnectedness is what makes the most distinct difference between the brain and a computer. Humans can make so incredibly much more sense of words than machines because our brains build up an enormous and intricate web of interrelationships in which the words of a language are embedded. Present-day computers do not have the comparable ability of approximate reasoning and they cannot cope with the potential infinity of the space of possible cases present in natural language.

4.5   The infinity of language

Language semantics is a continuum in the sense of Anaxagoras. (*"There is no smallest among the small and no largest among the large, but always something still smaller and something still larger."*) The characteristic of continuum is that it allows for the realization of infinity in a finite space. The world we live in is infinite. How do we cope with infinity?

An adult human brain has more than 10^{11} neurons [Damasio, 1999]. It is built up from neurons which communicate through connections that form increasingly complex circuits. Any particular neuron has between $10^4 - 10^5$ links. The total number of connections in the human brain exceeds 10^{15}. The number of ways the network in our brains can interconnect is amazing. The complexity of our neural structure reflects the infinity of the universe that we are able to deal with. That is visible in our language.

> In the human mind words are not isolated islands like they are in machines. Every thought, word and image is intricately connected to other related words and concepts through many subtle relationships. If we want machines to be able to understand our requests for information, and to respond with comprehensive and relevant results, then we need to give them a knowledge-base that is structured the way our own brains work. (Webpages, 5)

To enable generic experience and knowledge sharing among humans and computers the "different universe" problem for ontology must be solved.

5 Conclusions

The computer is epoch-making as a technical and conceptual tool and it presents a powerful metaphor in the same way as mechanical clockwork was the metaphor of Newtonian Universe. The Universe Computer metaphor may be read in two ways. Firstly, the Universe in its existence at some level of abstraction may be understood as an enormous informational and computational system. In a Computer Universe every physical process can be seen as computation.

Secondly, our own computers, conceived as earthly images of the Universe-computer show a tendency to contain the totality of ideas of the world as it appears to humanity of today. In that sense what is saved in the computers and communicable via computers becomes gradually all that there is.

The Semantic Web Project can be seen as an attempt to realize the grand Leibniz's dream. The World Wide Web as information space should be useful not only for human communication, but also for machines which must be able to participate and help in communicating and processing knowledge. Automated discovery is one of the goals that can free humans from time-consuming and repetitive work that is a considerable part of e.g. research or administration.

One of the impediments to the fulfillment of Leibniz's dream is that formal ontology is always embedded in a natural language with all of its ambiguity. The attempt to automate the communication between different ontologies encounters the problem of compatibility of concepts with different semantic origins. Coming from different universes, words with the same spelling may have a continuum of meanings – a problem that must be addressed.

In that way the formalization problem is related to the characteristics of the natural language semantic continuum. The human brain has through its evolution, developed the capability to communicate via natural languages. We need computers able to communicate in similar ways, which calls for a new and broader understanding far beyond the limits of formal axiomatic reasoning that characterizes computing today. The time has come for a new Renaissance, in which sciences and humanities, arts and engineering will reach a novel synthesis.

BIBLIOGRAPHY

[Bunge, 1977] M. Bunge. *Treatise on Basic Philosophy: Vol 3: Ontology I: The Furniture of the World.* Reidel, 1977.

[Bynum and Moor, 1998] T.W. Bynum and J.H. Moor, editors. *The Digital Phoenix: How Computers are Changing Philosophy.* Oxford: Blackwell, 1998.

[Cantwell Smith, 2003] B. Cantwell Smith. The wildfire spread of computational ideas. http://www.utoronto.ca/cat/whatson/kmdi.html, 2003. KMDI Lecture Series Seminar.

[Chaitin, 1987] G.J. Chaitin. *Algorithmic Information Theory.* Cambridge UP, 1987.

[Damasio, 1999] A.R. Damasio. *The Scientific American Book of the Brain.* New York: Scientific American, 1999.

[Davidson, 1984] D. Davidson. *Inquiries into Truth and Interpretation.* Oxford University Press, Oxford, 1984.

[Dodig-Crnkovic, 2001] G. Dodig-Crnkovic. What ultimately matters, indeed? Proc. Conf. for the Promotion of Research in IT at New Universities and at University Colleges in Sweden, http://www.idt.mdh.se/~gdc/work/what_ultimately_matters.pdf, 2001.

[Dodig-Crnkovic, 2003] G. Dodig-Crnkovic. Shifting the paradigm of the philosophy of science: the philosophy of information and a new renaissance. *Minds and Machines: Special Issue on the Philosophy of Information,* 2003. http://www.idt.mdh.se/gdc/work/shifting_paradigm_singlespace.pdf.

[Floridi, 2002] L. Floridi. *What is the Philosophy of Information?,* volume 33. 2002.

[Floridi, 2003] L. Floridi. *Blackwell Guide to the Philosophy of Computing and Information.* Oxford: Blackwell, 2003.

[Geach and Black, 1960] P. Geach and M. Black, editors. *Translations from the Philosophical Writings of Gottlob Frege.* Oxford: Blackwell, 1960.

[Gell-Mann, 1994] M. Gell-Mann. *The Quark and the Jaguar.* W.H. Freeman, 1994.

[Gödel, 1992] K. Gödel. *On Formally Undecidable Propositions Of Principia Mathematica And Related Systems.* Dover Pubns, reprint edition, 1992.

[Gruber, 1995] T.R. Gruber. Toward principles for the design of ontologies used for knowledge sharing. *Formal Ontology in Conceptual Analysis and Knowledge Representation,* 43(5/6), 1995. Special issue of the International Journal of Human-Computer Studies.

[Hofstadter, 2000] D. Hofstadter. Time 100: Kurt Gödel. http://www.time.com/time/time100/scientist/profile/godel.html, 2000.

[Nalimov, 1981] V.V. Nalimov. *The Labyrynths of Language: A Mathematician's Journey.* ISI Press, Philadelphia, 1981.

[Nalimov, 1982] V.V. Nalimov. *Realms of the Unconscious: The enchanted frontier.* ISI Press, 1982.

[Quine, 1964] W.V.O. Quine. *Word and Object.* The MIT Press, Cambridge, 1964.

[Russell, 1921] B. Russell. The analysis of mind, 1921. Essays
   http://www.literaturepage.com/read/russell-analysis-of-mind.html.
[Smith and Ceusters, 2003] B. Smith and W. Ceusters. The first industrial philosophy:
   How analytical ontology can be useful to medical informatics. *Interdisciplinary Science
   Reviews*, 28:106–111, 2003.
[Smith and Welty, 2001] B. Smith and C. Welty. Ontology: Toward a new synthesis. In
   Proceedings of FOIS '01, volume 2001, Ogunquit, ME, Oct. 17-19 2001.
[Weinberg, 2002] S. Weinberg. Is the universe a computer? *The New York Review of
   Books*, 49(16), 2002.
[Wolfram, 2002] S. Wolfram. *A New Kind of Science*. Wolfram Media, Inc., 2002.
[Wright, 1988] R. Wright. Edward fredkin. In *Three Scientists and Their Gods: Looking
   for Meaning in an Age of Information*. Times Books, 1988.

Webpages

1. http://www.w3.org/2001/sw/
   (Semantic Web)

2. http://www.w3.org/DesignIssues/Semantic.html
   (Semantic Web Road map)

3. http://infomesh.net/2001/swintro/
   (The Semantic Web: An Introduction)

4. http://jrscience.wcp.muohio.edu/lab/TaxonomyLab.html
   (The "Nuts and Bolts" of Taxonomy and Classification)

5. http://www.synaptica.com/
   (Synapse White Paper)

6. http://www.cogsci.princeton.edu/~wn/
   (WordNet A lexical database for the English)

Gordana Dodig-Crnkovic
Department of Computer Science and Engineering
Mälardalen University
Västerås, Sweden
Email: gordana.dodig-crnkovic@mdh.se

Applications of Anti-Realist Metaphysics to the Digital World

Matthew J. Dovey

ABSTRACT. Recently, we have been building a world whose reality subsists within electronic circuits and networks such as the Internet, World Wide Web and GRID. Now, this "digital reality" permeates much of our lives, although we only have a rudimentary comprehension of its ontological and metaphysical foundations. There is an uneasy relationship with this "digital reality": aspects of our lives subsist either completely or partially within it; whilst we ourselves exist completely outside of it. This external existence outside of the "digital world" raises a number of unresolved issues concerning truth. Without a full understanding or proper awareness, these issues can often result in uneasiness and misconceptions and a danger of not realizing the full potential of this domain. Traditional instruments of metaphysics can shed light upon and improve our understanding of the "digital world", albeit with a Wittgenstein sting in the tail: the mutability of "digital realities" provides a good medium for modeling metaphysical theories. This paper examines how ontology and metaphysics from the idealism of Leibniz and Berkeley to the anti-Realism of Wittgenstein can be used to examine our relationship with the digital world and help explain the problems that occur in using and developing solutions in information technology.

Over the latter half of the 20th century we have been engaged in building a world whose reality subsists in, for want of a better term, the world of electronic circuits, beginning with the development of computer systems and now, network computer systems such as the Internet, World Wide Web and GRID. At the beginning of the 21st century this "digital world" permeates many of our lives. However, we only have a rudimentary comprehension of the ontological and metaphysical foundations of the new "digital worlds" which we are building and in some sense living within. The motivation behind this work is to understand how philosophy can influence or at least help bring us to a better understanding of how we build these "digital realities" or "the digital world". By digital realities, I'm not really referring to virtual realities but to the day to day computer software we interact with

Lorenzo Magnani and Riccardo Dossena, editors, *Computing, Philosophy, and Cognition*, pp. 177–189 © 2005, M.J. Dovey

– operating systems, word processors, the internet – which form their own
reality and is very much a part of the world with which we both interact
and are constructing.

The essential premise to this paper is that this digital reality is potentially
very different from the real world even though it relies upon the real world
for its existence. Its apparent familiarity and similarity with the real world
is a misleading and dangerous fiction (in an anti–realist sense) and that this
digital reality is at best a distorting mirror of the physical world. In analogy
with an observation of Wittgenstein:

> It is clear that logic may not conflict with its application. But
> logic must have contact with its application. Therefore logic
> and its application may not overlap one another. [Wittgenstein,
> 1922]

so it is with digital and physical realities. They cannot overlap, although
the sense of one subsists within the sense of the other. Although concepts
in digital realities rely upon concepts in physical reality for their existence,
we cannot apply concepts from one reality to the other. An irony is that
these two conclusions are mutually contradictory, although we need the first
to derive the latter. Again, although with an obvious irony, we can draw
an analogy with Wittgenstein's Tractatus is applicable:

> My propositions are elucidatory in this way: he who understands
> me finally recognizes them as senseless, when he has claimed out
> through them, on them, over them (He must so to speak throw
> away the ladder, after he has climbed up on it) [Wittgenstein,
> 1922]

The activity of establishing what is "truth" within the digital world, is
not too dissimilar to that of determining within what mathematic truth
subsists. The various theories of mathematical truth from object Platonism
(namely that mathematical objects exist in some sense) through structural
Platonism (that mathematical truth exists in the relationship between abstract objects) to formalist views (that truth derives from definitions even
through as demonstrated by Lakatos [Lakatos, 1976], those definitions are
not constructed in isolation from theorems but in a feedback loop) all (again
ironically) have their analogues in determining truth within the digital reality. However, there is almost a spiritual or mysticism present when investigating this concept in digital realities.

Digital reality lends itself very well to the atomic ontologies of reality
propounded since Leucippus, whereby reality is constructed of indivisible

particles. In digital reality these "atoms" can be viewed as binary bits (note that this is not necessarily the case with virtual realities, as it is feasible that VR might be controlled by something other than a digital computer). These bits behave in a way analogous to Leibniz's monads, in that their perceptual properties are determined by their relationships to one another. Moreover their perceptual properties are also determined by their location in the digital world. A bit in the display memory for example has a different effect or meaning from a bit in the accumulator register of a CPU. It should be noted that this is not quite the same as Young's interpretation of the Tractatus as conceiving as a bit in logical space [Young, 2004]. In a Leibnizian sense, each bit reflects the entirety of DR within itself in that each bit could serve in all the possible meanings that a bit could obtain within DR, however, I do not think that we could take this to the extreme of regarding that the meaning of a bit is intrinsic to itself in the sense of Leibniz's monadology that "the predicate is in the subject" [Leibniz, 1696].

Given that the meaning of bits is determined by their location and interactions with each other, what *does* meaning involve in this context, given that unless we adopt the extremes of the monadic view of the bit being a reflection of the digital reality, meaning is not intrinsic to the bit,. For this we need a dualism resembling that of Descartes and Locke. Their dualism was between spirit and matter, in this context the matter is the bits of the digital reality and the "spirit" is the "how" of how we are lead to perceive these bits in their myriad ways. In more recent philosophy (such as Wittgenstein and later Dummett), we could argue that the meaning of the bit is determined by its use but this would leave us with the question of what determines the usage, and the answer is essentially the same as what the nature of this "spirit" is in digital reality. As an aside, given the nature of this argument, it is interesting to note that the 1919 Webster's New International Dictionary gives the definition of "virtuality" as "existing in essence or effect".

Ironically this "spirit" is best seen in the light of Berkeleian Idealism (ironic in the sense that Berkeley's Idealism was aimed at denying dualism) [Berkeley, 1713]. As in the Berkeleian veil of perception, what we perceive are the ideas or concepts of other minds, i.e. in the digital reality other minds shape how we perceive the bits. What is actually perceived as you traverse digital reality is a representation of the bits produced by the minds of programmers and engineers. In many cases it is a complex hybrid of many ideas of many such people if we trace the chain through the code of the software right down to the microcode of the CPU (and beyond). Indeed, this picture has dramatically changed over time; the early computers would be built and programmed by a few individuals – now they are complex interactions of BIOS, firmware, operating system, drivers, simultaneous (multi-tasking) applications, other computers on the network, etc. Once the province of lone programmers, today's software applications typically involve teams of programmers, designers, requirement engineers etc. – so the construction of this reality is now a truly co-operative process and no longer necessarily under the control of any particular individuals. Open Source projects are an example, when successful, of the software application having a life beyond that envisaged by its original creator.

However, in digital reality we have an opportunity of realising the Berkeleian sense of minds interacting directly by exchanging ideas. However within digital reality we no longer have the Berkeleian supreme regulatory mind. The lack of a single adjudicator has the potential of making digital reality a far richer and inconsistent than we would normally regard physical reality to be. Rather than the Berkeleian Supreme Mind, in the digital world, we actually have a kind of metaphysical tri–alism. Persistency in digital reality is determined by the arrangement of the atom or bits; meaning in digital reality is ascribed in some way by physical reality; our perception of digital realities through the minds of others. In this model physical reality is a meta–world of digital reality, in that the metaphysics of digital reality reside in physical reality. However, we could still collapse this into the Berkeleian Idealism, by arguing that the arrangements of bits and there interconnections in physical reality is precisely the Berkeleian mind in digital reality; this does not neglect the dependency of digital reality upon the physical – it just highlights that the physical has no "real" existence within digital reality. These two different philosophies are not mutually inconsistent as can be seen by returning to the Monadology of Leibniz

> the assemblage of all minds must make up the City of God [. . .]
> we have established a natural harmony between the two natural
> kingdoms [. . .] the physical kingdom of nature and the moral
> kingdom of grace; that is to say God as Architect of the machine
> of the universe, and God as Monarch of the divine City of Minds.
> [Leibniz, 1714]

although the "mind" in this sense may be no more than a convenient fiction.

The question of whether to apply pure Idealism to digital reality or this hybrid tri–alism reduces to whether we allow "mysticism" to feature as a valid concept in digital reality. Whilst this may at first seem somewhat surprising, however on reflection it can be seen that most realism versus anti-realism arguments in physical reality, are ultimately aimed at the justification or denial of the concept of a super-reality within the confines of physical reality. Most Eastern "mystical" philosophy is built around the existence of such super-realities, which can only be sensed at certain states of consciousness, or, as in Bergsonian philosophy, by "intuition" rather than "logic". The Berkeleian versus Locke and Leibniz debate centres on a form of Occam's Razor, namely that such super-realities are unneeded concepts. Any such super-reality by definition is unknowable. Hence mysticism does not greatly feature in the British tradition of philosophy – in the words of Wittgenstein:

> There is indeed the inexpressible. This shows itself; it is the mystical [...] whereof we cannot speak, thereof we must be silent. [Wittgenstein, 1922]

However, in this case, mysticism can be a very useful concept in building the argument, even if abandoned later like Wittgenstein's ladder. The relationship between physical and super realities is very similar to that between digital and physical realities; physical reality is the mystical "super-reality" within which digital reality resides. To borrow once more from Wittgenstein:

> The sense of the world must lie outside the world. In the world everything is as it is and happens as it does happen. What makes it non-accidental cannot lie *in* the world, for otherwise this would again be accidental. [Wittgenstein, 1922]

Physical reality's logic can be considered as a transcendental logic of digital reality; we can build limits within the logics of a computer system, so that a "being" within that system would not be able to comprehend the fuller logic available within physical reality. To quote Kant:

> it is impossible for the human intellect to know in *substantiis immaterialibus* these *relationes externas* which correspond to Space as the condition of the relation of material but only apparent things. [Kant, 1770]

However, the lack of a regulatory mind as mentioned above implies that digital reality is extremely rich in that the rules that govern the physics of its reality is limited only by the imagination of its creator. Again to quote Wittgenstein we have

> There is no causal nexus which justifies such an inference. The events of the future cannot be inferred from those of the present. Superstition is the belief in the causal nexus. [Wittgenstein, 1922]

The anti-realist stance of the argument as regard our perceptions of digital reality is that we can only perceive anything in digital reality through someone else's interpretation: we are always perceiving someone else's logical construct. Digital reality gives us an arena in which we can convert ideas into "reality". However, although we are the ultimate creators of this world, and in some sense omniscient (in that we can access the eternal states), our prescience is limited by the digital worlds complexity and both our prescience and omnipotence is limited by the collaborative nature of this world's construction. A modernist interpretation of the Berkeleian idealism analysis of digital reality (and indeed of the original intent of Berkeley) would be to view this collaborative meeting of minds within digital reality as a social network; the meaning and interpretation within digital reality thereby revolving around social and communal acceptance, comparable with linguistic based philosophy that the meaning of a word is determined by its usage.

To return to the question of our omniscience and omnipotence within digital reality (since we exist outside within a super-reality), it must be noted that what our ideas "become" when translated into the digital world, and hence are "realized" by taking on aspects of the digital atoms, may not fully resemble out original conceptions. Our world is not digital or discrete, whereas the digital reality is. There is a false, and hence dangerous, expectation that constructs from the physical will work in digital reality in an identical manner to which they work in physical reality, or the assumption that we fully understand digital reality because it is created by us. To fully comprehend this, and hence to better our understanding of how people react and work within digital reality, and as computers and the internet become even further embedded into common society, within hybrid reality, we need to understand the uneasy "mystical" relationship between physical reality and digital reality. The "unease" in this relationship is that although the meaning of concepts within digital reality subsists within physical reality, there is no necessary requirement for concepts within digital reality to have analogues in physical. In general, it is not a necessary fact that we can use the intellectual framework derived from our experiences in physical reality to comprehend digital reality. However, as can be seen from the ease at which we can apply philosophical concepts grounded in physical reality to digital reality, there does appear to be some contingent and unnervingly close relationship between concepts of both.

One a posteriori, empirical truth appears to be that the difference between the processes we build in the digital world and those in the real world are of degree rather than of nature. The degree part of this principle is fairly easy to explain. Computers are continually increasing in power and speed.

Advances in networking and communications are increasing the speed and ease by which computers communicate. Commercial pressures also bear on the situation; it is important to improve the functionality of both hardware and software in order to maintain a sellable commodity – often adding additional features that are not required by the user but that make it more attractive. The result is that time passes very quickly in digital reality with a number of unfortunate repercussions. One of these is that computer science is still, relatively speaking, a very young discipline, and in many ways poorly understood. However, peoples' perceptions greatly exaggerate where we really stand with this technology, with the result that there are many projects which fail due to too much being promised in too short a time frame. A more serious failing is the recognition of a fundamental bottleneck in any useful computer system, namely that of the human which participates in the digital reality being constructed. Internet communications is an example of this. Instant transmission of e-mail does not imply instant response. The computer industry has been overly concerned with the technical bottlenecks, but has paid little heed to the social ones.

The second part of our contingent principle that digital reality differs from physical reality in degree rather than nature can be analysed in terms of the Berkeleian Idealism expressed above. We can regard our interactions with digital reality as an exchange of ideas between minds: between that of the observer or participant in digital reality, and that of the designers and programmers behind that particular aspect of digital. Both these have a role to play in the perception of that aspect of digital reality: the programmer in that we can only ever perceive someone else's interpretation of the fundamental bits that ultimately constitute digital reality; and the ultimate observer will always place their own interpretation on what is being observed. I will consider the latter first, since, as will be show later, this also shapes the interpretations that the designers of digital reality try to project. Typically we interpret digital reality using the same inductive framework that we use for interpreting physical reality; we interpret our perceptions in both physical and digital realities based on our past experiences. As Hume writes

> the mind is convinced by reasoning of the principle that instances of which we have no experience, must necessarily resemble those of which we have. [Hume, 1739]

Typically our past experiences will be solely or primarily based in physical reality, and hence we superimpose our understanding of the principles of the physical into the digital. Viewed under this light it is not surprising that younger generations who have been brought up with computers find digital reality easier to deal with since their past experiences intrinsically include experiences of digital reality from a formative age. In effect we are building models grounded in physical reality to explain our experiences and interactions within digital reality. However these models are often extremely effective, proviso the principle mentioned above as regards differences in degree rather than nature. One explanation for this is that we are also using models grounded in physical reality to construct digital reality, as we will return to this later. However, it too surprising that we can construct effective models of digital reality in physical reality, without implying that either realities share concepts, if we consider anti-realist views of how we build mathematical models in the sciences. Essentially we perceive patterns in physical reality where none necessarily exist:

> Objects have no discoverable connection together; nor is it from
> any other principle but custom operating upon the imagination,
> that we can draw any inference from the appearance of one to
> the existence of another. [Hume, 1739]

This is similar to Wittgenstein's observation on the lack of a causal nexus quoted above. The instrumentalist stance to science claims that we construct models of the universe in physics; we are not really describing the universe, but instead creating mathematical fictions, which have certain predictive properties, which match the currently observed phenomenon. Entities such as electrons, which cannot be directly observed, do not have any "real" existence but are just convenient constructs in our model. This stance explains why the universe appears to be mathematical since mathematics is a language for describing patterns and relationships. The same can be applied to our perceptional models of digital reality. The mental framework we have constructed to interpret these fictional patterns in physical reality, is by its nature, also suited to interpreting fictional patterns in digital reality. As within the physical sciences, we need to be always ready to refine or even reject our existing perceptual models given new evidence. This is particularly pertinent to our models of digital reality, since digital reality can differ in quite subtle ways from our expectations based upon physical reality. For example, in user interface design, there is often a tendency to mimic physical objects [Hamilton, 2000]. This can cause confusion since the analogy can only go so far, and there will always be some difference between the replica in digital reality and the real version in physical reality, as anyone who has questioned the removal of a disk on a Mac by putting it in the trash bin can confirm. Curiously, there is sometimes more reluctance to drop our interpretations in DR than OR. Gregory gives some accounts when this happens, such as with the collection of Poll Tax system, whereby peoples' real addresses in physical reality, did not correspond to where the computer system thought they were [Gregory, 1997]. In such cases, people can quickly become stubbornly convinced that given a conflict between digital reality and physical reality, that digital reality should be the reference, whereas in other circumstances (for example where a credit transaction is involved) the same person would trust physical reality rather than digital reality.

The other reason for the contingent similarity between physical and digital realities, as touched on above, is due to the way we construct digital entities. Most of the time we build digital constructs which mirror the physical. There are two possible explanations for this.

The first is an assumption that for various reasons it is better to limit our digital constructions to those which mirror similar physical constructs. The assumption is either that people find it easier to work in digital reality when the constructs and principles are familiar to them from physical reality, or that the processes we have developed in physical reality are effective in digital reality. The fact that we interpret constructs in digital reality along physical reality lines could be argued to support these assumptions but I would claim that neither of these assumptions are necessarily valid premises. Whilst true that familiarity can reduce the learning curve, it is not necessarily the case that a system which involves a shallow learning curve is the most effective. There are many software packages that have a very complicated interface, but are more efficient when used by a competent user than a similar package with a simpler interface when also used by the same competent user. Whilst I would not propose abandoning principles of good user interface design, I would argue that we should not be limited to concepts grounded in analogy with physical reality when designing such things. Ultimately people have to learn to cope with extremely complex ideas in physical reality, and the same should be applicable to digital reality. Making digital reality overly familiar gives a false sense of security which often undermines the goal of making users more comfortable with digital reality when the differences become apparent. The above argument is based on purely philosophical reasoning but empirically it is also supported by evidence within the Information Science community on the problems associated with metaphor and logical analogues in interface design. For example, Grudin, in articulating the reasons why software applications fail indicates exception handling as one of the reasons, namely that the digital reality does not allow the flexibility and improvisation of physical reality in coping with unexpected conditions [Grudin, 1992]. At this point the analogy with the physical reality it is attempting to encapsulate breaks down to the discomfort of the user, who may respond in unexpected ways, such as believing digital reality rather than physical reality as regards to truth. The breakdown of the analogy in this case occurs because the logic of the system within digital reality does not encapsulate the logic of the process in physical reality, which is not surprising when we consider that the logic of digital is itself encapsulated by the logic of physical reality. This can lead to the system being represented in digital reality becoming out of synchronization with the system in physical reality, as in the Poll Tax example given above.

The second reason for the contingent resemblance between physical and digital realities stems from how we build computer systems which perform some task previously performed solely within physical reality. Often it is the case that the process in physical reality is modeled within digital reality without any major modifications to the process itself. As Joseph Weizenbaum observed in the computerization of social security systems "rather than use new technology to transform the process, we simply automated the existing flawed workpractices" [Weizenbaum, 1976]. This stems in part from the perceived need to maintain familiarity. There are strong social reasons for this claim since a totally alien process would probably be rejected by the existing users of the process, although this rejection may not be made on particularly strong grounds. As Grudin observes, another failure of software is when it attempts to disrupt the social process, violates social norms or threatens existing work practice i.e. "technology is not a bulldozer of cultures" [Grudin, 1992]. Hence whilst digital reality may offer radically new ways, and potentially better ways, of working, they may simply not be socially acceptable, even though the currently socially accepted process is not the best either in physical or digital realities. However, what is socially acceptable changes over time. Many established technologies (for example mass production) were at one point socially unacceptable (consider for example the Luddite Riots).

However we also have the perception that all that modeling the process in digital reality can offer is enhanced speed or changes in degree rather than nature. If digital reality can really offer nothing more that changes in degree, then it is sound that a process, which has been developed and refined over some, time in physical reality, should be transferred with little modification into digital reality. There are two dangers here. The first, as mentioned above, is that the different nature of digital reality results in the process itself being changed in subtle ways as it is translated into digital reality, particularly in the translation of the continuous to the discrete. The second danger is that is possible (not least because of this different in nature) that an entirely different process may be more effective in digital reality, but which either would not be so effective or possibly not even realizable in physical reality.

> A few weeks ago I received one of the greatest shocks of my life.
> I abruptly realized that all along, it has been the intention of
> many or most technical people to simulate hierarchy and simu-
> late paper [...] it had never occurred to me that a well-informed
> and clever person could intentionally and deliberately seek such
> an objective [...] I had simply assumed that [...] [these] sim-
> ulation[s] were temporary holding patterns [...] [but] many if
> not most computer people took [...] [these] simulation[s] to be
> the correct and final long term agenda because these represented
> the simulation of familiar reality. [Nelson, 2004]

There is, however, a severe problem of how to think in purely DR terms
without letting our pre-conceptions of the physical interfere. It may be that
we have to accept Hume's concepts behind the nature of ideas:

> That all out simple ideas in their first appearance are derived
> from simple impressions, which are correspondent to them, and
> which they exactly represent. [Hume, 1739]

that complex ideas are derived by combining these simple ideas which stem
ultimately from physical reality. Since interaction within digital reality is
essentially a direct interaction of minds and exchange of ideas, we are only
limited by our imagination as to what we can construct within digital reality.
However, if the philosophy of ideas are expounded by Hume is correct the
only ideas that we can exchange within digital reality are ideas which are
ultimately derived from our experiences in physical reality. Whilst in theory,
digital reality is not limited by the concepts or logics from physical reality,
in practice our exploration of digital reality is circumscribed by experiences
and logics of physical reality: we can never realise its full potential unless
we break out of the mental frameworks imposed upon us by our experience
of physical reality. There is a circularity here, in that digital reality if it
realized its full potential could provide a reality it which we can break out of
these bonds, but in order for us to make use of this potential digital reality
we already need to have broken out of these bonds. Whether digital reality
will ever realize its potential therefore revolves on whether all ideas must
derive from experience. Currently our constructs within digital reality seem
to support the Humean view of ideas, but this may be because of current
practice rather than necessary fact. However, there is evidence that as the
newer generations adopt the world hybrid world of both physical and digital
realities, and hence have experiences in both, that this is slowly pushing

the envelope of what can be conceived within digital reality a little further. There may, however, still be aspects of digital reality which necessarily lie outside of human comprehension and use – even though digital reality itself is a purely human construct.

To conclude, digital reality has the potential to far surpass the restrictions of our concepts of physical reality. However there seems to be a contingent truth that whilst digital reality is alien when compared to the physical, it in fact in most cases only differs from the physical by factors of degree rather than factors of nature. This may be due to current practices which perpetuate a myth believing that digital reality can only ever differ in degree and can offer little more that the physical in terms of nature or which feel we need to ground concepts of digital reality in the physical in order for digital reality to be comprehensible. However, it may be the case that this contingent resemblance between digital and physical realities is more deeply rooted in how we build our perceptual models of the universe. Whatever the case, whilst a human construct, digital reality has the potential to be very alien far surpassing what we may imagine or intended it to be.

BIBLIOGRAPHY

[Berkeley, 1713] G. Berkeley. Three dialogues between hydras and philonous. In *Berkeley – Philosophical Works*. John Dent and Sons, 1713. Edited by M.R. Ayers, 1975.

[Gregory, 1997] F.H. Gregory. Mapping information systems on to the real world. In R.L. Winder, S.K. Probert, and I.A. Beeson, editors, *Philosophical Aspects of Information Systems*. Taylor and Francis, 1997.

[Grudin, 1992] J. Grudin. Why cscw applications fail: Problems in the design and evaluation of organizational interfaces. In D. Marca and G. Bock, editors, *Groupware: Software for Computer-Supported Cooperative Work*, pages 552–560, Los Alamitos, CA, 1992. IEEE Press. Republication of conference paper.

[Hamilton, 2000] A. Hamilton. Interface metaphors and logical analogues. *Journal of the American Society for Information Science*, 50(2):111–122, 2000.

[Hume, 1739] D. Hume. *A Treatise of Human Nature*. Oxford University Press, 1739. Edited by L.A. Selby-Bigge, 1990.

[Kant, 1770] E. Kant. Inaugural dissertation on the two worlds. New York, 1770. Translated by W.G. Eckoff, 1894.

[Lakatos, 1976] I. Lakatos. Proofs and refutations, 1976.

[Leibniz, 1696] G.W. Leibniz. On the principle of indiscernibles. In *Liebniz – Philosophical Writings*. John Dent and Sons, 1696. Translated by M. Morris and G.H.R. Parkinson, 1973.

[Leibniz, 1714] G.W. Leibniz. Monadology. In *Liebniz – Philosophical Writings*. John Dent and Sons, 1714. Translated by M. Morris and G.H.R. Parkinson, 1973.

[Nelson, 2004] T.H. Nelson. New cosmology for information. Unpublished, 2004.

[Weizenbaum, 1976] J. Weizenbaum. *Computer Power and Human Reason: From Judgment to Calculation*. W.H. Freeman, 1976.

[Wittgenstein, 1922] L. Wittgenstein. *Tractatus Philosophicus*. Routledge, 1922. Translated by C.K. Ogden.

[Young, 2004] R.A. Young. Wittgenstein's tractatus project as philosophy of information. *Minds and Machines*, 14(1):119–132, 2004.

Matthew J. Dovey
Oxford e-Science Centre
Oxford University, Oxford, UK
Email: `matthew.dovey@oucs.ox.ac.uk`

The Role of the Internal Patterns
and the External Representations in Sustaining Creative Processes

Alberto Faro and Daniela Giordano

ABSTRACT. From the perspective of dynamic systems theory, the brain functions according to global patterns involving internal sensory-motor patterns and external sensorial stimuli. Developmental approaches assume that the brain functions by manipulating symbols that represent at the conceptual level what the perceptual system executes unconsciously in response to environmental stimuli. Conceptual re-representations (RR) support creative activities, but a criticism to RR is that it implies the existence of some entity in the mind that re-represents symbolically the world. A criticism to the dynamic systems approach is that it does not explain how the brain creates new patterns. The position of the paper is that the dynamic systems theory is suitable to explain how humans behave by coordinating the external stimuli and the neuronal groups according to global patterns, but it is argued that some re-organization processes of such patterns is needed to explain how people, aided by their own experience and by external representations, accomplish creative tasks. The role of the external representations is pointed out by considering the cognitive processes taking place at both the individual and social levels. Some evidence is provided supporting the proposed account for new pattern formation.

1 Introduction

Design, problem-solving and creativity have long been researched, with aims such as understanding the nature of the cognitive and social processes involved, or building computational models of creativity and concept formation (e.g. [Faro and Giordano, 1998]). In the past we have tackled the issue of supporting design creativity by developing suitable electronic environments, e.g., design memories [Faro and Giordano, 2000]. In this paper we are interested in theoretically analyzing the role that experience and external representations play in creating new artifacts such as in system designing. Is it enough to organize experience and related representations in design

Lorenzo Magnani and Riccardo Dossena, editors, *Computing, Philosophy, and Cognition*, pp. 191–208 © 2005, A. Faro and D. Giordano

cases from which the designer may take inspiration? How the psychology of the user behaviors hypothesized in these cases should be described in order to be suitably adapted to the current situation? To answer to these questions, we need a theory of mind which gives a strategy to consult the previous cases in order to have the maximum benefit from experience, and a methodology to decide the right affordances to offer to the system users.

For this reason the paper intends to study how people behave and how experience may be used in conjunction with the external representations for supporting creative activities. This implies taking a position with respect to one of the fundamental questions of cognition, i.e., how the brain functions at the conceptual level: is the brain a sort of symbolic processor where symbols are into correspondence with reality objects or is it a pattern classifier that operates in cooperation with its environment? These two positions have been recently well exemplified by the debate between Karmiloff-Smith and Thelen.

By studying cognition from the perspective of the dynamic systems theory, Thelen sustains that the brain functions following trajectories in two interconnected What-Where planes (e.g., [Thelen and Smith, 1988]). In both these planes the perceived objects are coded by activation levels (What). Concerning the Where dimension, in the first plane the object locations are coded by coordinates at which we address our look (Where-Look), whereas in the other plane the object locations are coded by the direction to follow to reach them (Where-Reach). Trajectories in such planes involving respectively observations and actions are into correspondence with the situations experienced by the subject. In the following we call such trajectories also action/observation patterns. This is in accordance with the existence, widely demonstrated in literature (e.g., [Kosslyn et al., 1990] and [Ungerleider and Miskhin, 1982]), of two neurological pathways in the human brain, also known as the what and where pathways, respectively dedicated to recognize the object features (i.e., color and shape), and the location of such objects in space.

Karmiloff-Smith in [Karmiloff-Smith, 1999] assumes that the brain functions by manipulating symbols that re-represent (RR) at the conceptual level what the perceptual system executes in an unconscious way in response to the environmental stimuli. Further conceptual re-descriptions allow the mind to invent new solutions to the problems. This developmental approach to cognition is explicated through four main steps. At level I the knowledge has the format of procedures governing human behavior in a given context. These procedures cannot be put in relation with each other neither they may be internally accessed. At level E1 humans are able, even if unconsciously, to interconnect the procedures I that share something between them and to extract some relevant parts of them. At level E2 and level E3 representations are understood consciously and may be expressed by non verbal (level E2) and verbal report (level E3).

The main criticism to RR is that it implies the existence of some entity in the mind that re-represents symbolically the world starting from the perceptual networks, whereas our criticism to the pattern approach is that it is not rich enough to explain how the brain is able to carry out complex activities, especially the ones aiming at the creation of new patterns that have a developmental nature because most likely a new pattern is formed by a step-by-step procedure starting from the existing ones.

We start from the position that the Thelen's point of view is suitable to explain how humans behave by coordinating the neuronal groups populating the mind according to (or *"by reusing"*) global patterns, previously learned, involving external representations. However, we argue that some dynamic re-organization of such patterns from which we take inspiration during the creative activity is needed too to explain how the mind, making use of external maps/drawings/sketching, and interacting with other people by a written/spoken language, may accomplish complex tasks such as system design.

The paper shows that solving new design problems or enhancing previous solutions require the joint operation of both these two brain attitudes, i.e., the one of dynamically organizing the action patterns so that the patterns most relevant to the current design step may emerge and the other attitude of reusing the patterns related to a situation more or less identical to the current one. In doing so, an account is proposed that dissolves the "ghost in the machine" present in the RR approach and extends the pattern theory into a non-representational theory of mind view as a black box capable not only of executing action/observation patterns depending on the context, but also of creating new patterns by suitably combining and recombining existing relevant patterns.

To avoid that not relevant patterns will be taken into account for reuse, section 2 claims that it is useful to consider patterns related not only to the mentioned what and where dimensions but also to other dimensions such as when, why and so on. Moreover it is pointed out that it is not necessary to reuse the entire trajectory to reach a certain goal, but also significant portions of it may be reused. In particular decomposing a pattern according to the synergetics approach to cognition [Haken, 2004] has not only the advantage of obtaining mini-patterns, called order states, more easy to reuse but also the one of identifying the affordances to be offered to people involved in the activity.

Section 3 claims that the activity patterns are classified in mind according to their interrelations to increase the number of relevant patterns to be "contemporaneously" taken into account to create a new pattern for solving a new problem. This implies that the patterns to be taken into account for reuse are not only the ones, say P_i, that refer to a more or less identical situation, but also the ones that belong to the same class to which P_i belongs to. The process of creating a new pattern is then discussed by motivating why this process is most likely performed by combing and re-combining the patterns (hopefully the mentioned mini-patterns and order states) belonging to the classes relevant to the problem at hand. Section 4 extends our theoretical framework to take into account the role played by the external representations at social level, especially by the representations circulating between people belonging to the same community (e.g., community of practices, the community of learners and so on). Finally in section 5 some evidence is provided supporting the proposed account.

2   The space of the activities: the mind in action

In this section, first the mind is described as a dynamic system able to reach a goal by suitably coordinating sensory inputs (observations) and bodily movements (actions). Each sequence of observations and actions is represented by a trajectory developing in an n-dimensional setting rather than in the What-Where plane proposed by Thelen. Secondly, the synergetics approach to cognition is applied to decompose these activity trajectories into smaller ones called order states. Passing from an order state to a next one depends on the values of some external stimuli that behave as the control variables that support humans in reaching their goals.

2.1 W^n Trajectories

The What-Where patterns constitute a plausible hypothesis of how an experience is learnt, i.e. by the ordering in time of sensorial inputs related to objects located in some place in coordination with bodily movements, if any, to reach them. As an example, a driver entering into a service station of a highway usually has at her/his disposal a certain number of W^2 trajectories depending on the service she/he intends to use, as shown in Figure 1 where the perceived objects are coded by the activation levels from 0 to 5, and an environment centered reference system is assumed for encoding the space. In the trajectory related to the fill with gasoline, the subject will perceive three objects in sequence: the entrance (level 1), the gasoline distributor (level 4), and the exit (level 0). With respect to the trajectory drawn in Figure 1, the movements performed by the driver in coordination with the three observations above are: moving towards the distributor from point A to point B and moving towards the exit from B to C.

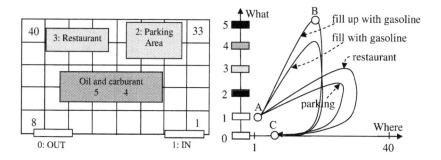

Figure 1. On the left we have: a) the layout of the service station indicating the objects, from 1 to 5, involved in the services needed by a driver and b) the linear coordinate, from 1 to 40, used to localize them. On the right the What-Where trajectories (in terms of actions and observations) performed by a driver entering into a service station.

Let us note that many trajectories in the W^2 plane could be active simultaneously even if they are mutually exclusive since they belong to different goals, e.g., the "fill with gasoline" and "fill up with gasoline" trajectories may be active, respectively, in the routine of everyday life or when the person is starting a journey. To decrease the cognitive load of deciding what trajectory should be executed among the potential ones and consequently limit the trials to be performed by the system in order to meet the sensorial offers coming from the environment, it seems natural to assume that the mind decomposes the What-Where (W^2) patterns into simpler ones more clearly linkable to the current context. For this reason, we assume that the W^2 patterns are articulated, while experience increases, by explicitly adding other dimensions, such as for_what (goal), why (motives), when (timing constraints), what can go wrong or wcgw (obstacles), that allow us to subdivide the set of all the possible W^2 patterns into subsets of W^n patterns, being each subset related to patterns that develop in a What-Where setting characterized by given goal, motives, timing constraints and what can go wrong, i.e., :

$$W^n = W_{\text{what, where}} \text{ (for\_what, why, when, wcgw)}.$$

Only after a goal has been reached or the activity has been aborted before reaching the goal, the mind will be able to execute another W^2 trajectory related to the new values of the conditions (i.e., goal, motives, timing constraints and what can go wrong). However, often a goal cannot be reached without interruptions since actions need a certain amount of time to be accomplished and the environment is not always able to offer the affordances needed for the action. As a consequence, it is useful to assume that a W^n trajectory can be articulated in a sequence of sub-trajectories, so that a trajectory may be temporarily suspended in order to give the possibility to start other behaviors related to other goals, and to be resumed later without restarting the activity from scratch. This assumption is in accordance with the re-description from level I (patterns W^2) to level E1 (patterns W^n) foreseen in the RR hypothesis, and may be expressed as follows:

Hypothesis I: the mind works as a set of cooperating neural subsystems that are able to jointly perform (after a suitable learning phase) patterns to reach some goal. Such patterns initially develop as trajectories in the W^2 space. As experience increases, accordingly with the RR hypothesis, the trajectories are organized into the mentioned W^n setting, where each W^n pattern is subdivided into a sequence of sub-trajectories to allow the mind to suspend temporarily a pattern to be resumed later without restarting from scratch. This not only makes activity more flexible, but it also allows us to recover possible activity breakdown, i.e., to activate some recovery pattern to manage the situation when something goes wrong and then to resume later the activity towards the goal.

2.2   Executing W^n trajectories: a synergetics based account

Turning to the problem of how the mentioned W^n trajectories are executed, it could be hypothesized that these trajectories are stored in the mind as the instructions of a program to be executed by some "entity". The problem of this "cognitivistic" approach is that we don't have any "entity" or processor in mind.

An alternative way is assuming that human knowledge is a repertoire of potential behaviors flexibly activated at interaction time with the environment, i.e., when subject and environment form a coupled system. For many years, due to the absence of a solid theory, this account remained a declaration of intents. Today, thanks to the results of a particular branch of the dynamic systems theory, called synergetics [Haken, 2004], it is possible to demonstrate that people execute in a very effective and intelligent way their patterns without any representation in mind. To show how this may be accomplished we have to introduce some elements of synergetics.

In synergetics terms, the mind, as a dynamic system, is characterized by *macroscopic order states*, e.g., walking, driving, eating, climbing the stairs etc., whereas *state transitions* (e.g., from driving to eating) are due to the change of some *control variables* in common between the current and the next order state. As an example, passing from our usual order state of bipedal climbing the stairs to another order state, e.g., the one of deciding of climbing the stairs by four legged clambering depends on an easily observable control variable, i.e., the ratio between the scaling riser height R and the leg length L: bipedal climbing is possible when the current value of the ratio R/L is less than 0.88 [Scott Kelso, 1999].

Let us note that this approach has been influenced by Gibson's researches (e.g., [Gibson, 1979]) about the perceptual invariants useful for action that are directly observable by the human minds (i.e., without any computation). But it differs from the Gibsonian school when it suggests, as pointed out in [Scott Kelso, 1999], that the action is decided by "something in the mind" able to control the range of the observed values of these invariants. According to synergetics, this is due to the coupling between mind and environment that near to the equilibrium may be modeled by a set of attractor states, i.e., the system order states, that are the minima of a function V that depends on the perceptual inputs and memory. An example of V function is as follows [Scott Kelso, 1999]:

$$V(x) = kx - x^2/2 + x^4/4$$

where x denotes the set of possible order states and k is the control parameter. Usually k depends on the sensorial inputs and on the memory, e.g., in case we have to decide how to climb the stairs, k is as follows [Haselager *et al.*, 2003]:

$$k = R/L + (N_{\text{climb}} - N_{\text{clamb}})S$$

where N_{climb} and N_{clamb} are, respectively, the number of times we have more or less recently climbed the stairs by bipedal climbing and by four legged clambering, whereas S depends on the perceptual characteristics of the observer.

Coming back to the patterns described by the W^n trajectories, in synergetics terms the sensory inputs, in the sequence indicated by the mentioned trajectory, are the control variables to be afforded by the subject to proceed towards the goal. Usually reaching the goal implies to pass through several order states, e.g., "to go to office" could be implemented by the sequence: a) driving the car, b) parking and c) entering into the office. Each order state polarizes the myriads of neurons involved in an activity and emerges as a behavior associated to a specific W^n sub-trajectory. Therefore passing from an order-state to the next one depends on the value of the control variables characterizing the sub-trajectories related to such states. A small example will clarify how the synegetics approach may be used to model the execution of the W^n trajectories without processor neither representations in mind.

Let us consider a driver entering into a service station of a highway to go to the restaurant. A possible pattern to follow, in W^n terms, is given by the trajectory drawn in Figure 2 where a view-centered reference system is assumed for encoding the space. The order variables involved in this plane and related sub-trajectories are shown in Table 1. Sometimes an order state implies the execution of only one control action (e.g., finding a restaurant implies the only action of seeing from the entrance if it is present or not), sometimes it requires the execution of more than one control action (e.g., approaching the restaurant implies to control the distance and the car velocity).

Order Variables (W^2 sub-trajectory)	Control variables
1 - Finding a restaurant	Existence of a building having some features
2 - Parking near the restaurant	Distance from the building and car velocity
3 - Finding a parking area (PA)	Existence of an area having some features
4 - Parking in PA	Distance from PA and car velocity
5 - Entering into the restaurant	Distance from the restaurant
6 - Leaving the service station	Distance from the exit and car velocity

To clarify how the control variables may determine the passage from one order state to another one, let us consider the first step of the mentioned W^n trajectory, i.e., finding a restaurant. Assuming that in the driver's experience, the restaurants, if any, are located at the border of the station as distant as possible from both the station entrance and the exit, the most likely trajectories are the one that have a vertex into the area A in Figure 2. But what is the decision of the driver if a building similar to a restaurant is located in an area partially within A and partially outside denoted B in Figure 2? Will s/he try to park the car to go inside the building or will she/he leave the station believing that the station is not provided with a restaurant? Applying the dynamic systems approach, it is easy to find that: a) if the building is located in the area A, then the driver will park the car, b) if the building is located outside the area A + B, then the driver will leave the station, c) if the building is located inside B, then the driver will park if $N_A > N_{A+B}$, i.e., if the number of times N_A the

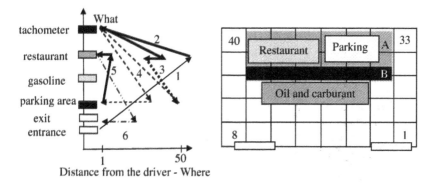

Figure 2. Decomposition of a trajectory into sub-trajectories related to order states (on the left). Layout of the service station pointing out the areas A and B used by the driver to decide if the station is provided with a restaurant (on the right).

restaurant has been found in A is greater than the number of times N_{A+B} the subject encountered a station not provided with a restaurant. This is due to a sort of hysteresis effect induced by the memory on the evaluation of the current context [Haselager et al., 2003]. Since human behaviors always show some hysteresis depending on the number of times they have been followed in previous similar contexts, "how frequently the patterns have been experimented" may be a way to measure the memory of the system without entering in any implementation details. This variable behave as an internal control variable that may influence the action too by amplifying or reducing the perceived sensorial inputs. Analogous considerations may be made to find the critical values of the other control variables.

3   The creative mind

The creative process cannot be explained by using the W^n patterns hypothesis alone. In fact this process seems to be understood more suitably as a process that develops according to a re-representation chain, as suggested by the revised RR hypothesis proposed in [Oxman, 1997], and [Faro and Giordano, 2000], that starts from a initial rough solution or sketch and evolves towards the final solution by a step by step procedure where a tentative solution (i.e., a tentative pattern) of each step is transformed into a better one by applying a suitable *"knowledge schema", i.e., a set of relevant patterns that favor a new interpretation of the problem* and consequently address a more advanced solution. In general, we assume that such multiple relevant patterns may be evoked by using notational, discursive or sketching systems [Goel, 1995]. Thus, for example, designing a new table by taking into account a "Swedish table" simply means to have in mind several patterns that cohere with the properties of such Swedish style and contribute, in the way we will show later, to the creation of the new design. This operative/constructive way of defining a "knowledge schema" is in accordance with the non-symbolic nature of the mind but it needs the existence of some patterns classification of the mind as follows:

Hypothesis II: the mind is founded on two spaces: the activity space (W^n space) consisting of all the activity patterns coded in the mind and the ontological space (O^n space) consisting of all the ontologies or schemas (e.g., task ontologies for system specifications, layout ontologies and so on) emerging from the classes obtained by classifying these patterns according to the relations existing between them [Faro and Giordano, 1998]. Examples of specific task ontologies are: seat reservation, club registration, dining at a restaurant and so on, whereas specific ontologies that govern the architectural 2D drawings may be circular disposition, axial symmetry and so on.

To understand why and how the brain "takes note" of relations between patterns that are at the basis of the above classification, it is enough to recall what happens when one tries to recover some fault. One of the first things the mind does is to try to apply the same actions followed in a similar previous case, i.e., the present pattern is influenced by a similar one. Similarity is one of the strategies that can be adopted, in fact other strategies may be taken into account, e.g., the actions to be performed may depend on the objects available for recovering the fault, the experience of the available consultants, and so on. In Minsky's terms [Minsky, 1988] experience is organized by knowledge lines (K-Lines) that link in the memory cases having some thing in common.

In any case, the present case is solved with the help of some other cases that influence in various way the current problem activity [Faro *et al.*, 1997]. Case-based reasoning (CBR) was the first approach aiming at reusing experience for producing a new artifact by suitably indexing the cases contained in an electronic memory [Kolodner, 1993]. Each index could be considered more or less a K-Line among several cases. Selecting more K-lines simultaneously produces the retrieval of a set of cases representing the experience needed for solving the problem at hands with high precision. In the paper we assume that the mind reaches a similar result by applying its innate ability of classifying patterns as follows:

Hypothesis III: the mind classifies the activity patterns by a neural mechanism in an unsupervised way. Each pattern may belong to several classes with a different degree. The number of classes is not fixed a-priori. It is found iteratively: the total number of classes may be conveniently increased by one if the passage from N to $N + 1$ classes produces an increase in the linkage energy.

Representing the patterns as nodes whose coordinates are the class membership degrees with respect to an N-dimensional setting having the classes as axes (as shown in Figure 3), maximizing the linkage energy might be obtained by imposing that $\sum d_i/N$ has to be the minimum, being d_i the distance from the axis i of the patterns belonging to the class i with a significant degree (e.g., > 0.5).

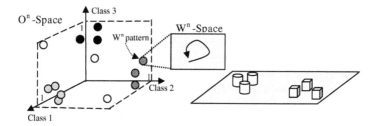

Figure 3. Physical and conceptual spaces respectively on the right and on the left.

All the mentioned hypotheses concerning the basic cognitive mechanisms governing human activity and reasoning and their neural implementation derive from having assumed that the mind is a neural machinery able to organize patterns in spaces in accordance with the "spatialization of form" hypothesis, expressed in different ways in the literature (e.g., [Lakoff, 1987], [Faro and Giordano, 2000] and [Gardenfors, 2000]). This hypothesis claims that the structure of the brain has to be understood in terms of physical spatial schemata (e.g., center-periphery, front-back, etc.) as the ones used in the W^n space, and a metaphorical mapping into a conceptual space such as the above O^n space.

Let us note that this picture differs from the one proposed by Thelen because she admits that classifying objects in different groups in the physical space has a symbolic value that we may appreciate non-linguistically and without having any symbols in mind as drawn in Figure 3b, but she does not mention the possibility of classifying brain patterns into patterns of patterns as shown in Figure 3a, most likely because there is no entity in mind able to "read" the mentioned classification. However, patterns classification may be effective for supporting action and reasoning even if there is no entity in mind. In fact, in accordance with Dreyfus et alii (e.g., [Dreyfus, 1998]) we assume that mind-situation is a coupled system in which the mind may model the environment according to the desired patterns and, on the other hand, the environment may force the mind to use/modify relevant patterns, if any, or to form new ones for managing the current situation. In this sense, human cognition is a dynamic system and the patterns are stable states of the system under certain conditions: changing conditions involve changing states. Therefore human mind is intermittently engaged on several patterns that we assume belonging to the areas of the O^n space activated by the current situation until a pattern prevails as the one indicated by the most stable W^n pattern depending on the conditions. This "attention process" is influenced by the environment but it may be sustained autonomously by the people according to their desires and often without any particular goal in mind. Exploration by freely focusing the areas of these spaces is very important to learn how to let regularities emerge, as is explained by the following fourth hypothesis.

Hypothesis IV: the problem at hand and some external representation (e.g, formulas or sketching) address the attention (in the above sense) towards some area of the O^n space that contains patterns that are relevant to the present situation (e.g., some commonality in goals or motives, more or less the same actors or objects involved, and so on).

From the previous hypothesis we may assume that we have several relevant patterns active in mind when we are creating a new pattern. But how do we create a new pattern? Here we claim that the new pattern, compatibly with the notion of neural darwinism proposed by Edelman (e.g., [Edelman, 1992]), emerges from selecting and synchronizing mini-patterns evaluated with respect to some fitness function. For example, in a design context the fitness function could be to guarantee the highest security degree when specifying an alarm procedure of an industrial plant, or to keep the user cognitive load to a minimum when specifying an interactive procedure of a business system, and so on. In Thagard's terms [Thagard, 2000], the new pattern is obtained by combining and recombining existing mini-patterns in such a way to obtain a pattern that reaches its goal by cohering (as much as possible) with the patterns belonging to the classes relevant for the problem at hand. For this reason we advance the following hypothesis:

Hypothesis V: a new pattern is created "genetically" by cross-over and mutation of relevant existing patterns. Cross-over may take into account either the feature bundle or the prototype of the classes to which the relevant patterns belong to (i.e., "knowledge schema"). The fitness function depends on the problem at hand.

It is important to note that combining and recombining mini-patterns to obtain a new patters results also in an external re-representation activity. However, this re-re-representation activity is not a process at a symbolic level, as the one Karmiloff-Smith assumes to arise at level E2 and E3 of her developmental theory, rather it derives from the genetic process of recombining patterns to produce new ones and aims at reinforcing the attention towards this recombining process.

To augment the recall of individuals patterns that may be useful to the mentioned genetic process, it may be useful "refocusing" the O^n space in search of other relevant patterns to "best fit" the prefixed design goal according to the following hypothesis:

Hypothesis VI: to effectively sustain the genetic process of the creation of a new pattern we assume that the we are able to relax or reinforce the relations or links between the patterns in mind so that old classes (primary knowledge schema) may disappear and new classes may emerge (secondary knowledge schema). We call the overall activity of extracting primary and secondary schema respectively as framing and re-framing the memory.

Although these new classes correspond to less experienced schema, they can be useful for the creation process too, especially for finding innovative solutions. Most likely, this ability, which has some points in contact with the cognitive flexibility theory proposed by Spiro in [Spiro *et al.*, 1988], is favored by the attitude or by the practice of exploring the O^n and W^n spaces.

4 Creative processes, social context and electronic tools

According to the previous hypotheses the creative process makes use of both the external representations and the experience coded in the mind in terms of patterns and "knowledge schema" which emerge from the pattern organization in classes. Thus designers invent new designs by re-representing their initial sketching or drawing in order to meet prefixed design requirements. This is obtained by a subsequent application of design schema emerging from the designers experience. Each schema produces a re-representation of the design that on its turn activates other schema until the design fits the requirements.

However, the distributed nature of cognition [Hutchins, 1996; Zhang, 1997] does not involve only external representations in the form of personal documents but also behaviors and suggestions coming from other people. In other words, many design patterns are activated and sustained by social interactions. For this reason, creative activities often make use of representations produced by other people that are considered useful for the problem at hand. This explains why a person enters into a network of people (community) to exchange representations and related patterns that are taken into account according to some shared values. As an example, design values that are typically shared in a community of design practice are: user centered design, reusable solutions, reliability and security, and so on. We assume that in the social context the external representations have the following role:

Hypothesis VII: in a social context, the external representations sustain the exchange of the patterns among people together with the values associated to them [Giordano, 2003]. For letting values emerge, the patterns are usually affected by oral or written comments depending on if the network is informal or not.

So the process of recombining patterns to produce a new one (resulting in an external re-representation activity) may be powered by having at disposal a good variety of representations of a community that suggest other patterns to reuse and patterns to avoid with respect to the value system agreed by the people involved in the community. Interestingly, a pure genetic system (as the natural one) would be too slow without the elitism implied by considering the best cases and the social variety that avoids that re-representation chain remains trapped within local minima [Faro and Giordano, 2003].

A first example of creating an electronic tool that sustains the creative process of a community, according to all the hypotheses advanced in the paper, is the STT (Story Telling Theory) based environment [Faro and Giordano, 1996] where the designs produced by novices are stored in an electronic shared memory. These designs are subdivided in modules; each module has a narrative structure that allows the novices to describe the specifications by W^n patterns. The designs are classified by an artificial neural agent according to the influence links existing between them. The links are inserted by the students together with some comments that point out what part and why they have reused of the designs from which they took inspiration. Patterns less frequently used are eliminated periodically from the memory.

5   Evidences and concluding remarks

In this section we show some evidence of the proposed account of the creative processes by illustrating the behavior of the novice designers that have learned system design in our University courses by using the mentioned STT environment. These evidences, reported in the following table, derive from having observed the learners at work and mainly aim at clarifying the hypotheses rather than at providing a rigorous verification of them. In the table below the term *concept* is used as a synonym of the term *knowledge schema* introduced above.

Hp.1	Situations or cases are coded by extended What-Where Patterns	Learners prefer to specify the objects within a narrative scheme consisting of extended dimensions. This will allow them to focus their attention to specific tasks and sub-tasks, and lets task semantics to be clearly expressed.
Hp.2	Patterns are classified by a spatial setting depending on how they influence each others	Learners request cases by indicating the task ontology they have to study or some "near" ontology thus expressing their preferences by a spatial metaphor. As an example those interested in the restaurant reservation are also satisfied by a case dealing with a medical visit reservation. Sometimes learners are interested in cases that have a good score or a positive peer review, thus pointing out that cases are linked in their mind according to different reasons or influences.
Hp.3	Classification lets ontologies or concepts emerge while each pattern exemplifies more than one concepts	Cases are understood by the learners as belonging with a certain degree to different task ontologies. As an example a restaurant reservation made by internet may belong to the e-commerce ontology too, even if the reservation does not imply any payment by internet.

Hp.4,5,6	Creative processes are based on a revisited version of RR approach implying classification and re-classification of memory to let primary and secondary concepts emerge. Cross-over and mutation of the relevant patterns produce a new solution.	Each new design clearly shows the initial patterns that have inspired the creative process. The learners often use intermediate representations to point out how their design was obtained. Let us note that the final pattern is not only due to the cross-over of the existing patterns but it derives also by a mutation due to the elements the learners introduce in the new designs coming from the lectures or belonging to their personal experience.
Hp.7	Patterns and concepts are exchanged between people of a community according to the values agreed. An evolutionary process takes place towards patterns that best fit the values of the community.	The above evolutionary process is more evident at the social level since all the artifacts are stored in an explicit memory of the community (e.g., the personal student libraries, the school library, an electronic datastore). Ethnographic and analytical studies performed by the authors [Faro and Giordano, 2003] support the genetic nature of the creative process of a community where cross-over and mutation mainly involve the external representations.

With respect to the existing approach to cognition the paper has the merit of posing a model of how the mind works that avoids to assume too much about the internal structure of the mind. The only hypotheses about the internal structure are that mind memorizes the observations and actions by global patterns in a flexible way after a learning phase, and that such patterns are organized in the mind according to a spatial metaphor so that more than one pattern is initially available to find a new pattern most suitable to a given context. Such two meta-cognitive abilities are hypothesized that operate in two interconnected spaces to sustain the developmental nature of human creativity: one is based on articulated procedural patterns that support cognitive flexibility (levels I and E1 of RR approach), the other supports symbolic reasoning without symbols in the mind (revised levels E2 and E3 of the RR approach) by using the ordering introduced among the patterns in a conceptual space due to their mutual influences (similarity, analogy and so on).

The same mechanism assumed by the dynamic systems approach when different order states are believed possible, it is here assumed for having simultaneously active more than one pattern. The most stable pattern that synchronizes the internal neural groups dedicated to specific tasks and the environment (stimuli, representations, language) is activated dynamically. Creation of a new pattern means to select mini-patterns coming from more or less coherent existing patterns to give rise (by combining and recombining them) to a new pattern that corresponds to some new goal and coheres, as much as possible, with the experience relevant for the problem at hands. No entity is assumed in the mind, but, accordingly to the distributed nature of cognition, a mind-environment coupling is hypothesized where individual and social representations, and values play an important role for sustaining both sensory motor behaviors and conceptual cognition.

BIBLIOGRAPHY

[Dreyfus, 1998] H.L. Dreyfus. Intelligence without representation, 1998.
    http://www.hfac.uh.edu/cogsci/index.html.
[Edelman, 1992] G.M. Edelman. *Bright Air, Brilliant Fire: On the Matter of the Mind).* HarperCollins Publishers, 1992.
[Faro and Giordano, 1996] A. Faro and D. Giordano. Story telling reasoning to learn information systems design. In P. Brna, A. Paiva, and J. Self, editors, *EuroAIED Conference on Artificial Intelligence in Education*, Lisbon, 1996.
[Faro and Giordano, 1998] A. Faro and D. Giordano. Concept formation from design cases. *Knowledge Based Systems Journal*, 7–8, 1998. Elsevier.
[Faro and Giordano, 2000] A. Faro and D. Giordano. From individual to distributed mind in creative design (the re-representation hypothesis revised). In *Conference of the Society for the study of Artificial Intelligence and Simulated Behavior AISB-2000*, University of Birmingham, 2000.
[Faro and Giordano, 2003] A. Faro and D. Giordano. Design memories as evolutionary systems (socio-technical architecture and genetics). In *IEEE Conference on Systems, Man and Cyernetics*, Washington, 2003.
[Faro et al., 1997] A. Faro, D. Giordano, and C. Santoro. In search of web forms. In *Proc. Webnet 97 Toronto AACE*, 1997. Best paper award.
[Gardenfors, 2000] P. Gardenfors. *Conceptual Spaces: The Geometry of Thought).* MIT Press, 2000.
[Gibson, 1979] J.J. Gibson. *The Ecological Approach to Visual Perception.* Houghton–Mifflin, Boston, 1979.
[Giordano, 2003] D. Giordano. Learning by sharing values in a virtual community of practice (a case study). In *Proc. of the Int. Conf. on Multimedia and ICT in Education, M-ICTE2003*, Badajoz, Spain, 2003.
[Goel, 1995] V. Goel. *Sketches of Thought.* The MIT Press, Cambridge, Massachusetts, 1995.
[Haken, 2004] H. Haken. *Synergetics.* Springer Verlag, 2004.
[Haselager et al., 2003] W.F.G. Haselager, R.M. Bongers, and I. Van Rooij. Cognitive science, representations and dynamical systems theory. In W. Tschacher and J.P. Dauwalder, editors, *The Dynamical Systems Approach to Cognition.* World Scientific, 2003.
[Hutchins, 1996] E. Hutchins. *Cognition in the Wild.* MIT Press, 1996.

[Karmiloff-Smith, 1999] A. Karmiloff-Smith. *Beyond Modularity: A Developmental Perspective on Cognitive Science).* MIT Press, 1999.

[Kolodner, 1993] J. Kolodner. *Case Based Reasoning.* Morgan Kaufmann, 1993.

[Kosslyn et al., 1990] S.M. Kosslyn, R.A. Flynn, J.B. Amsterdam, and G. Wang. Components of high level vision: a cognitive neuroscience analysis and accounts of neurological syndromes. *Cognition,* 34(3):203–77, 1990.

[Lakoff, 1987] G. Lakoff. *Women, Fire and Dangerous Things: What Categories Reveal about the Mind.* The Chicago University Press, 1987.

[Minsky, 1988] M. Minsky. *The Society of Mind.* Simon & Schuster, New York, 1988.

[Oxman, 1997] R. Oxman. Design by re-representation: a model of visual reasoning in design. *Design studies,* 18(4), 1997. Elsevier.

[Scott Kelso, 1999] J.A. Scott Kelso. *Dynamic Patterns.* MIT Press, 1999.

[Spiro et al., 1988] R.J. Spiro, R.L. Coulson, P.J. Feltovich, and D. Anderson. Cognitive flexibility theory: Advanced knowledge acquisition in ill-structured domains. In V. Patel, editor, *Proceedings of the 10^{t}h Annual Conference of the Cognitive Science Society.* Erlbaum Associates, 1988.

[Thagard, 2000] P. Thagard. *Coherence in Thought and Action.* MIT Press, 2000.

[Thelen and Smith, 1988] E. Thelen and L. Smith. *A Dynamic Systems Approach to the Development of Cognition and Action.* MIT Press, 1988.

[Ungerleider and Miskhin, 1982] L. Ungerleider and M. Miskhin. Two cortical visual systems. In D. Ingle, R. Mansfield, and M. Goodale, editors, *Analysis of Visual Behavior.* MIT Press, 1982.

[Zhang, 1997] J. Zhang. The nature of external representations in problem solving. *Cognitive Science,* 21(2):179–217, 1997.

Alberto Faro
Dipartimento di Ingegneria Informatica e delle Telecomunicazioni
University of Catania, Catania, Italy
Email: `Alberto.Faro@diit.unict.it`

Daniela Giordano
Dipartimento di Ingegneria Informatica e delle Telecomunicazioni
University of Catania, Catania, Italy
Email: `dgiordan@diit.unict.it`

Questioning External and Internal Representation
The Case of Scientific Models

TARJA KNUUTTILA AND TIMO HONKELA

ABSTRACT. This article approaches representation in cognitive science from the point of view of external representation. We ask what it means for something to be representation and what sort of relationship there is between representation and knowledge. We study these questions through a discussion of scientific models, taking the self-organizing map as an example. It is our claim that scientific knowledge is much more performative than the representational understanding of science would lead us to believe. Scientific models are not valued as much for their being true representations of some real target systems as they are for offering us self-contained artificial systems that we can experiment with. This view, in turn, is compatible with the claims attributed to distributed and embodied cognition.

1 Introduction

Despite its unquestioned importance as a central notion in cognitive science, representation has come under repeated attack. The critics of representation have been arguing for a sub-symbolic, non-computational or non-representationalist foundation of cognition. This has been motivated by new methods, above all by those of dynamical systems theory. However, mainstream cognitive science still seems largely wedded to the concept of "internal representation". The reason for this is not hard to come by: computer models of the mind have become central tools of cognitive science and it has seemed that all computational systems require internal representations as a medium of computation. Consequently, minds as well as computer models are thought of as functioning on the basis of internal representations.

So tight is the grip of this representational image of our brains that, as a result of various ways of conceptualizing or modeling our minds, wildly different things have come to be considered as representations. There is no consensus as to whether our minds house something akin to pictures or language, or perhaps holographic patterns. In classical cognitive science, internal representations are structured symbolic states, and discrete

Lorenzo Magnani and Riccardo Dossena, editors, *Computing, Philosophy, and Cognition*, pp. 209–226 © 2005, T. Knuuttila and T. Honkela

units of representation correspond to individual states of the world. The connectionist alternative to internal representation is far removed from the cognitivist one: here we asked to think of representation as something that is distributed according to the activation and connectivity of the whole network.

The obvious question is then what counts, or even worse what does not count as an internal representation? Stufflebeam, for instance, notes that given the right sort of interpretation, any internal pattern activation seems to count as an internal representation [Stufflebeam, 1999]. But does this not make the notion of internal representation trivial – and as such even futile? Moreover, why is it that we seem largely to agree that the concept of mental (or internal) representation is necessary for any account of the mind while, at the very same time, we are unable to say what we mean by mental representation?

Instead of trying to tackle head-on the difficult question of what there is in our minds and how that is supposed to represent the world, we take a somewhat roundabout route here. We ask rather what it is for something to count as representation and what sort of relationship there is between representation and knowledge. We will approach these questions from the point of view of external representation. It seems to us that as long as we keep on talking in terms of internal and external representation, we are justified in assuming that there is some conceptual core common to both. We also assume that since we are more acquainted with external than internal representation, an inquiry into our external practices of representation might help us to clarify that what we wish to affirm of representation more generally[1].

Not wanting, however, just to stay at the general philosophical level, we also study a specific model, the self-organizing map (SOM) [Kohonen, 2001]. With the SOM we try to illuminate how models give us knowledge and what part representation plays in science and knowledge acquisition. We hope that the example of the SOM also gives us an interesting reflexive loop to our argumentation, since in studying cognition, cognitive scientists often build models – and the self-organizing map is one such model.

---

[1] An inquiry into what is involved in external representation seems also to be needed because cognitive scientists have been in the habit of using external representations as evidence of "mental models" in our minds. From the semiotic point of view this step from external representations to internal ones seems too hasty. Granted that there are such things as mental models in our minds, what makes us to think that they resemble the external representations we produce? The cultural conventions and the history and availability of representative tools are more or less overlooked by this habit of blurring the differences between internal and external representation.

2   The concept of representation

The term "representation" has, of course, various uses and a complex semantic history, yet a certain uniform understanding of it seems to run through
the literature. Following this tradition, [Prendergast, 2000], in his recent
treatment of the concept of representation, discriminates between two basic
meanings of the term. Firstly, to represent means to *re*-present, meaning
the literal reappearance of an absent person or a thing or making present
again by means of a simulacrum. This sense of the term extends back to
antiquity. The second basic meaning of the term representation is that of
standing for [Pitkin, 1967][2]. For instance, a present term "b" can stand for
an absent term "a". Thus a relationship of representation is one of substitution. The substitution can take the form of a simulacrum, but it is a form
of making present (in the first sense of the term "representation") only if it
produces an illusion of presence by virtue of being a copy of the real thing.

Representation as "standing for" seems to be embedded in *representationalism*. According to representationalism, a sensing and knowing mind
cannot have direct acquaintance with its objects, but only indirectly through
ideas, which are supposed to represent those objects. Thus knowledge is conceived as an assemblage of representations that reproduce accurately, i.e.
stand truthfully for, what is outside the mind (see [Rorty, 1980, pp. 3–6]).
Representationalism typically makes use of the pictorial metaphor according to which we have true knowledge only if our representations correspond
to, or correctly map or mirror, the way the world is – independently of its
representations. In his *Age of the World Picture* Heidegger claims that it
is indeed characteristic of the modern epoch that it conceives of and grasps
the world as a picture. Everything that is, is only to the extent that it
is set up and represented [Heidegger, 1977]. Writing in the same spirit,
though within a different philosophical tradition, John Dewey has criticized
the "spectator theory of knowledge", the basis of our traditional epistemological beliefs. According to Dewey "the theory of knowing is modeled after
what was supposed to take place in the act of vision. The object refracts
light to the eye and is seen; it makes a difference to the eye and to the
person having an optical apparatus, but none to the thing seen" [Dewey,
1929, p. 19].

Taking into account the strong association between representation and
picturing, it is no wonder that mental representation is often discussed in
terms of seeing and images. As for vision, the recent views presented in
cognitive science testify to a curious marriage between constructivism and

---

[2]Pitkinmakes "standing for" *the* defining property of representation in her historical
study of the concept of representation, which covers both its epistemological and political
aspects.

representationalism, whereas in social sciences and philosophy, constructivism and representationalism are usually taken as diametrically opposing positions. Constructivism denies that the representation and the represented can be differentiated from each other in the way representationalism supposes, and it envisages instead *both* the representation and the represented as being constructed in the act of making knowledge. From the cognitive science point of view, our visual perceptions are often claimed to be constructed, since in perceiving we fill up the "whole picture" out of partial and gappy information given by saccadic eye movements. This constructedness of our vision has been taken to prove that what we see is actually represented to us by our brains. (The adequacy of this melting together of representationalism and constructivism depends on whether or not that what is presented to us by our sense organs and brains can actually be said to re-present something that exists as such independently of our perceiving it). Consequently, it has been reasoned that if already "direct" visual perception is a representation of some kind, then it might apply also to the rest of our mental content. It is not so easy, however, to understand the perceptions of the other senses involving acoustic, tactile or olfactory sensations according to the representational model. If in a dark room one touches a velvety material that one knows is on a certain chair, then what is the internal representation one is supposed to be having?

To be sure, for the cognitivists the internal representations that our minds house are symbolic structures. How have our intuitions of the mental images and the logical structures then run together into a language-of-thought? Building blocks toward an answer to this question are provided by Richard Rorty [Rorty, 1980], who in his *Philosophy and the Mirror of Nature* has given us a fascinating account of how the ideas, attributed to our minds by the earlier philosophical outlook, were after the "linguistic turn" in twentieth century philosophy externalized into linguistic descriptions. In the heyday of analytical philosophy any naturalistic explanations were to be avoided in favor of logical analysis (see [Kitcher, 1992]. It seems evident that the birth of the computer has helped to internalize logically rendered linguistic descriptions by showing how intentional states, understood as (formalisable) reason-giving relations that support the action in the external world, can be reducible to the patterns of causal transitions between physical states [Burwood *et al.*, 1999, pp. 56-57]. The "computational trick" that accomplished this was to devise representational vehicles whose physical, syntactic, and semantic properties converged [Clapin, 2002, p. 13]. In anticipating the further treatment of the epistemic value and functioning of models in science, it is noteworthy that the computer facilitated the cognitivist outlook into the mind *not* by giving a realistic representation of it *but* by offering a device with which it could be demonstrated how material states could bear content. Yet by doing this it paradoxically reified the traditional understanding of knowledge and reasoning as that of internal representing.

3 Models and scientific representation

Even though most of the explicit discussion on representation has taken place in aesthetics and the philosophy of art, the question of representation is perhaps even more critical for science than for art. After all, the traditional way of approaching science has been representational realism, according to which our best theories are (more or less) true descriptions of their real target objects and processes. The truth in turn is analyzed as a correspondence of some kind between a scientific representation and a natural phenomenon. The recent philosophical discussion on scientific representation has taken place especially in the context of models and modeling. This is, at least in part, due to the nearly exclusive interest of the conventional philosophy of science in theories and experiments, at the expense of modeling. As the hypothetico-deductive framework focused on hypotheses which were logically derived from formal theoretical frameworks and then tested by experimental methods, the question of representation did not arise explicitly. The case of modeling is different, if only because models exist in such a variety. Models can be diagrams, physical three-dimensional objects, mathematical equations, computer programs, organisms and even laboratory populations. This manifold diversity poses the question of how all these different things add to our knowledge.

Interestingly, the discussion concerning models and representation parallels that of mental representation. Nearly all recent writers on the topic of models and representation agree that in order to give us knowledge, models have to be representative. Nevertheless, their preferred accounts of representation differ widely from each other [Bailer-Jones, 2003; Da Costa and French, 2000; French and Ladyman, 1999; Frigg, 2002; Morrison and Morgan, 2003; Suárez, 2002; Giere, 2002]. We find this state of things puzzling: why is it that we seem to be so sure that cognition and knowledge have to be based on representation, and yet are unable to agree on what representation involves.

When it comes to scientific representation, the discussion has concentrated on what sort of relationship there is between the representation and the represented. The outcome of that discussion has been that representation is a triadic relation involving either the "users" or "interpretation" (e.g. [Bailer-Jones, 2003; Suárez, 2002; Giere, 2002]). This means a shift away from the semantic, or structuralist, conception of models, according to which representation is a dyadic relation between two things, the real system and its abstract and theoretical depiction. According to the structuralist conception, models are interpreted as structures, the relation of which to their target systems is analyzed in terms of isomorphism: a given structure represents its target systems if they are structurally isomorphic to each other. By isomorphism is meant that a mapping can be established between the two that preserves the relations among their elements. Consequently, the representative power of a structure derives from its being isomorphic to some real system or a part of it.

One of the advantages of speaking in terms of an isomorphic relation seems to be that isomorphism can be given a precise formal formulation, which cannot be done for instance to similarity, which is another candidate offered for the analysis of the representative relation [Giere, 1988]. The theoretical attractiveness of isomorphism vanishes, however, once it is noticed that the parts of the real world we aim to represent are not "structures" in any obvious way, at least not in the sense required by the structuralist theory. It is perhaps possible to ascribe a structure to some parts of the real world, but then they are already modeled (or represented) somehow. Even if we disregard the fact that the world does not present itself to us in ready-made structures, isomorphism does not seem to provide any adequate account of representation. Isomorphism is a symmetric relation whereas representation is not: we want a model to represent its target system but not vice versa[3]. Moreover, the isomorphism account does not accept false representations as representations. Either a representation is an accurate depiction of its object or then it is not a representation at all, which feature does not fit our actual representative practices. Both problems appear to be solved, once the pragmatic aspects of representation are taken into account. The users' intentions create the directionality needed for the representative relation: something is being used and/or interpreted as a model of something else, which makes the representative relation triadic, involving human agency. This also introduces indeterminateness into the representative relation: human beings as representers have to make choices regarding which aspects of a particular complex phenomenon are relevant or useful.

The dyadic conceptions of representation attempt, as Mauricio Suárez has put it, "to reduce the essentially intentional judgments of representation-users to facts about the source and target objects or systems and their properties" [Suárez, 2002, p. 3], whereas the point made by the pragmatic approaches is that no thing is a representation of something else in and

---

[3]This also applies to the similarity account of representation. For other properties that we might expect an acceptable concept of representation to satisfy, see [Suárez, 2002; Suárez, 2003; Frigg, 2002].

of itself. The relation between the representation and the represented has to be created – which is actually a specific scientific achievement, a result of scientific work. Thus, in order to understand representation better, we ought to take a closer look at our particular representational practices. Yet, from the point of view of actual practice, it seems that representation is not as central to the epistemic functioning of models as has been believed so far. In fact, it seems that models are especially valued for providing us a scientific object that can be manipulated and acted upon. This has emerged in various ways in studies in which models have been treated as mediators [Morrison and Morgan, 2003], epistemic mediators [Magnani, 2002], "unfolding and multiplex" epistemic things [Mertz, 1999] and, finally, as epistemic artefacts [Knuuttila and Voutilainen, 2003].

4   Mediation and the independence of models

Morrison and Morgan's *Models as Mediators* [Morrison and Morgan, 2003] has already proven to be an important forerunner in an attempt to approach models in a more practice-oriented way. Morrison and Morgan consider models as autonomous agents which through their construction gain independence from the theory-data framework typical of philosophy of science. In their view, models are comprised of both theory and data, but besides that models typically involve also "additional 'outside' elements" [Morrison and Morgan, 2003, p. 11], which makes them independent. Because of their independency, models can mediate in different ways. Although they can function as tools, scientific models are typically more than just instruments, they are "investigative instruments". Thus Morrison and Morgan stress the importance of the workability and manipulability of models for the scientific endeavor. By doing so, they distance themselves from the philosophical tradition which has tended to treat models as abstractions, idealizations or theoretical replicas of something external to themselves. This is built into the semantic view of models, for which only the "underlying" abstract structure matters. In contrast to this approach, the specific focus on models as independent entities makes us realize that scientific models typically are man-made things that are made out of a variety of ingredients. Even relatively simple mathematical models can consist of a multitude of ingredients. In his study of business cycle models [Boumans, 2003] found that analogies, metaphors, theoretical notions, mathematical concepts, mathematical techniques, stylized facts, empirical data and finally relevant policy views all played a part in their construction.

If mere mathematical formulas can be shown to be complex constructions, the same is obviously true of computer models, which form one of the most powerful tools of contemporary science. Being implemented computer programs designed to do certain things, they do not as such represent any target system in the world – not at least in any straightforward way. The modelers' primary goal is usually to get their models to produce proper output or interesting results. Moreover, rather than concentrating on the structure of the phenomenon of interest, one often strives to "simulate" its behavior. Thus the interest in the inner workings of models is channeled through their performance – one typically wants to know what kind of behavior is caused by certain kinds of features and solutions. This urges us to take a new look at the epistemic challenges of modeling.

The outlook on models as abstract theoretical structures usually assumes that models are constructed by idealizing and isolating the most important features of the target system into a theoretical description of it. However, in most cases we do not know enough about the phenomenon of our interest to be able to proceed in this way. In fact this seems to be exactly the point of modeling, which is only too familiar to modelers of mind. In modeling we strive to build artificial systems which exemplify some of the features or principles on the basis of which our minds are thought to be operating. Instead of being representations of what some external systems really are like, models are self-contained artificial systems from the workings of which we can infer what the phenomena we are interested in *might* be like. In modeling we are working with parallel artificial realities instead of picturing the one and the only reality.

5   Models as epistemic artefacts

Building on the insight that models are independent things, [Knuuttila and Voutilainen, 2003] discuss models as *epistemic artefacts*, which means that models can be conceived of as intentionally constructed things that are materialized in some medium and used in our epistemic endeavor in a multitude of ways. As parts and products of our scientific and other activities, models are endowed with intended uses, one of which is representation. In fact it is typical of modeling that the "same" models and modeling methods are used in a variety of ways as both *tools* and *objects* of enquiry. In their capacity as tools, models and modeling techniques are used largely as black-boxed technologies to accomplish various tasks. However, as modeling methods travel across disciplines, they are interpreted differently when they are applied to different kinds of problems. Consequently, models as tools are usually not transformed into full-fledged epistemic items until they come to embody different kinds of knowledge and data, depending on the scientific discipline in question. On the other hand, abstracted from all these various scientific uses, they also remain a research object for those who are developing the modeling method in question.

The epistemic productivity of models as epistemic artefacts is due to the way the intentionality and materiality of models intersect in their various scientific uses. Models are realized by exploiting specific material media, which influences the way the problems are designed and facilitates certain kinds of reasoning and solutions. Yet the diverse ways models are used and interpreted in scientific activity makes them open-ended and multiplex entities at the same time. Thus we see how the material dimension, which is actually required of models if they are to be "independent" in the sense that they can be applied to other tasks and contexts, is also critical for their productivity. Models often produce something unexpected and they typically breed new problems and lines of inquiry in addition to new applications.

To approach models as epistemic artefacts is to focus on their media-specific constraints and affordances in conveying knowledge. As material-ized things realized in specific media, models have their own construction and ways of functioning. They are not open to all possible interpretations and uses, which simplifies or modifies the cognitive tasks scientists face in their work. This is in line with the recent research in cognitive science that suggests that our knowledge is importantly bound to our ability to construct tools and manipulate our external material environment [Clark, 1997]. In scientific work one typically tries to transform the constraints built into a model into affordances: one devises the model in such a way that one can learn from using or "manipulating" it. Learning is thus made possible through the material dimension of models, which provides scientists a working object. Moreover, the stress on the artefactuality and material-ity of models can accommodate *thing knowledge*, which is often tacit and more bound to local environments and expertise than to explicit theoretical knowledge [Baird, 2003].

Treating models as artefacts stresses their multi-functionality in science and suggests that the links between models and reality are more complex than those who focus on representation only would have us believe. More-over, this approach leads us to consider representation differently than before. Whereas the traditional correspondence approach to representation abstracts largely away from the representative media themselves in treat-ing (a true) representation as an accurate depiction of reality as it is, the artefactual approach pinpoints the mediated nature of our knowledge. This makes visible both the means and processes of constructing and using rep-resentations. Consequently, the question becomes what kind of knowledge we gain through our different artefactual means and how do we acquire it. These are largely empirical problems. It is doubtful that any general ac-count of representation could be of much help in this respect, because it is difficult to see how it could determine once and for all how our diverse representative means can give us specific information about the world.

6   Self-organising maps

Among the specific properties of computer models as tools of science are obviously the vast computational capacities of computers in processing data
and the possibility to implement abstract models on a concrete machine,
thereby making them "experimentable". In fact, the distinct scientific affordances of computer models and simulations have emerged only gradually.
In her discussion of computer simulations [Fox Keller, 2003] notes how computational technology was first designed to meet existing needs and only
later to generate new opportunities and needs. As such she names "the
construction of models of [...] phenomena for which no general theory
exists and for which only rudimentary indications of the underlying dynamics of interaction are available" [Fox Keller, 2003, p. 202]. Unsupervised
learning methods can be seen as one such new approach to modeling that
computing has made available. Whereas modeling styles were previously
representational in the sense that one tried to specify the structure of the
model according to some pre-established theoretical insights, with unsupervised machine learning methods one specifies the operating principles and
is interested in how well the generated results mimic the overall behavior of
the process being studied. The epistemological implications of this kind of
modeling are potentially radical when we take into account the widely accepted assumption of philosophers of science that only structural knowledge
qualifies as proper scientific knowledge (see [Psillos, 2001]). In the following
we try to characterize in a preliminary way the role of self-organizing maps
in our scientific endeavor [Kohonen, 2001]. Kohonen's self-organizing map
(SOM; [Kohonen, 2001]) is an artificial neural network model and as such it
is entirely different from those models that make use of traditional physical
symbol systems. It is an example of a neural net that uses unsupervised
and competitive learning. The network architecture of the SOM consists of
a set of laterally interacting adaptive processing elements that we refer to as
adaptive prototypes. They are usually arranged as a two-dimensional grid
called a map. In Figure 1, the map on the left consists of 32 prototypes (a
4×8 grid) and the map on the right of 150 prototypes (a 10×15 grid). All
the prototypes are connected to a common set of inputs. Any activity pattern on the input results in the excitation of some local group of prototypes.
After learning, the spatial positions of the excited groups constitute the outline of a map. The learning process is based on similarity comparisons in
a continuous space. The result is a system that maps similar inputs close
to each other. The input may be highly complex multidimensional data,
as is often the case in real-life applications, such as in speech recognition

(e.g. [Kohonen, 1988]), recognition of handwritten characters (e.g. [Vuori *et al.*, 2001]), financial analysis (e.g. [Deboeck and Kohonen, 1998] , information retrieval and text mining (e.g. [Lin *et al.*, 1991; Honkela *et al.*, 1996; Kaski *et al.*, 1998]) and process monitoring (e.g. [Simula *et al.*, 1999]). The basic ideas in the algorithmic and mathematical formulation of the adaptation or learning process in the self-organizing map model are the following:

1. For each input sample vector the closest matching prototype vector (often denoted as the "winner") is sought for. The comparison can be based in any distance metrics. There are also formulations in which no explicit distance metrics are needed.

2. The closest matching prototype as well as the prototypes in its neighborhood on the map are adapted closer to the values of the input vector.

For different inputs the changes may be contradictory, but the net outcome in the process is that ordered values for prototypes on the map are finally obtained.

The SOM can be regarded as an artificial neural network model of experimentally found, ordered "maps" in the cortex. Neurophysiological evidence has been found to support the idea that the self-organizing map can serve as an abstract model of some of the fundamental adaptive processing principles of the brain [Kohonen, 1993]. Conceiving of the SOM in this way is compatible with an understanding of scientific models as abstract things, which give a theoretical representation of some aspect or part of a target system. This is not, however, an illuminating way to approach the epistemic value of SOMs. Most researchers developing and applying SOMs nowadays do not consider the original analogy of the SOM to the functioning of the human brain very relevant for their work, if only because they are applying SOMs to areas of inquiry that are rather remote from cognitive science or neuroscience. This is typical of neural networks in general, which are currently being used in disciplines as diverse as physics, economics and linguistics, for example. Rather than being a *model of*, or representation of, anything in particular, the SOM should be approached as an epistemic artefact that unfolds into many different epistemic tools and objects, depending on the task at hand. Representation is just one of the uses models such as the SOM can be put to. Consequently, the SOM can be considered to be, among other things, as (1) an artificial neural network model, (2) a statistical machine learning method, (3) a tool for data analysis and visualization within data and text mining, (4) a model component for some cognitive functions, and even (5) a framework for considering some epistemological questions.

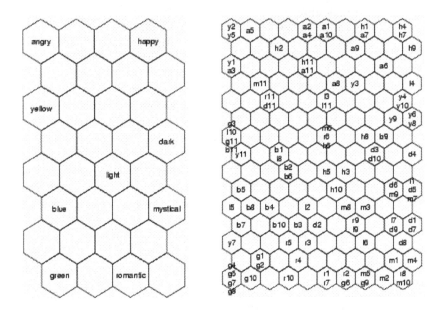

Figure 1. Two illustrative examples of self-organizing maps. The maps are based on data collected as responses from 11 test persons who were asked to assess whether a particular adjective is appropriate in a given context. The judgment was to be given on a scale from 1 to 5. The map on the left is a diagram that shows the relationships between the adjectives: the closer two adjectives are on the map, the more similar are the contexts in which the subjects, in the average, thought that the adjectives would be used in. The map on the right illustrates the use of the SOM to study the distribution of the individual judgments by the persons. The initial letters refer to the adjectives shown on the map at left ("g" = "green", "r" = "romantic", etc.). It becomes clear that such adjectives as "green" or "angry" were intersubjectively well shared, whereas such words as "happy" were more widely scattered on the map. Closer inspection reveals that subject 4 and subject 7 had relatively similar responses. This is clearly visible in their position within the same prototype in the lower left and upper right corner of the map (related to the words "green" and "happy", respectively).

As we are using the SOM here to consider epistemological questions concerning representation, we find that it is helpful in several ways. Firstly, as an example of a scientific model it shows that the epistemic value of a model does not necessarily derive from its being a straightforward representation of any real system. Even for cognitive scientists the SOM is, rather than being a realistic representation of a human brain, a machine that can produce some interesting results. Among these results are, secondly, the idea that a mind need not work with internal representations as traditionally understood but that a mind can be considered as a learning pattern matching device that works with the help of external artefacts – such as external representations. Finally, given that our minds could be in some respects similar to such a device, the SOM is useful as a visualization method for epistemic purposes, which present multidimensional data on a two-dimensional map – itself an external artefact, such as the maps in Figure 1.

7 Internal and external representation

What can be concluded about internal representation from the above excursion into the world of scientific representation and modeling? We suggest that the treatment of external representation is relevant to the question of internal representation at least in two ways. Firstly, we perceive some themes and problems that are common to both external and internal representation. As in the case of internal representation, we found out that knowledge has largely been believed to be dependent on representation, yet there is no consensus as to what representation involves. This has led to various analyzes of representation, many of them insightful, but not really accomplishing what might be expected from them, that is, revealing how our representations can give us knowledge of the external world. The outcome of the pragmatic accounts of representation has in a sense been the acceptance that "there is nothing there" in the *nature* of representation ([Hacking, 1983, p. 145]). If representation is complicated, constructive and inferential activity making use of specified similarities in view of diverse goals, we are far away from any general relationship that could once and for all be established by a neat philosophical analysis. The more complicated and artefactual are the processes in which our knowledge is constructed and mediated, the less work any philosophical general account of representation can be expected to do in explaining scientific knowledge. In the field of cognitive science an analogous finding about the explanatory program provided by the idea of representation can be made:

The most potent challenge to the representation-based understanding comes, we saw, from the cases in which the web of causal influence grows so wide and complex that it becomes practically impossible to isolate any "privileged elements" on which to spin the information-carrying adaptive roles [Clark, 1997, p. 166].

Secondly, in addition to the similarities between our ways of conceptualizing both internal and external representation, our practices of external representation give us some indirect evidence of how our minds function. From the point of view of scientific practice, representation in the sense of standing for is not so central to our knowledge-seeking activities. More often than not, models are considered rather as multi-functional tools and test-beds than representations: for ongoing scientific inquiry their experimentability and manipulability are more crucial than their ability to depict a certain target system accurately or even adequately. The most epistemic insight we get from models is not gained by *observing* ready-made models but by constructing them and interacting with them. All this resonates very well with the recent insights of distributed cognition, according to which human cognition arises in interaction between embodied humans and environment, the important part of which is artefactual, being created and shaped by purposeful human activity.

What is the role of internal representation in this dramatically changed cognitive landscape? Andy Clark is among those who have seriously considered the idea that cognition is extended outside the brain. However, after having admitted that a brain does not waste its time replicating the external media and environment, Clark joins others who still believe that internal representation has a place in cognitive science. The account Clark finally gives to representation, after a lucid treatment of it in cognitive science, is minimal, though. For Clark an inner state qualifying as representation is such that "it is *supposed* to carry a certain type of information and that its role relative to other inner systems and relative to the production of behavior is precisely to bear such information" [Clark, 1997, p. 146].

It seems to us that Clark's account of internal representation is both too deflationary and too superfluous. It does not distinguish those processes cognitive science is interested in from other bodily processes that can also be approached through the metaphor of information-processing. What is more, it remains redundant in the sense that calling these information-carrying states representations gives us actually no resources to tackle what Clark calls "representation-hungry" problems. It is precisely our "ability to track the non-existent (unicorn), the distal (the Eiffel Tower) and the abstract (acts of charity)" that makes us so sure of our capabilities to represent internally [Clark, 2002, p. 38]. Yet there is a big gap between these our experiences and Clark's preferred explanation of representation. It would not be fair to hold Clark responsible for this gap, though. In actuality, this gap is the one between the external and internal approach to what happens in the mind – and consequently related to the puzzle of explanation and understanding that has intrigued philosophers for long. Our internal experience of our thinking just does not easily fit into the external approach to our minds as information-processing devices. The question is whether the concept of representation can fill the gap; whether what we count as representation here can be linked with what we count as representation there? We do not know the answer.

However, considerable progress has been made concerning what part arte-facts and environment play in cognition and knowledge. It seems to us that studies of scientific representation in philosophy of science and in science and technology studies complement the picture of the "natural born cyborg" as painted by [Clark, 2003]. What comes out is the action-orientedness of any "representation", whether internal or external. At the same time it seems that the things we refer to with internal and external representation seem to be very different. Whatever there is in our minds, it seems to be more momentary and processual than our external representations. And this is exactly one important reason why we need such material scaffolding as external representation.

8 Conclusion

In this article we have focused on what external representation actually involves in examining the role of models in scientific inquiry. Moreover, we have asked what can be affirmed of internal representation on the basis of what we know of our external representative practices. What seems to us to be the case is that our scientific knowledge is bound to our specific scientific models and instruments to such an extent, that it does not make sense to talk about scientific knowledge abstracted from the means of making it. Interestingly, our scientific knowledge is much more performative than the representational "picture" of science would lead us to believe. Scientific models are not as much valued for their being true representations of some real target systems as for offering us self-contained artificial systems that we can experiment with and that embody mechanisms that might in some respects resemble real processes at work. The epistemological point of building machines lies exactly in the fact that we do not know how the world is; it does not (re)present itself to us in any obvious way. Thus we have to imagine what gives rise to the natural and other phenomena, and to be able to do this we have to build external representations that are materialized in various media. These artefacts, through and with the help of which we think and perceive, are historical and collective products, so in that sense whatever we succeed in thinking is already an intellectual accomplishment of some others at some other time and place (see [Latour, 1994]).

If our abilities to internally "represent" are thus largely a product of
the use of external representation, there seems to be no clear-cut and fixed
line between what should be counted as internal and what as external representation. It seems instead that cognition is a complicated process of
internalisation and externalisation mediated by our external means of representation. Our way of using metaphors and external artefacts to understand diverse phenomena, including our own minds, testify to this. Since
external representations, and other artefacts, are more familiar to us than
the supposed internal representations, at least part of the plausibility of
talking about internal representation actually derives from our familiarity
with external representation. Nevertheless, one of the aims of this article
has been to show that the things we call external representations do not
primarily function *representationally* – as has been traditionally assumed.
This should lead us to reconsider our understanding of mental content, or
"internal representation". We do not, however, propose that the insights
learned from external representation can be directly used to model that
what is internal. In fact, it seems to us that there is something basically
wrong with the whole idea of internal and external representation, which
somehow makes them analogous to each other. Where did this idea come
from?

Perhaps an artefact, the *camera obscura*, played a decisive role in creating
the problem of internal and external representation. The camera obscura
had a prominent place in the thought of both Locke and Descartes, who
extended the analogy of the camera and the eye to the subject thus placing
the "I" inside the box of the camera and creating a strict demarcation
between what is inside and what is outside. Moreover, what is inside was
approached as being isomorphic to what was outside (see [Bailey, 1988; Ihde,
2004]). Admitting the importance of artefacts for cognition as both means
and models, we can ask whether the new "epistemology machine" (Ihde)
put in place by the computer might eventually make the whole question of
internal and external representation appear dated by questioning both the
external/internal divide as well as the hegemony of representationalism.

BIBLIOGRAPHY

[Bailer-Jones, 2003] D. Bailer-Jones. When scientific models represent. *International Studies in the Philosophy of Science*, 17:59–74, 2003.
[Bailey, 1988] L.W. Bailey. Skull's dark room: The camera obscura and subjectivity. *Philosophy and Technology*, 6:63–79, 1988.
[Baird, 2003] D. Baird. Thing knowledge. In H. Radder, editor, *The Philosophy of Scientific Experimentation*, pages 39–67. University of Pittsburgh Press, Pittsburgh, 2003.
[Boumans, 2003] M. Boumans. Built-in justification, in: Models as mediators. In M. Morgan and M. Morrison, editors, *Models as Mediators*, pages 66–96. Cambridge University Press, Cambridge, 2003.

[Burwood *et al.*, 1999] S. Burwood, P. Gilbert, and K. Lennon. *Philosophy of Mind*. UCL Press, Padstow, 1999.

[Clapin, 2002] H. Clapin. Introduction. In H. Clapin, editor, *Philosophy of Mental Representation*, pages 1–20. Oxford University Press, Oxford, 2002.

[Clark, 1997] A. Clark. *Being There: Putting the Brain, Body, and World Together Again*. The MIT Press, Cambridge, MA, 1997.

[Clark, 2002] A. Clark. The roots of norm-hungriness. In H. Clapin, editor, *Philosophy of Mental Representation*, pages 37–43. Oxford University Press, Oxford, 2002.

[Clark, 2003] A. Clark. *Natural-Born Cyborgs. Minds, Technologies, and the Future of Human Intelligence*. Oxford University Press, New York, 2003.

[Da Costa and French, 2000] N. Da Costa and S. French. Models, theories and structures: thirty years on. *Philosophy of Science*, 67:116–127, 2000.

[Deboeck and Kohonen, 1998] G. Deboeck and T. Kohonen. *Visual Explorations in Finance with Self-Organizing Maps*. Springer, Berlin, 1998.

[Dewey, 1929] J. Dewey. *The Quest for Certainty. A Study of the Relation of Knowledge and Action*. George Allen and Unwin, London, 1929.

[Fox Keller, 2003] E. Fox Keller. Models, simulation, and computer experiments. In H. Radder, editor, *The Philosophy of Scientific Experimentation*, pages 198–215. University of Pittsburgh Press, Pittsburgh, 2003.

[French and Ladyman, 1999] S. French and J. Ladyman. Reinflating the semantic approach. *International Studies in the Philosophy of Science*, 13:103–121, 1999.

[Frigg, 2002] R. Frigg. Models and representation: why structures are not enough. Discussion Paper Series. Centre for Philosophy of Natural and Social Sciences, LSE., 2002.

[Giere, 1988] R.N. Giere. *Explaining Science: A Cognitive Approach*. The University of Chicago Press, Chicago and London, 1988.

[Giere, 2002] R.N. Giere. How models are used to represent physical reality. presented at PSA 2002, 2002. http://philsci-archive.pitt.edu/.

[Hacking, 1983] I. Hacking. *Representing and Intervening*. Cambridge University Press, Cambridge, 1983.

[Heidegger, 1977] M. Heidegger. *The Question Concerning Technology and Other Essays*. Harper & Row, New York, 1977.

[Honkela *et al.*, 1996] T. Honkela, S. Kaski, K. Lagus, and T. Kohonen. Exploration of full-text databases with self-organizing maps. In *Proceedings of ICNN'96, IEEE International Conference on Neural Networks, volume I*, pages 56–61, Piscataway, NJ, 1996. IEEE Service Center.

[Ihde, 2004] D. Ihde. Has the philosophy of technology arrived: a state-of-the-art review. *Philosophy of Science*, 71:117–131, 2004.

[Kaski *et al.*, 1998] S. Kaski, T. Honkela, K. Lagus, and T. Kohonen. Websom - self-organizing maps of document collections. *Neurocomputing*, 21:101–117, 1998.

[Kitcher, 1992] P. Kitcher. The naturalist's return. *Philosophical Review*, 101:53–113, 1992.

[Knuuttila and Voutilainen, 2003] T. Knuuttila and A. Voutilainen. A parser as an epistemic artefact: a material view on models. *Philosophy of Science*, 70:1484–1495, 2003.

[Kohonen, 1988] T. Kohonen. The 'neural' phonetic typewriter. *Computer*, 21(3):11–22, 1988.

[Kohonen, 1993] T. Kohonen. Physiolocigal interpretation of the self-organizing map algorithm. *Neural Networks*, 6/7:895–905, 1993.

[Kohonen, 2001] T. Kohonen. *Self-Organizing Maps*. 3rd extended edition, Springer, Berlin, 2001.

[Latour, 1994] B. Latour. On technical mediation-philosophy, sociology, genealogy. *Common Knowledge*, 3:29–64, 1994.

[Lin *et al.*, 1991] X. Lin, D. Soergel, and G. Marchionini. A self-organizing semantic map for information retrieval. In *Proceedings of 14th Annual International ACM/SIGIR Conference on R&D in Information Retrieval*, pages 262–269, 1991.

[Magnani, 2002] L. Magnani. Epistemic mediators and model-based discovery in science. In L. Magnani and N.J. Nersessian, editors, *Model-Based Reasoning. Scientific Discovery, Technology, Values*, pages 305–329. Kluwer Academic/Plenum, New York, 2002.

[Mertz, 1999] M. Mertz. Multiplex and unfolding: computer simulation in particle physics. *Science in Context*, 12(2):293–316, 1999.

[Morrison and Morgan, 2003] M. Morrison and M. Morgan. Models as mediating instruments. In M. Morgan and M. Morrison, editors, *Models as Mediators*, pages 66–96. Cambridge University Press, Cambridge, 2003.

[Pitkin, 1967] H.F. Pitkin. *The Concept of Representation*. University of California Press, Berkeley, 1967.

[Prendergast, 2000] C. Prendergast. *The Triangle of Representation*. Columbia University Press, New York, 2000.

[Psillos, 2001] S. Psillos. Is structural realism possible? *Philosophy of Science*, 68:S13–S24, 2001.

[Rorty, 1980] R. Rorty. *Philosophy and the Mirror of Nature*. Basil Blackwell, Oxford, 1980.

[Simula et al., 1999] O. Simula, J. Ahola, E. Alhoniemi, J. Himberg, and J. Vesanto. Self-organizing map in analysis of large-scale industrial systems. In E. Oja and S. Kaski, editors, *Kohonen Maps*. Elsevier, Amsterdam, 1999.

[Stufflebeam, 1999] R.S. Stufflebeam. Representation and computation. In W. Bechtel and G. Graham, editors, *A Companion to Cognitive Science*, pages 636–648. Blackwell, Padstow, 1999.

[Suárez, 2002] M. Suárez. An inferential conception of scientific representation. presented at PSA 2002, 2002. http://philsci-archive.pitt.edu/.

[Suárez, 2003] M. Suárez. Scientific representation: against similarity and isomorphism. *International Studies in the Philosophy of Science*, 17:225–244, 2003.

[Vuori et al., 2001] V. Vuori, J. Laaksonen, E. Oja, and J. Kangas. Experiments with adaptation strategies for a prototype-based recognition system for isolated handwritten characters. *International Journal on Document Analysis and Recognition*, 3:150–159, 2001.

Tarja Knuuttila
Center for Activity Theory and Developmental Work Research
University of Helsinki, Helsinki, Finland
Email: Tarja.Knuuttila@helsinki.fi

Timo Honkela
Laboratory of Computer and Information Science
Helsinki University of Technology, Helsinki, Finland
Email: Timo.Honkela@hut.fi

On the Representational Role of the Environment and on the Cognitive Nature of Manipulations

ALBERTO GATTI AND LORENZO MAGNANI

ABSTRACT. This article proposes some reflections about the status and the role of representations within cognition. It compares the traditional physical symbol system hypothesis with the more recent anti-representationalist approach. After a brief discussion about the definition of the notion of symbol, some arguments are proposed for illustrating the role of external structures in determining our cognitive behavior and a discussion is conducted about the nature and the origin of representations. The last part of the article is devoted to illustrate the cognitive role that the manipulations of the environment can play.

1 Physical symbol system hypothesis

When first attempts were made to understand human cognition, one of the concepts that emerged as central was that of representation. A classical paradigm in which the notion of representation grew up was the hypothesis that an agent capable of intelligent action must be a physical symbol system [Newell, 1980; Newell and Simon, 1976].

A physical symbol system is a sort of device that contains symbols and symbol structures in memory and can perform processes upon these symbol structures. In more detail, according to the physical symbol system hypothesis, a physical symbol system and, thus, cognition performs three functional processes that occur sequentially and that are controlled by a central information processor. The three functional processes are the following: 1) a symbolic representation of the environment is constructed by means of a perceptual process performed by a perception subsystem; 2) the symbolic representation that has been constructed is delivered to the central processor, which processes it in order to extract information and to be able to select a symbolic expression that stands for an action; 3) an action subsystem decodes the symbolic description of the action and converts it into a concrete action in the environment.

Lorenzo Magnani and Riccardo Dossena, editors, *Computing, Philosophy, and Cognition*, pp. 227–242 © 2005, A. Gatti and L. Magnani

It is important to understand what the terms "symbol" and "physical" mean. According to the classical definition given by [Newell, 1980], a symbol is an entity that stands for another entity. This kind of relation is called *designation* and its definition, with Newell's words, is:

> *Designation*: An entity X designates an entity Y relative to a process P, if, when P takes X as input, its behavior depends on Y. [Newell, 1980, p. 156]

Thus, a symbol is a syntactic element of a code and can be connected to other symbols to form symbol structures.

The term "physical" refers to the need for a physical implementation of a symbolic system in order for it to actually function and to actually act upon and affect or be affected by the environment.

Following these definitions, we can distinguish three levels of organization in which a cognitive system can be divided: the semantic level, the symbol level and the physical level [Pylyshyn, 1989]. At the semantic level, we have the content of knowledge and the goals that a system entertains. At the symbol level, the semantic content of the previous level is encoded by symbolic expressions. Finally, the physical level is constituted by the physical realization of the entire symbol system; in the case of humans, this level is represented by the biological level.

The postulation of a cognitive mechanism that works by means of symbols and symbol structures strictly implies the assumption that cognition takes place by means of internal representations and [Newell, 1980] considers "representation" as "simply another term to refer to a structure that designates" [Newell, 1980, p.176]:

> *X represents Y* if X designates aspects of Y, i.e., if there exist symbol processes that can take X as input and behave as if they had access to some aspects of Y. [Newell, 1980, 176]

Thus, according to the classical perspective we are describing the central notion is that of representation. Now what we have to pay attention to and to focus on are two characteristics that [Fodor and Pylyshyn, 1988] indicate as the ones that identify classical symbolic models. Such characteristics are the *combinatorial syntax and semantics of mental representations* and the *structure sensitivity of processes*.

Let us begin with the first concept. Classical symbolic theories distinguish between structurally atomic and structurally molecular representations; structurally molecular representations are constituted by other representations that can be either atomic or molecular and the semantic content

of a molecular representation is a function of the semantic contents of its syntactic constituents. According to this perspective, a *Language of Thought*
[Fodor, 1975] is postulated, with syntactic components and structural relations between these components.

The second point is the structure sensitivity of processes. What this assumption means is that the principles by which mental representations are
manipulated rely only on the structural properties of symbolic representations. More precisely, the formal, syntactic structure of a representation
specifies the role of the representation within an inference and can cause
the inferential process without reference to the semantic content. Hence,
the mental operations upon symbolic representations are activated only by
the form of the representations.

So far, we have tried to delineate the main features of the classical physical
symbol system hypothesis. Now we consider the radical different approach
that refutes the notion of representation as the central concept for explaining
cognition.

2   The anti-representationalist approach

Traditional Artificial Intelligence (AI) research has considered representation as the key to construct intelligent agents, that is, agents capable to
act in a way similar to human beings. One of the critiques that emerged
against traditional AI was that it was engaged in modeling high-level human activities such as problem solving in games, in geometry and in other
formal domains, but it did not deal with low-level intelligent activities such
as exploring an environment and interacting with it. In the former case we
have to do with stable domains that can easily be represented in a complete way; in the latter case, instead, we confront a dynamically changing
environment.

One of the most important approaches against the traditional AI notion
of central representations is constituted by Rodney Brooks's work. In this
section we take Brooks's [Brooks, 1991] research as a means to illustrate
some of the main assumptions of the anti-representationalist approach.

Brooks's goal is to construct intelligent autonomous agents capable of
acting in the real world and co-existing with human beings. These agents
are called by Brooks *Creatures*. In order to construct such autonomous
agents, Brooks adopts a different approach with respect to the one adopted
by traditional AI. He creates the intelligent system step by step by incre-
mentally adding the required capabilities. At each step, we must have a
complete intelligent system to be tested against the world.

Brooks states that, by following this procedure, he has reached an unexpected conclusion and has been led to a rather radical hypothesis. The

conclusion is that:

> When we examine very simple level intelligence we find that
> explicit representations and models of the world simply get in
> the way. It turns out to be better to use the world as its own
> model. [Brooks, 1991, p.140]

The radical hypothesis that Brooks presents is that:

> Representation is the wrong unit of abstraction in building the
> bulkiest parts of intelligent systems. [Brooks, 1991, p.140]

Now let us consider the methodology followed by Brooks in order to build
the autonomous agents that he calls Creatures. First of all, he considers
some of the requirements that the Creatures must meet. There are four
requirements. First, a Creature must cope adequately and in real time
with a dynamically changing environment. Second, it should be robust
with respect to its environment, in the sense that small changes in the
environment should not cause a general collapse of the Creature, but only
a local diminished capacity of acting. Third, a Creature should be able to
maintain multiple goals and to change a goal it is pursuing by adapting
itself to the environment and taking advantage of it. Fourth, a Creature
should have some purpose to pursue; it should do something in the world.

In order to achieve these requirements Brooks operates a particular kind
of decomposition of the intelligent system considered as a complex system.
Traditional AI decomposition of the intelligent system is a decomposition by
function, i.e., the intelligent system is considered as composed by a central
system, a perceptual subsystem and an action subsystem. The perceptual
subsystem delivers a symbolic representation of the world, the central system processes this representation in order to select a symbolic representation
of an action and the action subsystem takes the representation of action and
decodes it in order for the action to happen in the world.

The decomposition that Brooks chooses is a decomposition by activity.
The intelligent system is decomposed into activity producing subsystems,
each of which individually connects sensing to action. The activity producing subsystems are called *layers* and the architecture that Brooks's Creatures implement is called *subsumption architecture.*

Brooks's idea is that of gradually building an autonomous agent by first
constructing a very simple complete autonomous system and progressively
adding to it other activity producing systems. At each step, the complete
system that has been constructed has to be tested in the real world. The
activity-based decomposition allows Brooks to reach this goal, because we

have no longer a central system, a central control, but a series of behavior producing layers that act in parallel. Likewise, we have no longer central representations.

Such absence of a central representation and of a central system is considered by Brooks as the main and most important feature of his Creatures. In his robots there is not an identifiable single place to which perception would deliver a description of the world: data from the sensors can be connected to action by means of independent channels that act simultaneously. Moreover, Brooks's robots have not complex representations that have to be maintained: the idea is to use the environment as its own model and to sense it often in order to monitor it. The environment itself would be the "representation" used by the robots and the information used for an action is not maintained after the action is performed.

The absence of a central system is clear, due to the existence of multiple activity producing layers which act in parallel. Each layer connects perception to action directly, without the intervention of a central process and each layer extracts only those aspects of the world that it considers relevant to the action it has to perform. The consideration of the appropriate aspects of the environment and the connection between these aspects and the actions they cause are established and fixed for each layer; therefore, there is no choice to be made by matching, for example, the states of the world with the preconditions of a set of production rules. We can observe, in this line, that the robot system proposed has not an explicit representation of goals from which a central process selects a particular goal that the robot has to pursue.

Now we can summarize the assumptions that emerge from Brooks's research and that he shares with other anti-representationalist researchers. Such assumptions can be presented as follows:

(1) Rejection of a central system that controls peripheral subsystems and processes representations.

(2) Rejection of the need for representations of the world.

(3) Tendency to use the world as its best "representation".

(4) Rejection of the need for explicit representations of the goals.

3   Internal or external?

Brooks presents his robots as an example of intelligent systems that have no representation at all and that are not symbolic. Creatures would not be physical symbol systems. But not all of the researchers agree with this description of Brooks's Creatures.

At the implementational level, each layer of control in Brooks's robots is constituted by a network of finite state machines that send numerical information to each other. Now, after having analyzed the description of the way Brooks's Creatures function, Vera and [Vera and Simon, 1993] make the following assertion:

> Brooks's Creatures are very good examples of orthodox symbol systems: Sensory information is converted to symbols which are then processed and evaluated in order to determine the appropriate motor symbols that lead to behavior. [Vera and Simon, 1993, p. 34]

The reason why Vera and Simon treat Brooks's Creatures as symbol systems is that they adopt a definition of the notion of "symbol" which is different from the one adopted by other researchers who follow the physical symbol system hypothesis. [Touretzky and Pomerleau, 1994], for example, trying to refine the definition of the notion of symbol in order to give the physical symbol systems their own special status and referring to [Harnad, 1990], define symbols as follows:

- Symbols have arbitrary shapes unrelated to their meanings.
- Symbol structures are recursively composable by rule, forming a combinatorial representation. [Touretzky and Pomerleau, 1994, p. 346]

As a consequence, Touretzky and Pomerleau consider all of the analog representations as non-symbolic. In contrast, the notion of symbol used by Vera and Simon in their article is a broader one. The definition of the term "symbol" that they use is the one that defines a symbol as an entity that refers to or represents something. What is important for Vera and Simon is the relationship of denotation and not the features of this relationship, whether arbitrary or analogical [Vera and Simon, 1994].

Vera and Simon's approach about symbols, an approach that includes as symbolic also internal representations which take an analogical relationship with their external referents, makes us ask ourselves about the role of external environment and external structures in cognition. A good point of departure, according to us, is the theoretical discussion that [Vera and Simon, 1993] conduct about the concept of *affordance*.

This concept was coined by Gibson [Gibson, 1977; Gibson, 1979]. In Gibson's definition, an affordance is a property of things of the environment which is relevant relative to the action that an agent has to accomplish in that environment and which constitutes, therefore, an opportunity for that action to take place. According to Gibson's view, the affordances are invariants of the environment that can be directly "picked up" without any internal processing.

Gibson's approach is criticized by [Vera and Simon, 1993]. The two researchers argue that the affordance is not simply a property of the environment. The functional role played by a physical situation (i.e., the affordance) is the result of an elaborate symbolic perceptual process in which a translation into a functional language occurs of a physical situation whose functional significance is only implicit. Hence, the affordance, according to Vera and Simon, is a symbol that constitutes the encoding in functional terms of a complex physical scene. Using their words:

> Affordances are in the head, not in the external environment, and are the result of complex perceptual transduction processes. [Vera and Simon, 1993, p. 21]

The issue is very hard to be solved. Now, in order to make clear the role that external structures can directly play in cognitive tasks, we believe that it is well to state some plausible definitions about the notions of *cognitive process, information* and *representation* and pay greater attention to the "hardware" that implements the cognitive processes or parts of them, i.e., our brain.

We define a *cognitive process* as any process of gathering information and processing it in order to give a response or accomplishing a specific task. The important notion contained in this definition is that of information and this notion needs a definition too. We define *information* as any data that increase momentarily or permanently the knowledge base of a cognitive agent. Information is always given in a certain form and this form of the information can be considered the *representation* of the information. Thus, the general definition of representation that we use is that of representation as the form of the information.

The classic view on human cognition was a functional analysis of cognition and it did not pay much attention to the implementational details as important elements in determining cognitive processes. We do not think that the concerns about the "hardware" are merely details and we do not think that computer programs and computer models are always the key instrument for studying human cognition. The same behavioral results can be obtained by using different types of hardware and by using different programs, whether symbolic in the classic sense or connectionist, but this does not demonstrate that human beings reason in that particular way. Therefore, we think that it is necessary to pay more attention to the hardware that humans entertain, that is, the biological brain.

Human brain is a special organ and its most important peculiarity seems to be its great plasticity, that is, its great capacity to adapt itself to the external structures and the external tools of the environment. According to the neural constructivist approach ([Clark, 2003]; [Quartz and Sejnowski, 1997]), the growth of the brain and especially the synaptic and dendritic growth is profoundly determined by the environment in which we grow. This is to say that the structure of the environment, the structure of our experience shape the structure of our biological reasoning device, that "learning does not just alter the knowledge base for a fixed computational engine, it alters the internal computational architecture itself" [Clark, 2003, p.84]. If this approach is right, on the one hand we can explain why humans rely so deeply on the environment and, on the other hand, we must consider with more attention the nature of external representations and their role in shaping cognitive tasks. To do so, we consider the experimental study executed by [Zhang, 1997].

Zhang wants to examine the role that external representations play in problem solving and, to do so, he considers as an experimental case to study the common two-player game called Tic Tac Toe (TTT). In order to point out the different influence that different representations have on the solution strategy of the TTT problem, Zhang takes four isomorphs of the same TTT game. The isomorphism of the four versions of the TTT is constituted by a series of abstract structures that all the versions share. For our purposes, we will consider two of the four isomorphs used by Zhang: the *Line* version and the *Number* version.

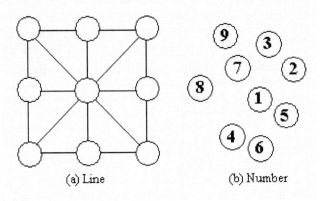

(a) Line   (b) Number

Figure 1. Two isomorphs of the TTT game. (a) *Line* version. (b) *Number* version.

The *Line* version is a minor variation of the original TTT. In this version, the nine elements of the game are constituted by nine circles arranged in a square structure and connected by means of eight straight lines (see Figure 1(a)). The task for the two players is to select the circles in turn by coloring them with different colors, one at a time. The one who first gets three circles on a straight line wins the game. In the *Number* version, the nine elements are constituted by nine numbers, exactly the numbers from 1 to 9 (see Figure 1(b)). The task for the two players is to select the numbers in turn by coloring them, one at a time. The one who first gets three numbers whose sum is exactly 15 wins the game.

As we have said, the isomorphs share some abstract structures and these structures are characteristics of the problem that are independent of specific representations. Among the abstract structures of TTT, we are interested here in the one that is called by Zhang *winning invariant*. The winning invariant is the number of winning triplets which an element is part of. The nine elements are divided into three symmetry categories (this is another abstract structure) and all the elements within a symmetry category share the same winning invariant. The three symmetry categories are, for the *Line* version, the center, the corners and the sides and, for the *Number* version, the number 5, the even numbers and the odd numbers and the winning invariants for the three categories are, respectively, 4, 3 and 2.

The winning invariants, if captured, can suggest some moves and, thus, influence the strategy adopted by a player. This is because an element with a major winning invariant gives more possibilities of winning than an element with a minor winning invariant and blocks more possibilities of winning for the opponent. Therefore, if the winning invariants were present in the environment, they could be considered as affordances. Zhang calls the bias generated by the winning invariants the "more-is-better" bias, that is, the more the winning triplets an element is involved in, the more preferable the move is that chooses that element.

Now, some of the experiments illustrated by [Zhang, 1997], in which human players played against a computer, showed that the more-is-better bias influenced the strategy adopted by the players in the *Line* version of the TTT, whereas it had no influence in the *Number* version of the game. Zhang explains this fact by stating that in the *Line* version the winning invariant structure is externally represented and, hence, is directly perceivable as an affordance in Gibson's terms, whereas in the *Number* version the winning invariant structure is not externally represented and, hence, is not directly perceivable, but has to be internally computed with a very great effort.

But the winning invariant is an abstract structure that is present both in the *Line* version and in the *Number* version. Therefore, if the affordances, as [Vera and Simon, 1993] argue, were the result of an elaborate internal symbolic process that extracts the functional significance of a physical situation, then we should expect that the winning invariant structure is equally captured and has the same influence in the *Line* version and in the *Number* version. But this is not the case. Hence, the results of Zhang's [Zhang, 1997] experiments seem to demonstrate that informational structures can indeed be embedded in the external environment and that external representations can directly affect the internal cognitive processes of an agent. Different representations of the same abstract structures of a problem influence in different ways the strategy of resolution. In particular, external representations seem to play a key role in shaping an agent's cognitive processes, because of the mind's limited capacity in working memory and attention.

An important consequence that seems to emerge from the discussion above and that we want to point out here is that human beings seem to be able to handle many different types of representational structures. With respect to this point, we can observe an important difference between computational machines and humans in the way they accomplish cognitive processes.

Computational machines, whether they use as representational code symbols and symbol structures in the classic sense or they use connectionist networks, they always handle the same representational code, whatever data are represented. In the case of humans, instead, the fact, as we have seen, that formally different representations of one same abstract structure of a problem influence in different ways the strategy of resolution of that problem seems to demonstrate that humans can use and actually use several different representational codes in their cognitive processes.

The neural constructivist approach could help give an explanation of this hypothesis of the use of different representational codes and shed light on the origin of the representations used by human beings. If neural constructivism is correct, since the structures of the environment shape the neural patterns of the brain, these neural patterns bear an analogical relationship to the structures of the environment. Now, the behavior that seems to emerge from Zhang's [Zhang, 1997] experiments and that we can observe in several other situations, i.e., a behavior in which it seems to be evident that humans handle different representational codes, could be explained by arguing that, when we reason by means of representations that originate in the interaction with the environment, we do not perform cognitive operations on the very synaptic pattern, that one is not the format of representation we use, nor do we use a single code, but we perform cognitive operations on the structure of data that the synaptic pattern has picked up in an analogical way from the environment.

Hence, the neural constructivist approach brings us to formulate the hypothesis that it is the structure of the environment that plays a fundamental role in generating the elements that constitute a cognitive representation. If we follow the neural constructivist perspective, we can assume that all of our representations either are external or have an external origin. We would use as format and syntax of the representations the format and syntax that can be found in the various structures that we take from the environment.

It must be clear that our approach does not exclude the existence of internal representations not directly generated by the immediate environment, such as goals, beliefs or, for example, mathematical models. What we argue is that also these kinds of representation may have different formats and that in most cases the elements that constitute them either have an external origin or are abstract symbols which, however, can be internally manipulated as external objects.

Our hypotheses about the origin of representations can give rise to a classification that divides the representations into three types:

(1) Totally external representations, when representations are formed by external elements.

(2) Internalized representations, when representations are internal reproductions of external representations.

(3) Internally constructed representations, when representations are internal, but are formed by elements that have an external origin or can be internally manipulated like external objects.

Since we have stressed the importance of the external world in shaping our representations, we want now to highlight the role that physical manipulations can play at a cognitive level and, in particular, we want to concentrate on the specific relationship between physical manipulations and cognitive representations.

4   Cognitive manipulating

If the structures of the environment play such an important role in shaping our representations and, hence, our cognitive processes, we can expect that physical manipulations of the environment receive a cognitive relevance.

Several authors have pointed out the role that physical actions can have at a cognitive level. In this sense [Kirsh and Maglio, 1994] distinguish actions into two categories, namely *pragmatic actions* and *epistemic actions*. Pragmatic actions are the actions that an agent performs in the environment in order to bring itself physically closer to a goal. In this case the action modifies the environment so that the latter acquires a configuration that helps the agent to reach a goal which is understood as physical, that is, as a desired state of affairs. Epistemic actions are the actions that an agent performs in the environment in order to discharge the mind of a cognitive load or to extract information that is hidden or that would be very hard to obtain only by internal computation.

In this section we want to focus specifically on the relationship that can exist between manipulations of the environment and representations. In particular, we want to examine whether external manipulations can be considered as means to construct representations. We propose a further analysis of the notion of epistemic action in which we make a distinction between two kinds of epistemic actions, which we call, respectively, *sensorial epistemic actions* and *eliciting epistemic actions*. These two kinds of epistemic actions together form the category of *cognitive manipulating*.

A sensorial epistemic action occurs when a cognitive agent gives a structure to its own sensorial action in order to receive from the environment a feedback sensation that is also structured and that contains specific information. This kind of epistemic action creates, in this way, a sensorial representation and the distinctive feature of a sensorial epistemic action is that the action that creates the representation is the same identical action that explores it.

An eliciting epistemic action occurs when a cognitive agent performs non-sensorial actions that are dedicated to changing the configuration of the world or to stimulate the world in such a way that the world gives previously unavailable information. In other words, an eliciting epistemic action gives rise to a configuration of the environment or to a reaction from the environment that can count as sensation-independent representations. Such representations are later examined to collect information and, therefore, the distinctive feature of an eliciting epistemic action is that the action that creates the representation is separate from the action that explores it.

The entire process through which an agent arrives at a physical action that can count as cognitive manipulating can be understood by means of the concept of manipulative abduction [Magnani, 2001]. Manipulative abduction is a specific cognitive process in which an agent, when faced with an external situation from which it is hard or impossible to extract information, selects or creates an action that structures the environment or explores it in such a way that it furnishes information which would be otherwise unavailable and which is used specifically to infer explanatory hypotheses.

An example that clarifies the notion of eliciting epistemic action and that can give an idea of the concept of manipulative abduction is the diagrammatic demonstration illustrated in Figure 2, taken from the field of geometry. In this case a simple manipulation of the triangle in fig. 2(a) gives rise to an external configuration (Figure 2(b)) that carries relevant information about the internal angles of a triangle.

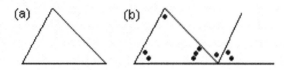

Figure 2. Diagrammatic demonstration that the sum of the internal angles of any triangle is 180°. (a) Triangle. (b) Diagrammatic manipulations.

A good example that, instead, makes the distinction between sensorial and eliciting epistemic actions clear and that we want to illustrate here is the one given by medical semeiology. Medical semeiology is the discipline that studies the connection between signs and pathologies and the adequate medical gestures to detect the diagnostic signs themselves. The four principles of physical semeiology that a physician follows during the examination of a patient are: inspection, palpation, percussion, auscultation [Caniggia, 1994; DeGowin and DeGowin, 1976; Gallone, 1987; Swartz, 2002]. During inspection, palpation and auscultation both sensorial and eliciting epistemic actions are present. In these three semeiological moments, respectively, the physician looks at, touches and listens to specific parts of the patient's body in specific ways in order to receive specific feedback sensations that carry diagnostic information. Therefore, the physician structures her own sensorial actions and construct three different kinds of sensorial representations: a visual representation, a tactile representation and an acoustical representation.

At the same time, however, eliciting epistemic actions are at work during the three semeiological moments we are taking into account. First of all, in all of the three cases the physician almost always asks the patient to change position or, for example, to breathe profoundly in order to evaluate what diagnostic signs emerge in a new setting. These actions are devoted to elicit new information which is immediately later examined and, therefore, they are eliciting epistemic actions. They are of a particular kind because these actions are executed by the patient under the physician's instructions. Besides these actions, during palpation the physician often uses specific gestures to provoke in the patient a pain reaction which is evaluated as a diagnostic sign and this is, again, a case of eliciting epistemic action. Furthermore, during the auscultation, for example, of an abdomen to evaluate the intestinal peristalsis, the physician often touches the abdominal wall in order to stimulate the peristalsis and then listens to the internal sound of the abdomen in order to evaluate if some changes in peristalsis have occurred. So, also in this case and eliciting epistemic action is used.

The percussion moment of a medical examination, instead, exhibits, as main epistemic actions, only eliciting epistemic actions. During the percussion procedure the physician beats, for example, the patient's abdomen with a specific gesture in order to provoke an acoustical reaction that she diagnostically evaluates. In addition, when an acoustically anomalous area is detected, the physician has to mark the boundary of such area and, to do so, she moves her hands on the abdomen, while beating, in search of all of the points that are close to each other and that exhibit acoustically anomalous features. This movement of the physician's hands draws an external configuration and, at the same time, attracts the visual attention of the physician herself toward such configuration. Hence, it can be said that the medical percussive gesture is an eliciting epistemic action that creates both an elicitied acoustical representation and an eliciting visual representation.

Epistemic Actions		Representations
Sensorial Epistemic Actions	Visual epistemic action	Visual representation
	Tactile epistemic action	Tactile representation
	Auditory epistemic action (stethoscope-mediated)	Acoustical representation
Eliciting Epistemic Actions	Interpersonal eliciting epistemic action (language-mediated)	Interpersonally structured representation
	Pain-eliciting tactile epistemic action	Elicited behavioral representation
	Sound-eliciting percussive epistemic	Elicited acoustical representation
		Elicited visual representation
	Sound-eliciting tactile epistemic action	Elicited acoustical representation

Table 1. Cognitive analysis of physical semeiology.

Table 1 summarizes in a schematic way the cognitive analysis of medical semeiology that we have proposed. Epistemic actions are connected to the respective representations that they create and are divided into the two categories of sensorial epistemic actions and eliciting epistemic actions.

Finally, if we consider both the medical examination and the subsequent diagnosis, then we can observe that two important elements previously discussed occur in the two processes respectively: 1) the physician inspects or manipulates the environment (the patient's body) in a specific way in order to gather specific diagnostic representations, thus there is *cognitive manipulating*; 2) the physician compares the discovered physical signs with an internalized representation externally generated by the repeated observation over time of signs of the same kind in order to make the diagnosis, thus we have *externally generated internal representations*.

5   Conclusion

In this article we have initially delineated the main features of the classic physical symbol system hypothesis and we have contrasted them to the position expressed by the opposite anti-representationalist approach.

Subsequently, we have specifically taken into account the notion of representation, we have pointed out the cognitive role of external representations and we have advanced some hypotheses about the formal structure and the origin of the representations used by humans. In particular, we have advanced the hypothesis that the representations used by human agents have not a single format, but can have various formats and that the origin of the representations is profoundly external.

Finally, we have examined the relationship between representations and manipulations of the environment and we have focused in particular on the idea of manipulations as embodied cognitive processes devoted to create representations in interaction with the environment.

Now one possible issue for further research might be whether our hypothesis about the use of multiple representational codes in human cognition can bring to the conclusion that the hypothesis of a Language of Thought in Fodor's terms has to be rejected.

BIBLIOGRAPHY

[Brooks, 1991] R.A. Brooks. Intelligence without representation. *Artificial Intelligence*, 47:139–159, 1991.

[Caniggia, 1994] A. Caniggia. *Metodologia Clinica*. Minerva Medica, Torino, 1994.

[Clark, 2003] A. Clark. *Natural-Born Cyborgs. Minds, Technologies, and the Future of Human Intelligence*. Oxford University Press, Oxford, 2003.

[DeGowin and DeGowin, 1976] E.L. DeGowin and R.L. DeGowin. *Bedside Diagnostic Examination*. Macmillan, Indianapolis, 1976.

[Fodor and Pylyshyn, 1988] J.A. Fodor and Z.W. Pylyshyn. Connectionism and cognitive architecture: A critical analysis. *Cognition*, 28:3–71, 1988.

[Fodor, 1975] J.A. Fodor. *The Language of Thought*. Harvard University Press, Cambridge (Mass.), 1975.

[Gallone, 1987] L. Gallone. *Semeiotica Chirurgica e Metodologia Clinica*. Ambrosiana, Milano, 1987.

[Gibson, 1977] J.J. Gibson. The theory of affordances. In R.E. Shaw and J. Bransford, editors, *Perceiving, Acting, and Knowing*. Lawrence Erlbaum Associates, 1977.

[Gibson, 1979] J.J. Gibson. *The Ecological Approach to Visual Perception*. Houghton Mifflin, New York, 1979.

[Giere, 1999a] R. Giere. Using models to represent reality. In L. Magnani, N. Nersessian, and P. Thagard, editors, *Model-Based Reasoning in Scientific Discovery*, New York, 1999a. Kluwer Academic Publishers.

[Harnad, 1990] S. Harnad. The symbol grounding problem. *Physica D*, 42:335–346, 1990.

[Kirsh and Maglio, 1994] D. Kirsh and P. Maglio. On distinguishing epistemic from pragmatic action. *Cognitive Science*, 18:513–549, 1994.

[Magnani, 2001] L. Magnani. *Abduction, Reason and Science. Processes of Discovery and Explanation*. Kluwer Academic/Plenum Publishers, New York, 2001.

[Newell and Simon, 1976] A. Newell and H.A. Simon. Computer science as empirical inquiry: Symbols and search. *Communications of the ACM*, 19:113–126, 1976.

[Newell, 1980] A. Newell. Physical symbol systems. *Cognitive Science*, 4:135–183, 1980.

[Pylyshyn, 1989] Z.W. Pylyshyn. Computing in cognitive science. In M. Posner, editor, *Foundations of Cognitive Science*. The MIT Press, 1989.

[Quartz and Sejnowski, 1997] S. Quartz and T. Sejnowski. The neural basis of cognitive development: A constructivist manifesto. *Behavioral and Brain Sciences*, 20:537–596, 1997.

[Swartz, 2002] M.H. Swartz. *Textbook of Physical Diagnosis: History and Examination*. W.B. Saunders Co, Philadelphia, 2002.

[Touretzky and Pomerleau, 1994] D.S. Touretzky and D.A. Pomerleau. Reconstructing physical symbol systems. *Cognitive Science*, 18:345–353, 1994.

[Vera and Simon, 1993] A.H. Vera and H.A. Simon. Situated action: A symbolic interpretation. *Cognitive Science*, 17:7–48, 1993.

[Vera and Simon, 1994] A.H. Vera and H.A. Simon. Reply to Touretzky and Pomerleau: Reconstructing physical symbol systems. *Cognitive Science*, 18:355–360, 1994.

[Zhang, 1997] J. Zhang. The nature of external representations in problem solving. *Cognitive Science*, 21(2):179–217, 1997.

Alberto Gatti
Department of Philosophy and Social Sciences
University of Siena, Siena, Italy
Email: gatti3@unisi.it

Lorenzo Magnani
Department of Philosophy and
Computational Philosophy Laboratory
University of Pavia, Pavia, Italy;
Department of Philosophy, Sun Yat-sen University
Guangzhou (Canton), P.R. China
Email: lmagnani@unipv.it

What is Embodiment?

ROY ELVETON

ABSTRACT. The Cognitive Revolution has become its own most thorough critic. Contrasting with the formalisms that characterize the initial models of cognition offered by the founders of the new science of cognition, the present generation of cognitive scientists has made "embodied cognition" a central focus of their work.

This paper will explore the concept of embodiment employed by the robotics research of Rodney Brooks. It will be argued that this concept falls significantly short of the concept of embodied consciousness that would be appropriate for the study of human cognition and experience. Brooks' concept is best understood within the historical context of von Uexkill's conception of the *Merkwelt* as well as within the context of contemporary models of functional analysis. It is suggested that both views of embodiment provide an inadequate framework for understanding important senses in which human cognition is a form of embodied cognition.

1 Introduction

The Cognitive Revolution has had its critics, but none more vigorous than its own self-criticism. Commenting on classical rule-governed models of cognitive processes, Terry Winograd remarked:

> If a model is to be of broader significance, it must be designed to cover a large range of the things we mean when we talk of understanding. The principles should derive from an attempt to deal with the basic cognitive structures. On the other hand, it is possible to devise abstract ideas of the logical structure of language – ideas which seem in theory to be applicable. Often, such systems, although interesting mathematically, are not valid as psychological models of human language, since they have not concerned themselves with the operational problems of a mental procedure. They often include types of representation and processes which are highly implausible, and which may be totally

Lorenzo Magnani and Riccardo Dossena, editors, *Computing, Philosophy, and Cognition*, pp. 243–258 © 2005, R. Elveton

inapplicable in complex situations because their very nature implies astronomically large amounts of computation for certain
kinds of computations. [Winograd, 1995]

Winograd's reservation is echoed by many others. For example, Andy
Clark has asked: "Why are even the best of our 'intelligent' artifacts still
so unspeakably, terminally dumb? One possibility is that we simply mis-
construed the nature of intelligence itself. We imagined mind as a kind of
logical reasoning device coupled with a store of explicit data [...] (But)
Minds are *not* disembodied logical reasoning devices". [Clark, 1997, p. 1]
    The work of Clark's that contains the sentences just quoted is entitled:
Being There: Putting Brain, Body and World Together Again. Clark's "embodied mind" manifesto is representative of the thinking of a growing number of researchers in artificial intelligence and the cognitive sciences who
attempt to develop a less abstract model of cognition by turning to a concept of cognitive embodiment, which, it is hoped, will lead to more realistic,
flexible and workable models of the mind[1]. It is more than of simply historical interest to note in passing that this change in thinking was anticipated
some time ago by Hubert Dreyfus' Heideggerian critique of artificial intelligence [Dreyfus, 1979].
    In one respect, we can trace this effort to rethink artificial intelligence in
terms of an "embodied consciousness" back to an earlier, and more classical,
symbolic AI model, proposed by Holland, Holyoak, Nisbett and Thagard.
Ignoring for the moment the general architecture of their model of inductive reasoning, they reject a restrictive reliance upon the abstract principles
of formal reasoning in modeling cognition and urge the incorporation of
"pragmatic reasoning schemas" [Holland *et al.*, 1989, p. 21]. Unlike more
abstract, purely syntactic reasoning principles, schemas are both context-
bound and goal-directed. The aim is to directly incorporate action and goal
oriented structures into our models of cognition, thus overcoming Winograd's complaint that too much emphasis has been placed upon "abstract
ideas of the logical structure of language".
    However, the theory that I would like to focus on here is the school
of thought that might be termed "robotic embodiment". I will outline
the central features of this approach shortly. My primary concern in the
discussion that follows will be to explore the notion of "embodiment" that
the robotic embodiment theory employs. This task may not be as simple
as it appears. Robotic embodiment proponents advocate beginning with
very simple robotic devices, whose interaction with their environment will
permit the "appearance" of centrally controlled behavior on the basis of

---

[1]As an additional example, see [Varela *et al.*, 1993].

such real, robot-world interaction. Unlike the Holland et. al. model, which begins with central cognitive processes "in the mind" (but processes that are also able to learn from its interaction with the world), robotic embodiment ignores central processes, or works its way up to such processes in a very exploratory, tentative and experimental way. As a result, the initial robotic "embodiments" in question will likely be extremely primitive in nature.

The central question I will take up concerns the concept of "embodiment" that is employed by "robotic embodiment" theory and practice. This concept may be too limited in content to be capable of being extended to human embodiment. This may not be disastrous in and of itself. But if human embodiment is in fact confused with a more impoverished conception of embodiment, then claims such as Clark's that "[...] minds are *not* disembodied logical reasoning devices" must be interpreted with great care. The inference I will draw is that robotic embodiment is best understood, not as "embodiment", but as a straightforward and technically restricted application of functional analysis to organism-world interaction.

The centrality of functional design in robotic embodiment suggests an additional subtlety in the general discussion of "embodied consciousness". It is difficult, if not impossible, to separate the analysis of embodied consciousness from certain qualitative dimensions of human experience. Furthermore, it may well be one of the more distinctive features of functional analysis (in the standard sense in which it will be used in this discussion) to abstract entirely from such qualitative features. If this is correct, it will not be surprising that the functional analysis of embodied consciousness falls short of the hoped for end of achieving clarity about the nature of "embodied" cognition and consciousness.

As the opening citation from Winograd reminds us, the combinatorial explosion of rule-based models of central cognitive processes poses a serious challenge to these models of cognition. It would be reasonable, then, to explore cognitive architectures that attempt to dispense with the computational limitations of vast amounts of central processing. The pursuit of such an option might even allow us to dispense with anything that might resemble Fodor's well-known "language of thought" hypothesis. Perhaps the integrated behavior characteristic of intelligence is the result of the emergence of a certain global integration that supervenes upon a complex assemblage of simpler devices that do not require "representations" (hence both the syntactic structure and the semantic content characteristic of the language of thought) and a computational medium for their manipulation. The concluding section of our discussion will suggest that this might be a misguided strategy with respect to embodied consciousness.

2   Autonomous agency

Rodney Brooks has been at the center of recent efforts to construct "autonomous mobile agents" that function in a goal-directed manner in the real world and in a manner that will effectively dispense with "mental representations" altogether [Brooks, 1997, p. 401]. Hereafter referred to as Brooks, followed by page reference. Since, in Brooks' view, symbolic A. I. has clearly failed to correctly identify the nature of central cognitive processes, an alternative path to artificial intelligence is necessary. The following are essential features of Brooks' approach:

> We must incrementally build up the capabilities of intelligent systems, having *complete* systems at each step, thus automatically ensuring that the pieces and their interfaces are valid.

> At each step, we should build complete intelligent systems that we let loose in the real world with real sensing and real action. Anything less provides a candidate with which we can delude ourselves. [Brooks, 1997, p. 395f]

The theoretical model Brooks embraces clearly follows the lines of a "practical" intelligence in contrast to a disembodied, symbol-manipulating intelligence. It is this conception of the mind as engaged and active that is one of the primary reasons that Clark views Brooks' work as an important implementation of the "embodied" mind perspective. At the same time, Brooks himself is careful to avoid an overly "human" and "perceptual" interpretation of his mobile agents. In so doing, however, and as we shall see, Brooks runs the risk of equivocating on the very notion of an embodied agent, which may of necessity carry reference to features of perceived, as opposed to simply "computed", experience.

In Classical AI "abstraction is usually used to factor out all aspects of perception and motor skills". Brooks argues that, on the contrary, "these are the hard problems solved by intelligent systems" [Brooks, 1997, p. 398]. Since there is no distinction between perception and "reasoning in the real world", the connection between Brooks' mobile agents and their environing world is a direct one, unmediated by vehicles of representation. Mobile agents do not represent their world to themselves in some appropriate linguistic medium; rather do they directly interact with the world, using the world as its own "representation". Brooks' general term for the view of robotic designs supported by this approach is "embodiment" [Brooks, 1997, p. 417].

Brooks' "engineering methodology" adopts the following platform:

A Creature must cope appropriately and in a timely fashion with changes in its dynamic environment.

A Creature should be robust with respect to its environment. Minor changes in the properties of the world should not lead to total collapse of the Creature's behavior; rather one should expect only a gradual change in capabilities of the Creature as the environment changes more and more.

A Creature should be able to maintain multiple goals and, depending on the circumstances it finds itself in, change which particular goals it is actively pursuing; thus it can both adapt to surroundings and capitalize on fortuitous circumstances.

A Creature should do *something* in the world; it should have some purpose in being. [Brooks, 1997, p. 402]

Since we are concerned with Brooks' use of the notion of embodiment and world, we shall not follow all of the details of the various mobile agents ("Creatures") Brooks' laboratory has constructed. The engineering goals outlined above presume that a mobile agent is capable of taking note of certain features of its world that are relevant to its goals. Its robustness and repertoire of capacities are dependent upon its reliably identifying such features despite the environmental noise it will inevitably encounter. As an example of such a construction, Brooks offers the following description of Herbert:

Herbert [...] used thirty infrared proximity sensors to navigate along walls and through doorways, a magnetic compass to maintain a global sense of direction, a laser scanner to find soda-can-like objects visually, and a host of sensors on an arm with a set of fifteen behaviors which, together, were sufficient to locate and pick up soda cans reliably. Herbert's task was to wander around people's offices looking for soda cans, pick one up, and bring it back to where the robot had started from. Herbert did succeed at this task. [...] In programming Herbert, it was decided that it should maintain no internal state longer than three seconds, and that there would be no internal communication between behavior generating modules. Each one was connected to sensors on the input side, and a fixed-priority arbitration network on the output side. The arbitration network drove the actuators. [...] Since Herbert maintained hardly any internal state – hardly any memory, it often had to rely on the world itself as its only available "model" of the world. Further, the world itself was the only effective medium of communication between Herbert's separate modules. [...] The advantage of this approach was that there was no need to set up internal expectations for what was going to happen next. That meant that the control system could both (1) be naturally opportunistic if fortuitous circumstances presented themselves, and (2) easily respond to changed circumstances – such as some other object approaching on a collision course. [Brooks, 1997, p. 412f]

In commenting on this correlation of world and agent, Brooks explicitly refers to the "perceptual world" theory of Jakob von Uexküll. According to this theory, "each animal species, and clearly each robot species with its own distinctly nonhuman sensor suites", will have its own special *Merkwelt* [Brooks, 1997, p. 400]. For Brooks, von Uexküll's notion of the *Merkwelt* delineates a particular environment and its pronounced perceptual features that correlate with the goal-directed activities of an individual species of organism. In apparently believing that the notion of perception in this context indeed represents one of the "hard problems solved by intelligent systems", Brooks' various intelligent agents are functionally designed experimental solutions for an analogous set of problems.

Von Uexküll's theory appeared in 1921. Several of von Uexkill's major works were devoted to its elaboration, including *Umwelt und Innenwelt der Tiere* and *Theoretische Biologie*. There is in fact much in von Uexkill's work that is relevant to robotic embodiment theory. Since Brooks makes his debt to von Uexkill's work explicit, this theory is worth examining in detail. In doing so, we shall turn to an early expositor and Neo-Kantian critic of von Uexkill's work, Ernst Cassirer.

Cassirer, writing in 1928, just a few years after the publication of Uexkill's major works, summarizes von Uexkill's "methodological basis" for the *Merkwelt* theory as follows:

The basic thought behind this biology consists in the claim that access to the different worlds of the individual forms of life can be had only through study of their "organization". If we submerge ourselves in the anatomical structure of a living creature and at the same time make as clear as possible to ourselves the extent of the achievements that this structure brings about, we thereby have delimited the field of its existence and its activities. This organization itself creates the environment of a living thing so that it is in no case a constant but, rather, different for every creature, since its varies with their organization. Just as environmental factors are objective, so too we must take as objective the effects called forth by them in the nervous system. They too can only be determined by reference to the body's structure, and from the outset they are seen and regulated through it. Now the totality of these effects is what we designate as the "inner world" of a living creature, so that – as Uexkill emphasizes – even establishing the existence of this inner world is "the unspoiled fruit of objective research", which "should not be clouded by psychological speculation [...]". [Cassirer, 1996, p. 42f]

This discussion of the theory occurs in the Fourth Volume of Ernst Cassirer's *The Philosophy of Symbolic Forms*, written in 1928, but only recently published (1995). Historically, von Uexkill's program has clear affinities to Cuvier's earlier functional reconstruction of prehistoric species, though now freed from Cuvier's attachment to a restricted set of a priori *Baupläne*. As Cassirer's discussion also makes clear, von Uexkill's analysis forms part of a broader discussion of animal cognition that occurred against the background of early twentieth century neo-Kantian psychology and anthropological theory[2].

Cassirer's own interests prompts him to elaborate upon von Uexkill's view of animal sensation. Cassirer notes that von Uexkill speaks of a "series of excitations" when describing the "inner life" of the pilgrim scallop:

A darkening of the horizon actuates the numerous, little tentacles, that surround the eye and cause them to open up so that the eye's field of vision becomes free. Thereafter the image of an approaching object is produced on the retina. The form and color of the object have no influence on the mollusk, that is, the image on the retina does not serve to cause excitement. This is different with the movement of the image. A movement of a certain speed – not too fast, not too slow – precisely the temps that the archenemy of all mollusks, the starfish Asterias, follows is the stimulus that causes excitement. At this, the tentacles surrounding the eye lose all their rigidity, the compressed water which causes it to swell is forced into the animal and the tentacles flap like long lashes at the moving object. If it is the starfish, then the receptors are excited by the slime and the tentacles are retracted. At the same time, however, the visceral ganglion receives a strong wave of movement and this reacts by moving the locomotive muscle whose quick strokes life the mollusk up

---

[2]Cassirer cites *Hans Volkelt's Uber die Verstellungen der Tiere: Ein Beitrag zur Entwicklunspsychologie* (1914).

and let it powerfully swim away from the dangerous area of the enemy[3].

Cassirer appends the following comment:

> [...] if we begin with a purely objective observation of its organi-
> zation, the animal has a large number of eyes that already reveal
> a very developed organization, possessing a retina and lenses and
> even indicating an apparatus of accommodation. Further con-
> sideration reveals, however, that the influences affecting these
> eyes do not affect or connect up with one another [...] Every
> eye makes use of the general reflex apparatus, which is set so
> that it springs into action from the same excitation that can
> come to it from any direction. Hence, if we say of higher ani-
> mals that they use their eyes, we must say of the pilgrim scallop
> that the eyes use the animal.

I have provided these two extended passages for two reasons. First, as we shall see, von Uexkill's analysis of the behavior of the pilgrim scallop precisely follows the style of functional analysis Rob Cummins called attention to several years ago. Second, Cassirer's comment concerning the functional role of the scallops' eyes highlights the difference between an organism's "seeing something" and an organism's "reacting to something".

Cummins' well-known definition of functional analysis seeks to avoid a host of problems associated with earlier definitions of functional explanations formulated, among others, by Charles Hempel and Ernest Nagle. Since our concern here is not with the history of the various explanations, examples and counter-examples in the dispute regarding the nature of functional explanations, but with identifying an appropriate way of characterizing Brooks' and Uexkill's approach to embodied agents, here I shall simply outline Cummin's proposed account of functional analysis and only remark that it is widely regarded as a useful definition of what a successful functional analysis entails.

Cummins' account contains two important requirements. First, any specification of a "function" is dependent upon a prior specification of a "containing-system" (s) within which the individual function in question will display its capacity to perform a specific functional role. "[...] It will be appropriate to say that x functions as a ϕ in s, or that the function of x in s is ϕ-ing, when we are speaking against the background of an analytical explanation of some capacity s which appeals to the fact that x has a capacity to ϕ in s" [Cummins, 1998, p. 189].

---

[3]Umwelt, p. 151 (Quoted in [Cassirer, 1996, p. 64]).

Second, functional explanations are of interest to the extent that the "analyzing capacities" are less sophisticated than and different in kind from the "analyzed capacities" [Cummins, 1998, p. 191].

The former requirement allows us to reject spurious functions, such as a claim that the function of the heart is to make a characteristic sound, when what we are in fact trying to explain is the heart's function within an organism's circulatory system. The second requirement is meant to insure that we have succeeded in explaining something by identifying the simpler mechanisms and their interrelationships that are responsible for more complex behaviors.

Brook's autonomous agent constructions implicitly follow these restrictions. Although the technology is contemporary, the logic behind the application of the technology has been well rehearsed. For example, Herbert's behavior easily meets the criteria stated above. The "containing system" is just Herbert's soda-can-to-be-picked up environment. The function of Herbert's arm in performing this function can be explained in terms of "less sophisticated" capacities: "[...] Consider actually grasping a soda can. The hand has a grasp reflex that operated whenever something broke an infrared beam between the fingers. When the arm located a soda can with its local sensors, it simply drove the hand so that the two fingers lined up on either side of the can. The hand then independently grasped the can" [Brooks, 1997, p. 413].

The fine correlations between an organism's sensory apparatus and the environment it inhabits is a feature of the biological world noted, not only by von Uexküll, but by Cuvier, Paley and Darwin as well. All have pursued some version of Cummins' functional analysis. It is only von Uexkill, however, who appears to have consciously noted the importance of Cummins' stipulation regarding a "containing-system" for the functional analysis of animal behavior. For every animal, writes von Uexkill, "The stimuli of the environment create at the same time a firm protective wall, which enclose the animal like the walls of a house and keep it from the whole foreign world" [Brooks, 1997, p. 62f]. The organism "floats" upon its reflexive triggers secure "in the immeasurable of the outer world" [Brooks, 1997]. The containing-system is not only the functional relationship holding between reflexes and environmental cues. Given a specification of what this is in any individual case, such as Herbert's soda-can-grasping behavior, we can proceed to an analytical delineation of the sub-processes and sub-functions that enable us to explain their role in the production of the more global behavior. Most significantly, it is equally important that such simpler functions are tightly fixed within the limits of the "world" (*Merkwelt*) in question. Just as an understanding that the proper function of the heart is to circulate blood depends upon a prior identification of the explanatory universe within which our functional attributions can be rendered unequivocal and explanatory, so does the world of the agent/organism require the introduction of an unequivocal *world-limit* in order for our engineering task to be clearly explanatory.

It is indeed just such a *world barrier* that Brooks engineers into his mobile agents. Von Uexküll's technical term for this functional complex was *Funktionskreis* ("functional circle") [Brooks, 1997, p. 43]. It is the impenetrable shell that every organism carries around with it during its entire lifetime [Cassirer, 1996, p. 62].

A quite definite description of this "functional circle" approach in Brooks' hands can be gained from several excerpts of his functional analysis of "Allen", Brooks' first embodied Creature. Allen is composed of three "layers" of functional control:

1. The lowest-level layer implements a behavior which makes the robot (the physical embodiment of the Creature) avoid hitting objects. It avoids both static objects and moving objects – even those that are actively attacking it. The finite state machine labeled *sonar* simply runs the sonar devices and every second emits an instantaneous map with the readings converted to polar coordinates. [...] This network of finite state machines generates behaviors which let the robot avoid objects. If it starts in the middle of an empty room it simply sits there. If someone walks up to it, the robot moves away. If it moves in the direction of other obstacles it halts.

2. The next layer makes the robot wander about, when not busy avoiding objects. The *wander* finite state machine generates a random heading for the robot every ten seconds or so. The *avoid* machine treats that heading as an attractive force and sums it with the repulsive force computed from the sonars. It uses the result to suppress the lower-level behavior, forcing the robot to move in a direction close to what *wander* decided but at the same time avoiding any obstacles. [...]

3. The third layer makes the robot try to explore. It looks for distance places, then tries to reach them. This layer suppresses the wander layer and observes how the bottom layer diverts the robot due to obstacles [...] [Brooks, 1997, p. 410f].

The general pattern of construction and analysis is clear. We have special-purpose computational devices (finite state machines) that return values for given environmental (*Merkwelt*) information and which override or allow the operation of other finite state machines. The interplay of these devices is designed so that a recognizable global pattern of behavior ("searching and avoiding") emerges from their interaction.

Brooks himself is clear that this specification of an embodied agent has nothing to do with what he terms "German philosophy," meaning, primarily, Heidegger. Of course, Brooks is free to define his core terminology as he wishes. Yet, what he describes is sufficiently remote from any ordinary sense of "embodied consciousness" so as to constitute a very technical definition indeed. In fact, the *Merkwelt* as employed by Brooks and the "functional circle" it designates has little resemblance to the "human" "perceptual world" [Brooks, 1997, p. 400]. But this is perhaps already strikingly obvious. As Cassirer rightly notes, "As little as the animal is able to ever penetrate this wall, so little is it ever able to notice it, to 'have' it as an object, as an obstacle" [Brooks, 1997, p. 63]. What goes unnoticed in Brooks' discussion is the constant but implicit assumption regarding the larger, surrounding world of objects available for our experience of which Herbert only "perceives" a restricted part.

Embodied consciousness is aware of a world of *objects*, not just stimuli that are correlated with sensory modules. It is aware that such objects form a part of a unified and continuingly harmoniously perceived *world*, whose essential structure is open-ended and incomplete. It is aware that its world is essentially temporal and spatial. It is continuously experiencing its immediately surrounding world (*Umwelt*) as related to the world in general as a "here" corresponding to a future "then and there." It is also aware that it is able to access its immediate surroundings *kinesthetically*. Finally, it is also aware that the world it perceives is an intersubjective one, containing, among other things, other embodied consciousnesses and cultural "entities" that serve to explicitly express the co-presence of others. Essential to all of these dimensions is the *bodily* nature of its consciousness and the *presumptive nature* of its perception of the world as intersubjective and embodied.

Rather than being contained within a shell that filters and restricts the "immeasurable" world to manageable stimuli, embodied consciousness is open to a world that exceeds it. If these intuitions indeed belong to "German Philosophy" and are worlds removed from the causal-functional engineering of Brooks' mobile agents, it is to this source that we can turn in order to see more clearly just how embodied consciousness is to be understood.

Of greater interest than both Heidegger and Dreyfus's early reliance upon
Heidegger in his critique of AI, is the work of Edmund Husserl on this
topic. According to Husserl, the lifeworld is "[...] the pregiven world. It is
pregiven to us all quite naturally, as persons within the horizon of our fellow
men, i.e., in every actual connection with others, as 'the' world common to
us all" [Husserl, 1970, p. 122].

A great deal of Husserl's discussion of the lifeworld focuses on the "privileged status of perception"[4]. For example, Husserl's introduction of the
theme of the lifeworld in the *Crisis* outlines four important lifeworld structures:

1. *Kinesthetic Processes.* "We soon note that these systems of 'exhibiting
   of' are related back to correlative multiplicities of kinesthetic processes
   having the peculiar character of the 'I do', 'I move' (to which even the
   'I hold still' must be added). The kinestheses are different from the
   movements of the living body which exhibit themselves merely as those
   of a physical body, yet they are somehow one with them, belonging to
   one's own living body with its two-sided character (internal kinetheses,
   external physical-real movements)" [Husserl, 1970].

2. *Alteration of Validity.* "Another extraordinarily important thematic
   direction has not yet been named; it is characterized by the phenomenon of the *alternation of validity* – for example, the alteration of
   being into illusion [...] It is easy to see that the change of appercep-
   tive sense takes place through a change of the expectation-horizon of
   the multiplicities anticipated as normal" [Husserl, 1970, p. 161f].

3. *Horizon Consciousness.* "For consciousness, the individual thing is
   not alone; the perception of a thing is perception of it within a *perceptual field.* And just as the individual thing in perception has meaning only through an open horizon of 'possible perceptions,' insofar as
   what is actually perceived 'points' to a systematic multiplicity of all
   possible perceptual exhibitings belonging to it harmoniously, so the
   thing has yet another horizon; besides this 'internal horizon' it has
   an 'external horizon' precisely as a thing within a *field of things*; and
   this points finally to the whole 'world as perceptual world'." [Husserl,
   1970, p. 162].

4. *Communalization of Experience.* "[...] In our continuously flowing
   world-perceiving we are not isolated but rather have, within it, contact
   with other human beings [...]. In *living with one another* each one

---

[4] *Crisis*, [Husserl, 1970, p. 161].

can take part in the life of the others. Thus in general the world exists not only for isolated men but for the community of men; and this is due to the fact that even what is straightforwardly perceptual is communalized" [Husserl, 1970, p. 163].

Each of these characteristics is an effective challenge to Brooks' conception of "embodied consciousness". The world, for an embodied consciousness in Husserl's sense, is not a circumscribing functional circle, but a horizon serving to incite perception and bodily movement to seek "more" rather than to remain confined to a functionally imposed "less." The mobility belonging to embodied consciousness is intimately connected to the "what if" of a consciousness of the future and to an awareness of the perceptual and experiential possibilities of the given here and now.

This suggests that a sharp line distinguishes the "functionally embedded" (the container-system model of the *Merkwelt*) from the "perceptually embodied". To confuse the two is to mistake a functional-analytical situation for a perceptual-embodied situation. This is not to claim that the former may not in some sense subserve the latter. It does, however, point out the dramatic difference between these two kinds of analysis.

We must forego a more extended treatment of these Husserlian themes that are representative of embodied consciousness. They clearly specify certain qualitative features of our perceptual experience that may not, by virtue of the very structure of a Cummins-style functional analysis, be readily analyzed "functionally". To the extent that a Husserlian embodied consciousness is characterized by the qualitatively experienced states of "mobility", an awareness of "illusion", an "open" perceptual field and a "community" of other subjects, it may fall outside of the purview of a functional analysis altogether. As Ned Block has argued, one of functionalism's basic problems is the problem of just those "qualitative" states that constitute the domain of psychology (whether it be Husserlian phenomenology or more recent psychological and philosophical discussions) [Block, 1980, p. 285]. If Block's analysis of functionalism is plausible, one would not even expect a program such as Brooks' to yield features constitutive of embodied consciousness, for functional analysis dispenses entirely with any significant reference to qualitative states such as those emphasized by Husserl.

To be sure, embodied consciousness inhabits a "world" that can in some sense be said to "contain" it. After all, an embodied consciousness cannot be construed as a worldless cognitive machine. And there may be a perfectly straightforward sense in which an embodied consciousness can be said to be physically contained by its surrounding environment. But the already noted horizontal consciousness of embodied consciousness's awareness of its surrounding environment prevents us from arguing that such a consciousness is contained by its environment in the same sense that pilgrim scallop's environment contains it.

3   Conclusion

There may be any number of reasons why one would wish to construct a Brooks autonomous agent. It may be useful not only to pick up empty soda cans in the environment, but to accomplish far more complex functional tasks. But Brook's program also serves to raise a more intriguing set of questions. Let us assume that, at one level or another, the difference that signals the difference between a functionally embedded robot and an embodied consciousness can be surmounted in one way or another. We might then ask: Can Brooks' approach serve to create autonomous agents whose "perceptual" experience of the world *differs* extensively from our own? Perhaps it can. What would we thereby gain? If we could successfully debrief such creatures, we might discover how these "autonomous agents" might perceive the world in remarkably different ways from our own. Perhaps one such an agent would be *immobile*, acting upon its world by remote devices, or perhaps not acting upon its environment at all. Perhaps its vastly complex system of sensory devices would permit it to "perceive" vastly larger areas of its environment than ourselves. Would its conception of its "environment" have a comparable meaning to our own? Would it still possess a horizon-consciousness? Might its perceptions be infallible? If it were the sole autonomous agent, would there be a qualitative difference in its perceptual experience in comparison with our intersubjectively structured experience? Would an intersubjective world have any meaning for it at all? And would its qualitative experience entail the senselessness for it of just such questions that we might wish to pose it? To imaginatively vary each of the four dimensions of embodied consciousness with respect to a Brooks autonomous agent may be an important way of confirming just how deeply rooted the primary features of our perceptual sensibility might be in such structures. Yet, however we might frame such questions, will they not always be posed *within* the horizon of our perceptual world as conscious agents aware of transcendent objects? Can we indeed coherently imagine a real perceptual consciousness that will not in some sense fall within the horizon of our "embodied consciousness"?

If our world is indeed the final horizon in terms of which we understand how agents of any type interact with worldly objects, perhaps the best we could do with a vastly different Brooks' agent would be to offer a Cummins-type functional analysis of what its experience might be like. On the basis of what has been said so far, such a strategy will have the effect subtly displacing our "perceptual" world with a world-as-container functional model of embodied consciousness. Suppose we substitute for the "what is it like to be a bat" question, the question "what is it like to be a Brooks' agent?" The answer, perhaps, will invariably take the form of "the world is experienced by the agent functionally in the following way", where "world" and "agent" have the Husserlian meanings they do, functioning as the "horizon" or implicit assumption in terms of which we attempt to make even some "functional" sense of how a differently structured organism might perceive its world.

The limitations of classical AI appear to be real ones. The impetus to develop alternative approaches, such as connectionism, dynamical systems theory and autonomous agents all appear to acknowledge that what appear to be largely implicit contextual "fringes" for classical AI also need to be fully captured by models of human cognition. Brooks' theory of robotic agents is an important participant in this recognition. Yet the identified limitations of his approach to modeling a genuinely embodied consciousness suggest just how difficult it may be to fully comprehend the foundationally *implicit* conditions of human cognition.

BIBLIOGRAPHY

[Block, 1980] N. Block. The trouble with functionalism. In N. Block, editor, *Readings in the Philosophy of Psychology: Volume One.* Harvard University Press, Cambridge, MA, 1980.

[Brooks, 1997] R.A. Brooks. Intelligence without representation. In J. Haugeland, editor, *Mind Design II*, Cambridge, MA, 1997. MIT Press.

[Cassirer, 1996] E. Cassirer. *The Philosophy of Symbolic Forms, Volume 4: The Metaphysics of Symbolic Forms.* Princeton University Press, New Haven, 1996.

[Clark, 1997] A. Clark. *Being There: Putting Brain, Body and World Together Again.* MIT Press, Cambridge, MA, 1997.

[Cummins, 1998] R. Cummins. Functional analysis. In C. Allen, M. Bekoff, and G. Lauder, editors, *Nature's Purposes: Analyses of Function and Design in Biology*, Cambridge, MA, 1998. MIT Press.

[Dreyfus, 1979] H. Dreyfus. *What Computers Can't Do.* Harper and Row, New York, 1979.

[Holland et al., 1989] J. Holland, K. Holyoak, R. Nisbett, and P. Thagard. *Induction: Processes of Inference, Learning and Discovery.* The MIT Press, Cambridge (Mass.), 1989.

[Husserl, 1970] E. Husserl. *The Crisis of European Sciences and Transcendental Phenomenology.* Northwestern University Press, Evanston, 1970.

[Varela et al., 1993] X. Varela, X. Thompson, and E. Rosch. *The Embodied Mind: Cognitive Science and Human Experience.* MIT Press, Cambridge, MA, 1993.

[Winograd, 1995] T. Winograd. A procedural model of language understanding. In *Computation & Intelligence: Collected Readings*, pages 203–234. American Association for Artificial Intelligence, Menlo Park, CA, 1995.

Roy Elveton
Department of Philosophy
Carleton College, Northfield, MN, USA
Email: relveton@carleton.edu

Unifying Approaches to the Unity of Consciousness
Minds, Brains and Machines

Susan Stuart

ABSTRACT. Whole landscapes of thought and literature have been
devoted to defining what is meant by the unity of consciousness, asking questions like who or what is doing the unifying and what it is that
is being unified. I will attempt to draw together two singularly different approaches to the problem. The first will be Cotterill's [Cotter-
ill, 1995] wherein he argues that consciousness is primarily associated
with movement and response, and that the necessary co-ordination of
movement and response requires a unity of conscious experience. The
second approach is Kant's [Kant, 1929] critical philosophy and, in particular, the claims he makes for the transcendental unity of apperception and the role of the cognitive imagination. Cotterill's argument
focuses on a neurophysiological approach to the problem and identifies the anterior cingulate as a possible "site" of consciousness. Kant's
approach is metaphysical though I will argue that Kant is committed to an active, sensorimotorily enmeshed view of consciousness. In
accepting Kant's metaphysics as prescriptive of the requirements for
conscious human experience, the kind that requires a unified subject
of experience, we can examine how Kant's functionalist [Sellars, 1970;
Brook, 1994] claims might be reinterpreted, recognized and possibly
even realized within the framework of contemporary neurophysiology.

1 Introduction

There is something that it is like to be a particular human being, cat, bat
or raven, that isn't simply its being the thing it is but also its interaction
with other things in its world. It is an embodied thing that is embedded
in its world; and when we use the term "human being" we think, though
not necessarily in a Cartesian way, of the problematic unity of a body and
a mind. The most we can say about ourselves, at least according to a strict
reading of Kant, is that we are logical subjects of thoughts, that we are
transcendental unities of apperception that are logically necessary for the

Lorenzo Magnani and Riccardo Dossena, editors, *Computing, Philosophy, and Cognition*,
pp. 259–269 © 2005, S. Stuart

very possibility of coherent cognition[1]. We look for the self, we reflect, and we find no thing, nothing that is the bearer of properties and we try to conjure it up in the concept of a soul or mental thing [Descartes, 1968], or a bundle of discrete perceptions in some kind of mental theater [Hume, 1739].

Self-consciousness requires the existence of a perceiving and conceiving being that acts and interacts with other objects and organisms in an objective world. It requires embodiment and embeddedness within its world; it is 'fallen' [Heidegger, 1962], necessarily adaptable, necessarily technological, extending itself through the use of tools, restoring lost functions and replacing lost organs and limbs, but also enhancing and reconfiguring itself, augmenting its capabilities and pushing itself further into its world. The self is not the body. The self is not the mind. The self is active agency within the world. I will argue that, although for Kant a unified self is simply the logical subject of thought, that is, a vehicle of concepts [B399/A341], in truth, because of, amongst other things, his commitment to inner experience being dependent on outer experience, he is committed to an embodied and embedded self.

2   Kant's basic architecture of the mind

Kant's account of the mind has two fundamental elements:

1. perceptual awareness or *intuitions* of our world

2. conceptualization of the perceptual experience of our world through *categories* or *concepts*

An intuition is a (re)presentation of an object, produced by either the faculty of Sensibility (*First Critique*) or the Imagination (*Third Critique*); it is

1. singular

2. direct

3. contains material passively received by the mind through one's sense organs.

A concept is a (re)presentation of an object, produced by the faculty of understanding; it is

---

[1]See, for example, "That the 'I' of apperception, and therefore the 'I' in every act of thought, is one, and cannot be resolved into a plurality of subjects, and consequently signifies a logically simple subject, is something already contained in the very concept of thought, and is therefore an analytic proposition". [B407]

1. general

2. indirect

3. actively produced by the mind.

And we can say exactly what Kant means when he claims that these elements are essential for experience by looking at two of his most famous phrases: "Thoughts without content are empty" and "Perceptions without concepts are blind" [Kant, 1929, A52/B76]. If our experience has no content, no experiential or perceptual input, our thoughts will be no thoughts at all for they will be empty. If we have perceptions or experience without any understanding to guide us in our organization of the data of that experience, we will be as good as blind, for all we will experience, if experience is what we would want to call it, is chaos. So what makes this experience unchaotic – well, the concepts in our understanding that act in some way to synthesize it, drawing together the unity of self-consciousness and the unity of objective experience. But let us examine this just a little further.

It must be the case that experience is possible only if it refers to an objective world, that is, if we are embedded in an experientially rich and changing environment, for how else would our thoughts have content. And, now it is possible to connect the following claims: "Unity of diverse experiences in a single consciousness [a self] requires experience of objects" [Strawson, 1966, p. 98] and, Kant's argument for the refutation of idealism, "that there are things in space outside me" [Kant, 1929, B275]. To demonstrate this latter claim Kant assumes Descartes' premise that I can determine my empirical consciousness in time without granting the existence of a physical world; but this will fail, for if inner experience is all I could have, then I could never arrive at a conception of myself as a temporally determined consciousness. Thus Kant concludes that inner experience cannot be all there is; there must be an outside world. It is really worth noting here that we see this most clearly set out in the argument for the second Analogy of Experience [A189–211/B233–56] where Kant claims that in being able to distinguish surveys from events, that is, in being able to distinguish stasis from movement even when we ourselves are moving, we are aware of our subjective experience as distinguishable from objective fact. It is this capability that makes self-conscious experiences possible.

And now let's look again at the claim that unity of consciousness requires consciousness of unity, that is, to be able to attach the "I think" to my thoughts they have to be ordered and unified by the application of the concepts and synthesized or brought together by the power of the imagination. This requirement is a bi-directional logical requirement, an interdependence claim, not a contingent relation, and the nomological force of this

claim clears the path for claiming that – because we have sensory awareness, understanding, a cognitive orproductive imagination[2], and a transcendental unity of apperception it is possible to recognize our thoughts
as our own, and all of this is made possible only because there is an external world with which we must engage if we are to have, even an illusory, sense of a continuing self [Hume, 1739; Brook, 1994; Strawson, 1997;
Strawson, 1999]. There is a strong sense in which it is possible to accept that
Kant is providing a notion of sensorimotorily enmeshed agent that interacts
with its, necessarily changing, world.

Thus, in ordinary cognitive judgement, the manifold of intuitions is "synthesized" which involves it being brought under concepts to produce judge-
ments. Synthesis occurs through the activity of the productive imagination.
Hence ordinary cognition is a product of interaction between the senses, the
understanding, and the imagination; it is the conceptualization and unification of experience with the potential – but only the potential – to be
expressed in the form of a judgement beginning: "I think". In unpicking
this Kantian picture we can begin to clarify what it is that must be resolved
if we are to understand the binding problem or how this synthesis operates.

3   The Binding Problem

I will begin by setting the problem out in broad terms: knowledge about
the world is stored all over the brain. How this knowledge is integrated
into one unitary perception to give us conscious experience is called the
binding problem. Currently there are two approaches to the resolution of
this problem:

1. Space-based binding which claims that there is a specific location or
   locations in the brain where information is brought together.

2. Time-based binding which claims that there is no one place where
   binding happens, because integration occurs over the entire brain and
   is regulated by some time-based process. Thus, time-based binding
   looks for when rather than where the binding occurs.

One definition of the binding problem, which is not nearly helpful enough,
is given by [Hardcastle]. Hardcastle says "Binding refers to the joining
together of the individually processed features at the 'psychological' level"
but fails to say what is meant by "the psychological level" whether, for
example, it is conscious or unconscious, and even, whether it refers to mind

---

[2]I use productive or cognitive imagination here in opposition to creative imagination,
and claim it to be a faculty but rather a power to synthesize or, rather differently, to
bring to mind something which is not wholly present.

states or brain states. I believe Cotterill [Cotterill, 1995] overcomes this problem with his use of the term "plenisentience" and I will develop this in the next section where I will also argue for a hybrid model of temporal and spatial-based binding.

4   The role of attention and synchrony in binding

There has been much talk of central executives [Baddeley, 1986] and supervisory attentional systems (SAS) [Norman and Shallice, 1980; Shallice, 1982] and their role in marshaling perceptual input and cognitive processes into making a unified experiential sense of the world; and a great deal has been said about the components that are being marshaled, for example, the visuo-spatial sketchpad and the phonological or articulatory loop; but very little has been said about the particular mechanism that must underpin the functioning of such executive or supervisory systems. In contrast to this Cotterill [Cotterill, 1995; Cotterill, 1998] goes out of his way to specify, in some detail, the role of the *master node* in drawing together efferent / afferent information into coherent action and thought. Crucial to Cotterill's theory are both synchrony and attentional processing. It is these we will concentrate on in analyzing his theory.

Much of the sensory system works as an outer sense, enabling the organism to determine its external state, and links – directly or indirectly – to actuators, making action, and hence interaction with the world, possible. But in more complex organisms "sensing" alsocomprises an "inner sense", not only enabling the organism to determine its goal(s) and compare its sensory input with its internal state(s), but also to monitor its position, movement and actions in the world. This is the view, a sensorimotorily enmeshed view of conscious experience, to which I am committing Kant; it is also Cotterill's view. It is the unity of experience which co-ordinates information from the senses, including the proprioceptive sense, with the agent's movement and appropriate responses.

In both Kant and Cotterill we see an emphasis on attention to movement for it is in attending to changes in our world, including changes in our body and position, being in a state of – what Cotterill describes as – "plenisentience", where inputs can be consciously sensed and unconsciously processed, that that, with, for example, the proper functioning of cells in the visual cortex, we are able to distinguish movement from stasis[3]. But Cotterill

---

[3]In humans and other primates, the vestibulo-ocular reflex [Churchland and Sejnowski, 1992] operates by direct feedback between sensory units (the semicircular canals) and actuators (motor neurons in the eye) with no "inner" representational or cognitive system intervening. Light in the eye falls on the retina and, depending on its intensity and wavelength or color, is translated by rod and cone cells into electrical impulses which are then transmitted along the optic nerves to the visual cortex at the back of the brain.

adds to this that the position of our muscles and our subsequent muscular movements are what makes it possible for us to ask questions about our environment and our position in our environment [Cotterill, 1995, p. 297]. In fact we can go much further than this, for if we were unable to move or unable to receive feedback through our senses, our interaction and knowledge of our world would be very limited. Now, if you are a tree this matters little but if you are an animal that must avoid being prey and instead become predator it is essential. Thus, if our sensory system including our proprioceptive sense – the ability to sense the position, location, orientation and movement of the body and its parts – is working well we will be in a position to receive and translate afferent signals and produce appropriate efferent impulses in response. In this way we become aware of our world and, though the development of a body schema, are able to conceive of ourselves in relation to but autonomous within our world.

We have a ready made counter-example to any opposition to this claim in those individuals who have lost their proprioceptive sense, for without their internal feedback system they rely on the external feedback provided by, in most cases, their visual sense to regain their sense of selfhood or identity. Meijsing [Meijsing, 2000, p. 42] says of the patient, Ian Waterman, "In the dark he did not know where his hand was; and even if he knew, he would not have been able to move it towards the bedside table without visual feedback". Yet, even this is insufficient for a fully unified sense of self[4]. Ian Waterman's sense of unity, his coherent sense of self, returned only when he had learned to move again. Thus, it is is not just the passively received information about a changing environment, but the interplay between this information and active self-movement that places the self, a unity of experience, firmly at the centre of its environment. It is active self-movement which gives a sense of agency, as the perceived environment changes as a result of the agent's purposive action [Meijsing, 2000, p. 46].

Miall and Wolpert [Miall and Wolpert, 1993] state that the brain structure should

---

It is in the visual cortex that this information is translated into perception of color, depth, objects and movement. The lens and retina act in some ways like a camera but the information that is transferred onwards to the visual cortex is in a different form altogether. There is no single visual cortex, rather there are assemblies of discrete cells some dedicated to discerning edges, some to motion, some to color, and so on. Neuropathological evidence shows us that damage to one batch of cells leaves others unaffected. For example, damage to the "color cells" will leave the individual able only to perceive in monochrome, and damage to the cells that determine objects might leave the individual able to perceive motion but without objects!

[4]She goes on to note that this is the replacement of an inner sense with an outer sense, and these may not equate to the same thing: the inner sense seems to be immune to error through misidentification [Evans, 1982; Brewer, 1995].

[...] receive as inputs an efferent copy of the motor command being sent to the [...] limb, and also proprioceptive information about the current state of the body. The latter is needed for an accurate internal representation of the limb, as the arm's mechanical properties depend on its position and motion. Hence, the internal dynamic model must be updated by proprioceptors. [p. 209]

If it isn't, then, like Ian Waterman, we lose our means of unifying our experience, and thus, we lose our sense of self.

Cotterill suggests that there is a hierarchy of muscular control over which there is a global control mechanism – which he justifies on the grounds that there are limits to the amount of information that can be handled by the system at any one time [Broadbent, 1958] – and, in accordance with the spatial-based binding approach, he proposes that it be the anterior cingulate that acts as this global control mechanism because it is neurally close to the higher motor hierarchical levels in the brain and because it is here – according to evidence from positron emission tomography [PET] scans (see [Pardo *et al.*, 1990]) – that a response is translated into a physical or motor directive. For example,

When I recognize a lemon, I am simultaneously detecting its pointed-oval shape, its dimpled skin, its yellow color, and possibly also its relative softness and its characteristic citrus smell. The first three of these attributes are all detected by the visual system, but by different parts of it. The fourth feature is detected by touch, while the last one is discerned by my olfactory sense. And where is the logical conclusion, *lemon*, located? It is nor deposited in some inner sanctum, farther up the hierarchy. On the contrary, its components are left in those same sensory modalities and areas. The concept *lemon* merely exists through the temporary binding together of its various attributes; and we are able to sense the lemon as a single unity because we can instantaneously detect what goes with what. [Cotterill, 1995, p. 305]

Kant would complete this last sentence by saying "[...] and we are able to sense the lemon as a single unity because we draw together the intuitions under concepts and with the synthesizing power of the imagination we are able to put together a thought which might be 'lemon' or, more complicatedly, 'I think it is a lemon'[5], and being able to unite the disparate parts of

---

[5]The complicated utterance "I think it is a lemon" would surely only be uttered where there is some doubt about the object's status.

my perceptual experience together into a thought is sufficient to reveal that the thought is being had in one head, that is, that it is 'my thought' ".

In his emphasis on the synchrony of input and output Cotterill presents us with a temporal-based response to the binding problem, but only in some circumstances. In the process of object recognition there is a great deal of neural activity which is a result of the information received through the modalities involved in the perception of an object, and that neural activity is distributed across the parietal-temporal-occipital association cortex. But we have also seen that synchrony of input alone cannot be the complete or sole explanation for binding. The detection of movement, both internal to the system and external to it, and the co-ordination of sensory input, including the proprioceptive sense, with the agent's movement and responses, is essential if there is to be a unity of consciousness, and a unity of consciousness is necessary if we are to have a coherent experience of our world. If Cotterill is right, this aspect of the neural activity must be located at the center for determining muscular direction in the brain, for it is with the proper functioning of the anterior cingulate, that we can ask questions about, and bring about changes within, our dynamically changing environment. Cotterill's picture is, then, of a hybrid model of how binding occurs; it is time-based in its synchrony and it is space-based in its possibly being located in the anterior cingulate.

5   Concluding remarks and future directions

Cotterill's account of consciousness is primarily associated with movement and response, but the necessary co-ordination of movement and response requires a unity of conscious experience. This is an interdependence claim not unlike Kant's claim that a unity of consciousness is possible only on condition that we have a consciousness of unity, and *vice versa*, and we have seen that Kant's argument for our being able to conceive of ourselves as unities of consciousness, that is, as temporally determined conscious agents, is based on our being able to discern and distinguish movement from stasis through the application of *a priori* concepts which order and unify our perceptual input. A great deal is implicit in Kant's notion of ordering and unifying, a great deal that is being excavated by current work in neurophysiology, robotics and cognitive architecture theories.

Cotterill's argument focuses on a neurophysiological approach to the problem and identifies the anterior cingulate as a possible 'site' of consciousness. This was not an approach available to Kant, yet in his metaphysical enquiry we find him committed to an active, sensorimotorily enmeshed view of consciousness, a view which is not just recognizable in but necessary to Cotterill's framework of enquiry.

One way in which this current work might be developed would be to examine how this framework is presented to us in Sloman's cognitive architecture theory [Sloman, 2003; Sloman, 2004], Aleksander's engineering approach that entails the integration of cognitive faculties into architectures [Aleksander and Dunmall, 2003], and robotics [Brooks, 2004; Browning, 1998].

Early hybrid cognitive architectures represented knowledge symbolically as rules and facts but had a neurally-based activation process that determined which facts and rules got deployed in which situations (see ACT-R and SOAR, [Anderson, 1983; Anderson, 1990; Anderson, 1993]). Sloman's Cog-Aff and H Cog-Aff architectures provide a more holistic approach to the requirements for consciousness experience, arguing that both cognitive and affective components must be combined in one architecture. Unlike early architectures H Cog-Aff is not algorithm and representation based, and although Sloman distinguishes between three types of processing and three cognitive levels, he does not offer any explicit account of a central processing element that acts to bind the information so it can be recognized as belonging to one consciousness.

In Browning's applied robotics work the fusing or integration of information operates on the basis of probability algorithms which must occur in both a temporal and a spatial framework if the system is to act appropriately in real time.

Fundamental to each of these approaches are the notions of embodiment, animation, perception, and imagination, but, in turn, each of these notions requires a system that has (i) the ability to bind its experiences as experience for it, (ii) the ability to order/tag its experience temporally if it is to be able to plan ahead and direct its attention in an effort to sustain its existence, and (iii) some element of affective processing that makes some things more desirable than others and provides the system with a will to act.

In bringing these approaches together a strong conclusion is clearly possible, that Kant, Cotterill, Sloman, Browning, Brooks, and Aleksander & Dunmall are all committed to a hybrid, that is, temporal and spatial model of binding/synthesis/integration. The future is exciting.

BIBLIOGRAPHY

[Aleksander and Dunmall, 2003] I. Aleksander and B. Dunmall. Axioms and tests for the presence of minimal consciousness in agents. *Journal of Consciousness Studies*, 10(4–5), 2003.

[Anderson, 1983] J. Anderson. *The Architecture of Cognition*. Harvard University Press, Cambridge, MA, 1983.

[Anderson, 1990] J. Anderson. *The Adaptive Character of Thought*. Erlbaum, Hillsdale, NJ, 1990.

[Anderson, 1993] J. Anderson. *Rules of the Mind*. Erlbaum, Hillsdale, NJ, 1993.

268   Susan Stuart

[Baddeley, 1986] A.D. Baddeley. *Working Memory*. Clarendon Press, Oxford, 1986.

[Brewer, 1995] B. Brewer. Bodily awareness and the self. In J. Bermudez, A.J. Marcel, and N. Eilan, editors, *The Body and the Self*, Cambridge, MA, 1995. MIT Press.

[Broadbent, 1958] D.E. Broadbent. *Perception and Communication*. Oxford University Press, Oxford, 1958.

[Brook, 1994] A. Brook. *Kant and the Mind*. Cambridge University Press, UK, 1994.

[Brooks, 1991] R. Brooks. Intelligence without representation. *Artificial Intelligence*, 47(1–3):139–159, 1991.

[Brooks, 2004] R. Brooks. Living machines overview, 2004. http://www.ai.mit.edu/projects/living-machines/overview/overview.shtml [accessed 1st August 2004].

[Browning, 1998] B. Browning. Neural systems for integrating robot behaviours. Australian Conference on Neural Networks, 1997, Brisbane, Queensland, Australia, 1998.

[Churchland and Sejnowski, 1992] P.S. Churchland and T.J. Sejnowski. *The Computational Brain*. MIT, Bradford Books, 1992.

[Cotterill, 1995] R.M.J. Cotterill. On the unity of conscious experience. *Journal of Consciousness Studies*, 2(4):290–311, 1995. Imprint Academic.

[Cotterill, 1998] R.M.J. Cotterill. *Enchanted Looms: Conscious Networks in Brains and Computers*. Cambridge University Press, Cambridge, UK, 1998.

[Descartes, 1968] R. Descartes. *Discourse on method, and the Meditations*. Penguin, Harmondsworth, 1968. translated with an introduction by F.E. Sutcliffe.

[Evans, 1982] G. Evans. *The Varieties of Reference*. Clarendon Press, Oxford, 1982. Edited by J. McDowell.

[Hardcastle,] V.G. Hardcastle. Synchronous oscillations and the Emperor's New Clothes? JCS-Online – Digest of the Key Debates. http://www.zynet.co.uk/imprint/online/hard.html.

[Hardcastle, 1994] V.G. Hardcastle. Psychology's 'binding problem' and possible neurobiological solutions. *Journal of Consciousness Studies*, 1(1), 1994. Imprint Academic.

[Heidegger, 1962] M. Heidegger. *Being and Time*. SCM Press, London, 1962. translated by J. Macquarrie and E. Robinson.

[Hume, 1739] D. Hume. *A Treatise of Human Nature*. Clarendon Press, Oxford, 1739. Edited, with an analytical index by L.A. Selby-Bigge.

[Humphrey, 2000] N. Humphrey. One self: A meditation on the unity of consciousness. *Social Research*, 67(4):32–39, 2000.

[Kant, 1783] I. Kant. *Prolegomena, and Metaphysical Foundations of Natural Science*. George Bell and Sons, London, 1783. translated by E.B. Bax, 1891.

[Kant, 1929] I. Kant. *The Critique of Pure Reason*. Macmillan Press, 1929. translated by N.K. Smith, (A edition 1781 + B edition 1787).

[Martin, 1998] C.M. Martin. Breaking out of the black box: A new approach to robot perception. *Mobile Robots XIII*, pages 126–137, November 1998 1998. Boston, MA.

[Meijsing, 2000] M. Meijsing. Self-consciousness and the body. *Journal of Consciousness Studies*, 7(6):34–52, 2000.

[Metzinger, 1995a] T. Metzinger. *Conscious Experience*. Imprint Academic, 1995a.

[Metzinger, 1995b] T. Metzinger. Faster than thought holism, homogeneity and temporal coding, 1995b.

[Miall and Wolpert, 1993] R.C. Miall and D.J. Wolpert. Is the cerebellum a Smith predictor? *Journal of Motor Behaviour*, 25(3):203–216, 1993.

[Norman and Shallice, 1980] D.A. Norman and T. Shallice. Attention to action. Willed and automatic control of behavior. Chip report 99, University of California San Diego, 1980.

[Pardo et al., 1990] J.V. Pardo, P.J. Pardo, K.W. Janer, and M.E. Raichle. The anterior cingulate cortex mediates processing selection in the Stroop attentional conflict paradigm. In *Proceedings of the National Academy of Sciences*, volume 87, pages 256–259, USA, 1990.

[Ramachandran and Blakeslee, 1998] V.S. Ramachandran and S. Blakeslee. *Phantoms in the Brain: Probing the Mysteries of the Human Mind*. William Morrow, New York, 1998.

[Roskies, 1999] A. Roskies. The binding problem. *Neuron*, 24(7–9), September 1999 1999. Cell Press.

[Sellars, 1970] W. Sellars. ... this I or he or it (the thing) which thinks .... In *Proceedings of the American Philosophical Association*, volume 44, pages 5–31, 1970.

[Sellars, 1978] W. Sellars. The role of the imagination in Kant's theory of experience. In H.W. Johnstone (Jr.), editor, *Categories: A Colloquium*. Pennsylvania State University, 1978.

[Shallice, 1982] T. Shallice. Specific impairments of planning. *Philosophical Transactions of the Royal Society London B 298*, pages 199–209, 1982.

[Sherrington, 1940] C. Sherrington. *Man on His Nature*. Cambridge University Press, Cambridge, 1940.

[Sloman, 2003] A. Sloman. Varieties of affect and learning in a complete human-like architecture, 2003. http://www.cs.bham.ac.uk/research/cogaff/talks/#talk24 [accessed July 2004].

[Sloman, 2004] A. Sloman. The cognition and affect project: Architectures, architecture-schemas, and the new science of mind, 2004. http://www.cs.bham.ac.uk/research/cogaff/gc/gc5-abstract-04-04.pdf [accessed July 2004].

[Strawson, 1966] P.F. Strawson. *The Bounds of Sense: An Essay on Kant's Critique of Pure Reason*. Methuen, London, 1966.

[Strawson, 1997] G. Strawson. The self. *Journal of Consciousness Studies*, 4(5–6):405–428, 1997.

[Strawson, 1999] G. Strawson. The self and the sesmet. *Journal of Consciousness Studies*, 6(4):99–135, 1999.

[Tirassa et al., 2000] M. Tirassa, A. Carassa, and G. Geminiani. A theoretical framework for the study of spatial cognition. In S. O'Nuallain, editor, *Spatial Cognition. Foundations and Applications*, pages 19–31, Amsterdam/Philadelphia, 2000. Benjamins.

[Von Der Malsburg, 1981] C. Von Der Malsburg. The correlation theory of brain function. *Biophysical Chemistry*, 1981. Technical Report 81-2, MPI.

[Young, 1988] J.M. Young. Kant's view of imagination. *Kant-Studien*, 79:140–164, 1988.

Susan Stuart
Humanities Advanced Technology and Information Institute
University of Glasgow, Glasgow, UK
Email: S.Stuart@philosophy.arts.gla.ac.uk
URL: www.gla.ac.uk/departments/philosophy/Personnel/susan/

Defining and Using Deductive Systems with Isabelle

F. Miguel Dionísio, Paula Gouveia, and João Marcos

ABSTRACT. The software Isabelle is a generic theorem-proving environment that allows for the definition and use of deductive systems for many different logics. The deduction rules may be specified in different formats: natural deduction rules, Hilbert-style axioms and rules, sequent-style rules, tableau rules, etc. In this way, using Isabelle, it is possible to define and experiment with different logics, since the user may implement the deduction rules she sees fit.

Obviously, some initial training is needed for the task of using Isabelle in order to define and experiment with new logics. However, it is our experience that only a few main concepts are, in fact, essential. The authors have been involved in teaching a logic course for undergraduate students. The system Isabelle was used for representation and use of natural deduction systems for propositional, first-order and modal logics. Students learned how to define logics and how to prove theorems and check inferences in those logics. From what they learned in one semester, most students were able to successfully deliver the final assignment that included the definition of a (new) hybrid logic, involving quantifiers and modalities. In this paper you will find the basic concepts needed to define and experiment with a logic in Isabelle.

1 Introduction

At the moment, there is a sizable number of models of logic software available, and seemingly there is still a strong impulse at the logic community to go and design their own personalized proof assistant, for their own preferred deductive systems. Some of the already existing logic software are highly flexible, and are intended as generic environments for doing a number of activities you would like the computer to help you with: doing interactive proofs, writing some formally verified mathematics, writing and checking formal specifications of all sorts, and, why not, doing some mechanized reasoning, that old dream of Leibniz.

Lorenzo Magnani and Riccardo Dossena, editors, *Computing, Philosophy, and Cognition*, pp. 271–293 © 2005, F.M. Dionísio, P. Gouveia, and J. Marcos

Such highly flexible models of logic software have a strong potentiality still largely to be unleashed in their use in computer-based learning and their integration to the standard set of teaching strategies and resources. Used as laboratories for experimentation with abstract entities, the right software can turn a computer into a sort of "bubble chamber" where ideas can be tested and improved – or rejected. Moreover, in the provocative words of Edward Feigenbaum [Gleick, 1987], computers can also help us in "creating intuition" about certain subjects. This outlook converts the computer into a genuine tool for doing philosophical and mathematical research.

We had a simple goal in mind: To use the computer to teach logic to undergraduate students. Our main aim, however, was not (only) to teach the students about this and that deductive system, but to provide them with some expertise on using an extensively customizable tool in which they would be able to define and work with *their own logics*, if that be the case. After some prospecting and experimentation with the existing proof assistants, Isabelle was chosen. Logic is carefully built-in in the design and implementation of this software. We are talking about a logical framework whose meta-*logic* is Intuitionistic Higher-Order Logic with three main components: (i) a meta-*implication* that can be used in laying down the object-logic rules (see section 2.2) of the specific object-logic being thereby represented and that takes care of the application of those rules and the discharge of assumptions; (ii) a meta-*universal quantification* that can be used in laying down a number of object-language quantifiers (see section 2.6); (iii) a meta-*equality* that can be used in laying down abbreviations as rewrite rules (see section 2.3). We are talking about a mechanizable theorem prover (see section 2.5) where: (i) object-logic formulas are λ-terms disambiguated by way of a priority grammar (see section 2.1); (ii) rules of the object-language are represented not as functions but as formulas of the underlying higher-order logic; (iii) the combination and application of those rules is performed by way of a uniform method of inference – higher-order resolution; (iv) tactics are implemented independently of the object-logic being represented (see section 2.4). We are talking about a simply typed environment where object-language formulas can be heavily structured (see sections 2.7 and 3), and very precise specifications can be met with.

Finally, it should be noted that Isabelle is written over ML [Paulson, 1996], a functional programming language that can come to help at any point where even more expressivity is needed. ML was designed precisely to serve as an implementation language for theorem provers.

This paper is not about the logic behind Isabelle (for that you may consult the appropriate handbooks), but about how Isabelle can be used to look ahead into a number of new user-defined logics. We will not be worried here about proving properties about our object-logics, but about how these very logics can be defined, changed, and used. To that intent, the following sections will systematically illustrate the USE of Isabelle in entirely pedestrian terms.

2   Defining logics in Isabelle

The system Isabelle [Nipkow *et al.*, 2002] has been developed by Lawrence C. Paulson (Univ. of Cambridge, UK) and Tobias Nipkow (Technical Univ. of Munich, DE) and is freely available on the web at

> http://www.cl.cam.ac.uk/Research/HVG/Isabelle/.

The relevant references about this system are also available on that site. For other mechanized reasoning systems see

> http://www-formal.stanford.edu/clt/ARS/systems.html,

where an extensive commented list is available.

Isabelle is a generic theorem-proving environment that allows for the representation and use of deductive systems for many different logics. In the following we briefly describe the basic concepts needed to define and experiment with a logic. We begin with simple examples concerning classical propositional logic. In particular we will refer to natural deduction, Hilbert- and sequent-style systems for this logic [Troelstra and Schwichtenberg, 1996]. More involved examples will be presented later on.

2.1   Language

The definition of the language and deductive system of a given logic constitutes a *theory* of Isabelle's meta-logic. Each theory must be specified in one file (with extension .thy).

Connectives are internally represented using λ-calculus and, therefore, understood as functions that for given argument formulas return a new formula. For example, conj(A,B) represents the conjunction of A and B. In this way conj is a function that, given two argument formulas, returns another a formula. The definition of this function is conj::[o,o]=>o, where o is the type of formulas. The more usual notation A&B may also be used (and is internally translated to conj(A,B)). Isabelle's code and notation for this connective is:

```
conj ::  [o, o] => o        ("_&_" [36,35] 35)
```

The values [36,35] 35 specify (using a priority grammar) the priority of conjunction (with respect to other connectives) and also that it is right-associative. In a priority grammar, priorities are assigned to occurrences of non-terminal symbols in a production, e.g. $A^{35} \Rightarrow A^{36} \wedge A^{35}$ (that corresponds to the priorities in rule `conj` above). Terminal symbols are assigned priority ∞. Derivations are as usual, with the difference that the occurrence of a non-terminal symbol can only be substituted using productions whose left-hand symbol has greater or equal priority. For example, in $A^{36} \wedge A^{35}$ only A^{35} can be substituted using $A^{35} \Rightarrow A^{36} \wedge A^{35}$ resulting in $A^{36} \wedge \boxed{A^{36} \wedge A^{35}}$. This process disambiguates the grammar and, in this example, justifies that conjunction is right-associative. Other connectives are dealt with in a similar way and the assignment of different priorities to different connectives sets its precedence. For example, the fact that conjunction has precedence over disjunction is coded by `disj::[o,o]=>o ("_|_" [31,30] 30)`.

2.2   Meta-logic and object propositional logics

Isabelle provides the logic `Pure`, a higher-order intuitionistic logic, as the framework for defining new logics. The logic `Pure` is called the *meta-logic*. Each new logic is called an *object-logic*. The deduction rules of each new logic must be coded in the meta-logic, using meta-implication. Consider, for example, a natural deduction elimination rule for conjunction:

$$\begin{array}{c} \mathcal{D} \\ \varphi_1 \wedge \varphi_2 \\ \hline \varphi_1 \end{array}$$

This rule is represented by the metaformula `P&Q ==> P` where meta-implication (`==>`) has the intuitive meaning that the consequent can be proved provided that the antecedent has been proved. On the other hand, the metaformula `P==>(Q==>P&Q)` means that `P&Q` can be proved provided that both `P` and `Q` have been proved. It can also be written as `[|P;Q|]==> P&Q` and it is a representation of the introduction rule for conjunction.

2.3   Example theories

The previous concepts are enough for defining, for example, a natural deduction system for classical propositional logic, or a Hilbert system for the same logic. We begin by displaying the theory `PROPOSITIONAL`, representing a natural deduction system for propositional logic. Note that: (i) this theory is an extension of `Pure`; (ii) the type o of formulas has to be declared; (iii) Isabelle must recognize the object-language formulas (that have type o) as atomic metaformulas (that have type `prop`) and this is achieved by declaring a function (`Trueprop`) that assigns to each object formula its corresponding metaformula (in fact, itself); (iv) rules must have names; (v) abbreviations may be defined as rewrite rules, using Isabelle's built-in meta-equality rules.

The function Trueprop has a strong semantic intuition behind it: it provides a way of internalizing Tarski's truth-predicate, so as to allow for the talk about the truth of the object-language formulas at the meta-logical level.

```
PROPOSITIONAL = Pure +
types
o
arities
o ::  logic
consts
Trueprop ::  o => prop ("(_)" 5)

(* Connectives *)
verum, falsum ::  o
neg ::  o => o ("~ _" [40] 40)
conj ::  [o, o] => o ("_&_" [36,35] 35)
disj ::  [o, o] => o ("_|_" [31,30] 30)
imp ::  [o, o] => o ("_-->_" [26,25] 25)
iff ::  [o, o] => o ("_<->_" [26,25] 25)

rules (* Natural deduction rules *)
conjI "[| P; Q |] ==> P&Q"
conjEr "P&Q ==> P"
conjEl "P&Q ==> Q"
disjIr "P ==> P|Q"
disjIl "Q ==> P|Q"
disjE "[| P|Q; P ==> R; Q ==> R |] ==> R"
impI "(P ==> Q) ==> P-->Q"
impE "[| P-->Q; P |] ==> Q"
abs "((P --> falsum) ==> falsum) ==> P"

(* Abbreviations *)
verum_def "verum == falsum-->falsum"
neg_def "~P == P-->falsum"
iff_def "P<->Q == (P-->Q) & (Q-->P)"
end
```

The theory Hilbert.thy that codes a Hilbert system for this logic can be written in a similar way. We omit the definition of the language (for simplicity we consider only implication and falsum as primitive connectives) and present a set of suitable axiom schemas and the accompanying inference rule.

```
Hilbert = Pure +
...
rules
ax1 "A --> (B --> A)"              (* Axioms *)
ax2 "(A-->(B-->C))-->((A-->B)-->(A-->C))"
ax3 "falsum-->A"
ax4 "((A-->falsum)-->falsum)-->A"
mp "[|A-->B;A|]==>B"              (* Rule *)
...
```

2.4 Using theories

In general, proofs in Isabelle are *backward proofs*, meaning that the user
starts by stating the goal and applies the inference rules backwards (from
the conclusion to the premises). Each premise constitutes a new subgoal to
be proved. The proof ends when no further subgoals remain to be proved.
The initial goal can be either a formula (e.g. A-->(B-->A)) or a metaformula
(e.g. [| A&B; B-->C |] ==> C). In the first case the goal corresponds to a
theorem and in the second to a derived rule of the deductive system.

Syntactic equation solving is called *unification*. The concept of unification
is fundamental to understanding how rules can be applied to a (sub)goal.
Rules are represented (internally) as schema metaformulas. For example
the rule conjI, i.e. [| P;Q |] ==> P&Q, is, in fact, represented as [| ?P;?Q |]
==> ?P&?Q. The variables ?P and ?Q are schema variables, that is, variables
that may be instantiated by any formula. This represents the fact that
this rule can be applied to any formula of the form ?P&?Q. In order to check
whether a given formula F has that form, an equation has to be solved,
namely the equation ?P&?Q=F. The equation ?P&?Q=A&(B-->C) has the solution
?P=A and ?Q=B-->C. In this way, the mechanism underlying the application of
a rule to a goal corresponds to the unification of the conclusion of the rule
with the goal. New subgoals appear corresponding to the premises of the
rule (where appropriate schema variables have been replaced by the corresponding solution of the equation). This mechanism is called *resolution*.
In the following example we establish [| A; C |] ==> A & (B-->C) using the
theory PROPOSITIONAL.

```
> Goal "[| A;C |] ==> A&(B-->C)";
Level 0 (1 subgoal)
[| A; C |] ==> A&(B-->C)
 1.  [| A; C |] ==> A&(B-->C)
val it = [] : Thm.thm list

> by (resolve_tac [conjI] 1);
```

```
Level 1 (2 subgoals)
[| A; C |] ==> A&(B-->C)
1.  [| A; C |] ==> A
2.  [| A; C |] ==> B-->C
val it = () :  unit

> by (assume_tac 1);
Level 2 (1 subgoal)
[| A; C |] ==> A&(B-->C)
1.  [| A; C |] ==> B-->C
val it = () :  unit

> by (resolve_tac [impI] 1);
Level 3 (1 subgoal)
[| A; C |] ==> A&(B-->C)
1.  [| A; C; B |] ==> C
val it = () :  unit

> by (assume_tac 1);
Level 4
[| A; C |] ==> A&(B-->C)
No subgoals!
```

The command by (resolve_tac [conjI] *number*) applies the rule conjI to the subgoal identified by *number* (similarly for by (resolve_tac [impI] *number*)). Some subgoals do not need rules to be proved since they are premises or unifiable with premises. These are proved using by (assume_tac *number*). In general, (sub)goals are proved *by* applying a *tactic*. The most important tactics are the previously referred tactics of resolution and assumption, the tactic resolve_tac [*rule*] *number* and the tactic assume_tac *number*. Moreover, rtac abbreviates resolve_tac and atac abbreviates assume_tac. Also, br *rule* *i* abbreviates by (rtac [*rule*] *i*) and ba *i* abbreviates by (atac *i*). The variable it contains the value of the presently evaluated expression. We will omit the corresponding output line whenever it is not relevant.

It is worth noticing that by establishing [| A; C |] ==> A&(B-->C) one has established a derived rule of the current deductive system. This rule can be used in other proofs. For that purpose a name has to be assigned to it using qed "newName";. Afterwards one may use by (resolve_tac [newName] *number*) to apply the new rule to a subgoal. The rule will only be available in the current session. A simple way of making new rules available in all sessions is to write down their proofs in a file with extension ML, named after the current theory, in this case PROPOSITIONAL.ML.

It is also possible to prove more complex metaformulas. For example the metaformula [|[|P==>Q;P|]==>R; P==>Q; P|]==>R is a rule having other rules (e.g. [|P==>Q;P|]==>R) as premises. Such rules may be taken as primitive rules in extensions of natural deduction systems like those proposed in [Schroeder-Heister, 1984]. Whenever the antecedent contains non-atomic metaformulas the result of Goal is the list of metarules associated to the premises.

```
> Goal "[|[|P==>Q;P|]==>R; P==>Q; P|]==>R";
Level 0 (1 subgoal)
R
1.  R
val it = ["[| P ==> Q; P |] ==> R" [.], "P ==> Q" [.], "P" [.]] :
Thm.thm list
```

Note that the goal to be established is simply R and there are three metarules, each one associated with a corresponding premise. These can also be recovered with premises(). Each metarule states that each premise is derivable from itself and is of the form [Pr] Pr (with the conclusion to the right). The previous output hides the metaformulas within [] (to see them use set show_hyps;). It is useful to assign a name to each metarule in the list, so that can be referred to later on. This can be achieved using val [pr1,pr2,pr3] = premises(); that assigns to the first element of the list the name pr1, to the second the name pr2 and to the third pr3. This can also be achieved directly by using

```
> val [pr1,pr2,pr3]=Goal "[|[|P==>Q;P|]==>R; P==>Q; P|]==>R";
Level 0 (1 subgoal)
R
1.  R
val pr1 = "[| P ==> Q; P |] ==> R" [.] :  Thm.thm
val pr2 = "P ==> Q" [.] :  Thm.thm
val pr3 = "P" [.] :  Thm.thm
```

The proof is as expected, noting that the names of the premises are used.

```
> br pr1 1;
Level 1 (2 subgoals)
R
1.  P ==> Q
2.  P
> br pr2 1;
Level 2 (2 subgoals)
```

```
R
1.  P ==> P
2.  P
> ba 1;
Level 3 (1 subgoal)
R
1.  P
> br pr3 1;
Level 4
R
No subgoals!
```

To establish a goal involving abbreviations, e.g. $\sim\sim$P<->P, the abbreviated expressions must be rewritten (using the convenient rewrite rules, in this case neg_def and iff_def). One way of doing this is by using the command Goalw [def1,def2,...] metaformula that rewrites the abbreviations in metaformula using the definitions in the argument list:

```
> Goalw [neg_def,iff_def] "~~P <-> P";
Level 0 (1 subgoal)
~~ P<->P
1.  (((P-->falsum)-->falsum)-->P)&(P-->(P-->falsum)-->falsum)
```

The proof can now be done as usual.

2.5   Sequents and automated deduction

Sequent calculus can provide an easy decision procedure for validity (in classical propositional logic). All one has to do is to repeatedly apply the rules to the goal sequent.

Sequents are represented in Isabelle by pairs of lists of formulas. For example,

$$\text{A, B-->C |- D, E\&F}$$

denotes a sequent with antecedent A,B-->C and consequent D, E&F. Variables prefixed by $ are list variables. The sequent

$$\text{"\$H, P, \$G |- \$E, P, \$F"}$$

represents an axiom schema and

$$\text{"[| \$H, \$G |- \$E, P; \$H, Q, \$G |- \$E |] ==> \$H, P-->Q, \$G |- \$E"}$$

codes the left-introduction rule for implication. Lists and sequents are provided by the theory Sequents.thy available in Isabelle's distribution. The following theory SPROP.thy defines the sequent calculus for classical propositional logic by providing the syntax of formulas and the sequent rules.

```
SPROP = Sequents +
consts
Trueprop ::   "two_seqi"
"@Trueprop" ::   "two_seqe" ("((_)/ |- (_))" [6,6] 5)

(* Connectives *)
falsum,verum ::  o
neg :: o => o ("~_" [40] 40)
conj :: [o, o] => o ("_&_" [36,35] 35)
disj :: [o, o] => o ("_|_" [31,30] 30)
imp :: [o, o] => o ("_-->_" [26,25] 25)
iff :: [o, o] => o ("_<->_" [26,25] 25)

rules (* Sequent Rules*)
axS "$H, P, $G |- $E, P, $F"
falsumL "$H, falsum, $G |- $E"
conjR "[| $H|- $E, P, $F; $H|- $E, Q, $F |] ==> $H|- $E, P&Q, $F"
conjL "$H, P, Q, $G |- $E ==> $H, P & Q, $G |- $E"
disjR "$H |- $E, P, Q, $F ==> $H |- $E, P|Q, $F"
disjL "[| $H, P, $G |- $E; $H, Q, $G |- $E |] ==> $H, P|Q, $G |- $E"
impR "$H, P |- $E, Q, $F ==> $H |- $E, P-->Q, $F"
impL "[| $H,$G |- $E,P; $H, Q, $G |- $E |] ==> $H, P-->Q, $G |- $E"

(* Abbreviations *)
verum_def "verum == falsum-->falsum"
iff_def "P<->Q == (P-->Q) & (Q-->P)"
neg_def "~P == P-->falsum"
end

ML
val parse_translation = [("@Trueprop",Sequents.two_seq_tr "Trueprop")];
val print_translation = [("Trueprop",Sequents.two_seq_tr' "@Trueprop")];
```

The reason for the use of both Trueprop and @Trueprop is that there are, in fact, two different representations of lists, the one referred above (and called the external representation) and a functional representation of lists (called the internal representation). @Trueprop(A,B), also written A|-B, is a sequent where the lists involved are written in the external representation. Trueprop(alpha,beta) is the sequent where the lists involved are written in the internal representation. The two lines in ML code at the end of the above theory provide functions that translate between the two representations of sequents.

In order to use this theory (with use_thy) the system must load the theory Sequents:

```
> isabelle Sequents
...
use_thy "SPROP";
```

Before illustrating the use of this theory with an example, we present the notion of *tactical*. Tacticals are forms of combining tactics. Useful tacticals are the iterative combinator of tactics REPEAT and the alternative combinator ORELSE. The tactic REPEAT *tactic* corresponds to the repeated application of the argument tactic until it fails. The tactic *tactic1* ORELSE *tactic2* corresponds to *tactic1* alone when the application of *tactic1* succeeds. Otherwise it corresponds to *tactic2* alone. Tacticals are useful in interactive proofs and they are the fundamental tools in developing automatic proving techniques.

The proof of |-(A-->(B-->C))-->((A-->B)-->(A-->C)) begins with three applications of resolution with impR to the first subgoal. These three steps may be simplified by using REPEAT (rtac impR 1).

```
> Goal "|- (A-->(B-->C))-->((A-->B)-->(A-->C))";
Level 0 (1 subgoal)
|- (A --> B --> C) --> (A --> B) --> A --> C
 1.   |- (A --> B --> C) --> (A --> B) --> A --> C

> by (REPEAT (rtac impR 1));
Level 1 (1 subgoal)
|- (A --> B --> C) --> (A --> B) --> A --> C
 1.   A --> B --> C, A --> B, A |- C
```

The next two steps are easy to follow.

```
> br impL 1;
Level 2 (2 subgoals)
|- (A --> B --> C) --> (A --> B) --> A --> C
 1.   A --> B, A |- C, A
 2.   B --> C, A --> B, A |- C

> br axS 1;
Level 3 (1 subgoal)
|- (A --> B --> C) --> (A --> B) --> A --> C
```

```
1.  B --> C, A --> B, A |- C
```

The final steps are by resolution with either axS or impL.

```
> by (REPEAT ((rtac axS 1) ORELSE (rtac impE 1)));
Level 4
|- (A --> B --> C) --> (A --> B) --> A --> C
No subgoals!
```

It may be helpful to exhibit parentheses making formulas more readable. The command set show_brackets; sets the corresponding flag to true.

```
> set show_brackets; Goal "|- (A-->(B-->C))-->((A-->B)-->(A-->C))";
Level 0 (1 subgoal)
( |- ((A --> (B --> C)) --> ((A --> B) --> (A --> C))))
1.  ( |- ((A --> (B --> C)) --> ((A --> B) --> (A --> C))))
```

As referred above, sequent calculus provides a decision procedure for validity (in classical propositional logic). In fact, each (backward) application of the rules decreases the complexity of the formulas involved in the sequent. In the end, subgoals consist of axioms or sequents without connectives that encode a counter-example for the original goal.

With this decision procedure in mind, one can easily write down a tactic that succeeds whenever the original goal is a valid sequent and fails otherwise. First one has to define a tactic that corresponds to the application of *some* rule. This tactic should try the rules in some order until it finds one that unifies. In this deductive system, the order of application of rules is irrelevant. It is more efficient to prefer rules that eliminate subgoals or introduce less new subgoals over other rules. One possible choice is to try application of rules in this order: axS,falsumL,impR,conjL,disjR,impL,conjR,disjL. The tactic

```
(rtac axS 1) ORELSE ... ORELSE (rtac disjL 1)
```

applies the axiom or some rule to the first subgoal and fails only if none is applicable. Repeated application of this tactic is achieved by

```
REPEAT ((rtac axS 1) ORELSE ... ORELSE (rtac disjL 1)).
```

Given a valid sequent, the application of this tactic succeeds, since the first subgoal is repeatedly simplified until an instance of the axiom axS is obtained and eliminated. At this point, if there are further subgoals, the second becomes the first and this process goes on until no subgoal is left.

If the original sequent is not valid, the tactic fails in the first subgoal consisting of a sequent without connectives that is not an axiom. In this case more subgoals can be left unworked. In the following example the original sequent is valid. The above tactic is given the name tacSeq1.

```
> val tacSeq1= REPEAT ((rtac axS 1) ORELSE ... ORELSE (rtac disjL 1));
> Goal " |- (A --> B --> C) --> (A --> B) --> A --> C";
Level 0 (1 subgoal)
|- (A --> B --> C) --> (A --> B) --> A --> C
1.  |- (A --> B --> C) --> (A --> B) --> A --> C
> by tacSeq1;
Level 1
|- (A --> B --> C) --> (A --> B) --> A --> C
No subgoals!
```

The next example corresponds to a sequent that is not valid.

```
> Goal "|- (A --> D --> C) --> (A --> B) --> A --> E";
Level 0 (1 subgoal)
|- (A --> D --> C) --> (A --> B) --> A --> E
1.  |- (A --> D --> C) --> (A --> B) --> A --> E
> by tacSeq1;
Level 1 (2 subgoals)
|- (A --> D --> C) --> (A --> B) --> A --> E
1.  B, A |- E, D
2.  C, A --> B, A |- E
```

It is not difficult to improve the previous tactic to also work out the remaining subgoals. In this way, for invalid sequents, the remaining subgoals will encode the counter-examples. For that purpose one simply has to rewrite the previous tactic in such a way that it can be applied to subgoals other than the first. The first step is to define a function that, to each subgoal i associates the tactic (rtac axS i) ORELSE ... ORELSE (rtac disjL i). This is achieved by val tacSeqfun = fn i => (rtac axS i) ORELSE ... ORELSE (rtac disjL i).

In the previous command the intended function (fn i => (rtac axS i) ...) is given the name tacSeqfun. Finally, the improved tactic is given by REPEAT_FIRST tacSeqfun that repeatedly applies tacSeqfun to each subgoal (starting with the first). When no further applications of tacSeqfun are possible, the next subgoal is worked out. For convenience, the name tacSeq is given to REPEAT_FIRST tacSeqfun. Note that the behavior of the new tactic on valid sequents is the same as the old tactic. We illustrate the new tactic using the previous (invalid) sequent.

```
> Goal "|- (A --> D --> C) --> (A --> B) --> A --> E";
Level 0 (1 subgoal)
|- (A --> D --> C) --> (A --> B) --> A --> E
1.  |- (A --> D --> C) --> (A --> B) --> A --> E
> by tacSeq;
Level 1 (2 subgoals)
|- (A --> D --> C) --> (A --> B) --> A --> E
1.  B, A |- E, D
2.  C, B, A |- E
```

2.6 Meta-universal quantification and first-order logic

Until now, different deductive systems for classical propositional logic have been presented. For the predicative version one needs terms, predicates and quantifiers. Terms belong to a type different from that of formulas and can be built in the usual way using variables and function symbols. Both formulas and terms are λ-calculus terms, i.e. λ-abstraction and λ-application are also available. Predicates are represented as functions that, to each term, associate a formula. For example, $\lambda x.P(x)$ associates to each term x the formula $P(x)$. The λ-term $\lambda x.P(x)$ is written %x. P(x). Quantifiers are represented as functions that associate a formula to a λ-term. For example, all(%x. P(x)) is a universally quantified formula. An alternative syntax (and a priority value) can be stated by (binder "ALL " 10). This means that ALL x. P(x) will abbreviate all(%x. P(x)).

For the purpose of defining propositional systems only meta-implication was needed. In the predicative context the introduction and elimination rules for quantifiers need the meta-universal quantification (of the built-in logic Pure). The metaformula !!x. P(x) means that P(t) is true for any arbitrary term t. In particular, the generalization (introduction) rule is represented by the metaformula (!!x. P(x))==>ALL x. P(x) and is represented internally by (!!x. ?P(x))==>ALL x. ?P(x). The rule can be read as follows: In order to prove ALL x. P(x) one has to prove P(x) for arbitrary x. The elimination rule for the universal quantifier is (ALL x. P(x))==>P(t) and is represented internally by (ALL x. ?P(x))==>?P(?t). The substitution of x by t in P corresponds, in the context of λ-calculus, to λ-application. Possible problems related to substitutions are dealt with by application of α-reduction (variable renaming) and β-reduction (function application).

Next we present the theory representing classical first-order logic.

```
CLASSIC = PROPOSITIONAL +
classes
```

```
term < logic

consts (* Quantifier functions *)
all ::  ('a::term => o) => o (binder "ALL " 10)
ex ::  ('a::term => o) => o (binder "EX " 10)

rules (* Quantifiers *)
allI "(!!x. P(x)) ==> (ALL x. P(x))"
allE "(ALL x. P(x)) ==> P(t)"
exI "P(t) ==> (EX x. P(x))"
exE "[| EX x. P(x); !!x. (P(x) ==> R) |] ==> R"
end
```

The theory uses the connectives and rules of classical propositional logic and
adds quantified formulas and their rules. It is noteworthy that term is not a
type but a class to which any term type must belong. For instance, noting
that 'a is a variable ranging over types, the function all :: ('a::term=>o)=>o
is a function that associates a formula to a predicate (on its turn, a function
that associates a formula to a term). Finally, in rule exE, the fact that R does
not depend on x codes the condition that x cannot occur free in R. In the
next example we want to establish [| ALL x. Q(f(x)); ALL x. (P(x)-->Q(x)) |]
==> ALL x. Q(f(g(x))) using the theory CLASSIC. It seems easy, at first glance,
since the conclusion follows from the first premise. We first apply rule allI
and then rule allE.

```
> Goal "[| ALL x. Q(f(x)); ALL x. (P(x)-->Q(x)) |] ==> ALL x. Q(f(g(x)))";
Level 0 (1 subgoal)
[|ALL x. Q(f(x)); ALL x. P(x)-->Q(x)|] ==> ALL x. Q(f(g(x)))
1.  [| ALL x. Q(f(x)); ALL x. P(x)-->Q(x) |] ==> ALL x. Q(f(g(x)))
> br allI 1;
Level 1 (1 subgoal)
[| ALL x. Q(f(x)); ALL x. P(x)-->Q(x) |] ==> ALL x. Q(f(g(x)))
1.  !!y.   [| ALL x. Q(f(x)); ALL x. P(x)-->Q(x) |] ==> Q(f(g(y)))
> br allE 1;
Level 2 (1 subgoal)
[| ALL x. Q(f(x)); ALL x. P(x)-->Q(x) |] ==> ALL x. Q(f(g(x)))
1.  !!y. [| ALL x. Q(f(x)); ALL x. P(x)-->Q(x) |] ==> ALL x. Q(x)
> ba 1;
*** by:  tactic failed Exception- ERROR raised
```

When applying allE, the unification of its conclusion %P. %t. P(t) with
Q(f(g(y))) has more than one solution. Isabelle displays first the result of β-
reducing %P. %t. P(t) into %t. Q(t) and the latter into Q(f(g(y))). In this case,

however, this is not the suitable solution since ALL x.Q(x) does not unify with the hypothesis ALL x.Q(f(x)). Isabelle's unifying procedure is clever in producing all possible solutions (and in first-order logic there can be an infinite number of them) by using lazy evaluation (evaluation on demand). To demand Isabelle to consider another solution we use the command back().

```
> back();
Level 2 (1 subgoal)
[| ALL x.Q(f(x)); ALL x.P(x)-->Q(x) |] ==> ALL x.Q(f(g(x)))
1.  !!y. [| ALL x.Q(f(x)); ALL x.P(x)-->Q(x) |] ==> ALL x.Q(f(x))
> ba 1;
Level 3
[| ALL x.Q(f(x)); ALL x.P(x)-->Q(x) |] ==> ALL x.Q(f(g(x)))
No subgoals!
```

The β-reduction of %P.%t.P(t) into %t.Q(f(t)) and the latter into Q(f(g(y))) is now considered. The rest of the proof is straightforward.

An alternative approach uses the tactic res_inst_tac [("v1","f1"),..., "vn","fn")] rule number, that corresponds to the use of resolution with rule to the subgoal identified by number forcing the schema variable v1 to be instantiated into f1 ... and vn into fn. In this case we can use res_inst_tac just after the application of the rule allI:

```
...
> by (res_inst_tac [("t","g(y)")] allE 1);
Level 2 (1 subgoal)
[| ALL x.Q(f(x)); ALL x.P(x)-->Q(x) |] ==> ALL x.Q(f(g(x)))
1.  !!y. [| ALL x.Q(f(x)); ALL x.P(x)-->Q(x) |] ==> ALL x.Q(f(x))
```

The last step of the proof is as before, using ba 1.

2.7 Labeled modal logics

The theories previously described are closely related to similar theories provided by Isabelle's distribution. Although theories for modal logics (including sequent calculus) are also available in that distribution we choose to present theories based on labeled deduction, as in [Viganò, 2000]. Labeled deduction internalizes semantic notions in the object-language and deductive system. Deductive systems for normal modal logics can thus become modular in the sense that they are obtained simply by adding suitable rules (representing the properties of the accessibility relation) to the deductive system of modal logic K. With labeled deduction as the choice of formalization for our modal languages we can escape the traditional difficulties that surface when the corresponding logical systems are represented, as advanced in [Paulson, 1990].

Formulas are obtained by prefixing a term (usually a variable) to a modal formula. For instance, $x : (\Box\Diamond\phi \to \psi)$ is a formula. Informally, this formula means that $(\Box\Diamond\phi \to \psi)$ holds in the world denoted by x. These are called *generalized modal formulas*. Formulas $x \, Rel \, y$ state that the world denoted by y is accessible from the world denoted by x and are called *relational modal formulas*. More generally, they may also involve terms as in $t_1 \, Rel \, t_2$. By the present construction, strings such as $(x : \phi) \lor (y : \psi)$ and $(\forall x)(x \, Rel \, x)$ are *not* formulas of K —but they *will* be formulas of the hybrid logic presented in the next section.

The theory for the minimal normal modal logic K is presented below. There are three types of syntactic entities involved in that theory: tm for terms (that prefix modal formulas), sbf for modal (sub)formulas and o for formulas. The latter are either generalized formulas (built with gf) or relational formulas (built with rf). The rules for $\Box$ ([]) and $\Diamond$ (<>) are similar to the rules for the universal and the existential quantifiers. For instance, the rule boxI (introduction of $\Box$) asserts that x: []P follows from the proof that P holds in y for arbitrary y related to x. We omit most of the propositional fragment as straightforward.

```
K = Pure +
classes
term < logic
types
tm (* the type of terms for labels *)
sbf (* the type of modal subformulas *)
o (* the type of formulas *)
arities
tm ::   term
sbf ::  logic
o ::    logic
consts (* Formula Generators *)
gf ::   [tm,sbf] => o ("_:_" [0,0] 10)
rf ::   [tm,tm] => o ("_ Rel _" [0,0] 10)
Trueprop ::  o => prop ("(_)" 5)
(* Modal (sub)formulas *)
and ::  [sbf, sbf] => sbf ("_&_" [36,35] 35)
...
box ::  sbf => sbf ("[]_" [40] 40)
dia ::  sbf => sbf ("<>_" [40] 40)
```

```
rules
(* Propositional *)
conjI "[| x:P; x:Q |] ==> x:P&Q"
...
(* Modal Operators *)
boxI "(!!y.(x Rel y ==> y:P)) ==> x:[]P"
boxE "[| x:[]P; x Rel y|] ==> y:P"
diaI "[| x Rel y; y:P|] ==> x:<>P"
diaE "[| x:<>P; (!!y.[|x Rel y; y:P|]==> z:Q)|]==> z:Q"
(* Abbreviations *)
verum_def "x:verum == x:falsum-->falsum"
neg_def "x:~P == x:P-->falsum"
iff_def "x:P<->Q == x:(P-->Q) & (Q-->P)"
```

The theory for KT can be obtained from the theory for K by adding the axiom (a rule with no premises) of reflexivity (x Rel x). The theory for KB adds to the theory for K the rule of symmetry (x Rel y ==> y Rel x), and the theory for $S5$ adds to the theory for K both the axiom of reflexivity and the rule of symmetry, together with the rule of transitivity ([|x Rel y; y Rel z|] ==> x Rel z). Many other modal systems can be formalized in a similar way. To define more complex systems such as the normal modal logic of confluence, one might make use of terms in the labels. In this case, we add to the theory for K a Skolem function as a new constructor of the form h :: [tm,tm,tm] => tm, and we add also the rules [|x Rel y; x Rel z|] ==> y Rel h(x,y,z) and [|x Rel y; x Rel z|] ==> z Rel h(x,y,z).

3 A hybrid logic

The issues addressed before are part of the syllabus of a course in logic for undergraduate students in Mathematics and in Computer Science, including the logics previously referred. The final assignment included the definition of a theory in Isabelle representing the hybrid logic described in the following. To learn more about hybrid languages, see [Blackburn and Seligman, 1998].

> The hybrid logic to be defined, using only Pure, is a labeled modal logic where quantification over worlds is allowed. Formulas like $\forall x (x\,Rel\,x) \rightarrow \forall x(x : \Box\psi \rightarrow x : \psi)$ can be written in the logic. In this logic the atomic formulas are generalized modal formulas and relational modal formulas, defined as in section 2.7. However, falsum, negation, disjunction and $\Box$ are the only connectives herein considered as primitive for the construction of the atomic formulas (verum, conjunction, implication, equivalence and $\Diamond$ are taken as abbreviations). The set of formulas is

obtained by closing the latter set of atomic formulas with negation, disjunction and the universal quantifier (conjunction, implication, equivalence and the existential quantifier are taken as
abbreviations). In particular, strings such as $(\forall x)\phi$ and $\Box(x : \phi)$
will *not* constitute formulas of the present language. Note that
the propositional connectives occur in formulas and also within
atomic formulas. For example, in the atomic formula $x : (\phi \vee \psi)$,
disjunction involves two modal subformulas whereas in the (non-
atomic) formula $(x : \phi) \vee (x : \psi)$ it involves two formulas of the
hybrid logic. The intended interpretation assigns to both formulas the same meaning (justification: $(\phi \vee \psi)$ is true at the
world x if and only if either ϕ is true at x or ψ is true at x)
and the deductive system must be able to prove them equiv-
alent. Moreover, the derived rules for all symbols defined by
abbreviation should be made available by the student.

Most students were able to successfully deliver the corresponding Isabelle
theory. One possible solution, using natural deduction, follows. In this
solution we use *polymorphism* to define the connectives that are common
to the two different types of "formulas", the modal subformulas and the
formulas themselves. For example, `not::('a::logic) => 'a` defines a polymorphic operation `not` that takes any type of class `logic` and returns a value
of that type. In our case we have two possible types, namely `sbf` (for modal
subformulas) and `o` (for formulas). In this way `not::('a::logic) => 'a` simultaneously defines the two functions (connectives) `not::sbf => sbf` and `not::o`
`=> o`. In general, one has to provide introduction and elimination rules for
both connectives. However, our solution provides rules only for `not::o =>`
`o` and provides further rules to transform subformulas into formulas and
vice-versa (when applicable). For example, in order to conclude `x:~P` one
may first conclude `~(x:P)` and then apply the rule that transforms it into
`x:~P`. The new rules for negation are `negOut "x:(~P) ==> ~(x:P)"` and `negIn`
`"~(x:P) ==> x:(~P)"`. By using such transformation rules the introduction
and elimination rules for `not::sbf => sbf` can be derived in this system. Similar considerations apply to other connectives.

```
HYBRID = Pure +
classes
term < logic
default
term
types
tm (* the type of terms for labels *)
```

```
sbf (* the type of modal subformulas *)
o (* the type of formulas *)
arities
tm ::  term
sbf ::  logic
o ::  logic
consts
(* Formula Generators *)
labf ::   [tm,sbf] => o ("_:_" [0,0] 45)
relf ::   [tm,tm] => o ("_ Rel _" [0,0] 45)
Trueprop ::   o => prop ("(_)" 5)
(* For modal subformulas only *)
verum, falsum ::   sbf
box ::   sbf => sbf ("[]_" [50] 50)
dia ::   sbf => sbf ("<>_" [50] 50)
(* Quantifiers (for formulas only) *)
all ::   ('a => o) => o (binder "ALL " 10)
ex ::   ('a => o) => o (binder "EX " 10)
(* Connectives for both modal subformulas and formulas *)
not ::   'a::logic => 'a ("~_" [40] 40)
and ::   ['a::logic, 'a] => 'a ("_&_" [36,35] 35)
or ::   ['a::logic, 'a] => 'a ("_|_" [31,30] 30)
imp ::   ['a::logic, 'a] => 'a ("_-->_" [26,25] 25)
iff ::   ['a::logic, 'a] => 'a ("_<->_" [26,25] 25)
rules
(* Connectives *)
abs "(~P ==> y:falsum) ==> P"
negE "[| ~P; P |] ==> Q"
negI "(P ==> y:falsum) ==> ~P"
negOut "x:(~P) ==> ~(x:P)"
negIn "~(x:P) ==> x:(~P)"
disjIr "P ==> P|Q"
disjIl "Q ==> P|Q"
disjE "[| P|Q; P ==> R; Q ==> R |] ==> R"
disjOut "x:(P|Q) ==> (x:P)|(x:Q)"
disjIn "(x:P)|(x:Q) ==> x:(P|Q)"
(* Modal Operators *)
boxI "(!!y. (x Rel y ==> y:P)) ==> x:[]P"
boxE "[| x:[]P; x Rel y |] ==> y:P"
(* Quantifier *)
allI "(!!y. P(y)) ==> (ALL x. P(x))"
```

```
allE "(ALL x.P(x)) ==> P(z)"
(* Abbreviations *)
verum_def "verum == falsum-->falsum"
conj_def "P&Q == ~((~P)|(~Q))"
imp_def "P-->Q == (~P)|Q"
iff_def "P<->Q == ~(~((~P)|Q) | ~(P|(~Q)))"
dia_def "<>P == ~([]~P)"
ex_def "EX x.P(x) == ~(ALL x.~P(x))"
end
```

Note a difference between the abbreviations of the theory HYBRID and those of the theory K, in section 2.7. In the present theory, a connective like <-> can be used to generate both atomic formulas (as in P<->Q) and formulas of the above hybrid logic (as in x Rel y <-> z:[]P). Therefore, the rewrite rules must now be laid down so as to apply to both situations.

We illustrate the theory with some examples. In the first one we prove the derived rule for the elimination of disjunction of modal subformulas. Recall from section 2.4 that when the antecedent contains non-atomic metaformulas it is convenient to associate a name to each of the elements of the result of Goal.

```
> val [mt1,mt2,mt3]= Goal "[|x:(P|Q); x:P==>y:R; x:Q==>y:R|]==> y:R";
Level 0 (1 subgoal)
y:R
1.  y:R
val mt1 = "x:P|Q" [.] :  Thm.thm
val mt2 = "x:P ==> y:R" [.] :  Thm.thm
val mt3 = "x:Q ==> y:R" [.] :  Thm.thm
> br disjE 1;
Level 1 (3 subgoals)
y:R
1.  ?P|?Q
2.  ?P ==> y:R
3.  ?Q ==> y:R
> br mt2 2; br mt3 3; ba 2; br disjOut 1; br mt1 1;
...
No subgoals!
> qed "disjmE";
val disjmE = "[| ?x:?P|?Q; ?x:?P ==> ?y:?R; ?x:?Q ==> ?y:?R |] ==> ?y:?R"
```

Other examples follow. Only the used rules are shown. In the very last example, we use the tactic rotate_tac *number steps*, that corresponds to a left permutation of the subgoal identified by *number* by a number of *steps*.

```
Goal "(x:(A&B))<->(x:A)&(x:B)";
br eqI 1; br conjOut 1; ba 1; br conjIn 1; ba 1;

Goal "(ALL x.(x:P))-->(ALL x.(x:[][]P))";
br impI 1; br allI 1; br boxI 1; br boxI 1; br allE 1; ba 1;

Goal "ALL x.  ((x Rel x)  --> ((x:[]P)-->(x:<>P)))";
br allI 1; br impI 1; br impI 1; br diaI 1; ba 1; br boxE 1; ba 1; ba 1;

Goal "(ALL x y.((x Rel y) --> (y Rel x)))-->(ALL x.((x:P)-->(x:[]<>P)))";
br impI 1; br allI 1; br impI 1; br boxI 1; br diaI 1; br impE 1;
br allE 1; br allE 1; by (REPEAT (atac 1));

Goal "(ALL x y z.((x Rel y) & (y Rel z) -->
(x Rel z)))-->(ALL x.(x:([]P-->[][]P)))";
br impI 1; br allI 1; br impIn 1; br impI 1; br boxI 1; br boxI 1; br boxE 1;
ba 1; br impE 1; br conjI 2; by (rotate_tac 2 2); by (rotate_tac 3 3); ba 2;
ba 2;
by (res_inst_tac [("z","yb")] allE 1); by (res_inst_tac [("z","ya")] allE 1);
by (res_inst_tac [("z","y")] allE 1); ba 1;
```

4 Concluding remarks

The system Isabelle is an appropriate tool for the definition and experimentation of new logics. The fundamental concepts underlying the definition of new Isabelle theories and their use are not too difficult to master. In this way, users can easily start to use the system for their own purposes. We have presented the most important concepts, illustrated by examples that undergraduate logic students are able to develop.

Obviously, there are other important features of Isabelle not described herein. There are many logics and useful tactics already provided by the distribution. There is a growing open collection of Isabelle proof libraries and examples at

http://afp.sourceforge.net/.

Moreover, proofs can be developed in more user-friendly environments, including management of theories and standard graphical notation for connectives and operators (see

http://proofgeneral.inf.ed.ac.uk/

for the ProofGeneral tool and its support for Isabelle). The language Isar provides syntactic sugar for developing proofs and is now becoming standard. Isar's manual and other relevant documentation are freely available on-line at

http://www.cl.cam.ac.uk/Research/HVG/Isabelle/docs.html.

Acknowledgements

This work was partially supported by FCT and FEDER, namely, via the Project FibLog POCTI/MAT/372 39/2001 of CLC (Centro de Lógica e Computação). The third author is partially supported by FCT grant SFRH / BD / 8825 / 2002.

BIBLIOGRAPHY

[Blackburn and Seligman, 1998] P. Blackburn and J. Seligman. What are hybrid languages? In M. Kracht, M. de Rijke, and H. Wansing, editors, *Advances in Modal Logic, Volume 1*, pages 41–62. CSLI Publications, Stanford, California, 1998.

[Gleick, 1987] J. Gleick. *Chaos, Making a New Science*. Penguin Books, New York, NY, 1987.

[Nipkow *et al.*, 2002] T. Nipkow, L.C. Paulson, and M. Wenzel. *Isabelle/HOL*, volume 2283 of *Lecture Notes in Computer Science*. Springer-Verlag, Berlin, 2002. A proof assistant for higher-order logic.

[Paulson, 1990] L.C. Paulson. Isabelle: The next 700 theorem provers. In P. Odifreddi, editor, *Logic and Computer Science*, pages 361–386. Academic Press, 1990.

[Paulson, 1996] L.C. Paulson. *ML for the Working Programmer*. Cambridge Univ. Press, 1996. 2nd edition.

[Paulson, 1999] L.C. Paulson. *Introduction to Isabelle*. University of Cambridge, 1999. 2nd edition.

[Schroeder-Heister, 1984] P. Schroeder-Heister. A natural extension of natural deduction. *The Journal of Symbolic Logic*, 49(4):1284–1300, 1984.

[Troelstra and Schwichtenberg, 1996] A. Troelstra and H. Schwichtenberg. *Basic Proof Theory*. Cambridge Univ. Press, 1996.

[Viganò, 2000] L. Viganò. *Labelled Non-Classical Logics*. Kluwer Academic Publishers, 2000.

F. Miguel Dionísio, Paula Gouveia, and João Marcos
CLC, Departamento de Matemática
Instituto Superior Técnico
Lisbon, Portugal
Email: {fmd,mpg,jmarcos}@math.ist.utl.pt

The Dynamic Nature of Meaning

CLAUDIA ARRIGHI AND ROBERTA FERRARIO

ABSTRACT. In this paper we investigate how the dynamic nature of words' meanings plays a role in a philosophical theory of meaning. For 'dynamic nature' we intend the characteristic of being flexible, of changing according to many factors (speakers, contexts, and more).

We consider meaning as something that gradually takes shape from the dynamic processes of communication. Accordingly, we present a draft of a theory of meaning that, on the one hand, describes how a *private* meaning is formed as a mental state of individual agents during a lifetime of experiences, and, on the other hand, shows how a *public* meaning emerges from the interaction of agents. When communicating with each other, agents need to converge on a shared meaning of the words used, by means of a negotiation process. A public meaning is the abstract product of many of these processes while, at the same time, the private meanings are continually reshaped by each negotiation.

Exploring this dynamics, we have been looking at the work done by computer scientists dealing with problems of heterogeneity of sources of information. We argue that a suitable solution for both disciplines lies in a systematic characterization of the processes of *meaning negotiation.*

1 Introduction

This paper wants to be a contribution, mainly of philosophical character, to a new current of thought and research in semantics that have been defined the "dynamic turn" in the study of meaning [Peregrin, 2003]. The central point of this approach to meaning is that there is not such a thing like a precise literal meaning of a word or expression, but meaning is something that gradually evolves from the dynamic processes of communication. This dynamic character is not some kind of secondary aspect of meaning, but it is instead a fundamental feature and we believe that it should receive more consideration in philosophical theories on meaning. What we are going to do is to stress the importance of this dynamic character and to make few steps towards a philosophical approach to meaning more focused on processes that shape meaning, instead of focusing on definitory issues.

Lorenzo Magnani and Riccardo Dossena, editors, *Computing, Philosophy, and Cognition*, pp. 295–312 © 2005, C. Arrighi and R. Ferrario

Even though the dynamic aspect of meaning may seem obvious, strangely enough it has been mostly neglected in philosophical theories. When dealing with meaning, some of the main currents in philosophy of language tend to focus on defining what meaning *is*, looking for something that can be circumscribed and pinned to a specific word; dynamics doesn't seem to be the main issue in these theories. We can also find a different tradition, the origin of which has been universally connected with Ludwig Wittgenstein's later work; this is engaged in the effort of showing a strong relation between what meaning is and what is the use we make of it, its relation with social interactions. Unfortunately, this approach to meaning still struggles to find a philosophical account that has not been accused of being 'foggy' or mere 'hand-waving'.

On the other hand, if we look outside of the philosophical circle, we can see that recently a lively debate related to meaning has animated computer scientists: the artificial agents they are dealing with don't always have access to a common and conveniently labeled ontology, they have their own representations of things, and maybe their own names, but they have to 'communicate' things to each other: how can this be done, practically? One of the solutions proposed is to imitate a way in which often humans manage to understand each other, i.e. by negotiating the intended meaning of words and expressions while engaged in conversations. How come that philosophers don't talk about meaning negotiation? It seems thus that the study of the processes of meaning negotiation is one of the points in which the studies in philosophy and in computer science can merge and therefore obtain reciprocal enhancement.

In this paper we would like to show that meaning cannot be defined independently from the practices in which it is used, but it can be more efficiently described as a tool used to pursue specific linguistic tasks. And, just as could happen to workshop tools, in the long run it itself is shaped by the many jobs done. We will consider the meaning of a word as a variable, the value of which slowly changes as a consequence of many individual negotiations of reference between speakers. The main idea is that repeated negotiations of a term in a social community *shape the meaning* of such terms, especially the meaning attributed to it by each individual agent, but also the one that has been called the "literal" meaning. To accomplish this, we need to reformulate the idea of negotiation taken from AI in a way that can be applied to real human communication; to this end we will refer to the work that Herbert Clark has done in psychology on collaborative processes in using language.

We start in section 1 by giving a brief account of the different approaches that have been historically developed in philosophy on the analysis of meaning and we single out four of these approaches, from which we try to extract interesting hints. Then we give a short survey of what has been done in computer science. In section 2 we look at the insights given by a theory of language use as a joint activity, while in section 3 we present our proposal and in section 4 we sketch some possible future developments.

2 Looking for a definition of meaning

2.1 Main theories in the philosophy of language

The idea of a tight connection between the meaning of words and the dynamics of social interactions has never been denied, but theories of meaning and reference that rely heavily on this connection have been considered in some kind of opposition to the other main stream in philosophy of language. This is well summarized by [Peregrin, 1995] at the beginning of a review of Robert Brandom's book "Making it explicit":

> The philosophy of language of the present century can be seen as dominated by two contrary tendencies. The first of them is to take language to be a kind of nomenclature, to take the word-meaning relation to be a basic and irreducible fact (either of the causal kind, or of a specific kind peculiar to "intentional" mediae of representation). The second is the tendency to view language rather as a toolbox; and to take the "intentional", representational capacities of words to be parasitic upon their involvement with human activities. According to this second view, "to have meaning" is to play a certain role within the structure of human conduct and within the social institutions which regulate it. [Peregrin, 1995, p. 84]

The second tendency described by Peregrin is the one we are going to follow. In order to do this, we feel compelled to compile a brief overview of the attempts made so far to define meaning, just to sketch the landscape that is framing this contribution. This is a list of what seem to be the essential features of the main traditional theories on the nature of meaning. They can be roughly summarized by the following slogans:

- the meaning of a word is the denoted object;
- meaning is something in the speaker's mind (idea, image, concept, intention);
- meaning is a set of conditions of satisfaction;
- meaning is determined by the use in a linguistic community.

The first position, taken literally, would assume a one-to-one relationship between words' meaning and entities in the world. More sophisticated and elaborated versions of theories of direct reference [Kripke, 1972] are able to account for more realistic relations many-to-many (the name "Mary" doesn't apply to just one thing in the world, and a certain object doesn't necessarily bear just one name), both in the case of correspondence of common names and "natural kinds" and in the case of proper names and single objects; nevertheless the central claim of these theories is that the meaning of a word is its denoted object. One of the main problems of this kind of approach has been underlined by the famous Fregean example of the morning and the evening star, that we rephrase here with a more prosaic example in everyday life: the words "entrance" and "exit", used to denote a unique door. In the example, one could be tempted to say that the two words denote the same object, but they mean different things, leaving space for an intermediary between word and object: from here the rise of the Fregean "sense". The merit of this position has been to underline the necessity of a connection between meaning and reference, i.e. between language and the world, but this relationship cannot be easily stated as a simple identity.

The second position in the list stresses the importance of an intermediate component between words and objects, and characterizes it as a subjective point of view on the object denoted. We use words to refer to things that we have in mind, so we could identify the meaning of a word with the mental content representing the object denoted. Let's take the example of the door again: whether this is an entrance or an exit depends on where I am and how that door is represented in my mind in a given moment. Or we could formulate the same idea using an intentional vocabulary: the door is an exit if I indicate it with the intention to indicate a way out from somewhere. But even this position presents hard problems. The main one is that in this way we have lost the connection to things in the world. If meaning is definable with what is inside one's head, how can we exchange thoughts with other speakers? A possible way out is that of assuming that the same word is simply connected to the same set of thoughts in every person. But if we assumed this, then we wouldn't have any misunderstanding in communication (clearly false), and if we don't assume this commonality, how is any communication possible at all given that we can't see directly in each other's mind?

The third position is one that characterizes the meaning of a word as the set of conditions to be satisfied by an object: whatever object satisfies the conditions, is the object denoted. This position has some useful features: it's able to connect the linguistic expression with states of the world, but without a one-to-one relationship; it doesn't need to be subjective, because the conditions can be the same for everyone (we could say "an exit is a door that goes outside with respect to the speaker, whoever he/she is"); then this definition doesn't identify meaning with a kind of entity, but rather with a procedure to check the relevant conditions. This view is really promising, but how to choose the relevant conditions to be satisfied is an open problem. The attempt to build a set of conditions defining the proper use of a word has proven to be hard to accomplish; the aim has been mainly to select a set of conditions individually necessary and jointly sufficient to describe the word, but it is often impossible to reach an agreement on such a set of conditions. The conditions approach could maybe rely on the help of pragmatic procedures to specify what kind of conditions have to be satisfied to accept a certain utterance, from a specific speaker, in a specific context. But it doesn't provide a convincing tool to describe general semantic knowledge.

In the fourth position there is an acknowledgment of the impossibility to set a fixed frame of conditions to specify what a word denotes, and instead it points out that the meaning of an expression consists in the actual use that can be made of that expression in social interaction. The spirit of this idea was suggested by Wittgenstein in the *Philosophical Investigations* (1958): one of the key paragraphs where Wittgenstein suggests this view is section 197, where he, talking about understanding a word, says:

> It becomes queer when we are led to think that the future development must in some way already be present in the act of grasping the use and yet isn't present. – For we say that there isn't any doubt that we understand the word, and on the other hand its meaning lies in its use. [Wittgenstein, 1958, section 197]

Following what seems to be his train of thought, if we consider the literal meaning of a word as a fixed set of things (rules, conditions, features), then we imply that when we learn that word, we are including in this knowledge any possible future usage of the word. According to Wittgenstein, something is weird in this view, and he promotes the idea that, in the end, to understand a word is the same thing as being able to use it properly, it is a practice; we don't need to be able to describe it in a finite and precise way, and maybe we wouldn't be able to do it (as for the practice of riding a bike). The problem with this view is that it doesn't provide a way to determine the details of a representation of meaning; just saying that the meaning of an expression consists in its use doesn't provide any information to represent this kind of knowledge. What is interesting in this view, however, is exactly what seems to be the source of its vagueness: if we want to determine a meaning, we have to look at the dynamic of linguistic practice, and not just at static rules and definitions. In this way this approach underlines the dynamics nature of language, and its social component. From this we could infer that, when looking for a representation of meaning, we can just represent the basic structures, the guidelines, the processes that we need to start and get involved in the practice of language.

Another potential problem in considering meaning as something subject to social practice that it would become a complete relativistic notion, different every time, something that cannot be decontextualized, there fore we could never talk about the *literal* meaning of a word. But the possibility of drawing a distinction between literal meaning and speaker's meaning is an important requirement, orthogonal to the positions about what meaning is. This distinction allows us to say that a certain sentence has a meaning, independently of any actual use: if I consider the sentence "the ball is green" without any other information, I can say that it has a meaning. In virtue of this distinction we can talk of an abstract literal meaning of a sentence as opposed to the specific referential function that the sentence is performing in a given context. In this way we can also account for the fact that the speaker is free to use the sentence, in an appropriate context, to perform an illocutionary act or to indicate a referent different from the literal meaning, but in order to do this we are supposed to know the a-contextual literal meaning. If we want to support a position that relates meaning with language use, we have to rethink this speaker's – literal meaning distinction.

We'll come back later to this issue; before doing that, we'll try to extract the most remarkable features from the approaches presented above.

2.2 Harvesting the best from the traditional theories

If we try to get the good qualities from the four positions on meaning that we have mentioned, but at the same time we try to avoid the major problems, we would have to draw a theory of meaning that has the following features:

- it must be able to identify a referent, but must not tie a meaning to a particular referent;

- it must be related with the mental contents of the speaker, but it must not be tied to this one either;

- it must take into account the conditions of satisfaction, but doesn't consider them as fixed;

- it must consider the variability of use of a linguistic expression important, but has to clarify the constraints and boundaries of this variation;

- finally, it has to give an account of the intuitive difference between a literal and a speaker's meaning.

This last point is particularly important: even if we are claiming that there is not a fixed meaning for a word, the classical difference between literal and speaker's meaning has to be accounted for.

The draft of a theory that meets all these requirements is twofold: on the one hand, it describes how the private meaning is formed as a mental state of individual agents and, on the other hand, it shows how a public meaning emerges from communication among agents and social practices; more than this, we would like to trace at least the outline of the structure of these "social practices".

Some interesting attempts in this direction have been made in computer science; even if originated by somewhat different motivations, these studies can be taken as inspiration for an analogous analysis in philosophy.

2.3 Theories of meaning in computer science

As already noted, theories of meaning in computer science are originated as attempts to give solutions to concrete problems of the everyday practices of storing and managing data. Many of these problems come from the so-called semantic heterogeneity, namely the diversity of meaning attributed to names and concepts by different information sources and users. More concretely, very often there is the need of merging information coming from different sources, that use different criteria to store and classify information.

If we want to merge information or to use information coming from different sources, we need a tool able to create communication among heterogeneous sources, such as databases using different schemas, document repositories using different classification structures, users' file systems etc.

In literature two main approaches have been proposed: the first is based on the creation of a shared model, a kind of "frame of reference" in which the concepts belonging to the different sources should be "translated". Even though this approach has proven useful in restricted or very specific domains, where the different parties seem to have similar goals and needs, it is less effective in open and dynamic environments. In order to deal with these, a second approach has been developed, that doesn't assume the presence of a shared model, but is based on a "peer-to-peer" philosophy. According to this approach, each peer keeps its own schema or conceptualization and they manage to communicate through two complementary processes: a process of *meaning coordination*, which is an attempt to find mappings between the meaning of a collection of expressions, and a process of *meaning negotiation*, that takes place when a direct mapping is not available and has the purpose of solving semantic conflicts among parties.

Now, if we try to draw a parallel with human language, the first, "centralized" approach can be seen as the process of compiling a dictionary or creating the frame of reference needed to account for the different uses of some words. In order to do this we must assume that some sort of common ground is already available, that there is a position from which the different uses can be observed and collected together. Instead the second, "distributed" approach is more similar to the way in which minor divergences in meaning are settled in everyday usage of language within a social community of speakers. We can have various kinds of difficulties in understanding each other in many occasions, and often we have to solve the problem on the spot, with no access to an already established common ground. From a philosophical perspective, this is the situation that is closer to the Quineian problem of *radical translation*, and this is also the dimension of language that is central in our approach, as we discuss in the next section.

3   Language use as a joint activity

The work of the psychologist Herbert Clark [Clark, 1996] presented in his book is one place where the connection between language and social practices has received a detailed and thorough formulation. In what follows, we summarize his reasons to claim that language use is a form of joint action. Then we outline Clark's general idea of joint actions and activities and we formulate an example to illustrate how the properties of an expression to "mean something" and to "refer to something" are properly described as special kinds of joint actions of speaker and listener .

At the very beginning of Herbert Clark's book, *Using language*, the author states his thesis:

> Language use is really a form of joint action [...] A joint action
> is one that is carried out by an ensemble of people acting in
> coordination with each other. [...] When Fred Astaire and
> Ginger Rogers waltz, they each move around the ballroom in
> a special way. But waltzing is different from the sum of their
> individual actions [...]. Waltzing is the joint action that emerges
> as Astaire and Rogers do their individual steps in coordination,
> as a couple. Doing things with language is likewise different
> from the sum of a speaker speaking and a listener listening.
> It is the joint action that emerges when speakers and listeners
> – or writers and readers – perform their individual actions in
> coordination, as ensembles. [Clark, 1996, p. 3]

One of the main representatives of this tendency in philosophy of language is Paul Grice [Grice, 1969], and Clark refers to his ideas a great deal, in particular regarding his concept of speaker's meaning and m-intention.

> Grice's m-intention – the heart of speaker's meaning – is a curious type of intention: it is one the speaker cannot discharge without the audience's participation [...] I can discharge my intention to shake a stick, an autonomous action, without anyone else's actions. But I cannot discharge my intention to do my part of our hand shake, a joint action, without you doing your part. [Clark, 1996, p. 130]

So, as a result of this character of the m-intention, the act of meaning something is what Clark calls "a participatory act in a joint act". In this way, Clark can formulate the principle he wants to defend:

> *Signal recognition principle*: signaling and recognizing in communicative acts are participatory acts. [Clark, 1996, p. 130]

where he's using "signaling" to indicate the speaker's action, and "recognizing" to indicate the listener's action. Together, they are participatory acts which constitute a "communicative act", the joint activity of communication.

In his book and in other articles, Clark takes the act of referring in particular consideration, describing how referring is a collaborative process [Clark and Wilkes-Gibbs, 1986] for a specific paper on the topic). He highlights the single steps of this process, that resemble very much the steps of a negotiation. We are going to give an example of this process that exemplifies some of the features pointed out by Clark.

In our example, Mary and Bob have a very general common goal, "keeping each other company", that doesn't necessarily need to have a linguistic component. During the pursuit of this goal, Bob comes out with an individual subplan, namely "to exchange opinions on a bike", and decides to present it to Mary as a candidate for a joint project. The presentation of this joint project, and the eventual achievement, can make very good use of language as a tool. Hence, Bob says: "Isn't that bike nice?" (let's call this the utterances). Bob has proposed this utterance as an opening of the subproject 'exchange opinions on a bike' on the basis of, at least, the following assumptions of common ground:

i) he and Mary both speak English

ii) they both have access to the same visual field

iii) they both are seeing a bike

iv) they both recognize "that bike" as salient.

It is now Mary's turn to take up or reject the project. Before that, however, she is engaged in the sub-sub-level joint activity of understanding Bob's utterance. This is what Clark calls principle of joint construal:

> *Principle of joint construal*: for each signal, the speaker and addressees try to create a joint construal of what the speaker is to be taken to mean by it.

Reaching a joint construal equals the mere linguistic problem of reaching convergence on the referent of an expression. To obtain this result, we need to engage in a specific kind of joint activity: this is the kind of joint activity where part of language is not just a tool, but is the product of the activity. So, what Clark calls "problem of joint construal", we are going to refer to as the "joint reference problem".

Let's go back to the example: if Bob is using their common ground correctly, the joint reference should be no problem at all, and if Mary goes ahead with a contribution to the "exchange opinions" project, they assume to have a joint referent, until otherwise proven. But in this case Mary has a problem with it, she doesn't know what Bob is referring to with "that bike", and so she proposes to solve this construal problem by asking: "Which bike?". The mistake is in Bob's assumption iv) about common ground, because there is not a clearly salient bike for Mary. Bob realizes this and answers "The green one", uptaking the "reach a joint reference for s" project, and proposing a correction. Now it is Mary's turn, and she says "Oh, I see...". In this way she accepts Bob's correction, and completes the "reach joint reference for s" project. Now she can go on and give her contribution in the project "exchange opinions on a bike", that has been suspended. She does so by saying "Well, I don't really like that bike", and the second level project can also be considered concluded, unless Bob or Mary disagree on the exit point, and makes another contribution, or opens another sublevel project and so on.

With this short example we want just to show how the process of *referring* to something is deeply connected with processes of interaction, collaboration, and this is also the main idea in the work by Clark that we have considered. But Clark himself traces precise boundaries to his goal. In [Clark and Wilkes-Gibbs, 1986] it is clearly stated that "our concern is not with semantic reference, but with the speaker's referent", (p. 2) and they provide a distinction between literary model and conversational model of linguistic exchange, claiming that the collaborative process for determining reference is active only in a conversational situation. On the one hand we agree on the peculiarity of tools used for this process during a "face-to-face" conversation (for example, the use of particular intonation of utterances), but on the other we think that the main features of this process can be generalized to give a more extensive account of words' meaning.

4   Our proposal

Starting from these positions, we want to take a further step: we not only want to show that in order to converge on the use of a word a negotiation is needed, we also want to claim that repeated negotiations *shape the meaning* of such word; they shape the 'private' meaning, attributed to the word by each individual agent, but negotiations also shape what has been called the 'literal' meaning, the meaning a word is supposed to *have* independently from context. In the two next subsections we'll show how these two different notions of meaning are characterized in our approach.

4.1   Private (or speaker's) meaning

We can say that the speaker's private meaning of a linguistic expression is a mental representation consisting of a variable set of conceptual features that don't represent a specific description that has to be satisfied by a candidate referent for the word, but rather must be considered just as tools to use when we engage in any linguistic exchange.

The linguistic exchange has a twofold purpose: the speakers try to find an agreement on the intended reference for a given word or expression, meshing their individual perspectives, and at the same time they refine their internal representation of the meaning in order to be more successful in future exchanges. The set of conceptual features is variable in two ways: it varies in time for the same speaker, due to the exposure to multiple linguistic interactions, hence to multiple refinement processes; it varies amongst different speakers, because there are hardly two speakers that have been through exactly the same series of refinement processes.

The private meaning is continually reshaped by the negotiation process, that creates new connections between words or concepts, strengthens some of these connections and weakens others etc.

As a possibility to represent private meaning as something shaped by interactions we could assume a flexible semantic network, where words (or concepts) are connected to one another when they frequently present themselves together in the experience of the agent.

The basic idea of a semantic network, as conceived in [Quillian, 1969], is to represent a semantic field as a graph where the nodes represent words (or concepts, or features), and the links between the nodes represent relationships. The links, or connections, between the nodes can have a different nature (similarity, inclusion, converse...), and different strength (more or less similar, for example). The nodes of such a network are activated when the corresponding concept is in use, and this activation spreads to the connected nodes, according to the distance, or the strength, or the nature of the connection. A psychological theory of spreading activation as a model for semantic processing was originally presented in [Collins and Loftus, 1975] and has been applied with success to explain psychological phenomena like semantic priming. Implemented examples of semantic networks include WordNet [Miller, 1990] or Semantica, an expansion of SemNet [Fisher, 2000]. What we are interested in is a flexible kind of semantic network, where nodes and connections can be reshaped as a consequence of use [Mitchell, 1993].

4.2 Literal or Public meaning

What has been called literal meaning, or also public meaning, of a word in a given language is also a set of conceptual features, but it is an abstract set and not the specific mental content of a person. It grows as a generalization from the most common conceptual features representing the speakers' meaning in widespread successful linguistic interactions[1]. We are then speaking of an abstraction, a "mean" value extracted from the speakers' usage of that meaning, and being the mean amongst values that vary in time, it also varies in time, even if slower. How is this mean value calculated? In everyday life it is not really calculated, but just estimated according to the best knowledge we have of a language. Compiling dictionaries is a professional performance of this estimation, which tries hard to extrapolate from as wide a basin of language usage as possible.

To sum up, our proposal consists of a treatment of meaning as emerging from processes of communication and negotiation taking place among agents: these processes can reshape the representation of private meaning, and in the long run the abstract representation of the literal meaning. As [Rapaport, 2003] puts it:

> We almost *always* fail [...]. Yet we almost always nearly succeed: This is the paradox of communication. [Rapaport, 2003, p. 402]

In order to understand how this process of negotiation determines a continuous transformation of the meaning of a word, in what follows we are going to describe a simplified example of negotiation where we can see the changes in the semantic representation.

---

[1]Language (or semantic) games, as described in [Hintikka, 1976] are a very interesting logical tool that has been proposed for the formalization of these processes.

4.3   A simple example of negotiation

Let's take the proper name "Socrates", pointing out the process that can transform someone's representation of such a name. If we are not learning a new word, the process of negotiation starts with a mental representation of the word/expression that has been consolidated through all the previous negotiations, that is what we have called private or speaker's meaning. The most common referent for "Socrates" is the well-known Greek philosopher, so we can imagine that the word "Socrates", inside a semantic network, is connected with words like "proper name, male, person, philosopher, past times, Greece, well-known, maieutic,..." (for the sake of simplicity, we describe here only simple word-to-word connections). The level of activation in these connections will be higher or lower in relation with the actual context, i.e. the general state of activity in the whole semantic network[2]. The number and the strength of the connections, instead, can be different in relation to my personal history of acquisition of the word; it is the product of a chain of previous linguistic exchanges that I have engaged in while learning and using this name, and maybe this chain could be followed backwards to trace the original source of the name, in this case the philosopher called Socrates[3].

The history of learning and usage of the name "Socrates" is even the source of the assumption that the person we are speaking with shares the same information about this name. There are words that we consider shared between anyone who speaks the same language, others that are shared between people of the same region, of the same social group, of the same degree of education, of the same technical background. All this information is related to what we know about the person we talk with, and what we know about the acquisition of a certain word.

So let's come to the conversation between two persons that we will call Massimo and Viola; this is taking place in Massimo's living room. Entering the living room, Viola notices the phonebook half-destroyed on the floor, and asks:

---

[2]For example, If I'm talking about gardening, the connections leading to "Socrates" in my network are supposedly not touched by the spreading of activation (unless at some point the conversation touches the word "hemlock").

[3]In this way, this theory can account for the crucial insight provided by the causal chain theory of reference. But there is a main difference with some of the accounts of the causal chain theory, as the one given by Kripke for example: according to Kripke, the connection between word and reference is transmitted through the causal chain as an constant connection, being a "rigid designator"; in the account of meaning as a dynamic result of negotiation, there is not space for such rigidity. Unsuccessful exchanges that didn't have a chance to be corrected and had wide resonance in a community can lead to permanent deformations of the connection established *ab initio*.

Viola: "My God, who has made this mess?"

Massimo: "Must have been Socrates"

Viola: "Socrates?"

Massimo: "Yes, he has even left a bone in here"

Viola: "Is the name of your dog Socrates?"

Massimo: "Yes"

Following freely the terminology used by Clark and Wilkes [Clark and Wilkes-Gibbs, 1986] on the psychological side and [Heeman and Hirst, 1995] on the computer scientce side, we can describe this conversation as follows: Viola and Massimo have engaged in a *referring plan*, Viola formulating a question that requires a referent as an answer (whoever has made the mess), Massimo responding with a *presentation* of a referring expression, identifying the author of the mess with the referent of the name "Socrates". Following the general schema given in Clark and Wilkes [Clark and Wilkes-Gibbs, 1986], after the *presentation* we need an *acceptance* (explicit or implicit) or a *rejection* from Viola. Asking "Socrates?", Viola is trying to manifest a rejection of the name as something able to pick up a referent. She is following a pragmatic principle of charity: there is no way to make sense of the fact that her referent for Socrates, the dead philosopher, is the one who made a mess in Massimo's living room. An internal revision process is in action: first of all, the association with past times has to be dismissed, because we are dealing with the agent of a recently happened event. Giving up on that means giving up several other connected features, or at least they become not likely (as philosopher, Greece, maieutic...). Let's imagine she is left with these connections: "proper name, male, living being, person". This is still not enough, so Viola asks for an *expansion* of the referring expression, trying to reach the goal of what we called *referring plan,* i.e. to find a common referent.

Now it's Massimo's turn, and he replies "Yes, he has even left a bone in here": Massimo has misunderstood Viola's rejection, in fact instead of thinking that Viola didn't get what the referent of "Socrates" is, he thinks Viola doubts that the actual referent of Socrates (in Massimo's use of the name) is also the author of the mess. Consequently, Massimo presents an *expansion*, to justify why he thinks that the reference of "Socrates" and the reference of "who has made the mess" are the same: "He has even left a bone in here". In Viola's representation system, the idea of an agent that leaves a bone on a floor in a house is connected with a pet, particularly a dog. Now the activation of "dog" helps to retrieve a background information, in fact she knows that Massimo has a puppy. The feature "person" can be deleted from her connections and she builds up a new hypothesis: "proper name, male, living being, dog, Massimo's pet". Viola, once again, has to *repair the referring plan*, as a consequence of her guessing, so she asks: "Is the name of your dog Socrates?". Finally, Massimo accepts this final correction, the negotiation is complete and the referential process is successful. End of the negotiation.

The referent of the word "Socrates" has been established, and so now she has extended her application of the word to a new usage and a new referent. This doesn't mean that this new referent has been fixed by the circumstance: any new linguistic act can require a new negotiation.

How do these changes in the speakers' meaning affect the general linguistic meaning of a word? In no relevant way. Actually, if Massimo was not a friend with whom Viola has frequent interactions, but just an occasional acquaintance, maybe the changes affecting her representation of Socrates in this conversation would be destined to weaken and dissolve in time. But saying this we don't mean to subscribe the view that this negotiation process is relevant only for the speaker's meaning. What we are arguing here is that this is also the starting point to define the more general linguistic meaning, that is nothing more that a large abstraction from the single speakers' meaning. We can imagine that these changes in the representation of the name "Socrates" can become relevant on a large scale if, for example, Massimo's dog becomes a movie star like Lassie. We are going to be more explicit about this in the next section, where we are going to sum up what has been said so far.

5   An alternative definition of meaning: conclusion and future issues

Let's summarize the view that we have delineated in the preceding sections. Using the traditional distinction between speaker's meaning and literal meaning, we can say that the private (speaker's) meaning of a linguistic expression is a mental representation consisting of a variable set of conceptual features, compositionally related to the syntactic structure of the expression. This set varies with every exchange in which such word or concept is involved.

What has been called literal meaning, or also public meaning, of an expression in a given language is also a set of conceptual features, but it is not something that can be clearly separated from the speakers' meaning: it emerges as an abstraction from the private meanings attributed to it by the speakers of a certain community. In common linguistic interactions, the literal meaning is the minimum set of features that we can assume to be shared by an unknown person who speaks our language: even in this case we just perform an heuristic estimation of what can safely be assumed. Any kind of knowledge of the background of our interlocutor can lead us to extend the set of assumption to be made[4].

How can such a process be formalized? We need to find an acceptable definition of the representation of the meaning of a word at the beginning of the exchange, for every agent engaged in the interaction. Then we follow the transformations of these representations while the dialogue is adding common information, and we can examine, at the end of the exchange, if the agents have reached a convergent structure, and what kind of structure it is: this will be the referent in that context. The kind of structure that has been the most successful in all of the linguistic interactions will be perceived as the linguistic meaning. The traditional relationship between private meaning and literal meaning is here inverted: we don't obtain the private meaning by applying pragmatic rules to the literal meaning, but rather we obtain a literal meaning when the negotiations about a word amongst speakers reach a large scale agreement[5].

Now, let's go back to the main question: can this kind of procedure be formalized and added to the grammar defining a language? In our opinion, this could be done by building a flexible semantic network that can represent ideally the main connections between concepts in an average speaker, and then describing the main processes that dynamically act on the network during the negotiation procedure with other speakers.

A concrete possibility to describe such processes could be the dynamic semantics proposed by [Groenendijk and Stokhof, 1991]. In the account given by [Veltman, 1996], the author stresses the dynamic component of this new kind of semantic stating:

> the slogan "You know the meaning of a sentence if you know the conditions under which it is true" is replaced by this one: "You know the meaning of a sentence if you know the change it brings about in the information state of anyone who accepts the news conveyed by it". [Veltman, 1996]

In computer science several attempts have been already made to describe and reproduce the way in which these processes work; we mention here only

---

[4]Maybe we could think of this process of formulating assumptions before a conversation as the result of a preliminary negotiation process with the context of conversation. In this case the process would take place between a speaker and a given situation, and not among speakers.

[5]A further consideration of this view can lead us to rethink the role of literal meaning. Outside an artificial and abstract description of language, is the idea of a literal meaning playing any role at all. A consideration of this view can be found in [Sperber and Wilson, 1998]

the more "semantically biased" approaches: the one based on ontologies [Masolo *et al.*, 2003], and on algorithms of semantic matching [Bouquet *et al.*, 2004] and [Giunchiglia *et al.*, 2004].

The direction shown by these studies is the one we believe is worth pursuing also in philosophy.

BIBLIOGRAPHY

[Bouquet *et al.*, 2004] P. Bouquet, L. Serafini, and S. Zanobini. Coordinating semantic peers. In *Proceedings of 11th AIMSA Conference*, Varna, Bulgaria, 2004.

[Clark and Wilkes-Gibbs, 1986] H.H. Clark and D. Wilkes-Gibbs. Referring as a collaborative process. *Cognition*, 22:1–39, 1986.

[Clark, 1996] H.H. Clark. *Using Language.* Cambridge University Press, New York, 1996.

[Collins and Loftus, 1975] A. M. Collins and E. F. Loftus. A spreading-activation theory of semantic processing. *Psychological Review*, 82(6):407–428, 1975.

[Fisher, 2000] K. M. Fisher. Semnet semantic networking. In J. H. Wandersee K. M. Fisher and D. Moody, editors, *Mapping Biology Knowledge*, pages 143–165. Kluwer, Dordrecht, Netherlands, 2000.

[Fllesdal, 1995] D. Fllesdal. In what sense is language public? In P. Leonardi, editor, *On Quine: New Essays.* Cambridge University Press, Cambridge, 1995.

[Giunchiglia *et al.*, 2004] F. Giunchiglia, P. Shvaiko, and M. Yatskevich. Semantic matching. In D. Fensel C. Bussler, J. Davies and R. Stuer, editors, *Proceedings of the 1st European semantic web symposium (ESWS'04)*, pages 61–75, Heraklion, 2004.

[Grice, 1969] H. P. Grice. Utterer's meaning and intentions. *Philosophical Review*, 78:147–177, 1969.

[Groenendijk and Stokhof, 1991] J. Groenendijk and M. Stokhof. Dynamic predicate logic, linguistics and philosophy. *Linguistics and Philosophy*, 14:39–100, 1991.

[Heeman and Hirst, 1995] P. Heeman and G. Hirst. Collaborating on referring expressions. *Computational Linguistics*, 21(3):351–382, 1995.

[Hintikka, 1976] J. Hintikka. Language-games. *Acta Philosophica Finnica*, XXVIII(1-3):105–125, 1976.

[Kripke, 1972] S. Kripke. *Naming and Necessity.* Harvard University Press, Cambridge (Mass.), 1972.

[Masolo *et al.*, 2003] C. Masolo, S. Borgo, Gangemi A., Guarino N., and A. Oltramari. Wonderweb deliverable d18. ontology library (final). Trento, Laboratory for Applied Ontology-ISTC-CNR, 2003.

[Miller, 1990] G. A. Miller. Wordnet: An on-line lexical database. *Inter. Journal of Lexicography*, 3(4):235–312, 1990.

[Mitchell, 1993] M. Mitchell. *Analogy-Making as Perception.* Bradford Books/MIT Press, Cambridge, 1993.

[Peregrin, 1995] J. Peregrin. Review of 'making it explicit' by robert brandom. *Canadian Philosophical Review*, XV:84–86, 1995.

[Peregrin, 2003] J. Peregrin, editor. *Meaning: The Dynamic Turn.* Elsevier, Amsterdam, 2003.

[Quillian, 1969] M.R. Quillian. Semantic memory. In M. Minsky, editor, *Semantic information processing.* The MIT Press, Cambridge (Mass.), 1969.

[Rapaport, 2003] W. J. Rapaport. What did you mean by that? misunderstanding, negotiation, and syntactic semantics. *Minds and Machines*, 13(3):397–427, 2003.

[Sperber and Wilson, 1998] D. Sperber and D. Wilson. The mapping between the mental and the public lexicon. In P. Carruthers and J. Boucher, editors, *Language and thought*, pages 184–200. Cambridge University Press, Cambridge, 1998.

[Veltman, 1996] F. Veltman. Defaults in update semantics. *Journal of Philosophical Logic*, 25:221–261, 1996.

[Wittgenstein, 1958] L. Wittgenstein. *Philosophical Investigations.* The Macmillan
Company, New York, 1958.

Claudia Arrighi
Philosophy Department
Stanford University, CA, USA
Email: carrighi@stanford.edu

Roberta Ferrario
Laboratorio di Ontologia Applicata
Consiglio Nazionale delle Ricerche, Trento, Italy
Email: roberta.ferrario@loa-cnr.it

A Modal Perspective on Proof Dynamics

PATRICK ALLO

ABSTRACT. Core aim of this paper is to focus on the dynamics of real proofs by introducing the block-semantics from [Batens, 1995] as a dynamical counterpart for classical semantics. This approach reveals an informational dynamics unknown to most dynamical logical systems. Viz. it adds an internal dynamics – due to deduction – to the better known external dynamics which is due to new information.

A block-based weakening of modal epistemic logic avoiding logical (deductive) omniscience is defined. It is subsequently extended with dynamic modal operators, in order to gradually recapture the initial strength of modal epistemic logic.

1 Introduction and motivation

Within recent research in formal approaches to human reasoning, two concepts seem to have acquired a predominant position: *dynamics* and *information*. As both have turned out to be very fertile, they have led in a short time to a true dynamical and informational turn in the domain of formal logic. While this revolution delivered a plurality of systems, it simultaneously yielded rather different views on the dynamics of information handling. As an illustration, one should certainly mention the gap between the approach in situation semantics - modeling how information flows from one situation to another - and that in dynamic epistemic logic (based on shifting ranges of alternative worlds in modal epistemic logic). [Van Benthem and van Rooy, 2003] characterizes the first one as *information as correlation*, and the latter approach – being his own – as *information as range*.

As to the concept of dynamics, most approaches seem to be concerned with changes due to new information. For instance, the underlying idea for Amsterdam-style dynamic logics is that information can be described as the change it induces on the knowledge (or belief) of a cognitive agent. This view – which models information as essentially *being informative* – has by now generated a series of very powerful logical tools for the representation of change in knowledge systems, see: [Van Benthem, 2003] for

Lorenzo Magnani and Riccardo Dossena, editors, *Computing, Philosophy, and Cognition*, pp. 313–327 © 2005, P. Allo

an overview. Despite its numerous existing applications like the dynamic epistemic logic presented in [Gerbrandy, 1997], the whole range of dynamic processes involved in human reasoning cannot fully be expressed within the present *information as range* setting. There is clearly more to the intuitive understanding of *being informative* than what is explicitly modeled by mainstream dynamic logics.

The problem we refer to is the following. Dynamic epistemic logic describes transitions of the kind induced by the new information that B is false, on the knowledge that A or B is true. Concretely it states that after every application of a program π – learning the falsehood of B – all epistemic alternatives contain A; formally $K_a(A \vee B) \supset [\pi]K_aA$. Such an approach relies on a notion of learning that is intrinsically stronger than our informal understanding of its meaning as "being told that ...". A more explicit interpretation of the interaction between a program π and an epistemic operator K (in dynamic epistemic logic) would be, learning the content of the information carried in π *and* computing all its consequences with respect to the present knowledge.

Considering the classical approaches in epistemic logic, it is easily seen that most of them model a logically and deductively omniscient agent. This means that the agent knows all logical truths, and all the logical consequences of his knowledge, see: [Girle, 2000, pp. 152–161]. At an informal level it should, however, not imply knowing proof-systems, feasible procedures, or accessing large amounts of computational time and space. Unfortunately such distinctions lie beyond the scope of traditional epistemic logic.

The tight connection between learning and computing, as presumed by classical epistemic logic and dynamic epistemic logic, is not as inevitable as it seems. Avoiding it mainly requires a broader view on cognitive dynamics, by the introduction of internal dynamics as a natural companion to external dynamics, for both are distinct parts of the intuitive notion of being informative. In a sense we only have to take Van Benthem's suggestion that the representation of information is tightly connected to processes of information handling even more seriously, and allow deductive processes to be treated as being equally informative.

By internal dynamics we refer to the changes in the knowledge of an agent that are due to a better insight through computing the consequences of one's initial knowledge. Hereby we insist on the fact that an increase of knowledge does not always rely on any new information; it is equally obtained by computing what is already given. This view not only rejects the deductive closure of one's knowledge, it even presupposes the stronger claim that knowing (and acquiring new information) does not imply any automatic (additional) deduction.

At the level of logics it asks for a blend of two systems. (i) Epistemic logics for knowing without computing; where *knowing that* has in itself no logical consequences. (ii) Dynamic operators expressing the effects of computing in a way that is analogous to what is known from dynamic epistemic logic. The necessity of such a radical distinction between computing and knowing is motivated on two levels: based on the need for logics yielding an explication of real cognitive processes, and, relying on a rather formal argument, based on the complexity of proof-procedures.

The first argument originates from philosophy of science. It is by now widely accepted that, with respect to the historical evolution of theories, requiring completeness is unrealistic, and in addition, the presumption of closure fails to explicate scientific change. This line of argument is, in conjunction with the undecidability of first-order logic, the core motivation for the study of adaptive logics as formal reconstructions of scientific and real-world reasoning, see: [Batens, 2000, pp. 52–54].

The second argument relies on computational and feasibility concerns, see [Urquhart, 2003] on the former and [Dubucs, 2002] on the latter. It has been argued that the traditional view on classical propositional logic, essentially based on its completeness and decidability, has to be reviewed with respect to the computational complexity of real proofs. From this perspective it turns out that even simple logical systems are not really decidable within limited resources of space and time, see [D'Agostino, 1999, pp. 45–46, 53–57] and [Urquhart, 1995]. For example, if we consider truth-tables for classical propositional logic, the well-known decision procedure is only feasible for a small number of propositional variables (it is exponential). More generally the classical propositional calculus in itself is $\mathcal{NP}$-complete whereas traditionally only the complexity-class $\mathcal{P}$ is considered practically solvable. This consideration extends the objections raised against deductive closure within the adaptive logics program for first order logics – due to undecidability results – to the plain propositional case. Besides that, thinking about computational complexity forces us to focus on real proof-systems instead of only relying on abstract consequence relations.

As the distinction between the derivability of a formula and an effectively derived formula is central to adaptive logics, it is no surprise that these logics already embody an implicit differentiation of knowing and computing. This is especially the case with the so-called block-semantics, the semantical counterpart of adaptive logics' dynamic proof-formats introduced in [Batens, 1995]. Within this context block-semantics have the advantage that they allow us to study internal dynamics independently from any specific proof-format. Therefore they can more easily be integrated in a different formal framework, viz tableau-proofs.

The aim of the planned connection between dynamic epistemic logic and internal proof dynamics is twofold. First it is intended as a general tool for studying the inherent dynamics of (adaptive and standard classical) proofs; next it can also be considered as an implementation of some results on omniscience from [Batens, 1995] within the framework of epistemic logics. This provides an alternative solution to the problem of omniscience in modal epistemic logic which only relies on a dynamic view of its propositional fragment (full insight is not instantaneous), and not on the more traditional weakening of its modal fragment. While the latter should be an immediate result of this paper, the former is more to be conceived as a methodological objective in the long run. Therefore I focus on the dynamics involved when writing down a proof, and argue that every step of such a proof is informative, hence has a pendant in some modal dynamic logic, viz, a dynamic operator representing the effect of a deductive step. Next to this, I show that adding the aforementioned operators to weak epistemic logics yields a logic with a deductive power comparable to some regular epistemic logics, but avoids uncontrolled deductive omniscience.

In a first part of the paper a basic account of block-semantics is given, related to standard natural deduction proofs (section 2.1), and subsequently reformulated with respect to tableau-proofs (section 2.2). A second part contains a reconstruction of internal dynamics with blocks and dynamic operators (section 2.3). In the third part a weak, block-based, epistemic logic is defined (section 3.1) and its interplay with dynamic operators outlined (section 3.2). Finally the presented approach to internal or proof-dynamics is further related to more general questions regarding information, being informative and the role of logic (section 4.1).

2 Internal dynamics starting from blocks

2.1 Proofs and blocks

In [Batens, 1995] classical proofs are reformulated in a way defining a consequence set that corresponds to the minimal understanding of the premises someone needs when writing down a specific line of a proof. This approach relies on the insight that making deductive moves in a proof does not presuppose a complete analysis of all involved complex formulas. Instead of rephrasing the whole setting of block-sematics and block-proofs, which is to be found in Batens' original paper, we tackle the problem through some examples.

The application of the *Disjunctive Syllogism* in the subsequent proof does, for instance, not imply a complete understanding of the disjuncts in (1). It is sufficient to distinguish that (1) consists out of a disjunction whose second term is negated in (2). This minimal analysis is precisely what is reflected in the block-analysis (right proof).

(1)	$(p \mathbin{\&} (\sim q \supset r)) \vee ((r \vee p) \supset q)$	(1)	$[\![(p \mathbin{\&} (\sim q \supset r))]\!] \vee [\![((r \vee p) \supset q)]\!]$	
(2)	$\sim ((r \vee p) \supset q)$	(2)	$\sim [\![((r \vee p) \supset q)]\!]$	
(3)	$p \mathbin{\&} (\sim q \supset r)$	(3)	$[\![p \mathbin{\&} (\sim q \supset r)]\!]$	

An obvious conclusion is that, given this block-analysis, $[\![p \mathbin{\&} (\sim q \supset r)]\!]$ is true at all block-models of the premises on line (1) and (2).

Comparing different natural deduction proofs within a block-based approach some peculiarities become apparent. More precisely, the comparison sheds a light on Batens' distinction between informative and uninformative moves in deductive systems – a Fitch-style one for the present case. While most classical proof-theories don't distinguish between the strength of various deductive rules, only few people familiar with real proofs would consider *Addition* and *Simplification* on the same level. Informally one could easily argue that moving from A to $A \vee B$ implies a move to a weaker statement. A similar argument would show that the move from $A \mathbin{\&} B$ to A and B at least does not involve a weakening. As the construction of proofs is merely a mechanical matter, such informal distinctions between deductive rules are not really a part of the game.

This objection does, as the following example shows, not apply to block-proofs. As may be easily checked, the application of SIMPL in the right-hand proof, restricts the set of all models satisfying $[\![A \mathbin{\&} B]\!]$ to the set of all models satisfying $[\![A]\!]$ and $[\![B]\!]$. More precisely, it restricts the set of all models satisfying $[\![A \mathbin{\&} B]\!]$, but allowing $[\![A]\!]$ and/or $[\![B]\!]$ to be false, to the set of all models satisfying $[\![A]\!]$ and $[\![B]\!]$ (and $[\![A \mathbin{\&} B]\!]$). On the contrary, the application of ADD in the left proof results in no restriction at all. As the block-analysis contains $[\![A]\!] \vee [\![B]\!]$ and $[\![A]\!]$, the set of models is not to be extended either. It involves no weakening of the consequence set, but only leads to the introduction of a new block.

(1)	$[\![A]\!]^1$		(1)	$[\![[\![A]\!]^1 \mathbin{\&} [\![B]\!]]\!]$	
(2)	$[\![A]\!]^1 \vee [\![B]\!]$	ADD	(2)	$[\![A]\!]^1$	SIMPL

As this example points out, proofs may contain some deductive steps we consider being uninformative. This does not entitle us to exclude these apparently useless rules from our proof-theory, for they are still useful (and obviously sound). At this point the distinction drawn between informative and uninformative steps is merely a heuristic feature (being helpful in the context of proof-search). It reveals the difference between steps that by themselves lead to a better insight in the premises, and steps that convert (at best) known information into a more convenient form for the application of another rule (see next section for an example).

2.2 Tableaus and blocks

Switching to the construction of tableaus, we get a completely different picture. Each tableau-rule leads, in its correspondent block-formulation, to a deeper block-analysis, and thus reveals the intrinsic informative nature of these rules. This conclusion is already reflected in the block-tableau for the previously mentioned application of DS.

In addition this example enables us to deal with the strange shift between tableaus – being informative in all their steps – and natural deduction proofs – necessarily relying on some uninformative steps. Whereas the structure of the given tableau fully relies on elementary analyzing rules, the proof consists of a single application of a derived rule. Comparing both, we cannot discern a single uninformative step, for the application of DS is in fact a shortcut, a combination of both elementary informative and uninformative steps (i.e. *Irrelevance* - $A/A \supset A$).

$$[[[(p \,\&\, (\sim q \supset r))] \vee [((r \vee p) \supset q)]]] \quad \text{Prem} \quad \surd$$
$$[\sim [((r \vee p) \supset q)]]] \quad \text{Prem}$$
$$\sim [p \,\&\, (\sim q \supset r)] \quad NC$$

$$\swarrow \quad \searrow$$
$$[(p \,\&\, (\sim q \supset r))] \;\bigm|\; [((r \vee p) \supset q)]$$
$$\times \qquad\qquad \times$$

Taking this result into account, and knowing that tableaus and natural deduction proofs are equivalent for classical propositional calculus, we conclude that for every elementary tableau-rule applied to the premises, an elementary or derived proof-rule providing us with the same insight in the premises exists. A proof for this claim can be reduced to the two cases we introduce further down: for tableau-rules on conjunctive formulas / blocks the correspondent proof-rule is SIMPL; for tableau-rules on disjunctive formulas / blocks the correspondent proof-rule is based on DS. This rather straightforward correspondence allows us to consider tableaus when studying internal proof-dynamics, and, at a later point, extend general conclusions to natural deduction proofs.

The use of tableaus has three major advantages:

(i) As mentioned, we don't have to deal with the distinction between informative and uninformative moves: tableau-rules are intrinsically informative and analyzing (the latter distinction between informative and analyzing from [Batens and Meheus, 2001, pp. 5–6] turns even out to be meaningless with respect to tableaus).

(ii) Some very useful derived rules have straightforward tableau-correspondents. This is particularly the case with so-called *de Morgan's laws* (NC, ND, and NI), which rely on rather complex (and also *unnatural*) natural deduction proofs. Precisely these cases are often mentioned as an objection against natural deduction, and as an argument in favor of tableau-systems (and sequent-calculus) as a more natural approach to deduction, see: [D'Agostino, 1999, pp. 63–67]. According to D'Agostino the contrived character of some proofs is mainly due to the constructive (intuitionistic) interpretation of the connectives reflected in natural deduction rules. From the standpoint of block-semantics, and especially considering the distinction drawn between informative and uninformative steps, one might prefer to blame the opaque interplay between informative and seemingly useless uninformative moves, for the "tricks" needed in some proofs. It even seems that the latter provides us with a more direct explanation for some flaws in natural deduction proofs, and the lack of these flaws in tableau-systems.

(iii) Whereas in natural deduction all introduction and elimination rules for the basic connectives are needed to obtain full deductive power (hence completeness), the number of tableau-rules can effectively be reduced. This can either be achieved by reformulating all connectives by means of (classical) negation and conjunction or disjunction, or by using Smullyan's distinction between rules applied on conjunctively (type A) and disjunctively (type B) acting (signed) formulas. In the sequel we choose to rely on the latter approach.

2.3 Modal description of block-analysis

As a last preliminary before turning to the modal dynamic perspective, we reformulate Smullyan's generalized approach for tableau-rules within the block-language. Starting from the distinction between formula's of type A and type B, it is possible to use only two tableau-rules, a linear and a branching one. As this is straightforward for anyone using the tableau-method, the only thing needed is a classification of the formulas using all connectives.

α	α_1	α_2
$T[\![X \& Y]\!]$	$T[\![X]\!]$	$T[\![Y]\!]$
$F[\![X \vee Y]\!]$	$F[\![X]\!]$	$F[\![Y]\!]$
$F[\![X \supset Y]\!]$	$T[\![X]\!]$	$F[\![Y]\!]$
$T[\![\sim X]\!]$	$F[\![X]\!]$	$F[\![X]\!]$
$F[\![\sim X]\!]$	$T[\![X]\!]$	$T[\![X]\!]$

$$\frac{\alpha}{\begin{array}{c}\alpha_1\\\alpha_2\end{array}}$$

β	β_1	β_2
$F[\![X \& Y]\!]$	$F[\![X]\!]$	$F[\![Y]\!]$
$T[\![X \vee Y]\!]$	$T[\![X]\!]$	$T[\![Y]\!]$
$T[\![X \supset Y]\!]$	$F[\![X]\!]$	$T[\![Y]\!]$

$$\frac{\beta}{\beta_1 \mid \beta_2}$$

The effect of both rules comes down to the analysis of a single block into its components. They represent one step out of a systematic construction of a Hintikka-set or downwards saturated set. Or, more precisely: the application of an α-rule extends a set of signed block-formulas with the components of one of its elements whereas the application of a β-rule extends a set of signed block-formulas to two alternative sets, each containing one component of an original element. Each analytic tableau can, as the subsequent example for the application of DS shows, be reconstructed by means of a labeled transition system (an abstract model of computation representing (i) states and (ii) transitions or programs, henceforth LTS).

$$\left\{\begin{array}{c} T[\![A \vee B]\!] \\ T[\![\sim B]\!] \\ \hline F[\![A]\!] \end{array}\right\} \quad \longrightarrow_\alpha \quad \left\{\begin{array}{c} T[\![A \vee B]\!] \\ T[\![\sim B]\!]\checkmark \\ F[\![B]\!] \\ \hline F[\![A]\!] \end{array}\right\}$$

$$\downarrow_\beta \qquad\qquad \searrow_\beta \qquad\qquad\qquad\qquad \downarrow_\beta \qquad\qquad\qquad \searrow_\beta$$

$$\left\{\begin{array}{c} T[\![A \vee B]\!]\checkmark \\ T[\![A]\!] \\ T[\![\sim B]\!] \\ \hline F[\![A]\!] \end{array}\right\} \quad \left\{\begin{array}{c} T[\![A \vee B]\!]\checkmark \\ T[\![B]\!] \\ T[\![\sim B]\!] \\ \hline F[\![A]\!] \end{array}\right\} \quad \left\{\begin{array}{c} T[\![A \vee B]\!]\checkmark \\ T[\![A]\!] \\ T[\![\sim B]\!]\checkmark \\ F[\![B]\!] \\ \hline F[\![A]\!] \end{array}\right\} \quad \left\{\begin{array}{c} T[\![A \vee B]\!]\checkmark \\ T[\![B]\!] \\ T[\![\sim B]\!]\checkmark \\ F[\![B]\!] \\ \hline F[\![A]\!] \end{array}\right\}$$

$$\searrow_\alpha \qquad\qquad \searrow_\alpha \qquad\qquad \longrightarrow_\alpha \qquad\qquad \nearrow_\alpha$$

Each node within this structure is labeled with two possibly empty sets of blocks: (1) Containing all block-premises (and – if analyzed – their sub-blocks); (2) Containing all negated block-conclusions (and – if analyzed – their sub-blocks). In what follows we will mainly focus on the first one.

From this simple case, we can deduce rather easily a few modal descriptions of the LTS for tableau constructions. E.g. in this structure it holds that: if $w \models T[\![A \vee B]\!]$ & $T[\![\sim B]\!]$, then $w \models \langle(\alpha;\beta) \cup (\beta;\alpha)\rangle T[\![A]\!]$, which means that from the state w, a state containing the information $[\![A]\!]$ can be reached through a number of α and β steps. In the next section we will extend this modal view in two ways: first with a block-formulation of modal epistemic logic, and secondly with a more precise formulation of the labelled transition system from this section.

3 A block approach to knowledge

3.1 Knowing blocks

As expected, replacing propositions with blocks allows for a possibilities model (see: [Gerbrandy, 1997]) for knowledge that validates necessitation and distribution, but simultaneously reduces their applicability. Let Ψ be the set of all blocks $[\![\ldots]\!]^b$. Each w is a possibility or block-model, and each S^{ba} is a set of possibilities or information state. In this case an information-state S^{ba} is the set of all models for a given block-analysis ba. On modal logic based on possibilities, see also: [Barwise, 1997].

(a) $w \models [\![\ldots]\!]^b$ iff $w([\![\ldots]\!]^b) = T$

(b) $w \models [\![\ldots]\!]^b \& [\![\ldots]\!]^{b'}$ iff $w \models [\![\ldots]\!]^b$ and $w \models [\![\ldots]\!]^{b'}$

(c) $w \models [\![\ldots]\!]^b \vee [\![\ldots]\!]^{b'}$ iff $w \models [\![\ldots]\!]^b$ or $w \models [\![\ldots]\!]^{b'}$

(d) $w \models [\![\ldots]\!]^b \supset [\![\ldots]\!]^{b'}$ iff $w \not\models [\![\ldots]\!]^b$ or $w \models [\![\ldots]\!]^{b'}$

(e) $w \models {\sim} [\![\ldots]\!]^b$ iff $w \not\models [\![\ldots]\!]^b$

(f) $w \models K[\![\ldots]\!]^b$ iff $w' \models [\![\ldots]\!]^b$ for all $w' \in S^{ba}$

(g) S^{ba} = the set of all classical models for a given block-analysis

Defining knowledge as such, it is clear that although $\models [\![\ldots]\!]^b \Rightarrow \models K[\![\ldots]\!]^b$, and $\models K[\![\ldots]\!]^b \& K([\![\ldots]\!]^b \supset [\![\ldots]\!]^{b'}) \Rightarrow \models K[\![\ldots]\!]^{b'}$ hold, deductive omniscience is restricted due to the failure of $\models K[\![A]\!]^b \& K[\![A \supset B]\!]^{b'} \Rightarrow \models K[\![B]\!]^{b''}$. So far, one might object that the presented block-approach to knowledge is merely an explicit representation of knowledge instead of a modeling of knowledge (see the discussion in [Fagin *et al.*, 1995, p. 320]).

There are, however, two major distinctions between the present approach and the explicit representations of knowledge. First, it should be mentioned that within the block-semantics for knowledge we impose some very specific constraints on the behaviour of K, viz. from (a)-(e) it follows that each $w \in S^{ba}$ defines a classical model, and from (f) and (g) it follows that the truth of $K[\![\ldots]\!]^b$ is defined with respect to all classical models satisfying $[\![\ldots]\!]^b$. Next, and more importantly, once we move up to a dynamic model, knowledge as truth in all possible worlds is recaptured step by step up to the level of litterals.

Before we turn to the elaboration of the dynamic setting, we still have to make the modal epistemic case explicit and show that it genuinely models knowledge. Consider the following case:

$$K[\![A \supset B]\!] \qquad\qquad K([\![A]\!] \supset [\![B]\!])$$

$$\left\{ \begin{array}{c} T[\![A \supset B]\!] \\ T[\![A]\!] \\ T[\![B]\!] \end{array} \right\} \;\leftrightarrow\; \left\{ \begin{array}{c} T[\![A \supset B]\!] \\ F[\![A]\!] \\ T[\![B]\!] \end{array} \right\} \qquad \left\{ \begin{array}{c} T[\![A]\!] \supset [\![B]\!] \\ T[\![A]\!] \\ T[\![B]\!] \end{array} \right\} \;\leftrightarrow\; \left\{ \begin{array}{c} T[\![A]\!] \supset [\![B]\!] \\ F[\![A]\!] \\ T[\![B]\!] \end{array} \right\}$$

$$\updownarrow \qquad\qquad \times \qquad\qquad\qquad\qquad \updownarrow \qquad\qquad \searrow\nwarrow$$

$$\left\{ \begin{array}{c} T[\![A \supset B]\!] \\ T[\![A]\!] \\ F[\![B]\!] \end{array} \right\} \;\leftrightarrow\; \left\{ \begin{array}{c} T[\![A \supset B]\!] \\ F[\![A]\!] \\ F[\![B]\!] \end{array} \right\} \qquad\qquad\qquad \left\{ \begin{array}{c} T[\![A]\!] \supset [\![B]\!] \\ F[\![A]\!] \\ F[\![B]\!] \end{array} \right\}$$

When comparing the epistemic possibilities matching an unanalyzed block with that of its analyzed counterpart, both turn out to model knowledge in the sense of *truth in all accessible states*, but they nevertheless remain clearly distinct. The proposed model simultaneously represents knowledge and one's insight in that knowledge. This becomes even clearer when we look at the effect of new information on a set of possibilities. For example, in this situation learning the truth of A excludes in both cases all possibilities in which A is false, but only leads to the knowledge of B in the right-hand case. In the left-hand case the falsehood of B remains possible. As the following structure points out, the effect of a program π – learning the truth of A – depends on the block-analysis, i.e. the insight in one's knowledge.

$$K[A \supset B] \qquad \longrightarrow_\beta \qquad K[[A] \supset [B]]$$
$$\downarrow \pi \qquad\qquad\qquad\qquad \downarrow \pi$$
$$K([A \supset B] \,\&\, [A]) \quad \longrightarrow_\beta \quad K([[A] \supset [B]] \,\&\, [A] \,\&\, [B])$$

It is, however, still possible to recover *learning and computing its consequences* by considering the compound program $\langle(\pi;\beta) \cup (\beta;\pi)\rangle$, which is – at least in this basic case – the block-correspondent for the program $[\pi]$ in dynamic epistemic logic.

As a final remark it should be noted that the use of blocks and block-valuations allows for possibilities such as classic-like models, hence excludes the need for non-normal possibilities to restrict logical omniscience. In the sequel we shall refer to such possibilities – e.g. where $[A \,\&\, B]$ is true whereas $[A]$ and/or $[B]$ are false – as incoherent but consistent possibilities. The next section will make this more formal.

3.2   Knowing and analyzing blocks

Informally, we have the following: (i) if an unanalyzed α-block is known, there is an α-action leading to the knowledge of α_1 and α_2, and (ii) if an unanalyzed β-block is known, there is a β-action leading to the knowledge that either β_1 or β_2 is true.

Consider an information state S^{ba} for a given block-analysis ba as the set of all classical models limited to that block-analysis. Each such a model corresponds to an epistemic possibility. If a known α-block is unanalysed – $[\ldots]_\alpha$ holds in all possibilities while its correspondent α_1 and α_2 sub-blocks do not necessarily hold in all possibilities – then there is an information state $\langle\alpha\rangle S^{ba}$ with all possibilities containing the corresponding α_1 and α_2 blocks. If a known β-block is unanalysed – $[\ldots]_\beta$ holds in all possibilities while some possibilities might contain none of its correspondent β_1 and β_2 sub-blocks – then there is an information state $\langle\beta\rangle S^{ba}$ with all possibilities containing at least one of the corresponding β_1 or β_2 blocks. This formulation and the subsequent properties makes the former informal characterization more precise.

(a) $\models K[\alpha] \supset \langle\alpha\rangle K([\alpha_1] \,\&\, [\alpha_2])$,   for $[\alpha]$ is an α-block
(b) $\models K[\beta] \supset \langle\beta\rangle K([\beta_1] \vee [\beta_2])$,   for $[\beta]$ is a β-block

Knowledge and logical consequence are restricted in this way:

$(\supset)$: $K([\![A \supset B]\!] \,\&\, [\![A]\!]) \supset \langle \beta \rangle K[\![B]\!]$
   or: $K[\![A \supset B]\!] \supset [\pi]\langle \beta \rangle K[\![B]\!]$, for π is learning the truth of A.
$(\sim)$: $K(([\![A]\!] \vee [\![B]\!]) \,\&\, [\![\sim B]\!]) \supset \langle \alpha \rangle K[\![A]\!]$
   or: $K(([\![A]\!] \vee [\![B]\!]) \supset [\pi]\langle \alpha \rangle [\![A]\!]$, for π is learning the falsehood of B.

It should be mentioned that the defined α and β programs are not deterministic, hence the information states $\langle \alpha \rangle S^{ba}$ and $\langle \beta \rangle S^{ba}$ are not unique sets with respect to a given information state S^{ba}. It is merely claimed that these analysed information states exist. Accordingly, we can define some general and straight-forward properties for the modal logic on which the operators $\langle \alpha \rangle$ and $\langle \beta \rangle$ rely. This logic describes a structure which is not connected, not transitive, but which is finitary, reflexive, and asymmetric.

As it is a (∗-free fragment of) propositional dynamic logic, it is clear that the LTS it describes should be a regular frame, which means that the relations for α and β are constructed in accordance to the following inductive clauses, see [Blackburn et al., 2001, pp. 22–23]:

(a) $R_{\pi 1 \cup \pi 2}$ $=$ $R_{\pi 1} \cup R_{\pi 2}$
(b) $R_{\pi 1 ; \pi 2}$ $=$ $R_{\pi 1} \circ R_{\pi 2}$ $(= \{(x,y) \mid \exists z (R_{\pi 1} xz \wedge R_{\pi 2} zy)\})$
(c) $R_{\pi_1^n}$ $=$ $(R_{\pi 1})^n$ $(= R_{\pi 1}^1 \circ \ldots \circ R_{\pi 1}^n)$

Introducing the notion of block-complexity (the number of logical connectives within a block, thus the complexity of $[\![A]\!]$ is 0, of $[\![\sim A]\!]$ and $[\![A \vee B]\!]$ is 1, ...), we have the following, more general, characterisation for a series of n blocks $[\![\ldots]\!]^i_{ci}$ of complexities ci as premises, and a block $[\![\ldots]\!]^j_{cj}$ of complexity cj as a conclusion.

(a) if $\bigwedge_{i=1}^{n} [\![\ldots]\!]^i_{ci} \vdash_{BCL} [\![\ldots]\!]^j_{cj}$, and $K_a \bigwedge_{i=1}^{n} [\![\ldots]\!]^i_{ci}$, then

$(\exists k)\langle (\alpha \cup \beta)^k \rangle K_a [\![\ldots]\!]_j$ for $\left(\left(\sum_{i=1}^{n} ci \right) - cj \right)$ is an upper-bound

for k.

Remark that the consequence-relation $\vdash_{BCL}$ is defined with respect to block-proofs as presented in [Batens, 1995, pp. 297–299], or equivalently with respect to block-tableaux. Given the existence of a faithful embedding of **BCL** in **CL**, this approach fits nicely with the prior characterization of knowledge over blocks. Let Γ be a set of block-formulas, and tr a translation-function.

(a) $\Gamma \vdash_{BCL} A$ iff $tr(\Gamma) \vdash_{CL} tr(A)$
(b) $\Gamma \models_{BCL} A$ iff $tr(\Gamma) \models_{CL} tr(A)$

Due to the non deterministic character of the LTS for block-analysis, the general characterization based on the compound program $\langle(\alpha \cup \beta)^k$ for a given k refers to one possible way to analyze a given set of blocks. The latter is equivalent to the shortest closing tableau, starting from the set of premise-blocks and the negated conclusion-block, and allowing for a closing rule based on blocks instead of atomic formulas (a branch in a block-tableau is closed iff both a block and its negation occur on two of its nodes. This implies both blocks must be identified).

Before reporting to the final conclusions, we should emphasize some important features on which the dynamic fragment of the given system and that of dynamic epistemic logic stand apart. The first difference was already mentioned, viz. the non-deterministic character of internal dynamics vs. the deterministic character of external dynamics. Although it is (technically) possible to construct a logic with deterministic programs for block-analysis this would not enhance our insight into proof-dynamics. It is therefore preferable to stick with the non-deterministic version and keep the intuitive connection between $\langle(\alpha \cup \beta)^k\rangle$ and the notion of knowability.

A second remark applies to the consciousness of updates in the sense of *learning that π has been executed*. Despite its importance in dynamic epistemic logic, the topic was not treated independently with respect to programs for block-analysis (in fact, the internal structure of a program π as $?\phi$ was also left aside). Again, this omission is not harmful for our present purpose, for the notion of consciousness of update cannot – at least at the conceptual level – be separated in a sensible way from the notion of gaining insight into one's knowledge. Nevertheless it remains necessary to give a formal account of block-analysis which models a conscious update. A complete formal description of these programs will have to incorporate this in the sense that a program for analyzing a given block is the conscious update of an information state with the given block's sub-blocks (see [Gerbrandy and Groeneveld, 1997, pp. 6–7] on conscious updates with respect to possibility semantics).

Combining both previous remarks, we come to a third and last one, which leads to a very appealing reformulation of internal dynamics using deterministic programs as its basic building blocks. For a given information state S^{ba} containing n α-blocks and m β-blocks we have that:

$$\alpha =_{def} \quad (U^*\pi_1 \cup \ldots \cup U^*\pi_n) \quad \text{for } U^*\pi_i \text{ is conscious updating with the conjunction of the sub-blocks of } \alpha_i.$$

$$\beta =_{def} \quad (U^*\pi_1' \cup \ldots \cup U^*\pi_m') \quad \text{for } U^*\pi_i' \text{ is conscious updating with the disjunction of the sub-blocks of } \beta_i.$$

This traces back the intrinsic non-deterministic character of block-analysis described by the generic α and β programs with respect to an information state containing more than one block of each kind, to the use of non-deterministic choice program constructors in its reformulation.

4 Concluding remarks

4.1 Logic, information and being informative

In the previous sections an alternative method for avoiding the classical problems of logical and deductive omniscience in epistemic logic was outlined. Contrary to other ways to tackle the problem, it does not rely on the mere rejection of necessitation or distribution. It was argued that the introduction of internal dynamics solves the problem in a very natural way by retaining the notion of knowledge as truth in all possibilities. Seen from a different perspective, the proposed approach only restricts the idealisation of full (instantaneous) insight in the premises, and reintroduces it step by step afterwards.

Note that this approach, viz. situating the problem of omniscience at the level of the propositional fragment of epistemic logic, is in a sense closer to the proposal by [Dubucs, 2002], who puts forward a substructural approach (e.g. linear logic with exponentials, see: [Marion and Sadrzadeh, 2004]) to restrict the idealization of unlimited resources from classical logic. In other words, both approaches claim that the problem with (logical) omniscience is rather related to the way we use classical logic unrestrictedly, than to the behavior of the modal operators in epistemic logic.

Put in a broader perspective, the introduction of internal dynamics is relevant for the way we perceive information. Although the starting-point of our investigation is closely related to Veltman's view that 'You know the meaning of a sentence if you know the change it brings about in the information state of anyone who accepts the news conveyed by it,' (see [Gerbrandy and Groeneveld, 1997, p. 147]), its consequences are only accepted in a weakened sense. That is, related to effective insight in knowledge.

Compared to other logical approaches to the nature of information, the presented framework concentrates more on the question of what it means to *be informative*, than on *being information* as such (distinction pointed out by L. Floridi during E-CAP2004). Taking informativeness as the core feature of information is considered a fruitful approach for it reduces the ontological commitments with respect to information to a minimum. Concretely it means that rejecting the necessary truthfulness of information offers a more flexible approach: e.g. information and misinformation are handled in the same way. Besides, it encompasses a view on information handling which fits naturally adaptive logics' way of non-monotonic reasoning based on *provisional deduction unless and until it effectively leads to an abnormality*, see: [Batens, 2001, pp. 45–47]. Or, reformulated to match the informational approach: treat information-like objects (i.e. information and misinformation) as if it were information; that is, use it to perform an update, unless and until that update leads to an abnormality.

Finally, the topics of omniscience and information come together when considering the question from [Bremer, 2003] whether logical truths carry information. The benefit of the block-approach is such that, even if it does not solve the problem of logical truths (necessitation is retained, except in the context of adaptive logics where the empty set has no models of its own, see [Batens, 2001, p. 56]), it offers a framework in which putting the logical tools at work is informative. This means that updating with a theorem of classical logic has no effect at all, but making a deduction – and it was shown that this can be reconstructed as an update – does have an effect in the sense that it genuinely reduces the set of possibilities.

4.2 Further research

As this paper essentially contains the outline of the reconstruction of internal dynamics within the framework of dynamic epistemic logic, further research and the elaboration of a decent meta-theoretical framework, showing that the present approach captures all proof-dynamics, is still needed. On the other hand, the sketched approach exhibits some nice properties and touches upon several topics within the philosophy of information. Therefore the further integration of this framework within a broader informational setting deserves further attention as well.

BIBLIOGRAPHY

[Barwise, 1997] J. Barwise. Information and impossibilities. *Notre Dame Journal of Formal Logic*, 38(4):488–515, 1997.
[Batens and Meheus, 2001] D. Batens and J. Meheus. On the logic and pragmatics of the process of explanation. In M. Kiikeri and P. Ylikoski, editors, *Explanatory Connections. Electronic Essays Dedicated to Matti Sintonen*, 2001. http://www.valt.helsinki.fi/kfil/matti/.
[Batens, 1995] D. Batens. Blocks. The clue to dynamic aspects of logic. *Logique & Analyse*, 150–152:285–328, 1995.
[Batens, 2000] D. Batens. A survey of inconsistency-adaptive logics. In D. Batens, C. Mortensen, G. Priest, and J.P. Van Bendegem, editors, *Frontiers of Paraconsistent Logic*, pages 49–73, Baldock, 2000. Research Studies Press.
[Batens, 2001] D. Batens. A general characterization of adaptive logics. *Logique & Analyse*, 173–175:45–68, 2001.
[Blackburn et al., 2001] P. Blackburn, M. de Rijke, and Y. Venema. *Modal Logic*. Cambridge University Press, Cambridge, 2001.
[Bremer, 2003] M. Bremer. Do logical truths carry information? *Minds & Machines*, 13(4):567–575, 2003.
[D'Agostino, 1999] M. D'Agostino. Tableau methods for classical propositional logic. In M. D'Agostino, D. Gabbay, R. Hähnle, and J. Posegga, editors, *Handbook of Tableau Methods*, pages 45–123, Dordrecht/Boston/London, 1999. Kluwer Academic Publishers.
[Dubucs, 2002] J. Dubucs. Feasibility in logic. *Synthese*, 132:213–237, 2002.

[Fagin *et al.*, 1995] R. Fagin, J.Y. Halpern, Y. Moses, and M.Y. Vardi. *Reasoning about Knowledge*. MIT Press, Cambridge/London, 1995.

[Fitting, 1999] M. Fitting. Introduction. In M. D'Agostino, D. Gabbay, R. Hähnle, and J. Posegga, editors, *Handbook of Tableau Methods*, page 143, Dordrecht/Boston/London, 1999. Kluwer Academic Publishers.

[Gerbrandy and Groeneveld, 1997] J. Gerbrandy and W. Groeneveld. Reasoning about information change. *Journal of Logic, Language and Information*, 6(2):147–169, 1997.

[Gerbrandy, 1997] J. Gerbrandy. Dynamic epistemic logic. In L. Moss, J. Ginzburg, and M. de Rijke, editors, *Logic, Language, and Information*, volume 2, Stanford, 1997. CSLI Publications.

[Girle, 2000] R. Girle. *Modal Logics and Philosophy*. Acumen, Teddington, 2000.

[Marion and Sadrzadeh, 2004] M. Marion and M. Sadrzadeh. Reasoning about knowledge in linear logic: Modalities and complexity. In D. Gabbay, S. Rahman, J. Symons, and J.P. Van Bendegem, editors, *Logic, Epistemology and the Unity of Science*, pages 327–350, Dordrecht/Boston/London, 2004. Kluwer Academic Publishers.

[Smullyan, 1968] R. Smullyan. *First-Order Logic*. Springer Verlag, New York, 1968. (reprinted by Dover, New York, 1995).

[Urquhart, 1995] A. Urquhart. The complexity of propositional proofs. *The Bulletin of Symbolic Logic*, 1(4):425–467, 1995.

[Urquhart, 2003] A. Urquhart. Complexity. In L. Floridi, editor, *The Blackwell Guide to the Philosophy of Computing and Information*, pages 18–27, Oxford, 2003. Blackwell Publishing.

[Van Benthem and van Rooy, 2003] J. Van Benthem and R. van Rooy. Connecting the different faces of information. *Journal of Logic, Language and Information*, 12(4):375–379, 2003.

[Van Benthem, 2003] J. Van Benthem. Logic and the dynamics of information. *Minds & Machines*, 13(4):503–519, 2003.

Patrick Allo
Centre for Logic and Philosophy of Science
Vrije Universiteit Brussel, Belgium
Email: patrick.allo@vub.ac.be
URL: homepages.vub.ac.be/~pallo/

Exemplar-Based Explanation

RENS BOD

ABSTRACT.   This article proposes a formal, computational model
of exemplar-based reasoning which explains novel phenomena on the
basis of a corpus of previously explained phenomena. By representing explanations in terms of *derivation trees* (which incorporate not
only laws and initial conditions but also empirical corrections and adjustments), I will show that explanations of novel phenomena can be
constructed by combining *subtrees* of explanations of previous phenomena. I will introduce the notion of *derivational similarity*, and
suggest that scientists solve a new problem by maximizing derivational similarity with respect to previously solved problems. I will
give a concrete instantiation of this exemplar-based model, using a
corpus of phenomena from classical and fluid mechanics, and argue
that the approach integrates theoretical and phenomenological modeling in hydraulics.

1   Introduction

The idea that natural phenomena can be explained by modeling them on
exemplars has often been proposed in the literature. Yet, to the best of
my knowledge, no exact mechanism exists that models new phenomena on
previously explained phenomena, or that describes how problem solutions
can be reused to explain new cases in science. In this article I will propose
such a mechanism.

It is not difficult to find inspiration in the literature for constructing an
exemplar-based model of explanation. In his account on normal science,
Thomas Kuhn urged that exemplars are "concrete problem solutions that
students encounter from the start of their scientific education" [Kuhn, 1970,
p. 187] and that "scientists solve puzzles by modeling them on previous
puzzle-solutions" [Kuhn, 1970, p. 189]. Scientists possess what Kuhn called
"acquired similarity relations" that allow them "to see situations as like
each other, as subjects for the application of the same scientific law or law-
sketch" [Kuhn, 1970, p. 190].

According to Frederick Suppe, implicit in Kuhn's work is an account of
theory as "symbolic generalizations empirically interpreted by exemplars

Lorenzo Magnani and Riccardo Dossena, editors, *Computing, Philosophy, and Cognition*,
pp. 329–348 © 2005, R. Bod

and modeling of other applications on the exemplars" [Suppe, 1977, p. 149]. In a similar vein, Ronald Giere argues that "Scientists have at their disposal an inventory of various known phenomena and the sorts of models that fit these phenomena. When faced with a new phenomenon, scientists may look for known phenomena that are in various ways similar to, which is to say, analogous with, the new phenomenon. Once found, the sort of models that successfully accounted for the known phenomena can be adapted to the new phenomenon" [Giere, 1999a]. Giere thus interprets Kuhn's exemplars as models [Da Costa and French, 2003].

Thomas Nickles relates Kuhn's theory of normal science to Case-Based Reasoning [Nickles, 2003, p. 161]. Case-Based Reasoning (CBR) provides an alternative to rule-based problem solving. Instead of solving each new problem from scratch, CBR tries to match the new problem to one or more problems-plus-solutions already available in a database of previous cases. The idea that previous derivational patterns may be reapplied to new situations has also been proposed by Philip Kitcher: "Science advances our understanding of nature by showing us how to derive descriptions of many phenomena, using the same patterns of derivation again and again" [Kitcher, 1989, p. 432].

But neither Giere, Nickles or Kitcher, let alone Kuhn, provide an exact mechanism that describes how previous problem solutions can be reused and adapted to solve new problems and phenomena. The development of such a mechanism is exactly the goal of this paper: *given a corpus of previously explained phenomena, how can we explain new phenomena on the basis of this corpus?*

This goal is important not only from a cognitive perspective, as Kuhn argued, but also from an epistemic point of view. It has become increasingly clear that many real-world phenomena cannot be formally deduced from laws but that their derivations involve various non-deductive elements such as intermediate phenomenological models, approximation schemes, empirical corrections and normalizations that do not follow from laws or bridge principles (see [Cartwright, 1983; Cartwright, 1999; Giere, 1988; Giere, 1999b; Morgan and Morrison, 1999], and the examples therein). Exemplars, then, provide examples of how laws, models, boundary conditions, approximations, corrections etc. are used to solve a problem – that is, how deductive and non-deductive patterns are *de facto* combined in scientific reasoning. A corpus of exemplary problem solutions thus offers a toolkit of strategies, together with their applications to real-world cases, that aid scientists in deriving new phenomena. The underlying idea of exemplar-based explanation is that once you have learned how to construct derivations for a number of (exemplary) phenomena, you can apply parts of these derivations

– i.e. sequences of derivation steps – to other, similar phenomena.

In order to develop a formal model of exemplar-based explanation, we need to instantiate the following two parameters:

1. a corpus of explanations of prior phenomena, and

2. a matching procedure that specifies how partial explanations from prior

phenomena can be reused to explain new phenomena.

Note that these parameters allow for a wide range of different models of explanation. The exemplar-based view hypothesizes that scientific explanation can be modeled as a matching process between a new phenomenon and a corpus of previously explained phenomena, but it leaves open how the explanations in the corpus are represented and how parts from these explanations may be combined.

In this article I will focus on one notion of exemplars only, namely as "concrete problem solutions" [Kuhn, 1970, p. 187]. I realize that there are various other interpretations of "exemplars", for instance as category representations or concepts (e.g. [Nosofsky, 1988]), but I will not deal with these here. I will provide a formalization of problem solutions in terms of *trees* and develop a matching mechanism (based on a notion of *derivational similarity*) that explains novel phenomena by combining *subtrees* of explanations of previous phenomena. I will start by illustrating this exemplar-based model on idealized, exactly solvable phenomena from classical mechanics. Such phenomena do not occur in the real world, but they do form the typical examples of introductory textbooks, thereby constituting the exemplars all physicists learn. Next, in section 3, I will show how my account can be extended to real-world phenomena from fluid mechanics for which there are no deductive solutions but for which recourse is made to empirical corrections and coefficients. I argue that my exemplar-based model aptly integrates deductive and non-deductive patterns of scientific reasoning.

2 An exemplar-based model for idealized, exactly solvable phenomena

To pave the way for real-world phenomena, it is convenient to first explain the exemplar-based view for idealized cases. Physics textbooks provide the typical examples where solutions of exemplary problems are subsequently used for solving new problems. As an illustration, consider the following problem of deriving the Earth's mass from the Earth-Moon system as given by Alonso and Finn in their textbook *Physics* [Alonso and Finn, 1996, p. 247]:

Suppose that a satellite of mass m describes, with a period P, a circular orbit of radius r around a planet of mass M. The force of attraction between the planet and the satellite is $F = GMm/r^2$. This force must be equal to m times the centripetal acceleration $v^2/r = 4\pi^2 r/P^2$ of the satellite. Thus,

$$\frac{4\pi^2 mr}{P^2} = \frac{GMm}{r^2}$$

Canceling the common factor m and solving for M gives

$$M = \frac{4\pi^2 r^3}{GP^2}.$$

Figure 1. Derivation of the Earth's mass according to [Alonso and Finn, 1996].

By substituting the data for the Moon, $r = 3.84 \times 10^8$ m and $P = 2.36 \times 10^6$ s, Alonso and Finn compute the mass of the Earth: $M = 5.98 \times 10^{24}$ kg. Note that Alonso and Finn abstract from many features of the actual Earth-Moon system, such as the gravitational forces of the Sun and other planets, the magnetic fields, the solar wind, etc. Moreover, Alonso and Finn do not correct for these abstractions (which would be very well possible and which is often accomplished in the more advanced textbooks). That's why the represented system is called an idealized system, or better, an idealized model of the system. Albeit idealized, the derivation in Figure 1 can be used as an exemplar to derive various other (idealized) phenomena. To show this, it is convenient to represent the derivation in Figure 1 in a step-by-step way by a *derivation tree*, given in Figure 2.

The derivation tree in Figure 2 represents the various derivation steps (insofar as they are mentioned in Figure 1) from higher-level laws to an equation of the mass of a planet. A derivation tree is a labeled tree in which each node is annotated or labeled with a formula (the boxes are only convenient representations of these labels). The formulas at the top of each "vee" (i.e. a connected pair of branches) in the tree can be viewed as premises, and the formula at the bottom as a conclusion. In this tree, the only derivational action consist of term substitution, except for the last derivation step, which is not formed by a vee but consists in a unary branch that solves the directly preceding formula for M. The reader is referred to [Baader and Nipkow, 1998] for an overview on term rewriting and equational

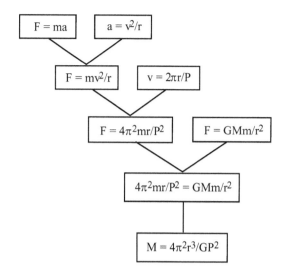

Figure 2. Derivation tree for the derivation in Figure 1.

reasoning.

Note that a derivation tree captures the notion of a deductive-nomological (D-N) explanation of [Hempel and Oppenheim, 1948]. In the D-N account, a phenomenon is explained by deducing it from general laws and antecedent conditions. It is well known that the D-N account has serious shortcomings as a model of explanation (see e.g. [Salmon, 1989]), and I will come back to this in the next section.

But a derivation tree represents more than just a D-N explanation: there is also an implicit theoretical model in the tree in Figure 2. A theoretical model is a representation of a phenomenon for which the laws of the theory are true [Suppes, 1961; Suppes, 1967; van Fraassen, 1980]. By equating the centripetal force of circular motion $4\pi^2 mr/P^2$ with the gravitational force GMm/r^2 the model that is implied in Figure 2 is a two particle model where one particle describes a circular orbit around the other one due to gravitational interaction and for which the mass of the first particle is negligible compared to the other. Theoretical models have been claimed to be the primary representational entities in science. [Suppes, 1967] shows how the field of classical particle mechanics can be described in terms of a set-theoretical notion of model. However, while theoretical models can represent idealized systems, it has been widely argued that they fail to represent reality. Applying a theoretical model to a real system is a matter of intricate approximation and de-idealization [Cartwright, 1999; Morrison, 1999]. In section 3, I will show how derivation trees can be extended to include not only theoretical models but also phenomenological models and how these two models can be integrated within the same representation. For the moment it suffices to keep in mind that derivation trees are not just representations of the D-N account but that they also refer to an underlying theoretical model.

Turning back to the derivation tree in Figure 2, we can extract the following fragment or subtree by leaving out the last derivation step in the derivation tree in Figure 2 (i.e. the solution for the mass M). This subtree is given in Figure 3, and reflects a theoretical model of a general planet-satellite or sun-planet system (or any other orbiting system where the mass of one particle is negligible compared to the other).

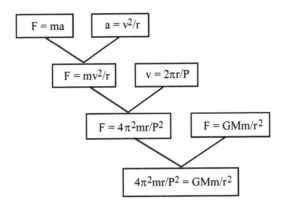

Figure 3. A subtree from Figure 2 reflecting a theoretical model of a planet-satellite system.

This subtree can be applied to various other, analogous situations. For example, in deriving Kepler's third law (which states that r^3/P^2 is constant for all planets orbiting around the sun) the subtree in Figure 3 needs only to be extended with a derivation step that solves the last equation for r^3/P^2, as represented in Figure 4.

Thus we can productively reuse parts from previous derivations to derive new phenomena. Instead of starting each time from scratch, we learn from previous derivations and partially reuse them for new problems. This is exactly what the exemplar-based view entails: a theory is viewed as a prior corpus of derivations (our body of physical knowledge, if you wish) by which new phenomena are predicted and explained. In a similar way we can derive

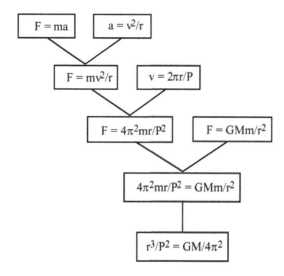

Figure 4. Derivation tree for Kepler's third law from the subtree in Figure 3.

the distance of a geostationary satellite, namely by solving the subtree in Figure 3 for r.

However, it is not typically the case that derivations involve only one subtree. For example, in deriving the velocity of a satellite at a certain distance from a planet, we cannot directly use the large subtree in Figure 3, but need to extract two smaller subtrees from Figure 2 that are first combined by term substitution (represented by the operation "o"[1]) and then solved for v in Figure 5.

Although exceedingly simple, Figure 5 shows that we can create new derivations by combining different parts from previous derivations, i.e. from exemplars. The result could be used as an exemplar itself. But what is the advantage of using partial derivations rather than laws? First, as noted above, by using the same derivational patterns we do not have to explain

---

[1]The *substitution operation* or *combination operation* "o" is a partial function on pairs of labeled trees; its range is the set of labeled trees. The combination of tree t and tree u, written as $t \circ u$, is defined iff the equation at the root node of u can be substituted in the equation at the root node of t (i.e. iff the lefthandside of the equation at the root node of u literally appears in the equation at the root node of t). If $t \circ u$ is defined, it yields a tree that expands the root nodes of copies of t and u to a new root node where the righthandside of the equation at the root node of u is substituted in the equation at the root node of t. Note that the substitution operation can be iteratively applied to a sequence of trees, with the convention that o is left-associative.

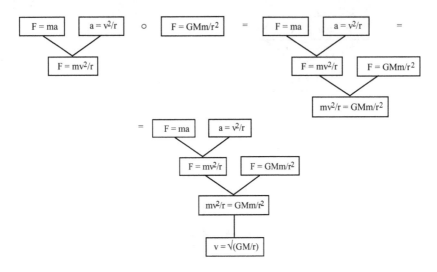

Figure 5. Constructing a derivation tree for a satellite's velocity by combining two subtrees from Figure 2.

each new phenomenon from scratch if we have derived similar phenomena before. More than that, as we will see in the next section, derivations of *real-world* phenomena typically involve corrections and coefficients that are not dictated by laws or initial conditions. The advantage of exemplar-based explanation is then that it integrates theoretical laws and ad hoc rules that can be productively reused by means of subtrees.

We have thus instantiated a first model of exemplar-based explanation to which I will refer as "EBE". EBE employs (1) a corpus of derivation trees representing exemplars and (2) a matching procedure that combines subtrees from the corpus into new derivation trees by means of term substitution. Given a corpus C of derivation trees $T_1, T_2, \ldots, T_n$ and a term substitution operation $\circ$, an explanation of a phenomenon P with respect to C is a derivation tree E such that (i) there are subtrees $t_1, t_2, \ldots, t_k$ in $T_1, T_2, \ldots, T_n$ for which $t_1 \circ t_2 \circ \ldots \circ t_k = E$, (ii) the root node of E is equivalent to P and (iii) the leaf nodes of E are either general laws or antecedent conditions. (Of course there may be mathematical operations between any composition of two subtrees, to which I will come back in the next section.) Note that subtrees can be of any size: from single equations to any combination of laws up to entire models and derivations. This reflects the continuum between laws and derivations in the exemplar-based approach.

How do we know which subtrees from previous explanations can be reused if confronted with a new phenomenon – rather than trying out all combinations? Kuhn's (and also Giere's) answer is that scientists see similarity relations between a new phenomenon and previous problem solutions and therefore know which law patterns can be applied to derive the new phenomenon. This similarity relationship remains a rather vague notion in most accounts and some believe it cannot be formalized. What can our model say about it? Since EBE's matching procedure is entirely derivational, it is convenient to interpret the notion of similarity in terms of *derivational* or *explanatory similarity*. In EBE, a new phenomenon is derivationally similar to a previously explained phenomenon if the derivation of the previous phenomenon can be (partially) reused to explain the new phenomenon, that is, if their resulting derivation trees share one or more subtrees. The more and larger subtrees they share – i.e. the larger the portion of common subtrees in the two trees – the more (derivationally) similar they are. The fraction of common subtrees (w.r.t. all subtrees in the two trees) is a measure of their similarity.

Still this similarity measure does not a priori tell us which subtrees from previous derivation trees can be used to explain a new phenomenon. Sure enough, we could exhaustively enumerate all possible combinations of subtrees that result in a derivation of the phenomenon, and next establish the similarity relations by determining the largest partial matches with previous derivations. But this is highly inefficient. Moreover, it only tells us *after the fact* which partial matches could be used. Fortunately, there exist algorithms that can establish the largest partial match in one go by computing the so-called *shortest derivation* of a given phenomenon. The shortest derivation of a phenomenon is the derivation that consists of the smallest number of subtrees from the corpus. Given a set of subtrees and a (new) phenomenon, the shortest derivation can be computed by means of a best-first beam search procedure [Bod, 2000; Cormen *et al.*, 2002]. Since subtrees are allowed to be of arbitrary size, the shortest derivation corresponds to the derivation tree which consists of largest partial matches with previous derivation trees in the corpus. Thus derivational similarity is maximized by minimizing derivation length. We hypothesize that scientists try to explain a new phenomenon by maximizing derivational similarity between the new phenomenon and previously derived phenomena. And the shortest derivation provides a computationally efficient way to attain this goal.

For example, the phenomenon known as Kepler's third law in Figure 4 is maximally similar (modulo equivalence) to the problem of deriving the

Earth's mass from the Moon's orbit in Figure 2, because only one big sub-tree from the Earth's mass problem is needed to derive Kepler's law (Figure 3). Even if the two problems may seem different to the layman, for the physicist they are nearly equal, except for the final solution of a certain variable. The new problem can be solved by almost entirely reusing a previous problem solution. Also the phenomenon of the velocity of a satellite in Figure 5 is quite similar to the Earth-Moon system, though somewhat less than Kepler's third law since it involves two (smaller) subtrees that result in a smaller fraction of common derivation steps, as can be seen by comparing resp. Figures 5 and 4 with Figure 2.

Note that it is possible for a certain phenomenon to have different derivations with (virtually) no common subtrees. For example, the Earth's mass can be derived not only from an orbiting planet-satellite model (as in Figure 2), but also from a planet-object system at rest, namely by equating the gravitational acceleration at the Earth's surface g with GM/R^2 where R is the Earth's radius and M the Earth's mass. Thus our notion of similarity only tells us something about the similarity of the *derivations* of phenomena rather than about the phenomena themselves. If one phenomenon has two different derivations with no common subtrees, then these derivations refer to different underlying models.

We should keep in mind that the examples in this section are highly idealized and could just as well be solved by means of laws rather than by exemplars. In the next section I will extend the EBE model to real-world systems and phenomena. As an intermediate step, I could also have dealt with idealized phenomena that are *not* exactly solvable. A typical example is the three-body problem in Newtonian dynamics. Even if we make the problem unrealistically simple (e.g. by assuming that the bodies are perfect spheres that lie in the same plane), the motion of three bodies due to their gravitational interaction can only be approximated by techniques such as perturbation calculus. However, in perturbation calculus every derivation step still follows numerically from higher-level laws. The actual challenge lies in real-world phenomena and systems for which there are derivation steps that are *not* dictated by any higher-level law.

3 An exemplar-based model for real systems and phenomena

Derivations of real systems are strikingly absent in most physics textbooks. But they are abundant in engineering practice and engineering textbooks. As an example I will discuss how a general engineering textbook treats a real system from fluid mechanics: the velocity of a jet through a small orifice, known as Torricelli's theorem, and to which I will also refer as an *orifice system.* I have chosen this system because it is very simple and yet it has no rigorous solution from higher-level laws but involves ad hoc coefficients. I will show how a "derivation" of the orifice system allows us to develop an EBE model for real-world systems which can derive a range of other systems, such as weirs and water breaks.

The orifice system is usually derived from Bernoulli's equation, which is in turn derived from the Principle of Conservation of Energy[2]. According to the Principle of Conservation of Energy the total energy of a system of particles remains constant. The total energy is the sum of kinetic energy (E_k), internal potential energy ($E_{p,\text{int}}$) and external potential energy ($E_{p,\text{ext}}$):

$$\sum E = E_k + E_{p,\text{int}} + E_{p,\text{ext}} = \text{constant}$$

Applied to an incompressible fluid, the principle comes down to saying that the total energy per unit volume of a fluid in motion remains constant, which is expressed by Bernoulli's equation:

$$\rho g z + \rho v^2/2 + p = \text{constant}$$

The term $\rho g z$ is the external potential energy per unit volume due to gravity, where ρ is the fluid's density and z the height of the unit (note the "resemblance" with mgh in classical mechanics). The term $\rho v^2/2$ is the kinetic energy per unit volume (which "resembles" $mv^2/2$ in classical mechanics). And p is the potential energy per unit volume associated with pressure. Bernoulli's equation is also written as

$$\rho g z_1 + \rho v_1^2/2 + p_1 = \rho g z_2 + \rho v_2^2/2 + p_2$$

which says that the total energy of a fluid in motion is the same at any two unit volumes along its path.

Figure 6 shows the engineering textbook *Advanced Design and Technology* derives Torricelli's theorem from Bernoulli's equation [Norman *et al.*, 1990, p. 497]:

> We can use Bernoulli's equation to estimate the velocity of a jet emerging from a small circular hole or orifice in a tank, Figure 12.12a. Suppose the subscripts 1 and 2 refer to a point in the surface of the liquid in the tank, and a section of the jet just outside the orifice. If the orifice is small we can assume that the velocity of the jet is v at all points in this section.

---

[2]Bernoulli's equation is often treated as a special case of the Navier-Stokes equations in the more specialized textbooks.

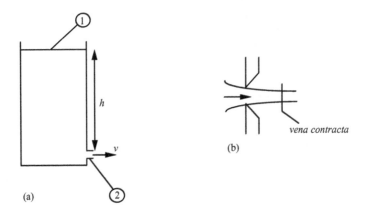

Figure 12.12.

The pressure is atmospheric at points 1 and 2 and therefore $p_1 = p_2$. In addition the velocity v_1 is negligible, provided the liquid in the tank has a large surface area. Let the difference in level between 1 and 2 be h as shown, so that $z_1 - z_2 = h$. With these values, Bernoulli's equation becomes:

$$h = v^2/2g \quad \text{from which} \quad v = \sqrt{2gh}$$

This result is known as Torricelli's theorem. If the area of the orifice is A the theoretical discharge is:

$$Q(\text{theoretical}) = vA = A\sqrt{2gh}$$

The actual discharge will be less than this. In practice the liquid in the tank converges on the orifice as shown in Figure 12.12b. The flow does not become parallel until it is a short distance away from the orifice. The section at which this occurs has the Latin name *vena contracta* (*vena* = vein) and the diameter of the jet there is less than that of the orifice. The actual discharge can be written:

$$Q(\text{actual}) = C_d A\sqrt{2gh}$$

where C_d is the coefficient of discharge. Its value depends on the profile of the orifice. For a sharp-edged orifice, as shown in Figure 12.12b, it is about 0.62.

Figure 6. Derivation of Torricelli's theorem in [Norman *et al.*, 1990].

Thus the theoretically derived discharge of the system differs substantially from the actual discharge and is corrected by a coefficient of discharge, C_d. This is mainly due to an additional phenomenon that occurs in any orifice system: the *vena contracta*. Although this phenomenon is known for more than three centuries, no rigorous derivation exists for it and it is taken care of by a correction factor. Note that the correction factor is not an adjustment of a few percent, but of almost 40%. The value of the factor varies however with the profile of the orifice and can range from 0.5 (the so-called Borda mouthpiece) to 0.97 (a rounded orifice).

Introductory engineering textbooks tell us that coefficients of discharge are experimentally derived corrections that need to be established for each orifice separately (see [Norman *et al.*, 1990; Douglas and Matthews, 1996]). While this is true for real-world three-dimensional orifices, it must be stressed that there are analytical solutions for idealized two-dimensional orifice models by using free-streamline theory (see [Batchelor, 1967, p. 497]). [Sadri and Floryan, 2002]) have recently shown that the *vena contracta* can also be simulated by a numerical solution of the general Navier-Stokes equations which is, however, *again* based on a two-dimensional model. For three-dimensional orifice models there are no analytical or numerical solutions [Munson, 2002; Graebel, 2001]. The coefficients of discharge are then derived by physical modeling, i.e. by experiment. This explains perhaps why *physics* textbooks usually neglect the *vena contracta*. And some physics textbooks don't deal with Torricelli's theorem at all. To the best of my knowledge, all engineering textbooks that cover Torricelli's theorem also deal with the coefficient of discharge. (One may claim that the *vena contracta* can still be qualitatively explained: since the liquid converges on the orifice, the area of the issuing jet is less than the area of the orifice. But there exists no quantitative explanation of C_d for a three-dimensional jet.)

Although no analytical or numerical derivations exist for real-world orifice systems, engineering textbooks still link such systems via experimentally derived corrections to the theoretical law of Bernoulli, as if there were some deductive scheme. Why do they do that? One reason for enforcing such a link is that theory does explain some important features of orifice systems: the derivation in Figure 6, albeit not fully rigorous, explains why the discharge of the system is proportional to the square-root of the height h of the tank, and it also generalizes over different heights h and orifice areas A. Another reason for enforcing a link to higher-level laws is that the resulting derivation can be used as an exemplar for solving new problems and systems. To formally show this, I will first turn the derivation in Figure 6 into its corresponding derivation tree. But how can we create such a derivation tree if the coefficient of discharge is not derived from any higher-level equation? The orifice system indicates that there can be phenomenological models that are not derived from the theoretical model of the system. Yet, when we write the coefficient of discharge as the empirical generalization $Q(\text{actual}) = C_d Q(\text{theoretical})$, which is in fact implicit in the derivation in Figure 6, we can again create a derivation tree and "save" the phenomenon. This is shown in Figure 7 (where we added at the top the principle of conservation of energy, from which Bernoulli's equation is derived in [Norman et al., 1990]).

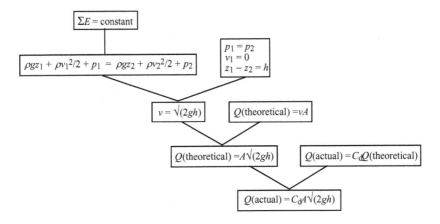

Figure 7. Derivation tree for the derivation in Figure 6.

The tree in Figure 7 closely follows the derivation given in Figure 6, where the initial conditions for p_1, p_2, v_1, z_1 and z_2 are represented by a separate label in the tree. The coefficient of discharge in Figure 7 is introduced in the tree by the equation $Q(\text{actual}) = C_d Q(\text{theoretical})$. Although this equation does not follow from any higher-level law or principle, we can use it *as if* it were a law. Of course it is not a law in the universal sense; it is a correction, a rule of thumb, but it can be reused for a range of other hydraulic systems, ranging from nozzles, nappes, notches, weirs, open channels and many pipeline problems – see [Douglas and Matthews, 1996]. Does the derivation tree in Figure 7 represent a deductive-nomological (D-N) explanation? Different from the derivation trees in section 2, the final result $Q(\text{actual}) = C_d A \sqrt{2gh}$ in Figure 7 is not logically deduced from general laws and antecedent conditions only. Additional knowledge in the form of an ad hoc correction is needed to enforce a link. While this correction can be expressed in terms of a mathematical equation, it clearly goes beyond the notion of fundamental law or antecedent condition that are said to be essential to a D-N explanation (see [Hempel, 1965, p. 337])[3]. Of course, the correction can be viewed as an *auxiliary hypothesis*, but it should be kept in mind that it is not derived from any higher-level law. Yet it can be straightforwardly integrated in a derivation tree, obtaining *de facto* the same status as a law. It is also difficult to frame the derivation tree in Figure 7 into the semantic notion of theoretical model, since the formula $Q(\text{actual}) = C_d A\sqrt{2gh}$ is not true in the theoretical model of the system, except if C_d were equal to 1, which never occurs. The derivation tree in Figure 7 reflects two models: a model of the theory and a model of the phenomenon that are connected by the factor C_d.

What does this all mean for EBE? By using the derivation tree in Figure 7 and by using the same substitution mechanism for combining subtrees as in section 2 together with a mathematical procedure that can solve an equation (i.e. that effectively substitutes a subtree by a mathematically equivalent one), we obtain an exemplar-based model that can explain a range of new real-world systems. For example, the following three subtrees in Figure 8 can be extracted from the derivation tree in Figure 7 and can be reused in deriving the rate of flow of a rectangular *weir* (or *dam*) of width B and height h (see e.g. [Norman *et al.*, 1990, p. 498]):

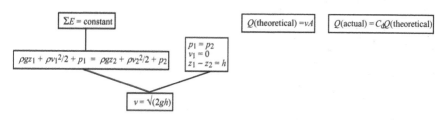

Figure 8. Three subtrees from Figure 7 that can be reused to derive a weir.

By adding the equation $dA = Bdh$, which follows from the definition of a rectangular weir, and the mathematical equivalence $vA = \int v dA$, we can create the derivation tree in Figure 9 for the discharge of a weir.

The derivation tree in Figure 9 closely follows the derivations given in [Norman *et al.*, 1990, p. 498] and [Douglas and Matthews, 1996, p. 117], where a weir system is constructed out of an orifice system. This corresponds to engineering practice where new systems are almost literally built

---

[3]Note that the correction factor does neither fit the notion of what Hempel called a *proviso* [Hempel, 1988]. A proviso would consist of the condition that there are no additional phenomena and thus *no vena contracta*. Under this proviso, the derivation of the discharge would need no correction factor, but it would be far from the truth.

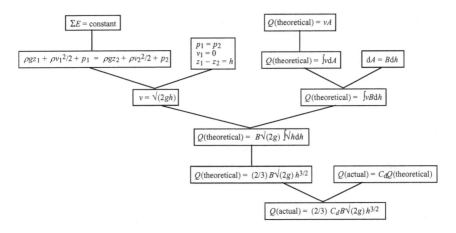

Figure 9. Derivation tree for a weir constructed by combining the subtrees from Figure 8.

upon or constructed out of similar previous systems. EBE simulates this modeling process by using partial derivations from one system to explain a new system. Note the analogy with Figure 5 in section 2, where we also constructed a new derivation tree by combining subtrees from a previous derivation tree (i.e. a satellite's velocity from a derivation of the Earth's mass). But there is a very important difference: while the phenomenon represented in Figure 5 can just as well be derived from laws rather than from previous subtrees, this is *not* the case for the phenomenon represented in Figure 9. For deriving the weir system, we need to make recourse to the rule $Q(\text{actual}) = C_d Q(\text{theoretical})$ which is taken from a previously explained phenomenon that functions as an exemplar. Our new exemplar-based model thus integrates and recombines three sources of knowledge: theoretical laws, antecedent conditions and phenomenological rules. As long as non-deductive knowledge such as corrections or empirical rules can be stated in terms of mathematical equations they can be integrated by a derivation tree, and be reused to solve new problems.

This means that we have to modify our previous definition of EBE given in section 2. There we stated that the leaf nodes of an explanation, i.e. of a derivation tree E, should either refer to general laws or to antecedent conditions. In the new EBE model, the leaf nodes of E may also be corrections or other kinds of adjustments. We will merge these three kinds of knowledge as knowledge that is not derived from anything else. Furthermore, the new EBE model also allows subtrees to be substituted by mathematically equivalent ones (as in Figure 9). Our new definition for EBE becomes:

> Given a corpus C of derivation trees $T_1, T_2, \ldots, T_n$ and a term
> substitution operation $\circ$, an explanation of a phenomenon P
> with respect to C is a derivation tree E such that (1) there are
> subtrees $\tau_1, \tau_2, \ldots, \tau_k$ which are mathematically equivalent to
> subtrees in $T_1, T_2, \ldots, T_n$ for which $\tau_1 \circ \tau_2 \circ \ldots \circ \tau_k = E$, (2) the
> root node of E is equivalent to P, and (3) the leaf nodes of E
> cannot be further derived.

We also need to adapt the notion of derivational similarity in EBE. That
is, a new phenomenon is derivationally similar to a previously explained phenomenon if their resulting derivation trees contain mathematically equivalent subtrees. The fraction of mathematically equivalent subtrees is a
measure of the similarity of two derivation trees. This fraction can be maximized by computing the shortest derivation of a phenomenon. E.g. the
three subtrees in Figure 8 correspond to the minimal set of subtrees from
the orifice system needed to construct a derivation tree for the weir system
in Figure 9.

The final formula in Figure 9 is widely used in hydraulic engineering,
where the coefficient C_d is usually established experimentally. It should
be stressed that the coefficient C_d is not a meaningless fudge factor. For
example, for the class of rectangular weirs there exists an empirical generalization that computes C_d from two other quantities. This generalization
was first formulated by Henry Bazin, the assistant of the celebrated hy-
daulician Henry Darcy [Darcy and Bazin, 1865], and is commonly referred
to as Bazin formula (also called "Bazin weir formula", to distinguish it from
"Bazin open channel formula" – see Douglas and [Douglas and Matthews,
1996, p. 199]):

$$C_d = (0.607 + 0.00451/H) \times (1 + 0.55(H/(P + H)^2))$$

In this formula H = head over sill in metres, and P = height of sill
above floor in metres of the weir. Thus C_d can be stated in terms of two
meaningful variables. Bazin formula is an empirical regularity derived from
a number of concrete weir systems, and as such it can be used in derivation
trees for new weir systems. Although the regularity is known for more than
150 years, there exists no derivation from higher-level laws. Yet this does
not prevent us from using and reusing the regularity in designing real world
systems that have to work accurately and reliably. Hydraulics is replete
with formulas like Bazin's, each describing particular regularities within
a certain flow system. There are, for example, Francis formula, Rehbock

formula, Kutter formula, Manning formula, Chezy formula, Darcy formula, Colebrook-White formula, Keulegan formula, to name a few (see [Chanson, 2002]). Many of these formulas are known for more than a century but none of them has been deduced from higher-level laws. They are entirely based on previous systems and form the lubricant that makes new systems work.

In passing it may be noteworthy that we cannot derive the phenomena from classical mechanics discussed in section 2 by means of the derived phenomena from fluid mechanics given in this section. For instance, Kepler's third law cannot be derived by subtrees from the orifice system. However, there are various other classical phenomena that *can* be derived by subtrees from the derivations in fluid mechanics given in this section. An example is Torricelli's theorem, which gives the idealized velocity of the jet from a tank of height h, $v = \sqrt{2gh}$. This equation is "equal" to the speed that an object would attain in free fall from a height h in Newtonian mechanics. So what happens if we use EBE to construct a derivation for a phenomenon which is merely described by $v = \sqrt{2gh}$ on the basis of a corpus which contains both Torricelli's result and the Newtonian analogue for a falling object? Then EBE obtains two different derivations for this phenomenon: one derived from Bernoulli's theorem and one from Newton's laws. Since the derivations are both maximally similar to at least one derivation in the corpus, which of the two should be chosen? If no distinction is made between the velocity of a fluid and that of a point mass, $v = \sqrt{2gh}$ is inherently ambiguous and two different models and derivations apply to it. This is not as strange as it seems, since historically, Daniel Bernoulli solved the problem of the velocity of water from an orifice by treating a flow in terms of Newtonian-like particles, which makes the two phenomena indeed "equivalent"[4]. But if we want to avoid EBE mixing up derivations from different fields, we should introduce different variables for point mass velocity and fluid velocity. This can be accomplished by using subcategorizations, e.g. v_p for the velocity of a particle and v_f for a fluid. This way, the two velocities cannot be substituted, and the phenomena $v_p = \sqrt{2gh}$ and $v_f = \sqrt{2gh}$ get different derivations. But Bernoulli's historical example suggests that mixing up variables may also be productive.

4   Conclusion

I have given a formal model of exemplar-based explanation, termed EBE, that constructs derivation trees for new phenomena by combining subtrees from a corpus of previous derivation trees that function as exemplars. I have

---

[4]Moreover, the fields of classical and fluid mechanics can be seen as subfields of the more encompassing field known as classical continuum mechanics (cf. [Truesdell and Noll, 1992]).

shown how this model operates for both idealized and real-world phenomena, and argued that the approach integrates theoretical and phenomenological modeling in hydraulics. Although the examples of real-world phenomena were limited to fluid mechanics, the situation is basically the same for other areas: real-world phenomena are not formally deduced from laws and antecedent conditions but also rely on other knowledge, such as intermediate models, phenomenological corrections and coefficients, approximation schemes, normalizations etc. As long as this other knowledge can be expressed in terms of mathematical equations, it can be fit into a derivation tree, and be reused by EBE to explain new phenomena.

What happens if a phenomenon cannot be explained by any combination of subtrees – even if we had a corpus of all previously explained phenomena? This situation clearly goes beyond the scope of EBE. It is an enormous challenge for a scientist to find an explanation for a novel phenomenon that does not seem to correspond to any known theory or previous explanation. Such an anomaly may touch upon a Kuhnian crisis and, possibly, a revolution. I have not yet attempted to develop a formal model of revolutionary science – if at all possible. But I hope that an implementation of the proposed EBE model may aid scientists in dealing with a range of new problems. That is, by considering *all* subtrees from *all* previous phenomena (rather than only "familiar" subtrees from "familiar" phenomena), the model may come up with unconventional explanations and predictions, possibly suggesting new directions.

BIBLIOGRAPHY

[Alonso and Finn, 1996] M. Alonso and E. Finn. *Physics.* Addison-Wesley, New York, 1996.

[Baader and Nipkow, 1998] F. Baader and T. Nipkow. *Term Rewriting and All That.* Cambridge University Press, Cambridge, 1998.

[Batchelor, 1967] G. Batchelor. *An Introduction to Fluid Dynamics.* Cambridge University Press, Cambridge, 1967.

[Bod, 2000] R. Bod. Parsing with the shortest derivation. In *Proceedings COLING'2000*, pages 69–76, 2000.

[Cartwright, 1983] N. Cartwright. *How the Laws of Physics Lie.* Oxford University Press, Oxford, 1983.

[Cartwright, 1999] N. Cartwright. *The Dappled World.* Cambridge University Press, Cambridge, 1999.

[Chanson, 2002] H. Chanson. *The Hydraulics of Open Channel Flow.* Butterworth-Heinemann, 2002.

[Cormen *et al.*, 2002] T. Cormen, C. Leiserson, and R. Rivest. *Introduction to Algorithms.* The MIT Press., Cambridge (Mass.), 2002.

[Da Costa and French, 2003] N. Da Costa and S. French. *Science and Partial Truth – A Unitary Approach to Models and Scientific Reasoning.* Oxford University Press, Oxford, 2003.

[Darcy and Bazin, 1865] H. Darcy and H. Bazin. *Recherches Hydrauliques.* Imprimerie Nationale, Paris, 1865.

[Douglas and Matthews, 1996] J. Douglas and R. Matthews. *Fluid Mechanics*. Vol. 1, 3rd edition, Longman., 1996.

[Giere, 1988] R. Giere. *Explaining Science: A Cognitive Approach*. University of Chicago Press, Chicago, 1988.

[Giere, 1999a] R. Giere. Using models to represent reality. In L. Magnani, N. Nersessian, and P. Thagard, editors, *Model-Based Reasoning in Scientific Discovery*, New York, 1999a. Kluwer Academic Publishers.

[Giere, 1999b] R. Giere. *Science without Laws*. University of Chicago Press, Chicago, 1999b.

[Graebel, 2001] W. Graebel. *Engineering Fluid Mechanics*. Taylor & Francis, New York, 2001.

[Hempel and Oppenheim, 1948] C. Hempel and P. Oppenheim. Studies in the logic of explanation. *Philosophy of Science*, 15:135–175, 1948.

[Hempel, 1965] C. Hempel. *Aspects of Scientific Explanation and Other Essays in the Philosophy of Science*. The Free Press, New York, 1965.

[Hempel, 1988] C. Hempel. Provisoes: a problem concerning the inferential function of scientific theories. *Erkenntnis*, 28:147–164, 1988.

[Kitcher, 1989] P. Kitcher. Explanatory unification and the causal structure of the world. In P. Kitcher and W. Salmon, editors, *Scientific Explanation*. University of Minnesota Press, 1989.

[Kuhn, 1970] T. Kuhn. *The Structure of Scientific Revolutions*. 2nd edition, University of Chicago Press, Chicago, 1970.

[Morgan and Morrison, 1999] M. Morgan and M. Morrison. *Models as Mediators*. Cambridge University Press, Cambridge, 1999.

[Morrison, 1999] M. Morrison. Models as autonomous agents. In M. Morgan and M. Morrison, editors, *Models as Mediators*. Cambridge University Press, 1999.

[Munson, 2002] B. Munson. *Fundamentals of Fluid Mechanics*. Wiley, New York, 2002.

[Nickles, 2003] T. Nickles. Normal science: from logic to case-based and model-based reasoning. In T. Nickles, editor, *Thomas Kuhn*. Cambridge University Press, 2003.

[Norman et al., 1990] E. Norman, J. Riley, and M. Whittaker. *Advanced Design and Technology*. Longman, New York, 1990.

[Nosofsky, 1988] R. Nosofsky. Exemplar-based accounts of relations between classification, recognition, and typicality. *Journal of Experimental Psychology: Learning, Memory and Cognition*, 14:700–708, 1988.

[Sadri and Floryan, 2002] R. Sadri and J.M. Floryan. Entry flow in a channel. *Computers and Fluids*, 31:133–157, 2002.

[Salmon, 1989] W. Salmon. *Four Decades of Scientific Explanation*. University of Minnesota Press, Minnesota, 1989.

[Suppe, 1977] F. Suppe, editor. *The Structure of Scientific Theories*. 2nd edition, University of Illinois Press, Illinois, 1977.

[Suppes, 1961] P. Suppes. A comparison of the meaning and use of models in the mathematical and empirical sciences. In H. Freudenthal, editor, *The Concept and Role of the Model in Mathematics and Natural and Social Sciences*. Reidel, 1961.

[Suppes, 1967] P. Suppes. What is a scientific theory? In S. Morgenbesser, editor, *Philosophy of Science Today*. Basic Books, 1967.

[Truesdell and Noll, 1992] C. Truesdell and W. Noll. *The Non-Linear Field Theories of Mechanics*. Springer Verlag, Berlin, 1992.

[van Fraassen, 1980] B. van Fraassen. *The Scientific Image*. Oxford University Press, Oxford, 1980.

Rens Bod
Institute for Logic, Language and Computation
University of Amsterdam, Amsterdam, The Netherlands
Email: rens@science.uva.nl

The Frame Problem and the Treatment of Prediction

MARK SPREVAK

ABSTRACT.   The frame problem is a problem in artificial intelligence that a number of philosophers have claimed has philosophical relevance. The structure of this paper is as follows: (1) An account of the frame problem is given; (2) The frame problem is distinguished from related problems; (3) The main strategies for dealing with the frame problem are outlined; (4) A difference between commonsense reasoning and prediction using a scientific theory is argued for; (5) Some implications for the computational theory of mind are discussed.

1   Introduction

The frame problem is a problem in artificial intelligence that was first described in by John McCarthy and Patrick Hayes in 1969. As a problem in artificial intelligence, it has been extremely difficult to solve. A number of philosophers, including Daniel Dennett, Jerry Fodor, Clark Glymour, and John Haugeland have suggested that the frame problem is either indicative of a new problem in philosophy, or has important connections to existing problems. Unfortunately, no one can agree what those connections are, or what the frame problem is. In this paper, I argue for two things. First, I argue for a view of what the frame problem is. Second, I argue that there is at least one sense in which the frame problem is relevant to philosophy: the frame problem provides a precise way of discriminating commonsense reasoning from prediction using scientific theory. Some people already believe that these two forms of reasoning are distinct. However, even for these people, it has proved remarkably difficult to say exactly where the difference lies. I believe that the frame problem can help.

2   What is the frame problem?

The frame problem concerns how to represent a complex changing world. In artificial intelligence (AI), the standard way to represent a changing world is to use time-slices or situations. Time-slices represent what is true in the world at a particular moment in time; for example, they represent

Lorenzo Magnani and Riccardo Dossena, editors, *Computing, Philosophy, and Cognition*, pp. 349–359 © 2005, M. Sprevak.

where a thing is located at an instant, or what the temperature is at an instant. Changes and events are represented as functions between time-slices. Applying an event to a particular time-slice yields another time-slice that represents the state of the world that the system thinks would be the result of that event. These functions or relations between time-slices are called the "laws of motion": they describe how the agent thinks the world changes over time. This approach seems sensible, but it quickly runs into problems.

Consider how the functions that represent events are specified. For each object or state of affairs in the world one needs to specify how its state before the event relates to its state after the event. For example, imagine a function that represents the action of the agent moving through a door into another room. This function maps the agent's location before the event to a new location after the event. Part of the function would be specified as:

F the agent is in room $R1$ in situation S

AND IF the door D from $R1$ to $R2$ is open in situation S

THEN the agent is in $R2$ in situation goThrough(D, S).

This specification accounts for the *position* of the agent – it maps the position of the agent before the event to a new position after the event – but what about the rest of the world, how does the application of the goThrough function affect that? Most of the world will be unaffected by the agent going through the door. The agent's hair will remain the same color. Paris will still be the capital of France, the walls of the room will still be the same, and so on. How does the system know this? The answer is that it doesn't: that information is not deductively entailed by the rule about position. The system has to be told about these other properties. How does one tell it? One way is to explicitly specify the information, for example:

IF the agent has hair color C in situation S

THEN the agent has hair color C in situation goThrough(D, S).

However, this specification needs to be repeated for nearly every property and relation in situation S. A huge number of no-change rules are needed in order for the system to know that moving rooms will not dramatically change the world. These no-change rules are called "frame axioms". The frame problem is that AI systems seem to need a lot of frame axioms. If there are 100 actions and 500 instantaneous facts, then the system will need up to 50,000 frame axioms. Worse, as the system learns more about the world, the number of frame axioms will come to dwarf everything else it knows.

The frame problem is the problem of getting a system to infer that the world remains largely the same before and after an action: it is the problem of getting the system to infer a large number of obvious non-changes. More precisely, the frame problem is the problem of getting the system to infer that the world remains the same *unless it has good reason for supposing otherwise.* It is worth clarifying a few things that the frame problem is not:

1. *Computational complexity.* The frame problem is not a point about computational complexity. Even if one had an infinitely fast machine the frame problem would still be present. It is representational systems that suffer from the frame problem, not individual machines. An infinitely machine has to be programmed. *We* have to decide what representational system to give it. If the representational system requires a vast number of no-change frame axioms, then we would still be stuck with the task of having to explicitly specify those axioms. In an even moderately complex world, this looks like an impossible task.

2. *Infallibility.* Humans make mistakes all the time; we are not infallible with our model of a changing world, so why should we expect our AI system to do better? Infallibility is not in question in the frame problem. The requirement is *not* that an AI system be infallible, but that it be reasonably reliable and robust. A system is reasonably reliable and robust if: (1) the system is right more often than not; and (2) the system does not fail catastrophically when changes that we would consider quite minor are made to the world. This specification is not precise, but it is clear that current AI systems fail to satisfy it.

3. *Hume's problem of induction.* Hume's problem of induction concerns how to justify our inductive inferences. The problem is to find a non-circular reason for trusting our inductive practices in the future. This is not the frame problem. The frame is not concerned with how to justify inferential systems, it is concerned with how to *construct* such systems. While Hume is interested in whether our inductive beliefs are justified, AI researchers are interested in developing systems that simply possess those beliefs.

4. *The problem of knowing when to stop making inferences.* Real-world AI systems have to stop making inferences at some point and act. This is a familiar problem in decision theory: when does the expected cost of acquiring further information relevant to a decision exceed the

expected value of that information? This is a problem of interest to many AI researchers, but it is not the frame problem.

5. *The problem of acquiring inductive beliefs (abduction).* Abduction concerns how one generates inductive hypotheses from a finite set of observations. (This problem is distinct from Hume's problem of *justifying* the generated hypotheses). The problem of abduction is of great interest to AI researchers, but it is not the frame problem. For the purposes of the frame problem, we are happy to lend our AI system as much of our hard-won inductive knowledge as possible. The system is not required to infer its inductive beliefs from scratch.

6. *The problem of belief revision.* The problem of belief revision is how a system should react to new information. The problem of belief revision is distinct from the frame problem. Systems that suffer from the frame problem need not suffer from the belief revision problem. An example from [Hayes, 1987]: Imagine a program which has to plan a sequence of movements of a robot arm across a table crowded with objects. Let the program have a complete representation of this world and its dynamics so that no new information will come its way. This program will have the frame problem in spades, but no belief revision problem.

7. *The ceteris paribus problem.* Problems associated with *ceteris paribus* clauses are the problems most commonly conflated with the frame problem. What I am calling the *ceteris paribus* problem is referred to in the AI literature as the *qualification problem*. The qualification problem is how to specify inductive inferences in such a way that they are defeasible. Inductive inferences only hold provided certain blocking circumstances do not obtain. There can be an unlimited number of blocking circumstances. We cannot specify all such circumstances, much less check that they do not obtain. As epistemic agents, what we tend to do is assume that they do not obtain, and then if a good reason to the contrary comes along, we consider our inference defeated. The qualification problem concerns how to formalize this feature of our reasoning. More specifically, the qualification problem concerns how to formalize the inference rule: "If X is true and all else is equal, then conclude Y".

The frame problem is also concerned with formalizing inductive inference rules, but it is a different problem. The frame problem concerns the consequent, rather than the antecedent of inferences. It concerns how to formalize: "Conclude Y *and* conclude that all else is unchanged unless there is good reason to suppose otherwise".

Ceteris paribus   If X & . . . then Y (1)

Frame problem   If X then Y & . . .   (2)

The *ceteris paribus* problem concerns how to formalize schema (1) in a way that does not require an explicit specification of the antecedents. The frame problem concerns how to formalize schema (2) in a way that does not require an explicit specification of the consequents. The *ceteris paribus* problem and the frame problem concern formalizing inductive inference rules, but they concern different aspects of those rules.

To summarize: the frame problem is the problem of getting a system to infer that the world remains the same unless it already has a good reason to suppose otherwise.

3 Approaches to solutions

There is an enormous amount of literature on solving the frame problem, but no agreed solution. Rather than summarize all the approaches, I will describe one popular logic-based approach to solving the frame problem.

One might think of the frame problem as the problem of getting extra entailments out of limited assumptions. A tempting way to solve this problem is therefore to strengthen one's inferential system to get the extra entailments out. The aim is to build something like the following principle into an inferential system: "Conclude that something stays the same, unless there is good reason to think otherwise". Unfortunately, this principle is remarkably hard to formalize.

First, try a simple formalization. Formalize the principle as: "If there is no explicit rule for a property, then assume that property stays the same". This formalization has the virtue of being easy to implement in the original situation calculus. Does it solve the frame problem? Let us see how it works.

Imagine an AI system that reasons about a world containing colored blocks. Suppose that this AI system, like the one described above, has axioms predicting what happens when a given events occurs. For example, the system may have axioms predicting what happens if a block is moved. Moving a block changes its location, so one of the axioms may be:

IF the location of block B is L in situation S

THEN the location of block B is $L + D$ in situation moveBlock(B, D).

This may be just one of many axioms specifying how the moveBlock event affects the world. However, unlike the system described above, this system does not need a moveBlock axiom for *every* property in situation S. The system can use its no-change rule – "If there is no explicit rule for a property, then assume that property stays the same" – to deduce the state of other properties for itself. For example, it unnecessary to explicitly tell the system that the block will be the same color before and after a move, or that Paris will be the capital of France, or that the walls of the room will be the same color. The system can infer these consequences for itself. Therefore, this system does not need the vast number of frame axioms that our first system needed. Does it thereby solve the frame problem? Unfortunately, it does not.

Imagine that the world contains a blue spray-can that continuously sprays paint against a wall. Suppose that the system knows all about spray-cans, paint, and what paint can do to colored blocks. Now suppose that the system is queried on what would happen if a red block were moved between the spray-can and the wall such that it is in the path of the blue paint. What will the system predict? The system will reason as follows. First, it will follow its explicit rules for moving blocks, such as its rule for how moving affects location. Then, the system will consider the properties for which changes are not explicitly specified. It will infer the state of these properties using its no-change rule: those properties will be marked as unchanged, since they lack explicit rules specifying otherwise.

The system will therefore make the following predictions. It will correctly predict that the position of the block changes when it is moved, but it will incorrectly predict that the red block will still be red when moved into the path of the blue paint. This is disappointing. We would have liked our system to make a correct prediction. But what makes this situation intolerable is that the system makes this prediction *despite the fact that it knows all about spray-cans, blue paint, and what they can do to colored blocks*. The problem is not that the system does not know about spray-cans and paint, but that it cannot bring this information to bear to defeat its no-change rule. The no-change rule is too inflexible, it is not sensitive to being overridden in appropriate ways. What we would like is for the no-change rule to be defeated *when the system has good reason to think that a property will change*. This would be a better implementation of the original principle that we were trying to capture.

The failed formalization we have just tried was: "If there is no explicit rule for a property, then assume that property stays the same". There are many ways to improve on it. Here are three popular example. First: "Assume that a property stays the same, unless believing so results in a contradictory belief set." Second: "Assume that a property stays the same, so long as it is not believed that it changes." Third: "Assume that the maximal set of properties stay the same, consistent with the system's knowledge of the situation." These three principles are associated with default logics, autoepistemic logics, and circumspection logics respectively[1]. All three formalizations produce different kinds of logic. None gives the same results, and none is as well-behaved as the original situational calculus. More importantly, none of the logics give results that match up with our intuitive understanding of the no-change principle. There are counterexamples, like the blue spray-can example, on which any given formalization performs catastrophically badly. There seems to be no silver logical bullet to solve the frame problem[2].

4 The frame problem and scientific theory

The purpose of the preceding section was to show that the frame problem is hard. In this section, I will argue that the frame problem provides a precise way in which commonsense reasoning can be distinguished from prediction using scientific theory.

The frame problem's most obvious application is in commonsense reasoning. Does the frame problem also affect prediction using scientific theory? The standard way of treating prediction using scientific theory is with the DN-model[3]. According to the DN-model, making a prediction is simple: a prediction deductively follows from a scientific theory conjoined with a numerical description of the current situation. This is familiar to anyone who has used a scientific theory: one has a theory, one plugs in the numbers, and the prediction deductively pops out. The DN-model has been criticized in other contexts, but its treatment of prediction has proved resilient. The main critics of the deductive model of prediction have been the DN-model's creator Carl Hempel [Hempel, 1988], and Nancy Cartwright [Cartwright, 1983]. Their criticism is that real scientific theories only entail their predictions *ceteris paribus* and the DN-model has difficulty modeling *ceteris paribus* clauses.

The DN-model also has difficulty modeling frame-type consequents. This

---

[1] See [Gabbay *et al.*, 1994] and [Ginsberg, 1987].

[2] For a survey of problems with recent approaches to the frame problem see [Morgenstern, 1996]. For recent logical approaches that hold promise for the future, see [Levesque *et al.*, 1997], [Reiter, 1991], and [Shanahan, 1997].

[3] Strictly speaking, the DN-model is a model of explanation, not prediction. However, the DN-model includes a deductive model of prediction. For the purpose of this paper, I focus only on this component of the DN-model. There is no special name for the component, so I will refer to it as the "DN-model". It is primarily this component that Cartwright targets in her criticism of the DN-model ([Cartwright, 1983] essays 7, 8).

is why the frame problem is so hard. If the DN-model could easily model frame-type consequents, then the frame problem would be easy, since formal AI models of inference are usually just variations on the DN-model. There-fore, the DN-model of prediction has difficulty with both *ceteris paribus* clauses and frame-problem-type consequents. Both features of inductive inference are clearly important. Does this mean that the frame problem, like the *ceteris paribus* problem, causes trouble for the DN-model of sci-entific inference? Does the frame problem demonstrate problems with the DN-model that *add* to those of Hempel and Cartwright?

I do not think so. The frame problem does not affect scientific inference. Consider an astronomical theory for predicting eclipses. Such a theory will almost certainly have *ceteris paribus* clauses: the theory will predict eclipses *provided* other planets do not upset the orbits, and so on. We would expect this feature to cause difficulties for a DN-type model of prediction using that theory. Does the frame problem introduce additional difficulties? It does not. What one wants from a theory of eclipses are times of eclipses, and this is exactly what the theory provides. One does not require that the theory *also* predict the non-change of other aspects of the world into the bargain. One does not ask for a *total* future world state from a scientific theory, only the state of certain properties – a partial future world state. We can fill in the other properties for ourselves using cognitive resources *outside* the scientific theory. In this sense, scientific theories are like spe-cialized instruments for predicting the values of particular properties. They do a different job from commonsense reasoning, which fills in the rest of the world-state. The frame problem only bites if one tries to model this commonsense background in a DN-type way. Therefore, the frame problem affects commonsense reasoning, but not prediction using scientific theory.

The fact that models of these two forms of reasoning face different prob-lems suggests that they are different forms of reasoning. Consider the grounds on which one justifies that two things are the same or different. A common reason for saying that two things are different is that accounts of those two things face different problems. One might claim that the phys-iological nature of horses is different to that of cows because, if one tries to give a physiological theory of horses, that theory faces significantly different problems from a physiological theory of cows. In contrast, a physiologi-cal theory of Betsy the cow does not face significantly different problems from a physiological theory of Daisy the cow (assuming Betsy and Daisy are normal cows). At the appropriate level of abstraction, different problems indicate different things. We have seen that at the level of abstraction at issue, accounts of commonsense reasoning faces different problems from ac-counts of scientific inference. Accounts of the commonsense reasoning face the frame problem, while accounts of prediction using scientific theory do not. This difference is not trivial because, as we saw, the frame problem is extremely hard to solve. Furthermore, the difference is not shown up by other epistemological problems – for example, the *ceteris paribus* problem affects both commonsense reasoning and prediction using scientific theory. Therefore, the frame problem appears to provide at least a *prima facie* reason for saying that prediction using commonsense reasoning and prediction using scientific theory are different.

Whether this claim is ultimately correct is a delicate issue. One might feel that there is too much at stake for the issue to be settled on just one problem. However, even if one resists the claim above – that the two forms of reasoning are distinct – one still has to accept the claim that *accounts* of the two forms of reasoning face different problems. An account of commonsense reasoning faces different demands from an account of prediction using scientific theory: the former faces the frame problem while the latter does not. I wish to draw two implications of this claim.

First, since accounts of the two forms of reasoning faces different demands, one should be careful when proposing a model of scientific inference not to try to do too much. In particular, one should be careful not to try to implicitly model commonsense reasoning too. A good account of one need not be a good account of the other. The point is general but it suggests a way of defending the DN-model against Hempel and Cartwright's criticism. Hempel and Cartwright attack the DN-model for its inability to cope with *ceteris paribus* clauses. But perhaps *ceteris paribus* clauses, like frame-problem-type consequents, are better seen as part of the commonsense component of reasoning. A scientific theory may DN-entail its prediction and then our commonsense reasoning decides whether that theory applies in that circumstance. On this view, a scientific theory is like an instrument for predicting values of properties in a straightforward DN-type way, but we decide on the basis of our commonsense reasoning whether to use that instrument, just as we decide on the basis of commonsense reasoning what the state of the rest of the world is likely to be. A two-tier approach to inference has already been forced on us by the frame problem. It does not seem unreasonable to apply this distinction to *ceteris paribus* clauses.

The second implication is as follows. Since accounts of the two forms of reasoning face different problems, treating commonsense reasoning as a kind of scientific inference may be a mistake. The computational theory of mind models commonsense reasoning in exactly this way: as a kind of scientific theory. If the two forms of reasoning are distinct, or require radically different treatments, then there is something seriously wrong with this approach. This seems to be borne out both in Fodor's comments that the frame problem creates serious trouble for the computational theory of mind, and in the difficulty that AI researchers have had in creating successful commonsense reasoning systems [Fodor, 2000]. The computational theory of mind works well for automated scientific reasoning systems, but it quickly breaks down when asked to produce anything commonsensical. This should be unsurprising given that the DN-model that works for scientific inference was not designed to deal problems like the frame problem that face models of commonsense reasoning.

5   Conclusion

The frame problem provides a diagnostic difference between commonsense reasoning and prediction using scientific theory: the frame problem affects one but not the other. This difference can be taken in two ways. It can be taken either as evidence that the two forms of reasoning are essentially different; or, it can taken in a weaker way, as demonstrating that accounts of the two forms of reasoning face different demands. Either way, the difference has consequences for both the computational theory of mind and the treatment of prediction in scientific theories.

BIBLIOGRAPHY

[Cartwright, 1983] N. Cartwright. *How the Laws of Physics Lie.* Oxford University Press, Oxford, 1983.
[Dennett, 1987] D.C. Dennett. Cognitive wheels: the frame problem of ai. In Z. W. Pylyshyn, editor, *The Robot's Dilemma*, pages 41–64. Ablex, Norwood, 1987.
[Fodor, 1987] J.A. Fodor. Modules, frames, fridgeons, sleeping dogs and the music of the spheres. In Z.W. Pylyshyn, editor, *The Robot's Dilemma*, pages 139–150. Ablex, Norwood, 1987.
[Fodor, 2000] J.A. Fodor. *The Mind Doesn't Work That Way.* The MIT Press, Cambridge (Mass.), 2000.
[Gabbay *et al.*, 1994] D. Gabbay, C. Hogger, and J. Robinson, editors. *Handbook of Logic in Artificial Intelligence and Logic Programming, volume 3.* Oxford University Press, Oxford, 1994.
[Ginsberg, 1987] M. Ginsberg, editor. *Readings in Nonmonotonic Reasoning.* Morgan Kauffman, Los Altos, CA., 1987.
[Glymour, 1987] C. Glymour. Android epistemology and the frame problem: comments on dennett's 'cognitive wheels'. In Z.W. Pylyshyn, editor, *The Robot's Dilemma*, pages 65–76. Ablex, Norwood, 1987.
[Haugeland, 1987] J. Haugeland. An overview of the frame problem. In Z.W. Pylyshyn, editor, *The Robot's Dilemma*, pages 77–95. Ablex, Norwood, 1987.
[Hayes, 1987] P.J. Hayes. What the frame problem is and isn't. In Z.W. Pylyshyn, editor, *The Robot's Dilemma*, pages 123–138. Ablex, Norwood, 1987.
[Hempel, 1988] C.G. Hempel. Provisos: a problem concerning the inferential function of scientific theories. *Erkenntnis*, 28:147–164, 1988.
[Levesque *et al.*, 1997] H. Levesque, R. Reiter, Y. Lesperance, F. Lin, and R. Scherl. A logic programming language for dynamic domains. *Journal of Logic Programming*, 31:59–84, 1997.

[McCarthy and Hayes, 1969] J. McCarthy and P.J. Hayes. Some philosophical problems
from the standpoint of artificial intelligence. In B. Meltzer and D. Michie, editors,
Machine Intelligence 4, pages 463–502. Edinburgh University Press, Edinburgh, 1969.
[Morgenstern, 1996] L. Morgenstern. The problem with solutions to the frame problem.
In K. Ford and Z. Pylyshyn, editors, *The Robot's Dilemma Revisited*, pages 99–133.
Ablex, Norwood, 1996.
[Reiter, 1991] R. Reiter. The frame problem in the situation calculus: A simple solution
(sometimes) and a completeness result for goal regression. In V. Lifschitz, editor,
*Artificial intelligence and mathematical theory of computation: Papers in honor of
John McCarthy*, pages 359–380. Academic Press, Boston, 1991.
[Shanahan, 1997] M.P. Shanahan. *Solving the Frame Problem: A Mathematical Inves-
tigation of the Common Sense Law of Inertia*. The MIT Press, Cambridge (Mass.),
1997.

Mark Sprevak
Dept. History and Philosophy of Science,
University of Cambridge, Cambridge, UK
Email: mds26@hermes.cam.ac.uk

Can Vision Be Computational?

ROSARIA GRAZIA DOMENELLA AND ALESSIO PLEBE

ABSTRACT. To anticipate the disappointment of readers: at the end of this paper there will be no "yes"or "no" answer, and we would not even attempt to give one. The purpose of this work is rather to take the question in the title as a starting point for a reflection on the role of computation today in investigating human vision. As soon as one tries to give an answer, it appears that the word *computation* is too ill defined to take the question seriously. To be honest, there is a precise meaning, inside formal mathematics, but the very abstract meaning of *computational* is perhaps scarcely productive for an understanding of vision. But the term in the tradition of vision computation is loaded with many attributes, as in the theory of Marr, where several concepts of computer science has been borrowed for explaining the human visual system. This flavor of *computational* is definitely more fruitful, but also more exposed to difficulties when related to the other areas of research currently dealing with vision like philosophy, psychology and neuroscience. This latter, today, is also bearing an other sense of *computational*, that used in *computational neuroscience*, where the role of the computer is weaker than in other scenarios. At the end of the discussion this seems to be a possible way of pursuing a concept of computational which can still produce new insights, but can better fit in a multi-disciplinary approach to human vision.

1 Introduction

Image processing has been a well-established research area in computer science since the early days [Nagy, 1968], though scarcely related with the philosophy and the physiology of human visual perception for a long time. In the meantime the basic elements of the biological computation in vision were discovered by David Hubel and Torsten Wiesel [Hubel and Wiesel, 1962]. David Marr first bridged these two domains, with the approach to the natural vision as an engineering problem of information processing [Marr, 1982]. His paradigm shift has been fruitful for both image processing and the new wave of cognitive research of vision.

Now, twenty years later, we wonder how far can be brought the connection between image processing software and natural vision, hence the

Lorenzo Magnani and Riccardo Dossena, editors, *Computing, Philosophy, and Cognition*, pp. 361–379 © 2005, R.G. Domenella and A. Plebe.

question if human vision can be computational. Part of the question we
believe boils down in the meaning of its terms, first of all *computational*,
a relatively new word, used with a rather broad span of different meaning.
Ascribing the *computational* predicate to vision therefore can lead to a variety of consequences, depending on the adopted meaning of this term. While
human vision is certainly not a new term, with a seemingly precise linguistic
use, it is not less problematic. In the light of the current knowledge of the
neurophysiology of vision it looks far from trivial to define exactly the borders of what can be called a *human visual system*, especially if the format
should be compatible with the requirements of a *computational* system.

To assess the meaning of *computational*, there is a first reference dating
back to Hilbert, Post and Turing, of *computable* meaning anything expressed
by a mathematical function that can be executed in a finite number of steps
by a definite method like the Turing Machine (TM hereafter) [Turing, 1936].
If vision can be characterized in terms of some mathematical function - however complicated - then in that very abstract sense, it may be computable.
Closely related there is another important abstract concept, that of *algorithm*, the definite sequence of steps solving a general problem. Even if for
a mathematician *algorithmic, computable by a TM, decidable, effective* are
just synonymous, here the difference exists, inasmuch the *algorithm* can be
raised at the same level of a scientific explanation, thanks to its linguistic
form.

For both the above interpretations of *computational* it will be arduous
to give to the question "is vision computational?" an answer saleable to
a mathematician. But the main point is to understand if answering "no"
or "yes" to the question if vision is computable in such abstract senses will
reveal anything useful on how vision actually works in humans. Maybe a
stone falling in a puddle or the noise of a crank are also computable in such
senses, but then this shared prerogative is not very informative.

Another sense, more familiar to the traditional Artificial Intelligence research is that of *computational* as runnable on a digital computer, therefore
equivalent with some software executable on a machine. For the functionalist stream in philosophy of mind, the analogy between brain and computer
works because the essence is the algorithm, the software, and the hardware where this software runs does not count. Moreover, computers are
the fertile ground where image processing theories have grown, and where
several concepts have been borrowed by Marr's theory, like the software
engineering approach. The computer metaphor has been a fruitful source
of interesting insights, but it also brought dangerous consequences, when
taken too literally. The main concepts of computer science here shown to
be cumbersome for an explanation of human vision are that of identifying

Input/Output, of a modular organization of the processes, and finally the relevance of computational complexity.

At the end, there is another meaning to *computational*, which is used for example in the research domain called *computational neuroscience*. It is the possibility of simulating within a computer some components of the biological visual perception, not necessarily in full details, but at least in their essential functions. This weaker meaning can sound rather trivial: "computational vision" could be feasible, exactly as "computational meteorology", being possible to simulate the atmospheric dynamics in a computer. But of course, the atmosphere by itself has nothing to share with a computer. There is actually something more, in this context "computational" also betokens the evidence that what is being modeled by the computer is itself a kind of computation, albeit one quite unlike that running on the serial digital machines called computers. This latter meaning of computation is close to that of signal processing: the purposeful modification of measurable entities.

2   Turing Machine equivalence

The most familiar notion of computational is the TM, a system evolving by changing the internal states, depending on symbols read on a sequential storage, where it can also write. It is an abstract concept, formally equivalent to a bunch of others like *λ-calculus* [Church, 1941], rewriting systems [Post, 1921], *semi-Thue* systems [Thue, 1912], Markov algorithms [Markov, 1954] and phrase structure grammars [Chomsky, 1958]. While all the other systems are mainly known by mathematicians, the TM spread its fame on the wave of the real machines designed using its paradigm, which later everybody would have used for doing computations. There are two ways of challenging the equivalence of vision with the Turing Machine concept.

2.1   The equivalence is mathematically scabrous

First of all one can engage himself in formal mathematics, realizing soon that the path to the equivalence of vision with TM is beset with difficulties. There are at least two crucial thorny steps:

1. formulating vision as a computational problem;

2. claiming the existence of a TM solving vision.

The first step is the basic presupposition for something to be computable: to be characterized in terms of some mathematical problem, however complicated. A typical definition of "problem" suitable for computation is that of deciding over a set of instances. That is, a problem P is a binary relation from the set of instances I to truth values:

(1) $P : I \to \{\texttt{true}, \texttt{false}\}$.

It is actually a restriction over a more general notion of problem:

(2) $P : I \to S$

where S is now the set of all possible solutions. Problems originally in the form (2) most of the time can be recast as (1) [Garey and Johnson, 1979].

It is far from obvious if vision can be stated in terms of (1) or even (2). A typical position of computationalism in vision is to claim that vision can be formulated as a relation between possible visual scene and possible actions. It follows that P_V, the problem of vision, could have a formulation like:

(3) $P_V : I \to \{\texttt{true}, \texttt{false}\}$; $I = V \times A$

where V is the set of all possible visual scenes, and A the collection of all possible actions. Not only this position is too abstract for a possible demonstration, but the agreement with any empirical evidence seems weak. No human would ever react the same way in front of the same visual scene. This point will be discussed again in section 4.2.

However, if the previous point can be overcome somehow, and vision can be formulated as (3) or anything like that, then the other chapter of the story should be to show that a TM can solve this problem. Clearly until someone comes along with a solving TM, or with a formal demonstration of the impossibility of a solution, no more words can be added to the riddle. Due to the extreme generality of the problem formulation, it is very doubtful that any step in either directions can be made.

2.2 Vision system and circulatory system

There is a second and more important way of challenging the TM equivalence, that is to reflect on the epistemological consequences of claiming that vision is a TM or not. It may appear that vision is not like a TM not because there is mathematical incompatibility, but just because there is nothing in the concept of a TM useful to explain visual mechanisms.

Let us take for example some other human function, like the circulatory system. Is it equivalent to a TM? It may, or may not, but no one cares, and probably nobody has ever attempted to demonstrate either answer. It seems that for some reason the property of being a TM is pertinent to the vision and not to the circulatory system, although the latter looks more like a pure mechanical device. In fact, there are several abstract models of blood circulation, but the mathematics used there has nothing to do with TM, rather with tools like dynamic systems and differential equations [Peskin and McQueen, 1997]. The moral is that for a system to exhibit computational properties does not necessarily mean that the TM is the best way of characterizing it. The vision computationalist will probably argue that there is something more in vision than in the circulatory system: it is not only possible to model the vision, but what is being modeled is itself a kind of computation. It is a point that can be agreed upon, but still it does not means that a TM is an epistemological valuable model of that computation. The TM catches perfectly the essence of digital computers, not only, also of several other phenomena like the parsing of a language syntax, but it does not seem to adhere to any particular feature of the computations done in biological visual systems, from the current status of knowledge.

3   Vision as an algorithm

The concept of algorithm is formally so close to that of TM that it is not useful any more to put ourselves in a mathematician's shoes and dissert about possible equivalence. It will be more or less the same discussion done in section 2.1. The possibility of vision to be an algorithm deserves its own place not just for its mathematical properties, rather for its linguistic properties, of being a kind of explanation in natural language.

The idea that vision should be algorithmic for inescapable epistemological motivations is often a hidden presupposition, but sometimes it is also an overt claim, like in this statement:

> Appeals to non-algorithmic explanations cannot seriously be en-
> tertained because, by definition of algorithm, they would not
> give a step-by-step procedure for achieving a solution to a prob-
> lem. [...] Since biological scientists provide algorithmic expla-
> nation, computational plausibility is not only an appropriate but
> a necessary consideration. [Tsotsos, 1993, p. 273]

It is an argument resonant of *petitio principi* like saying that an expli-cation of vision cannot be other than an algorithm because nothing but an algorithm is a valid explanation.

3.1   Algorithms in the primary visual cortex

But let us try to understand better what kind of explanation an algorithm should provide in the case of vision, using a simple example from the cortical processes. In the still almost dark picture of how the brain works, one of the best known mechanism is primary vision, taking place in areas V1 and V2 of the occipital cortex. One of the relevant structures is an aggregation of a few thousands neurons called "macrocolumn", where all cells seem to be engaged in processing the same visual area, giving rise to complex receptive fields. Several measured shapes of such fields closely resemble

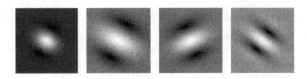

Figure 1. Example of Gabor functions. Each should be read as a mask to be applied to a retinal field, where dark areas will contribute negatively and brighter areas positively.

some mathematical functions called Gabor filters, shown in Figure 1. For image applications their equations are:

$$(4) \quad f(x,y) = e^{-\frac{\left(\omega_x^2+\omega_y^2\right)\left(x^2+y^2\right)}{2\sigma^2} - \imath(x+y)}.$$

These functions where first introduced by D. Gabor in the field of telecommunication signal analysis [Gabor, 1946]. Just a funny coincidence? Probably not: a peculiar property of these functions is the optimal projection of the principal component of a broad class of signals. It has recently been demonstrated for generic natural pictures [Hancock *et al.*, 1992]. The shape of such clever receptive fields seems to arise in the cortical macrocolumns as one of the auto-organization processes taking place in the early ontogenesis of the visual system [von der Malsburg, 1990; von der Malsburg, 1995], in which an important role is played by lateral connections in the macrocolumns [Grinvald *et al.*, 1994; Miikkulainen *et al.*, 1997].

Now, what should an algorithm tell as an explanation of this story? At first glance, it seems straightforward: the application of (4) to an image can easily be described with an algorithm. But the claim that such algorithm is the visual phenomena will be manifestly false. Nothing in the macrocolumns happens like "taking an x, squaring it, adding to the square of y, ...", the neural computation taking place is a very different sort of business, giving rise collectively to a shape resembling a Gabor function, thanks to earlier auto-organization processes.

One may grant that also the actual computation of neural macrocolumns is not a mystery, in principle it can be expressed by extending the application of a basic model like Hodgkin-Huxley reaction-diffusion equations of neural activity [Hodgkin and Huxley, 1952; Rinzel, 1990; Hille, 1992]:

$$\frac{\partial V}{\partial t} = \delta\frac{\partial^2 V}{\partial x^2} + I + F\left(V, y_{Na^+}, y_{K^+}, y_L\right), \qquad (5)$$

$$\frac{\partial y_{Na^+}}{\partial t} = \gamma_{Na^+}\left(V\right) y_{Na^+} + \alpha_{Na^+}\left(V\right),$$

$$\frac{\partial y_{K^+}}{\partial t} = \gamma_{K^+}\left(V\right) y_{K^+} + \alpha_{K^+}\left(V\right),$$

$$\frac{\partial y_L}{\partial t} = \gamma_L\left(V\right) y_L + \alpha_L\left(V\right).$$

where V is the electric voltage, I is electric current, x a mono-dimensional space, y_X chemical concentrations, and F, γ_i e α_i non-linear auxiliary functions. Even if not straightforward, one may also grant that (5) together with all what is needed for modeling macrocolumns can be described in a (rather lengthy) algorithm. But now, this algorithm is not explaining anything about the phenomena. Every brain function from perceiving tickle to speculate about pure reason is supported by this sort of computation. Gabor functions have now disappeared.

One may insist that in principle it is possible to express in a single algorithm the whole auto-organization process giving rise to Gabor functions which will be later applied by the neural structure. Not far from true, in fact there are several attempts of modeling the emergence of Gabor-like functions in visual cortex, for example the adaptive-subspace self-organizing map model [Kohonen, 1995a; Kohonen, 1995b; Kohonen et al., 1997].

This can be stuffed in an algorithm, which tells something like "take the input visual scenes and adapt the neural columns with a self-organization procedure, until some stability measure reaches a threshold, and then apply these columns to whatever image is in input". That's the explanation of the story. It is, indeed, trying not to be too finical about the details: this algorithm probably catches the essence of the phenomena, explaining how it emerges, and how it is applied in the vision process. But still, it would be false to claim that such algorithm is the visual computation. Quoting von der Malsburg, the self-organizing map model is nothing more than

> an algorithmic caricature of the [self-organization] mechanism. [von der Malsburg, 1995]

The point will be serious if someone pretends to investigate further the inside of the algorithm for speculating about the inside of the phenomena: this will be an easy epistemological error in the use of the algorithm as equivalent to the vision process.

4 The computer metaphor

A pervasive understanding of *computational* is clearly associated with the most familiar equipment capable of computing: the computer. As mentioned in the introduction, the question dealt in this work would probably never be asked without important disciplines like machine vision and digital image processing. The focus of these research fields is not human vision but the possibility of computers to implement some capability of processing visual inputs. Computers became crucial for understanding human vision when Marr argued that the efforts and the difficulties in designing artificial visual systems may shed light on the equivalent problems solved by biological evolution in human vision [Marr, 1982]. On the other hand, progresses in neuroscience of vision may help computer engineers in developing more efficient image processing software borrowing strategies from biological vision. This close and fruitful interchange is often taken a step further, with the more or less implicit assumption that there is no difference in principle between computations going on in a digital computer connected with a camera and the human visual system.

But taking too literally the computer metaphor of vision can soon mislead the direction in the research on human vision.

4.1 Hardware and software

In computers there is a sharp division between these two aspects, that can be identified immediately in every equipment. The temptation to extend this metaphor to humans is strong, and is indeed the base of the *functionalism* stream in philosophy: there is something like a software which can be studied independently from the hardware. This is just a conceptual and methodological dichotomy, nothing real corresponding to it. This difference simply does not exist in the brain: as in the biological computing elements the physical properties are inseparable from the processes they are doing.

One may object that in the computer world the distinction between hardware and software today is rather blurred. But this will be just to mistake the design level with the execution level. Truly, there is a broad choice in deciding what will go in the hardware or in the software when designing a computer. But whenever you consider the execution of a program in an existing computer, the distinction between the flux of instructions (software), and the circuits implementing the instruction set (hardware) is perfectly sharp .

It is possible to identify also in biological systems several levels of organization, ranging from ion selective channels in membranes to dendritic spines, dendrites, neurons, microcolumns, neural networks and so on, but none of these levels can be singled out as the hardware, opposed to some software [Churchland and Sejnowski, 1994; Bell, 1999; Churchland, 2002]. This can be easily realized trying to apply to humans one of the most typical properties of software: portability. While computer software can be reproduced exactly, transferred to another system , copied and modified, nothing in the brain can be managed in this way, because there is nothing like a software.

4.2 Input and output

In any computation carried out by a computer a fundamental specification is the input and the output of the process. The identification of what entities are the input and the output is consequently always straightforward in every computer operation. In machine vision, the input is a well defined signal from a camera or a file-carrying image information, and the output is some kind of result from the recognition process, coded in a precisely specified format. On the contrary, it becomes highly problematic to tell what are the input and the output when dealing with human vision. While many researcher will agree about the difficulty to assess what the output of vision is, a similar problem for the input is usually neglected, taking for granted that it can be identified with the incoming light to the eyes. There are reasons to doubt about this simple position, but let us first start with the output.

For those following the classical theory of Marr the output of vision is the geometry of all recognized objects in the scene. What is exactly the format of the *geometry* of an object is controversial [Cummins, 1989]; for Marr it should be a reconstructed three dimensional metric description. There are good philosophical reasons to doubt such kind of representational format, from Berkeley, through Kant's schematism [Kant, 1787, Part II.I, section 2] up to the current philosophy of mind [Cummins, 1989]. But most of all, all computational attempts in the 80's to implement something similar have failed and today this approach has been almost abandoned [Edelman and Wienshall, 1998]. Other alternatives have been proposed recently, like structural descriptions based on a set of primitive components [Biederman, 1987], or locations in a multidimensional image featured space, in particular a shape space [Edelman, 1999].

This concept of visual output has been strongly challenged by Gibson, who argued that recognition cannot be a final task, disconnected from a biological motivation [Gibson, 1979]. In his view the product of the visual system is to guide actions, the basic reason for vision to come into existence in the history of evolution. From this perspective object recognition itself is not unbiased, but driven by the physical actions the seen objects can afford. The point of view of Gibson has been taken into account by several people in the computational community, for example by Rodney Brooks in robotics [Brooks, 1990], where vision is not delivering a high level representation of the word, instead it cooperates with motor controls enabling survival behavior in the environment. This position is in line with the formalization of vision mentioned in section 2.1, where the input is a scene and the output a possible action (3). While it is very sensible that the main goal of vision in humans is to contribute to moving and acting with objects in the word, it is highly improbable that a set of actions can be identified as the output of vision. Otherwise, vision must include all sort of computations contributing to the acting behavior in that set: it is like saying that vision should cover more or less the whole brain activity.

A compromise which has been sometimes proposed is that vision includes two distinct functions, like a recognition system and a direct perception system [Neisser, 1994] or a perceptual system and an object-directed action control system [Goodale and Humphrey, 1998]. What is missing anyway is the account of an important feature of human vision: the phenomenological aspect of perception, which is different from either object recognition and motor control, yet so important in the experience of seeing.

It is time now to get back to the other site of the computation, the Input, which we promised to demonstrate as not being so immune from problems as it seems at the first glance. That visual input has little to do with the "scene" as collected by a camera was known since the early studies of Yarbus about saccades [Yarbus, 1967]. Our phenomenological experience of a "scene" is the brain construction based on hundreds of saccadic movements foveating salient features of the world. The image processing adept can reply that using the scene as input to the visual process is valid either if the scene is acquired as a single snapshot or integrated over several scans. It is hard to digest, when tracked saccadic movements reveal themselves to be organized around discernible goals and sensitive to attentional goals [Land and Lee, 1994], and this is just a last tract of the complex process driving the eyes on constructing what will be our perceived "scene" [Domenella, 2002]. But there is more.

Another challenge to a simplistic assumption of identifying the input as the light incident to the retinas are the well known phenomena of visual imagery and dreams, where phenomenological experiences similar to seeing are generated by the brain in absence of any similar external signal. It is known that these experiences involve the same neural circuits engaged in normal vision [Kosslyn, 1980; Kosslyn, 1994].

A fan of computers may still argue that it is not different from what a machine vision can do: to take as input a live signal from a camera or a video clip stored as a file in the hard disk. But the concept of input as

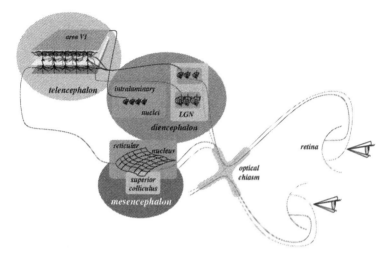

Figure 2. The path of signals from the retina to the primary visual area in the cortex (V1). LGN is the lateral geniculate nucleus.

in use in computer science means the only data affecting the output of a process. The main problem for human vision is exactly to single out an isolate bunch of data as input in the computer metaphor. The interaction between what is sensed in the external world by the eyes and what comes internally by other parts of the brain is not at all a matter of switching between camera and files, mental imagery and dreams being just special cases of a continuum.

Figure 2 shows the path of connections between the retinas and the first area in the cortex involved in vision: the striate primary visual area, or area V1. All the cortex is organized in six layers, and layer IV is where most thalamic axons project. The thalamus is the center in the diencephalon where all sensory information (except the olfactory system) passes through before reaching the cortex, in particular the visual signals reach a specific part of the thalamus called lateral geniculate nucleus (LGN).

There is a separated path from the retina reaching the superior colliculus in the mesencephalon, a phylogenetic earlier part of the brain. The puzzling fact is that in V1 the thalamic projections account for no more then 20% of all synaptic connections in layer IV [LeVay and Gilbert, 1976]. So where do all the other inputs originate? Mostly from other areas of the cortex, as well as from other non-thalamic nuclei, like the intralaminar nuclei projecting mostly in layer I. Moreover, the V1 projects back many more axons than what it receives from the thalamus. In the LGN the number of axons coming from V1 is ten times larger that optic nerve axons [Wilson *et al.*, 1984]. Clearly the sensory input is necessary for vision, in absence there is no externally guided function, but this input accounts for a minority of all synaptic contacts in the cortex.

If it is possible to assign a meaning to neural connection in the brain following a path from the periphery, it is much harder to understand the function of connections projected by non specific areas: certainly this large amount of input from inside the brain to the primary visual area should be purposeful. A reasonable consideration is to think how the visual process is constructed using much more knowledge and beliefs than what is purely delivered by the eyes. Rodolfo Llinás found close similarity in the MEG (magnetoencephalography) patterns of subjects during REM dream and awake state, lacking in deep sleep conditions, characterized by 40Hz frequency burst. This oscillation may arise in the corticothalamic feedback connections including the reticular nucleus, shown in Figure 2, where axons of layer VI of V1 project [Llinás and Ribary, 1992]. The striking similarities of this resonant activity in the two states lead to a strong hypothesis:

> [...] the brain is essentially a closed system capable of self-generated oscillatory activity that determines the functionality of events specified by the sensory stimuli. [...] sensory input plays an extraordinarily important but, nevertheless, mainly modulatory role. [...] In other words, sensory cues gain their significance by virtue of triggering a preexisting disposition of the brain to be active in a particular way. [Llinás and Ribary, 1994, pp. 114–115]

4.3   The software engineering paradigm

Software engineering is the attempt to rationalize and optimize the process of software design, akin engineering practice in more conventional fields like mechanical design or building. This domain grew in the 80's, and is still an important discipline, especially for large software projects [Fairey, 1985]. One of the first methodological prescriptions has been the concept of *modular* organization [Parnas, 1972]. Complex tasks are tackled decomposing them into smaller systems, each one solved by an independent piece of software: a module. The modules are arranged in a hierarchical fashion, from the input data up to the desired output. Each module is a closed box communicating externally only by means of specified Input/Output.

This strategy has proved fruitful in computers, and today it is the most obvious first choice in developing software. And it has been largely imported in the study of vision, one of the first advocate being Marr. In the same period it also became popular in the functionalist stream of philosophy, as a general principle of how the entire mind is organized [Fodor, 1983].

Restricting here the discussion on human vision, there is today a large evidence that it is very far from the computational inspired modular conception. Since 1994 a seminal work, *A Critique of Pure Vision*, has brought evidences from many different points of view [Churchland *et al.*, 1994], and is still today a useful reference for the discussion. Quoting from this paper:

> [...] The recognition [...] in the real-world case depends on richly recurrent networks, some of which involve recognition of visuo-motor patterns such as, roughly, "this critter will make bad smell if I chase it," "that looks like a rock but it sounds like a rattlesnake, which might bite me". Consequently, the degree to which sensory processing can usefully be described as hierarchical is moot. [Churchland *et al.*, 1994, p. 27]

The supporting arguments are drawn from the three main categories here listed in a synthesis.

1. **From visual psychophysics**, a striking example being the illusory motion of a dot behind an occluder. This motion is perceived when other elements surrounding that dot have a parallel movement, otherwise it just seems to blink. The illusion can even be induced in absence of any other moving elements, by an auditory clue [Ramachandran and Anstis, 1986]. Therefore not only the "module" responsible for motion detection is not isolated from other processing results of the visual scene, but it is even influenced by other modalities. The deep interaction between proprioception and visual processing was already identified by Gibson in the concept of *optical flow* [Gibson, 1966].

2. **From neuroanatomy**, here in section 4.2 it has been already mentioned the impressive projection from the primary visual cortex down to the LGN; the same fact has been discovered in all the other cortical visual areas [Van Essen and Anderson, 1990], even between not consecutive areas, as the case of temporal cortex down to V2 and V1 [Rockland, 1990].

3. **From neurophysiology**, among the many experimental examples, outstanding is the discovery of some V1 neurons responding to illusory contours [Grosof *et al.*, 1992].

4.4 How complex is vision

An important domain in computer science is the theory of complexity, where this generic term is loaded with a precise technical meaning: it is the function of the steps required by an algorithm to solve a problem, versus the dimension of problem instances, expressed in asymptotic notations [Lewis and Papadimitriou, 1981; Papadimitriou and Steiglitz, 1982]. For example the O-notation (spelled "big O") is the asymptotic upper bound, and defines a class of functions:

(6) $O\left(g(n)\right) = \{f(n) : \exists c, n_0 \ \forall n \geq n_0 \left(0 \leq f(n) \leq cg(n)\right) \}$

where n is the dimension of the problem instance. One of the main results of the theory is to split problems in two classes: $\mathcal{P}$ and $\mathcal{NP}$, where the former have polynomial complexity, like $O(n^2)$, in the latter class the complexity is higher, for example $O(e^n)$, but at least it is possible to verify a solution in polynomial time. Conversely, problems in $\mathcal{P}$ are feasible while problems in $\mathcal{NP}$ are considered intractable.

This theory has also been borrowed to investigate how difficult is vision, and how adequate can be a computational theory of vision:

> [...] in principle solutions are not necessarily realizable and thus are not necessarily acceptable. A necessary condition on their validity is that they must also satisfy the complexity constraints of the problem and the resources allocated to its solution. [Tsotsos, 1993, p. 282]

It is certainly wise to take into consideration the computational resources of the biological system in assessing the validity of a vision theory, the problem being to assume that the methodology developed inside computer science can be ported as it is to a totally different kind of computational systems. The classical complexity theory is perfect for assessing the performances of software or in general of symbolic elaboration algorithms.

Let us take for example a typical $\mathcal{NP}$-class problem, the so-called TSP (*Traveling Salesman Problem*), of finding the shortest circular path between a given set of cities, visiting each one only once. This problem is proved to be $\in \mathcal{NP}$ [Lawler et al., 1985], and the solution using exhaustive search grows exponentially with an increase in the number of cities. However, this is strictly true for any computational system aimed to find the exact solution, while analogical biological systems in general can only offer approximate solution, which can be very good anyway in practice. Ant colonies are able to spontaneously develop shortest routes just by pheromone release [Dorigo and Gambardella, 1997], artificial self-organizing neural networks can find approximate solutions to large instances almost in linear time [Plebe and Anile, 2001; Plebe, 2002].

On the other hand, the most trivial problems in class $\mathcal{P}$ for a digital computer can be terribly hard for the human brain, for example computing the cube root.

A theory of complexity of biological computational systems would be welcome, but is still far from being available, and certainly cannot be a photocopy of the theory developed for digital computers. There are some early attempts in this direction, recently Marco Gori introduced the concept of *Computational Suspiciousness* as a putative equivalent of the classical computational complexity for neural networks [Gori and Meer, 2002; Gori, 2003], treated as a continuous universal approximator. The degree of *suspiciousness* of a problem is a kind of measure of the chance for the network of being trapped in local minima while reaching for the optimal solution.

Up to now, it is clear that vision is a hard problem for both human and machines, but there is no support for claiming that if a part of the process is complex for the computer, it should be the same also for the human vision, and the other way round.

5   Conclusions

The analysis exposed in the previous sections has been often drawn following two different lines: the mathematical possibility and the epistemological validity of asserting the computational property to the human visual system. It appeared that while on the first line the question remains open, the second line will bring more strongly to a denial of the equivalence, under several of the possible meaning of the term *computational*. The methodological consequence seems quite heavy, it is like saying that the computational approach is not useful in the investigation of human vision. Yes, but only within the equivalence supposed in the main question. Paradoxically we believe that the computational approach would be of great help when stripped of the claim that vision is computational.

Running software in computers to execute image processing algorithms is an irreplaceable tool for exploring and validating theories about biological vision, once dismissed the dangerous temptation of extending computational analogies too far, up to the full equivalence, sticking to a weaker but fruitful role, which can be called simulation.

A pertinent example is the meaning of *computational* in the domain today called *computational neuroscience*. Quoting from the coiners of this term:

> [...] As we use the term, "computational neuroscience" aims for biological realism in computational models of neural networks, though *en route*, rather simplified and artificial models may be used to help test and explore computational principles. [...] The expression "computational" in computational neuroscience reflects the role of the computers as a research tool in modeling

complex systems such as networks, ganglia, and brains. Using the word in that sense, one could have also computational astronomy or computational geology. In the present context, however, the word's primary force is descriptive connotation, which here betokens the deep-seated conviction that what is being modeled by a computer is itself a kind of computer, albeit one quite unlike the serial, digital machines on which computer science cut its teeth. [Churchland and Sejnowski, 1994, pp. 6–7]

The computational approach, dismissing its hegemonic state, will be a powerful tool for explaining vision, together with several others like psychology, psychophysics and neuroscience, each with its own language but understandable to each other.

BIBLIOGRAPHY

[Bell, 1999] A. Bell. Levels and loops: the future of artificial intelligence and neuroscience. *Philosophical transactions of the Royal Society of London*, 354:2013–2020, 1999.

[Biederman, 1987] I. Biederman. Recognition-by-components: A theory of human image understanding. *Psychological Review*, 94:115–147, 1987.

[Brooks, 1990] R.A. Brooks. Elephants don't play chess. *Robotics and Autonomous Systems*, 6:3–15, 1990.

[Chomsky, 1958] N. Chomsky. On certain formal properties of grammars. *Information and Control*, 1:91–112, 1958.

[Church, 1941] A. Church. *The Calculi of Lambda Conversion*. Princeton University Press, Princeton (NJ), 1941.

[Churchland and Sejnowski, 1994] P.S. Churchland and T. Sejnowski. *The Computational Brain*. MIT Press, Cambridge (MA), 1994.

[Churchland et al., 1994] P.S. Churchland, V. Ramachandran, and T. Sejnowski. A critique of pure vision. In Christof Koch and Joel Davis, editors, *Large-Scale Neuronal Theories of the Brain*. MIT Press, Cambridge (MA), 1994.

[Churchland, 2002] P.S. Churchland. *Brain-Wise. Studies in Neurophilosophy*. MIT Press, Cambridge (MA), 2002.

[Cummins, 1989] R. Cummins. *Meaning and Mental Representation*. MIT Press, Cambridge (MA), 1989.

[Domenella, 2002] R.G. Domenella. La coda dell'occhio. Cinema e percezione visiva. In *Raccolta di scritti in memoria di Antonio Villani*, pages 907–921. Istituto Suor Orsola Benincasa, Napoli, (IT), 2002.

[Dorigo and Gambardella, 1997] M. Dorigo and L.M. Gambardella. Ant colony system: A cooperative learning approach to the traveling salesman problem. *IEEE Transactions on Evolutionary Computation*, 1:53–66, 1997.

[Edelman and Wienshall, 1998] S. Edelman and D. Wienshall. Computational approaches to shape constancy. In V. Walsh and J. Kulikowski, editors, *Perceptual constancy: Why things look as they do*. Cambridge University Press, Cambridge (UK), 1998.

[Edelman, 1999] S. Edelman. *Representation and Recognition in Vision*. MIT Press, Cambridge (MA), 1999.

[Fairey, 1985] R. Fairey. *Software Engineering Concepts*. Mc Graw Hill, New York, 1985.

[Fodor, 1983] J. Fodor. *Modularity of Mind: and Essay on Faculty Psychology*. MIT Press, Cambridge (MA), 1983.

[Gabor, 1946] D. Gabor. Theory of communication. *Journal IEE*, 93:429–459, 1946.

[Garey and Johnson, 1979] M.R. Garey and D.S. Johnson. *Computers and Intractability: a Guide to the Theory of NP-Completeness.* San Francisco (CA), W. H. Freeman, 1979.

[Gibson, 1966] J. Gibson. *The Ecological Approach to Perception.* Houghton Miflin, Boston (MA), 1966.

[Gibson, 1979] J. Gibson. *The Ecological Approach to Perception.* Houghton Miflin, Boston (MA), 1979.

[Goodale and Humphrey, 1998] M.A. Goodale and G.K. Humphrey. The objects of actions and perception. In M.J. Tarr and H.H. Bülthoff, editors, *Object Recognition in Man, Monkey, and Machine.* MIT Press, Cambridge (MA), 1998.

[Gori and Meer, 2002] M. Gori and K. Meer. A step towards a complexity theory for analog systems. *Mathematical Logic Quarterly*, 48:45–59, 2002.

[Gori, 2003] M. Gori. Continuous problem solving and computational suspiciousness. In S. Ablameyko, L. Goras, M. Gori, and V. Piuri, editors, *Limitations and future trends in neural computation.* IOS Publishing, 2003.

[Grinvald et al., 1994] A. Grinvald, E.E. Lieke, R.D. Frostig, and R. Hildesheim. Cortical point-spread function and long-range lateral interactions revealed by real-time optical imaging of macaque monkey primary visual cortex. *Journal of Neuroscience*, 14:2545–2568, 1994.

[Grosof et al., 1992] D.H. Grosof, R.M. Shapley, and M.J. Hawken. Macaques striate responses to anomalous contours? *Investigations in Ophthalmology and Visual Science*, 33:1257, 1992.

[Hancock et al., 1992] P.J.B. Hancock, R.J. Baddeley, and L.S. Smith. The principal components of natural images. *Network*, 3:61–70, 1992.

[Hille, 1992] B. Hille. *Ionic Channels of Excitable Membranes.* Sinauer, Sunderland (MA), 1992.

[Hodgkin and Huxley, 1952] A.L. Hodgkin and A.F. Huxley. A quantitative description of ion currents and its applications to conduction and excitation in nerve membranes. *Journal of Physiology*, 117:500–544, 1952.

[Hubel and Wiesel, 1962] V. Hubel and T. Wiesel. Receptive fields, binocular interaction, and functional architecture in the cat's visual cortex. *Journal of Physiology*, 160:106–154, 1962.

[Kant, 1787] I. Kant. Kritik der reinen Vernunft. In *Gesammelte Schriften.* Berlin, 1787.

[Kohonen et al., 1997] T. Kohonen, S. Kaski, and H. Lappalainen. Self-organized formation of various invariant-feature filters in the Adaptive-Subspace SOM. *Neural Computation*, 9:1321–1344, 1997.

[Kohonen, 1995a] T. Kohonen. The Adaptive-Subspace SOM (ASSOM) and its use for the implementation of invariant feature detection. In F. Fogelman-Soulié and P. Gallinari, editors, *Proceedings ICANN'95, International Conference on Artificial Neural Networks*, volume I, pages 3–10, Nanterre, France, 1995. EC2.

[Kohonen, 1995b] T. Kohonen. *Self-Organizing Maps.* Springer-Verlag, Berlin, 1995.

[Kosslyn, 1980] S.M. Kosslyn. *Image and Mind.* Harvard University Press, Cambridge (MA), 1980.

[Kosslyn, 1994] S.M. Kosslyn. *Image and Brain: the Resolution of the Imagery Debate.* MIT Press, Cambridge (MA), 1994.

[Land and Lee, 1994] M.F. Land and D.N. Lee. Where we look when we steer. *Nature*, 369:742–744, 1994.

[Lawler et al., 1985] E.L. Lawler, J.K. Lenstra, A.H.G. Rinnooy Kan, and D.B. Shmoys, editors. *The travelling salesman problem: a guided tour of combinatorial optimization.* John Wiley, New York, 1985.

[LeVay and Gilbert, 1976] S. LeVay and C.D. Gilbert. Laminar patterns of genicuolcortical projection in the cat. *Brain Research*, 113:1–19, 1976.

[Lewis and Papadimitriou, 1981] H.R. Lewis and C.H. Papadimitriou. *Elements of the Theory of Computation.* Prentice Hall, Englewood Cliffs (NJ), 1981.

[Llinás and Ribary, 1992] R. Llinás and U. Ribary. Rostrocaudal scan in human brain: a global characteristic of the 40-Hz response during sensory input. In E. Basar and T. Bullock, editors, *Induced Rhythms in the Brain*. Birkhäuser, Boston, 1992.

[Llinás and Ribary, 1994] R. Llinás and U. Ribary. Perception as an oneiric-like state modulated by the senses. In C. Koch and J. Davis, editors, *Large-Scale Neuronal Theories of the Brain*. MIT Press, Cambridge (MA), 1994.

[Markov, 1954] A.A. Markov. *Teoriya algorfmov*. Academy of Sciences USSR, Moskva, 1954. Trad. *Theory of Algorithms*, Israel Program for Scientific Translation, 1962.

[Marr, 1982] D. Marr. *Vision: A Computational Investigation into the Human Representation and Processing of Visual Information*. W. H. Freeman, San Francisco (CA), 1982.

[Miikkulainen et al., 1997] R. Miikkulainen, J. Bednar, Y. Choe, and J. Sirosh. Self-organization, plasticity, and low-level visual phenomena in a laterally connected map model of the primary visual cortex. In R.L. Goldstone, P.G. Schyns, and D.L. Medin, editors, *Psychology of Learning and Motivation*, volume 36, pages 257–308. Academic Press, New York, 1997.

[Nagy, 1968] G. Nagy. State of the art in pattern recognition. *Proc. of the IEEE*, 56:836–862, 1968.

[Neisser, 1994] U. Neisser. Multiple systems: a new approach to cognitive theory. *European Journal of Cognitive Psychology*, 6:225–241, 1994.

[Papadimitriou and Steiglitz, 1982] C.H. Papadimitriou and K. Steiglitz. *Combinatorial Optimization: Algorithms and Complexity*. Prentice Hall, Englewood Cliffs (NJ), 1982.

[Parnas, 1972] D.L. Parnas. On the criteria to be used in decomposing systems into modules. *Communications of the Association for Computing Machinery*, 15(12), 1972.

[Peskin and McQueen, 1997] C.S. Peskin and D.M. McQueen. Fluid dynamics of the heart and its valves. In H.G. Othmer, F.R. Adler, M.A. Lewis, and J.C. Dallon, editors, *Case Studies in Mathematical Modeling—Ecology, Physiology, and Cell Biology*. Prentice Hall, Englewood Cliffs (NJ), 1997.

[Plebe and Anile, 2001] A. Plebe and A.M. Anile. A neural-network-based approach to the double traveling salesman problem. *Neural Computation*, 14(2):437–471, 2001.

[Plebe, 2002] A. Plebe. An effective traveling salesman problem solver based on self-organizing map. In J.R. Dorronsoro, editor, *Artificial Neural Networks – ICANN 2002 International Conference, Madrid, Spain, August 2002*, pages 908–913, Berlin, 2002. Springer-Verlag. ISBN: 3540440747.

[Post, 1921] E. Post. Introduction to a general thoery of elementary propositions. *Journal of Mathematics*, 43:163–185, 1921.

[Ramachandran and Anstis, 1986] V. Ramachandran and S.M. Anstis. Perception of apparent motion. *Scientific American*, 254:102–109, 1986.

[Rinzel, 1990] J. Rinzel. Electrical excitability of cells, theory and experiment: review of the Hodgkin-Huxley foundation and an update. *Bulletin of Mathematical Biology*, 52:5–23, 1990.

[Rockland, 1990] K.S. Rockland. Configuration, in serial reconstructions, of individual axons projecting from area V2 to V4 in the macaque monkey. *Cerebral Cortex*, 2:353–374, 1990.

[Thue, 1912] A. Thue. Über die gegnseitige Lage gleiche Teile gewisser Zeichenreihen. *Norske Vid. Selsk. Skr. I. Mat. Nat. Kl.*, 10:1–67, 1912.

[Tsotsos, 1993] J. Tsotsos. The role of computational complexity in perceptual theory. In S. Masin, editor, *Foundations of Perceptual Theory*. North Holland, Amsterdam, 1993.

[Turing, 1936] A. Turing. On computable numbers, with an application to the Entscheidungsproblem. *Proceedings of the London Mathematical Society*, 42:230–265, 1936.

[Van Essen and Anderson, 1990] D.C. Van Essen and C.H. Anderson. Information processing strategies and pathways in the primate retina and visual cortex. In S. F. Zornetzer, J. Davis, and C. Lau, editors, *An Introduction to Neural and Electronic Networks*. Academic Press, New York, 1990.

[von der Malsburg, 1990] C. von der Malsburg. Network self-organization. In S.F. Zornetzer, J. Davis, and C. Lau, editors, *An Introduction to Neural and Electronic Networks*. Academic Press, New York, 1990.

[von der Malsburg, 1995] C. von der Malsburg. Network self-organization in the ontogenesis of the mammalian visual system. In S.F. Zornetzer, J. Davis, C. Lau, and Th. McKenna, editors, *An Introduction to Neural and Electronic Networks*, pages 447–462. Academic Press, New York, 1995. (Second Edition).

[Wilson *et al.*, 1984] M.A. Wilson, M.J. Friedlander, and S.M. Sherman. Ultrastructural morphology of identified X- and Y- cells in the cat's lateral geniculate nucleus. *Proceedings of the Royal Society of London*, 221:411–436, 1984.

[Yarbus, 1967] A.L. Yarbus. *Eye Movements and Vision*. Plenum Press, New York, 1967.

Rosaria Grazia Domenella and Alessio Plebe
Department of Cognitive Science,
University of Messina, Italy
Email: {rdomenella,aplebe}@unime.it

Category Learning by Formation of Regions in Conceptual Spaces

MIKKO BERG, JAN-HENDRIK SCHLEIMER, JAAKKO SÄRELÄ, AND TIMO HONKELA

ABSTRACT. In this paper, we discuss the issue of conceptualization. The traditional view is that concepts are essentially linguistic. Recently, Gärdenfors has proposed a contradicting view stating that the concepts get associated to language terms, but essentially belong into other domain called conceptual spaces defined by quality dimensions. These dimensions form meaningful representations of the concept domains in hand and they should be formable by mappings from the sensory input and possibly from other more basic quality dimensions as well.

In the space spanned by the quality dimensions, natural concepts form convex regions. The borders of these regions can be hard or soft and can vary according to the context. In the present work, we have decided to code the regions by prototypes, so that instances closest to a particular prototype in the conceptual space form a region. In other words, the regions are defined by the Voronoi tessallations of the prototypes, which later define hard-bordered regions. In the case of soft borders, the prototypes can consist of probabilistic density functions defining graded membership function for each point in the conceptual space.

This paper explores the idea of quality dimensions by trying to realize contextual categorization in such a domain. That is, trying to form prototypes and regions. As addition, the connections to the lower, connectionist level and to the higher, symbolic level are discussed briefly.

1 Introduction

Intelligent systems generalize and compress the complex input they receive through their perceptual organs. This is clearly necessary to survive in a complex and potentially hostile world. Human beings have an exceptional capacity to utilize this process. We often rise from the basic regularities of the world to more abstract interpretations. This makes it possible to exploit

Lorenzo Magnani and Riccardo Dossena, editors, *Computing, Philosophy, and Cognition*, pp. 381–396 © 2005, M. Berg, J.-H. Schleimer, J. Särelä, and T. Honkela

even very distant (in time or place) similarities to make effective predictions of the state of the world. Another trait of humans is the capability for complex communication. Probably, to attain robustness, this communication in general takes place using discrete symbols, words.

Until now, a very central issue in artificial intelligence (AI) is arguably the relation between these very central traits: effective modeling of the world (accessed by sensory organs) and effective communication of the relevant parts of these models (language).

The traditional view, formulated by Newell & Simon [Newell *et al.*, 1958] is that we are physical symbol manipulating systems. This is to claim that the models we have of the world, are essentially linguistic. The modern view relies on dynamic systems theory [Kelso, 1995]. It claims that symbols emerge from dynamic interaction processes.

Connectionism is regarded to be a specific version of this dynamic hypothesis [Van Gelder, 1995]. The connectionist paradigm for AI gained popularity, in the early 90's, mainly through the books by the PDP research group [McClelland *et al.*, 1987; Kohonen, 1984]. They argued that human information processing is mainly continuous not discrete. Furthermore, the essential feature of human intelligence is learning, thus making the conceptual system a dynamic process rather than a static one.

One drawback of most of the connectionist algorithms is their distributed knowledge representation, which does not allow explicit interpretations of the inference process. That is why these systems are sometimes referred to as "blackboxes". A famous example is the NetTalk system from Seinowski and Rosenberg, a multi-layerd perceptron capable of reading English texts. The system was trained in a supervised manner with text as input and corresponding phonemes as output. Although achieving an accuracy of 95% the neural network did not extract rules for the decision making, that could be interpreted by linguistic processing. This example underlines the gap between the connectionist models and symbol manipulation systems.

Connectionism can be interpreted as a special case of associationism using ANN (Artificial Neural Networks). Gärdenfors [Gärdenfors, 2000] has presented a new level on top of these neural models trying to reach the symbolic level processes that humans are naturally capable of. The model being functional, Gärdenfors states that conceptual spaces can be seen as a set of attractor points of dynamic systems. Yet, his model retains the possibility of classical symbol manipulation with the three-level-model: 1) connectionism as the lowest, 2) conceptual spaces in between, and 3) classical symbol manipulation as the highest level.

Domains in conceptual spaces are an attempt to give functional and contextual focus for otherwise ambiguous symbolic level. One concept can be evaluated in several domains using different salience weights, where as properties are domain specific. Scale of the particular dimension in a domain is obtained using contrast classes. In another words, the continuous mapping to the subspace is performed within the boundaries of contextual extreme values. For example, what is considered to be (phenomenological) hot for bathing water is merely warm for coffee. In general, different abstractions are created with the corresponding *quality dimensions* having specific metrics.

This article does not try to rescue the idea of quality dimensions from its weaknesses. Most importantly, the satisfactory explanation of how these domains and quality dimensions come about is missing from [Gärdenfors, 2000], Here the dimensions are taken as given, assuming that some of them result from innate biological structures with evolutionary background. This is of course not true to all dimensions that are more abstract and which can be learned.

In conceptual spaces, (natural) concepts are defined as (convex) regions[1]. Voronoi tessellations necessarily result in convex spaces when Euclidean metrics is used. Voronoi tessellation partitions given space based on prototypical attractors. Clustering methods tackle the reverse problem, by defining regions which detect the prototypes.

The nature of a concept in conceptual spaces is

1. prototypical, coding of the structure

2. regional, geometric area instead of points (objects are very narrow concepts, perhaps even points), this makes the concepts vague or fuzzy, which relates to frame theory

In a sense, prototype and frame theory are combined here.

As addition to concept borders, there are also other reasons for modeling vagueness in concept formation and communication. Our dynamic scheme is thought to have three interacting parties: 1) cognitive concepts (including laws of psychology), 2) language and social interaction, and 3) phenomenal common world (including laws of physics). These entities have influence on the prototypes, and their connection is considered to be a source of impreciseness or fuzziness.

Next section explains further what is meant by dynamical hypothesis, followed by two sections discussing how conceptual spaces model extends this, relying first on traditional prototypes and second on convex regions. After that, in section 2 we review two clustering methods, as well as discuss

---

[1] According to Gärdenfors, natural concepts are the only concepts that can participate in inductive reasoning.

the possibility to combine similar concepts into more general concepts corresponding to larger regions in the conceptual space. Finally, in section 3 we apply these clustering methods to divide a space with color quality dimensions into concepts according to two images differing in characteristics.

1.1 Dynamical hypothesis

As a result from the ability to adapt to the environment and learn from experiences, our concepts change in time. Considering this, it would be implausible to assume nativist perspective for conceptual modeling and use innate rules for all categorization. Instead some rules, namely learning rules, could be used to guide the concept formation process, but not the concepts itself.

Concepts are assumed to emerge through self-organization process guided by top-down (global) and bottom-up (local) influence. The dichotomy results from modeling levels, where complex global behavior emerges from local interaction of simple and homogenous elements [Van Gelder, 1995]. For instance, the limitations of short-term memory could be seen as boundary condition for conscious analyzes of features of an object. In conceptual domain, it would seem natural for the regions to influence the location of prototypes and vice versa, until stable categories are obtained.

The challenge of an emergence theory is to explain the relationship between the chosen levels. By the definition, it is impossible to witness more global phenomena from the local level, but according to microreductionism (weak version of emergentism, [Buchmann, 2001]) top-down constraints are result of bottom-up effects. In fact, there is no level with ontological priority according to constructive reductionism [Kelso, 1995]. However, in this case the relationship between distributed neural level and symbols need not to be merely descriptive, and that is not what the mentioned three-party-interaction scheme implies. The existence of a symbol that groups observations naturally affects perception. This can take form of Categorical Perception to concept borders [Harnad *et al.*, 1991] or paradigm shift [Kuhn, 1996] to entire conceptual system. The effect of symbols becomes more apparent in next section with the notion of prototypicality.

1.2 Prototype theory

Prototype theory was formulated by Rosch and got started from findings relating to typicality (not yet having prototypical structure) among the category members. Findings of Rosch and Mervis [Rosch and Mervis, 1975] emphasized typicality as opposed to all category members representing the category equally. Rosch [Rosch and Lloyd, 1978] found that there are more typical members that are learned faster and serve as cognitive reference. The membership was considered to be graded and it was shown not to result from frequency or familiarity of the particular test items. The correlations with frequencies turned out to be useful in many cases, but not definitive. As an exception, chicken is frequent, but not typical bird. The results of Rosch & al. [Rosch et al., 1976] supported this finding, but only when structural relations between items were held constant.

After that, the characterizing properties were the target of the research. First, Wittgenstein's family resemblance rate was found to describe categories better. There were no explicit definitions, but similarities between individual group members, that could be modeled with locally similar cells. Second, exclusiveness (not total) was also proposed as typicality measure. Then the typicality would not only relate to the features of particular group, but also to the shortage of important features from other groups (contrast category). This is the phenomenon that Gärdenfors' [Gärdenfors, 2000] quality dimensions are explained to obtain their scaling. Contrast categories are difficult to verify empirically, because it would involve all the (other) categories. Third, it was found that broader knowledge structures and top-down processing play their part in this as well. For example functionalities can be inherited to sub-categories [Rosch and Mervis, 1975]. Barsalou [Barsalou, 1985] later repeated the related experiments.

The actual prototype theory was based on one summary representation of all the members, not as commonly misunderstood on the best match. Based on psychological experiments, Strauss [Strauss, 1979] proposed a method, in which features of the prototype should be averaged if their distribution is small and counted distinctively if it is sparse. The counting was explained by subject's interpretation as qualitative differences, not on one continuous axis. There is an analogy to how Gäärdenfors' dimensions evolve from integral, having correlation, to distinct separable dimensions, for example when child learns to separate shape from color. Feature correlations are method for applying prototypes and correlations alone are not sufficient for categorization. In terms of conceptual spaces, after arbitrary mapping, any two points in space can be close to each other. It has been claimed that people use hierarchical clusters. The intermediate groupings effect the typicalities, for example the statement that robin is a typical bird may be overlooking the fact that it is small, chirping, worm- or seed-eating tree bird [Malt and Smith, 1984].

Rosch [Rosch and Lloyd, 1978] describes the vertical dimension of the structure as taxonomy of category relations. There is inclusiveness of subordinate (lower-level) through basic level into superordinate (higher-level). The basic level categories is a topic with much empirical research. Read more from [Rosch and Lloyd, 1978]. The horizontal dimension is segmented structure without clear-cut boundaries. There is only the judgment for clearness of the case, the prototypicality.

There has been the idea of using probabilities to increase the accuracy of categorization and for example Churchland [Churchland, 1989] uses term warranty for uncertainty of chosen prototype. Experiments of Ross and Murphy [Ross and Murphy, 1996] showed that this was not actually accounted and turned the focus on preciseness of categorization.

There should be discussion about to what extent can human cognition be modeled with prototypes or with ANN (Artificial Neural Networks) algorithms. It is argued that theories should be verified using the evidence from psychological research, instead of mere speculations. Some of such attempts to find the limitations of the prototype theory in the past are exemplar effect of context model (started by Medin & Schaffer [Medin and Schaffer, 1978]) and the research on human memory, and different models about the use of background knowledge (e.g. [Murphy and Medin, 1985], read more from "Theory-Theory" in [Laurence and Margolis, 1999])

A vector in ANN model as Roschian prototype represents a summary of all the members of the cell, and not the best match. The prototype theory does not provide any model for the process, representation or learning. It only presents constraints and a possibility to deal with abstractions without any context. One of such constraints or descriptions is that there is correlation structure of the neighbors in nature of family resemblance [Rosch and Lloyd, 1978]. For instance, this is the way in which input of SOM [Kohonen, 1984] map is connected, because it gives emphasis on retaining the local level structure. There is no explicit way to define how SOM creates the model vectors, because the process is a result from heuristic principles. Neither is there any evidence there should be such for prototype theory. For example independent cue model [Medin and Schaffer, 1978] is only one ineffective implementation.

2   Discovering regions in conceptual spaces

Identifying concepts with regions in the space already adds an element of vagueness to the conceptual representation, because it subsumes objects $x \in \mathbb{R}^d$ with a variety of different attributes as one concept.

It is argued that there is a another vague element, namely that objects do not utterly belong to concepts or putting it in probabilistic terms, there are varying probabilities with which different objects are explained by a concept. Then the hard margins of the regions, representing concepts, in the plainly geometric approach make it difficult to incorporate this vagueness. A possible solution is to define a probability distribution in the conceptual space, that itself corresponds to a concept.

Finding the regions can be solved by clustering methods, but it is as well necessary to infer how many clusters are needed, and in an dynamical environment, the decision whether to split or combine regions, respectively concepts, arises. This question can be partly solved by hierarchical clustering methods or moving to Bayesian versions of clustering algorithms that give evidence on the model complexity, e.g. the number of concepts needed.

In the following sections we discuss three methods for finding these regions and defining a vague concept in them. It is assumed that the objects, perceived in nature or encountered in a more abstract way in our mind, are represented in as points in a conceptual space [Gärdenfors, 2000].

2.1 K-means clustering

The *k-means clustering algorithm* [Bishop, 1995] moves a chosen number of k cluster centers, so that they cover the whole data and thereby partitioning it for $i \in [1, k]$ into subsets S_i, defined by their center μ_i and containing the N_i nearest data points. It does it via minimizing the sum-of-squares error function,

$$E = \sum_{j=1}^{k} \sum_{n \in S_i} ||x_n - \mu_i||^2 \tag{1}$$

but other distance measures can be used as well. The batch version of the algorithm has an update rule $\Delta\mu_i = \eta(x_n - \mu_i)$ quite similar to that of SOM, only lacking the neighborhood function. With the help of the mean vectors a Voronoi tessellation can be found, as used by Gärdenfors for concept representation.

The defined regions are vague representations of concepts. But if the euclidean distance is used to identify the k nearest neighbors or even a tessellation, than there are hard margin between concepts, which does not seem to be a natural representation.

2.2 Density estimation

As shown in [Bishop, 1995] the k-mean algorithm can be regarded as a limit of the EM optimization of a *Gaussian mixture model* (MOG) with a common variance, when $\sigma^2 \to 0$. In a Gaussian mixture model the probability density of the data $p(x) = \prod_{n=1}^{N} p(x_n)$ is modeled as a weighted sum of Gaussians

$$p(x_n) = \sum_{i=1}^{k} p(x_n|i)p(i). \tag{2}$$

with a soft max prior $p(i) = \frac{\exp(\gamma_i)}{\sum_j \exp(\gamma_j)}$ and $p(\boldsymbol{x}_n|i) \sim \mathcal{N}(\boldsymbol{\mu}_i, \sigma_i)$. The negative log-likelihood of the data

$$-\log(p(\boldsymbol{x})) = -\sum_{n=1}^{N} \log \left\{ \sum_{i=1}^{k} p(\boldsymbol{x}_n|i) p(i) \right\} \tag{3}$$

can be used as an error function. Finding the minimum by setting the derivatives for $\boldsymbol{\mu}_i$, σ_i^2 and γ_i to zero and using the the Bayes' theorem to get the corresponding posterior $p(i|\boldsymbol{x}_n) = \frac{p(\boldsymbol{x}_n|i)p(i)}{p(\boldsymbol{x}_n)}$, the following updating rules can be derived

$$\hat{\boldsymbol{\mu}}_i = \frac{\sum_n p(i|\boldsymbol{x}_n)\boldsymbol{x}_n}{\sum_n p(i|\boldsymbol{x}_n)} \tag{4}$$

$$\hat{\sigma}_i^2 = \frac{\sum_n p(i|\boldsymbol{x}_n)||\boldsymbol{x}_n - \hat{\boldsymbol{\mu}}_i||}{d \sum_n p(i|\boldsymbol{x}_n)} \tag{5}$$

$$\hat{p}(i) = \frac{1}{N} \sum_n p(i|\boldsymbol{x}_n) \tag{6}$$

Due to the nonlinear dependencies in the equation a iterative update scheme is used to solve the problem. Start ing with random initial values for the parameters and then calculating the posterior and the new parameter values. It can be shown that repeating this process will converge to a maximum likelihood solution.

Applying this algorithm to points in a conceptual space results in a probability density function that covers the structure of the points arrangement in the space. This distribution can be identified with a certain concept, where the mean vectors of the Gaussian mixture components are prototype like examples of them. The individual Gaussians can represent more detailed sub-concepts. But still remains the question of how many centers shall be used.

Another unsolved problem is that, when operating the algorithm on every object of the conceptual space one large MOG distribution will result and therefore only one concept. So one has to use the clustering in a hierarchical way. For example first tessellate in a crude way to find different concepts using the k-means algorithm and than find the distributions in the cluster with the help of a Gaussian mixture model.

2.3   Hierarchical clustering

Instead of applying the above mentioned clustering methods repeatedly one can utilize a *hierarchical clustering* in the first place. A possible class of methods are called single linkage algorithms for a detailed description see

[Rohlf, 1982]. These algorithm start by treating every data point as one cluster and than combine the "most similar" according to the used metric. This is done repeatedly using minimum, maximum, the average distance or the distance of the centers of gravity[2] for comparing clusters containing more than one data point, and thereby creating a hierarchical structure.

The lower branches in the hierarchy can be cut away, meeting the concerns of difference only to a certain level of detail. But how is it then that a concept generating process in an intelligent system could find a level that is meaningful to use? There are two answers at hand: (i) just use any detail level for a start, and then, by a process similar to natural selection in living creatures or maximizing the model evidence in AI, it will turn out to be more useful to go into a more detailed version of the concepts or to thin them out and therefore have broader concepts; (ii) in a Bayesian version of the clustering algorithms, in spirit closer to density estimation, it is possible to combine the data likelihood with a prior distribution, representing the anticipation for the number of concepts needed, which can itself result from previous knowledge and experience in the world, and hence get a posterior probability distribution over the needed number of concepts.

2.4   Bayesian mixture model

Deriving concepts from available facts, e.g. sensory data and existing knowledge of the world - in this case represented in conceptual spaces, is an inferential task with statistical properties, resulting from the irregularities in the frequency of the data and the incertitude of the already gained knowledge, respectively.

A mathematical framework for describing statistical inference problems is the Bayesian statistics, where a basic idea is to interpret the probability of an event as the *degree of belief* on the occurrence of that event. Learning the attributes θ of a model structure $\mathcal{H}$ e.g. the shape and location of the gaussians forming the distribution associated with a concept, is achieved by combining prior knowledge, described by a distribution indicating the believe in certain facts, with new information from data x, described by a likelihood of the data given the learned quantity and the model structure. A possibility to calculate the posterior distribution of the attributes, which combines old and new knowledge is given by Bayes' theorem

$$p(\theta|x, \mathcal{H}) \quad = \quad \frac{p(x|\theta, \mathcal{H})p(\theta|\mathcal{H})}{p(x|\mathcal{H})}, \tag{7}$$

with $p(x|\mathcal{H}) = \int p(x|\theta)p(\theta|\mathcal{H})d\theta$ being known as the *model evidence*. This

---

[2]This relates to discussions in prototype theory about which set member, if any (as Roschian prototype theory suggests) should be used as the representative.

integral over all possible parameter values is, for difficult distributions not always solvable, but maximizing it with respect to $\mathcal{H}$ would lead to more optimal model structures.

This calculation of the posterior can be conducted each time new data is available and if the posterior distribution of the former inference step is used as the prior in the next execution of the Bayes' rule, it will lead to an adaptive learning mechanism. An intelligent system acting in a new environment and starting to conceptualize from scratch might in some circumstances not have prior knowledge for the shape of concepts, and therefor the categorization of the new and unknown. Still it is possible to define *non-informative priors*, that do not influence the finding of the posterior for the attributes, but "let the data speak for its self".

As mentioned earlier, one can express the density estimation problem in the bayesian framework (see [Attias, 2000] for a detailed derivation). One advantage is that this treatment allows searching for optimal model structure, e.g. the number of gaussians in the mixture model, whereas this is not feasible in the ML solution (paragraph 2.2) without empirical regularization terms. This is due to the fact that the ML solution from the EM algorithm prefers more complex model structures, that fit better to the data.

The approach in [Attias, 2000] is from the structure of the algorithm related to EM, but utilizes a helpful technique in bayesian inference called variational learning. There the posterior distribution of the parameter, that is often complicated to calculate, due to the difficult integral in (7), is approximated by a distribution with desired properties. In the case where the best model structure should be determined the requirement is that the approximate model evidence needed to optimize the number of gaussian components can be obtained in closed form.

It should be mentioned that there are many other model selection techniques like bootstrapping [Efron and Tibshirani, 1993], cross-validation, Markov-Chain-Monte Carlo sampling and Bayesian Information Criterion (BIC), see [Gelman *et al.*, 2003], which all somehow work in practice, but most of them are theoretically only justified for infinite data sets, whereas concepts can certainly emerge from only few examples.

3   Clustering of color spaces for concepts

As a simple example, the conceptualization of colors in two pictures, originating from a landscape in summer and winter, was studied. Choosing these pictures it can be expected that the process of conceptualization in our model depends on the encountered examples, a peculiarity of concept forming, that can be observed in the real world, e.g. considering various ethnic groups, that divide the color spectrum into differently detailed colors

[Bornstein, 1973; Hardin, 1993].

The color code for the pixel elements of the pictures is the hue-saturation-value color map, which is a intuitive representation for humans. The colors are coded with three numbers, firstly the *hue*, ranging from 0 to 360 degree in a circular arrangement and indicating the color type according to its wavelength, secondly the *saturation* or intensity between 0-100%, telling how grayish the color is and finally the *value* in percentage, that tells the brightness or the spread of wavelength. The hsv color space is redundant because there exists white and black for every color. Therefore, a color spindle instead of the cylinder in HSV model has been suggested [Kamvysselis and Marina, 1999]. It is achieved by reducing the range of the saturation linearly as the intensity approaches 0 or 100%. This modified color code has been used in the experiments and the intervals were scaled to unity.

A representative set of the data points for the summer and winter pictures can be seen in Figures 1 and 2 respectively. The prototypes for the MOG model, i.e., the means of the Gaussians have been marked there with x's as well. As expected, the MOG model has used more resources that is, more prototypes to account for areas having more data points. Observing that they cover the distribution of the color samples quite well, the corresponding colors can be expected to cover the coloring, present in the picture, appropriately. But the results depend completely on how many initial mixture components are chosen.

Thus the clusters given by the EM algorithm were further combined to bigger clusters by the hierarchical linkage algorithm. The resulting colors as well as the hierarchy can be seem in Figsures 1 and 2 for the summer and winter pictures respectively. Now one can see the grouping of different shades of white an brown to a more general concept of the color.

Definite differences in the prototype colors can be seen. While the clusters formed from the summer picture have several shades of green and dark gray, the colors in the winter picture are concentrated in lighter shades of gray and white.

[More inferences of the results are made, when we have the results of the spindle model. Now there are, for example, very dark colors that do not appear to be close to each others. This is due to the significant difference in the hue.]

4   Discussion

We issued some implementation aspects left open by Gärdenfors' Conceptual spaces [Gärdenfors, 2000]. We mainly discussed the formation of the concepts as regions in a given conceptual space. The significance of these results to the understanding of actual implementation of human intelligence

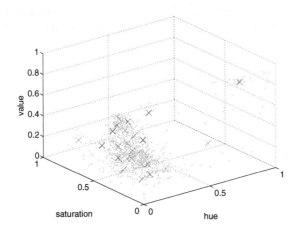

Figure 1. The color vectors of the summer picture with 27 centers for a mixture of Gaussian model after 30 iterations of training with EM algorithm.

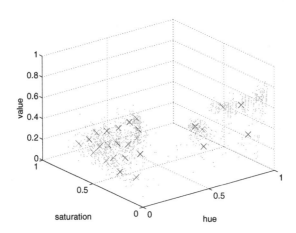

Figure 2. The color vectors of the winter picture with 27 centers for a mixture of Gaussian model after 30 iterations of training with EM algorithm.

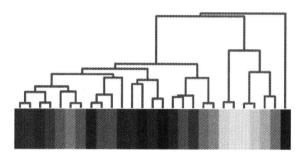

Figure 3. The 27 colors of the summer picture in a dendrogram.

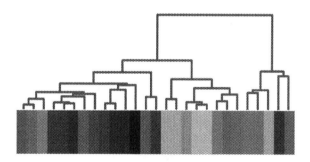

Figure 4. The 27 colors of the winter picture in a dendrogram.

might be questionable or at least modest. However, the central contribution of this paper does not lie therein, but in simulation of the intelligence as an AI project.

We only paid attention to the categorization in already acquired conceptual spaces. We now discuss in brief the connection of the conceptual level to the connectionist, namely the acquisition of the quality dimensions, and the symbolic levels, namely thought processes and language.

A natural way to connect the conceptual level to the basic sensory input level is provided by the connectionist approach. The quality dimensions are determined by the sensory input as well as possibly some other more basic quality dimensions using a flexible nonlinear mapping. However, Gärdenfors usually takes the quality dimensions as given, though clearly this cannot be true for all concepts. The principles guiding the learning are not easy to state, because they should include at least, capacity constraints, generalization of properties and finally, the relevance of different structures in the sensory data for the particular task the concepts are needed for.

Dynamical interaction framework was described as a starting point to explain the emergence of concepts. One possible way to advance into the direction of dynamic systems theories is to have behavioral models with discrete attractor basins (e.g. energy minima) [Cariani, 2001]. Kelso [Kelso, 1995] has studied these extensively and hinted that such basins could be interpret as prototypes. This is significant, because prototype theory itself does not deal with learning or concept formation, but only structure.

Furthermore, to really bridge the conceptual level to the symbolic level, one needs to explain the relation between the acquired concepts and language. We see it plausible to assume that language terms get associated to the regions in the conceptual spaces, that is concepts. Then concepts that get instantiated due to sensory input or voluntary thought processes may trigger the use of language, internally or in a speech act.

Another property of concepts in the influence of natural language, is their context sensitivity. As an example, one could think of the different meanings of hot when going to sauna or having fever. Gärdenfors suggests that by a magnification or scaling of the quality dimensions (see the skin color example on page 119f of [Gärdenfors, 2000]) could amount to this property. In the bayesian framework context sensitivity can be achieved by the use of different priors, that modify the mean and variance of the gaussians to meant the contextual environment.

5   Acknowledgements

We would like to thank all the participants of the course of conceptual modeling at HUT, Autumn 2003, for their valuable input, especially Mr.

Janne Hukkinen and Mr. Karthikesh Raju. We would like to thank the Neural network research centre for providing the infrastrucutre for working on this subject.

BIBLIOGRAPHY

[Attias, 2000] H. Attias. A variational bayesian framework for graphical models. In T. et al Leen, editor, *Advances in Neural Information Processing Systems*, volume 12. MIT Press, Cambridge, MA, 2000.

[Barsalou, 1985] L. Barsalou. Ideals, central tendency and frequency of instantiation as determinants of graded structure in categories. *Journal of Experimental Psychology: Learning, Memory, and Cognition*, 11:629–654, 1985.

[Bishop et al., 1996] C. M. Bishop, M. Svensen, and C. K. I. Williams. GTM: a principled alternative to the self-organizing map. In C. von der Malsburg, W. von Seelen, J. C. Vorbruggen, and B. Sendhoff, editors, *Artificial Neural Networks—ICANN 96. 1996 International Conference Proceedings*, pages 165–70. Springer-Verlag, Berlin, Germany, 1996.

[Bishop et al., 1998] Christopher M. Bishop, Markus Svensen, and Christopher K. I. Williams. GTM: The generative topographic mapping. *Neural Computation*, 10(1):215–234, 1998.

[Bishop, 1995] Christopher M. Bishop. *Neural Networks for Pattern Recognition*. Oxford University Press, 1995.

[Bornstein, 1973] M.H. Bornstein. Color vision and color naming: A psychological hypothesis of cultural difference. *Psychological Bulletin*, 80:257–285, 1973.

[Buchmann, 2001] M. Buchmann. Emergent properties. In N. Smelser and P. Baltes, editors, *International Encyclopedia of the Social, and Behavioral Sciences*, pages 4424–4428. Elsevier Science, Oxford, 2001.

[Cariani, 2001] P. Cariani. Symbols and dynamics in the brain. *BioSystems*, 60:59–83, 2001.

[Churchland, 1989] P.M. Churchland. *A neurocomputational perspective: The nature of mind and the structure of science*. Cambridge, MA: MIT Press, 1989.

[Efron and Tibshirani, 1993] B. Efron and R. Tibshirani. *An introduction to the bootstrap*. Chapman & Hall, 1993.

[Gärdenfors, 2000] Peter Gärdenfors. *Conceptual Spaces: The Geometry of Thought*. MIT Press, 2000.

[Gelman et al., 2003] Andrew Gelman, John B. Carlin, Hal S. Stern, and Donald B. Rubin. *Bayesian Data Analysis*. Chapman & Hall/CRC, 2 edition, 2003.

[Goldstein, 1999] B. Goldstein. *Sensation and Perception*. International Thomson Publishing Company, 5 edition, 1999.

[Hardin, 1993] C.L. Hardin. *Color for Philosophers*. Indianapolis/Cambridge: Hackett Publishing Company, expanded edition, 1993.

[Harnad et al., 1991] S. Harnad, S.J. Hanson, and J. Lubin. Categorical perception and the evolution of supervised learning in neural nets. *Working Papers of the AAAI Spring Symposium on Machine Learning of Natural Language and Ontology*, pages 65–74, 1991.

[Hård and Sivik, 1981] A. Hård and L. Sivik. NCS–natural color system: a Swedish standard for color notation. *Color research and application*, 6:129–138, 1981.

[Kamvysselis and Marina, 1999] M. Kamvysselis and O. Marina. *Imagina: A Cognitive Abstraction Approach to Sketch-Based Image Retrieval*. MIT Press, Cambridge, MA, 1999.

[Kelso, 1995] J. A. S. Kelso. *Dynamic Patterns: The Self-Organization of Brain and Behavior (Complex Adaptive Systems)*. Cambridge: MIT press, 1995.

[Kohonen, 1984] T. Kohonen. *Self-Organization and Associative Memory*. Berlin, Heidelberg: Springer, 1984.

[Kohonen, 1995] T. Kohonen. *Self-Organizing Maps*. Berlin: Springer-Verlag, 1995.

[Kuhn, 1996] T.S. Kuhn. *The structure of scientific revolutions (3rd edition)*. Chicago: University of Chicago Press, 1996.

[Lakoff and Johnson, 1999] G. Lakoff and M. Johnson. *Philosophy in the flesh: The embodied mind and its challenge to western thought*. N.Y. : Basic Books publishing, 1999.

[Laurence and Margolis, 1999] S. Laurence and E. Margolis. *Concepts: Core Readings*, chapter 1, pages 3–81. Cambridge, MA: MIT Press, 1999.

[Malt and Smith, 1984] Barbara C. Malt and Edward E. Smith. Correlated properties in natural categories. *Journal of verbal learning and verbal behavior*, 23:250–269, 1984.

[McClelland et al., 1986] J. L. McClelland, D. E. Rumelhart, et al., editors. *Parallel distributed processing: Volume2: Psychological and Biological Models*. Cambridge: MIT press, 1986.

[McClelland et al., 1987] J. L. McClelland, D. E. Rumelhart, et al., editors. *Parallel distributed processing: Volume1: Foundations*. Cambridge: MIT press, 1987.

[Medin and Schaffer, 1978] D. Medin and M. Schaffer. Context theory of classification learning. *Psychological Review*, 85:207–238, 1978.

[Murphy and Medin, 1985] G. Murphy and D. Medin. The role of theories in concept coherence. *Psychological Review*, 92:289–316, 1985.

[Murphy and Wisnewski, 1989] G. Murphy and E. Wisnewski. Categorizing objects in isolation and in scenes: What a superordinate is good for. *Journal of Experimental Psychology: Learning, Memory, and Cognition*, 15:572–586, 1989.

[Newell et al., 1958] A. Newell, H.A. Simon, and J.C. Shaw. Elements of a theory of human problem solving. *Psychological Review*, 65:151–166, 1958.

[Rohlf, 1982] F. James Rohlf. Single-link clustering algorithms. In P.R. Krishnaiah and L.N. Kanal, editors, *Handbook of Statistics*, volume 2, pages 267–284. Elsevier Science Publishers, Amsterdam, The Netherlands, 1982.

[Rosch and Lloyd, 1978] E. Rosch and B. Lloyd. *Cognition and Categorization*. Hillsdale, NJ: Lawrence Erlbaum, 1978.

[Rosch and Mervis, 1975] E. Rosch and C. Mervis. Family resemblance: Studies in the internal structure of categories. *Cognitive Psychology*, 7:573–605, 1975.

[Rosch et al., 1976] E. Rosch, C. Simpson, and R. Miller. Structural bases of typicality effects. *Journal of Experimental Psychology: Human Perception and Performance*, 2:491–502, 1976.

[Ross and Murphy, 1996] B. Ross and G. Murphy. Category-based predictions: Influence of uncertainty and feature associations. *Journal of Experimental Psychology: Learning, Memory, and Cognition*, 25:51–63, 1996.

[Stephens, 1998] M. Stephens. Bayesian analysis of mixture models with an unknown number of components. *Journal of the Royal Statistical Society*, 59:731–792, 1998.

[Strauss, 1979] M. Strauss. Abstraction of prototypical information by adults and 10-month-old infants. *Journal of Experimental Psychology: Human Learning and Memory*, 5:618–632, 1979.

[Van Gelder, 1995] T. Van Gelder. What might cognition be, if not computation? *Journal of Philosophy*, 92:345–381, 1995.

[Zadeh, 1965] L. Zadeh. Fuzzy sets. *Information and Control*, 8:338–353, 1965.

Mikko Berg, Jan-Hendrik Schleimer, Jaakko Särelä, and Timo Honkela
Neural Network Research Centre
Helsinki University of Technology, Helsinki, Finland
Email: {mikko.berg,schleime,jaakkos,timo.honkela}@hut.fi

Bio-Robotic Experiments and Scientific Method

Edoardo Datteri and Guglielmo Tamburrini

ABSTRACT. Principled robotic implementations can be used to test hypothetical models of biological sensorimotor capabilities. Distinguishing features of this experimental strategy, often referred to as "bio-robotics" or "neuro-robotics", include the construction of some robot based on a theoretical model of the biological system under examination, and model-based comparisons between biological and robotic behaviors. This use of robots goes beyond mere replication of biological capacities in robotic systems (which is pursued in many biologically inspired robotic investigations), and significantly differs from analogous attempts to understand biological capacities by means of computer (non robotic) simulations. This paper explores ways in which biorobotic experiments connect to theoretical hypotheses about adaptive behaviors, along the dimensions of falsification, corroboration, and heuristic role in the discovery of unexpected facts. Significant methodological issues arising in bio-robotic experiments are addressed too, such as the problem of ensuring the correctness of bio-robotic implementations with respect to the underlying theoretical models, and the problem of identifying appropriate boundary conditions for the regular behavior of both biological and artificial systems.

1 Introduction

After wandering for dozens of meters in search of food, desert ant *Cataglyphis* reaches its nest following a straight path. This impressive homing capacity is not readily explained: it cannot be accounted for in terms of chemiotaxis, as chemical traces evaporate rapidly in desert heat. Path integration – requiring non-trivial computation and memory capacities, in addition to specialized sensors – is not fully adequate either: in view of massive error increase over time, path integration does not account for this insect homing precision. The now prevailing explanation combines path integration and snapshot navigation. The former accounts for how *Cataglyphis* reaches nest vicinities, whereas the latter accounts for how the ant zeroes in on the nest

Lorenzo Magnani and Riccardo Dossena, editors, *Computing, Philosophy, and Cognition*, pp. 397–416 © 2005, E. Datteri and G. Tamburrini

small aperture. Snapshot navigation involves repeated comparisons between perceived visual scenario and a memorized snapshot taken at target location [Cartwright and Collett, 1987]. This hypothesized mechanism was tested by means of robotic implementations. In particular, the snapshot model was implemented in the robotic system *Sahabot*, whose behavior was observed in the same desert environment where data about *Cataglyphis* were originally collected [Lambrinos *et al.*, 2000]. Similarity of observed behaviors by artificial and biological systems in the same environment was taken to corroborate the proposed theoretical model.

A variety of theoretical models of biological sensorimotor mechanisms have been probed or tested by means of robotic systems, including chemiotaxis in crickets [Webb, 2002] and lobsters [Grasso *et al.*, 2000], and hippocampus control in rat navigation [Burgess *et al.*, 1997]. Similar approaches have been adopted in investigations of human sensorimotor systems: arm posture maintenance was investigated by implementing the hypothesized neural control model [Chou and Hannaford, 1997] onto an artificial arm equipped with a robotic muscle spindle [Jaax and Hannaford, 2002]; features of the primate optomotor system were investigated by means of a VLSI implementation [Horiuchi and Koch, 1996]; the role of basal ganglia in action selection [Prescott *et al.*, 2002] and characteristic patterns of human arm trajectories [Schaal and Sternad, 2001] were investigated on a similar basis.

These various inquiries share a common pattern: construction of some robotic system, driven by a *theoretical model* of the biological system under examination; experiments involving *model-based comparisons* between biological and robotic behaviors; methodological decisions about corroboration or falsification of the theoretical model on the basis of such behavioral experiments. This style of inquiry, crucially involving experiments with robotic systems, has been referred to as "bio-robotics" [Webb, 2001] or "neuro-robotics" [Dario *et al.*, 2002].

In contrast with non-robotic computer simulations, bio-robotic experiments involve the testing of sensorimotor coordination models in real environments, possibly in the same ecological niche of target biological systems. Notably, model-based comparisons between biological and robotic behaviors enable one to identify *ceteris paribus* conditions for theoretical models, to spot previously neglected features of theoretical models, to corroborate or falsify specific hypotheses on adaptive sensorimotor coordination capacities in animals and human beings, without relying on the background hypotheses about system environment that are required to set up computer simulations.

A rich taxonomy of bio-robotic models is presented in [Webb, 2001]. The bio-robotic modeling and explanation of non-intentional, adaptive behaviors is examined in [Tamburrini and Datteri, forthcoming], against the background of the prominent historical antecedent of Cybernetics. A comparative analysis of pre-cybernetic, machine-supported inquiries into adaptive behaviors is developed in [Cordeschi, 2002]. Here, we examine model-based comparisons between biological and robotic behaviors along the dimensions of falsification, corroboration, and heuristic role in the discovery of new, unexpected phenomena. The proposed classification of bio-robotic experiments enables one to envisage a rich landscape of experimental possibilities in biorobotics, which is conceptually akin to classifications of experimental possibilities in physics and other scientific domains [Franklin, 1981].

Commonalities with experimental practices in other fields of scientific inquiry can help one isolating more stringent criteria for "good" bio-robotic experiments: current bio-robotic investigations are often based on inaccurate robotic implementations of the functional models to be tested; criteria underlying principled comparisons between biological and artificial system behaviors are often missing; theoretical implications of experimental results are accordingly difficult to identify.

Various stages of bio-robotic inquiry are contextually involved in the present examination of bio-robotic experiments: identification of explananda, design of explanatory theoretical models, robotic implementations, model revision. The formulation of *explananda* is examined in section 2, by reference to how-does-it-work models of scientific explanation advanced in the philosophy of science. In particular, descriptions of mechanisms as sources of scientific explanations are examined focussing on attending modularity, *ceteris paribus*, and functionalist assumptions. The implementation of bio-robots based on descriptions of mechanisms is discussed in section 3. A classification of bio-robotic experiments, inspired to Franklin's taxonomy of experiments in physics [Franklin, 1981], is proposed in section 4.

2 Explanandum and explanans in bio-robotic investigations

2.1 Explanandum

Bio-robotics addresses explanation requests concerning events ("why did ant #11 follow this homing trajectory on trial #3?"), law-like regularities ("why recurring homing patterns are observed in ants?"), and capacities ("why is *Cataglyphis* capable of straight-line homing even when the nest is not in the range of its sensory apparatus?"). However, one may reasonably doubt that capacities and law-like regularities are substantively different bio-robotic *explananda*. In fact, pre-theoretical talk of capacities appears to be translated, in bio-robotic investigations, into talk about law-like connections involving environmental variables, physical properties of the system,

sensor, and motor data. For example, the lobster navigation capacity investigated in [Grasso *et al.*, 2000] is identified with a law-like relationship
between an initial agent-environment situation (the lobster being immersed
in a chemical plume) and a final one (the lobster being in the vicinity of
the plume source). Occasionally, the capacity to be explained is understood
as a law-like connection between system properties, involving no reference
to external environment. For example, the bio-robotic inquiry described
in [Schaal and Sternad, 2001] is based on hypothesized regular connections
between tangential velocity and radius of curvature of arm trajectories. It
is worth noting that a deflationary view of capacities is adopted in major models of explanation which admit system capacities as pre-theoretical
explananda. Notably, Cummins identifies psychological and biological capacities with dispositional regularities [Cummins, 1975], and claims that
ascribing a dispositional regularity to some given system is tantamount to
asserting that the system exhibits a certain law-like I/O regularity between
precipitating conditions (its inputs) and behavioral manifestations (its outputs). A similar view is upheld in recent epistemological analyzes of biological mechanistic models of biological explanation [Craver, 2001]. In accordance with this widespread deflationary attitude in both epistemological
analysis and experimental inquiry, we concentrate on bio-robotic explanations of law-like regularities and events, leaving aside the difficult ontological
question whether capacities are in fact reducible to law-like regularities, and
the related epistemological question whether the explanation of biological
system capacities requires a different treatment from the explanation of
law-like regularities.

Law-like behavioral regularities are supposed to hold *ceteris paribus*.
Conjecturing a law-like connection R starting from some finite set of observed data is typically concurrent to the identification of a set BCS of
boundary conditions associated to R itself, that is, conditions that are necessary for the regularity to be manifested by system S. The identification
of BCS, which enables one to circumscribe more precisely bio-robotic *explananda*, may involve experimental tests, whereby R is checked in varying
environmental conditions (experiments of this sort are reported in [O'Keefe
and Dostrovsky, 1971], concerning the firing of hippocampal "place cells" in
rats). Clearly, the experimental identification of relevant BCS for biological
system behavioral regularities is needed also at later stages of bio-robotic
inquiry. It is needed, for example, in order to proceed to a proper evaluation
of mismatches arising in experimental comparisons with behaviors exhibited
by robotic systems: rather than revealing the empirical inadequacy of the
theoretical model proper, these mismatches might depend on previously
unidentified boundary conditions that are necessary for the regularity to

obtain.

2.2 Functional description of mechanisms as the explanans of bio-robotic investigations

Theoretical models in bio-robotics are the source of explanatory accounts of *why* biological systems possess some capacity or exhibit some (regular) behavior. According to [Lambrinos *et al.*, 2000], Cataglyphis is capable of straight homing *because* various sub-capacities are put to work in a coordinated fashion. A path-integration system generates straight homing paths, that is, provides nest heading and distance information when the ant is far from the nest. When the ant reaches the vicinity of the target, another system is activated, iteratively comparing perceived and memorized visual scenarios. The matching response of the comparison system is used to compute precise homing direction. This how-does-it-work explanation for the overall ant homing capacity makes appeal to theoretical model consisting of a set modular items, functionally characterized in terms of their mutual interconnections and the mappings each one of them performs. Functional accounts of this sort are possibly enriched by structural information about the localization of these various functions in the ant's nervous system.

Bio-robotic theoretical models, which take the form of functional mechanism descriptions, play a variety of epistemologically significant roles in bio-robotics: in addition to providing behavioral explanations, mechanism descriptions constrain the implementation of bio-robots and guide bio-robotic experimental work [Tamburrini and Datteri, forthcoming]. Even incompletely or imprecisely specified mechanism descriptions can play these roles in bio-robotic inquiry [Webb, 2001]. Accordingly, in the ensuing epistemological analysis, we adopt descriptive and regulative perspectives - rather than a strictly normative one - on precision, completeness and other desirable features of "good" bio-robotic mechanism descriptions.

2.3 Sharp and unsharp I/O models

The restrictive conditions on mechanism descriptions[1] proposed by Woodward provide a suitable entry point to a discussion of bio-robotic theoretical models:

> a necessary condition for a representation to be an acceptable model of a mechanism is that the representation (i) describe an

---

[1]Related features of mechanisms are discussed by Cummins, who maintains that systems consist of coordinated capacities [Cummins, 1975]. Glennan claims that mechanisms specify "direct causal laws" (or, in a later work, "invariances under interventions") holding between system components [Glennan, 1996]. Distinctive features of biological mechanisms are extensively examined in [Machamer *et al.*, 2000].

402 Edoardo Datteri and Guglielmo Tamburrini

organized or structured set of parts or components, where (ii)
the behavior of each component is described by a generalization
that is invariant under interventions, and where (iii) the generalizations governing each component are also independently
changeable, and where (iv) the representation allows us to see
how, in virtue of (i), (ii) and (iii), the overall output of the
mechanism will vary under manipulation of the input to each
component and changes in the components themselves. [Wood-
ward, 2002]

Fulfillment of condition (i), which is contingent on near-decomposability
of biological systems [Tamburrini and Datteri, forthcoming], is typically met
by bio-robotic functional decomposition of sensorimotor systems. Condition
(ii) requires that the behavior of each modular component be invariant
under intervention (that is, causal dependencies should hold between each
module I/O variables). Many biological models specify parts behaviors
as mathematical functions $O = f(I)$, and mathematical techniques may be
adopted to predict the overall I/O behavior of the whole system on the basis
of combined part behaviors, thus satisfying constraint (iv); by dynamical
system analysis, for example, one may draw information about the coarse
structure of state spaces in neuronal assemblies or behavior-based systems
[Beer, 1997].

Let us consider the possibility that condition (ii) is not fulfilled by some
mechanism description, and distinguish accordingly between "sharp I/O
models" which satisfy constraint (ii), and "unsharp I/O models" which do
not. The former are ideal cases, hardly ever satisfied in robotics or bio-
robotics. The more typical bio-robotic models are unsharp I/O models,
which fail to specify modules in the way required by condition (ii). In unsharp I/O models, the behavior of some modular component is left unspecified or is imprecisely specified. Cases in point are bio-robotic theoretical
models specifying just the number of modules and their connectivity ("the
output of module A is passed on as input to module C"), illustrating the I/O
behavior of the whole system by means of a limited sample of I/O pairs, or
else specifying I/O behavior by means of some $O = f(I, k_1, \ldots, k_n)$, where
the value of parameters $k_1, \ldots, k_n$ is not fixed. Notably, unsharp I/O theoretical models provided a basis for the above-mentioned bio-robotic investigations on Cataglyphis, lobsters and rat navigation, and basal ganglia in
action selection[2].

---

[2]Unsharp models come in different varieties. A relatively precise, but still unsharp I/O
model is the muscle spindle model described in [Jaax and Hannaford, 2002], for only few
parameters mentioned in the I/O relationships characterizing its modules are assigned a
precise value (from heuristic extrapolations of experimental data relative to the biological

Unsharp I/O models impose loose constraints on material model implementation, insofar as the functional organization of material models is incompletely or imprecisely specified. Accordingly, one may doubt whether unsharp I/O models are suitable bases for genuinely bio-robotic investigations on adaptive behaviors, for bio-robots widely differing in their functional organization may be regarded as instances of the same unsharp I/O model. A possible strategy to overcome this inadequacy of unsharp I/O models will be discussed in the next section, in connection with calibration experiments on bio-robots, which may be performed to fill in unsharp theoretical models.

2.4   Functional isolation assumptions

A "functional isolation" assumption underlies bio-robotic investigations on *Cataglyphis*: the theoretical model implemented in *Sahabot* suffices to explain the conjectured behavioral regularities. No other concomitant mechanism contributes to determine the ant's navigation behavior. The role of similar isolation assumptions is evident in the evaluation of bio-robotic experiments on human arm sensorimotor coordination based on the Anthroform arm. Human subjects were asked to impose three different levels of resistance to arm perturbations, and these levels of resistance were modeled in the bio-robotic system as different co-contraction values for flexor and extensor muscles. The underlying isolation assumption is that adjustment of arm viscoelastic properties is sufficient to model voluntary resistance to perturbations, and that no properly motivational mechanisms have to be included in the theoretical model. This isolation assumption was questioned on the basis of experimental data: behavioral discrepancies between artificial and human arm was attributed to motivational factors unduly neglected in the theoretical model.

Bio-robotic experiments are useful to test functional isolation hypotheses about theoretical models, as interferences may emerge in the presence of particular boundary conditions or in connection with restricted sets of inputs. In the bio-robotic study of lobster navigation [Grasso *et al.*, 2000], for example, iterated failures of RoboLobster to replicate lobster behavior at 100 cm distance from plume sources are ascribed to insufficient gradient information to determine robot's heading. Accordingly, the proposed theoretical model, exclusively based on chemical gradient detection, is discarded, and a presently unfathomed mechanism is thought to be at work in

---

system). Unsharp I/O models may prove adequate for some explanatory purposes: a shallow or vaguely formulated explanation may happen to satisfy the need underlying an explanation request about some observed biological behaviors. However, explanatory adequacy of some unsharp I/O model does not entail that this model provides a suitable basis for properly bio-robotic investigations.

lobsters, which controls heading even when no chemical gradient information is available.

2.5 Boundary conditions BCM for M

The formulation of theoretical models M is typically concurrent to the identification of a set BCM of relevant boundary conditions [Tamburrini and Datteri, forthcoming]. The relation between BCS and BCM must be carefully investigated, insofar as BCM does not necessarily coincide with BCS. For example, if the presence of a polarized light source may be regarded as essential to *any* instantiation of the snapshot model, allowing one to include it in the set BCM, other factors might be essential only to particular instantiations, that is, to particular ants or robotic machines ("the environmental temperature should not exceed 50°C" is an example that probably holds for *Sahabot*, without holding necessarily for all the biological systems living in the desert). The relations between BCM and BCA, that is, the set of boundary conditions associated to robotic implementations of M, are also relevant in bio-robotics; the set BCM is likely to hold for any bio-robotic implementation A of M, and the identification of boundary conditions for A may be brought to bear on M itself, thus leading to the refinement of the set BCM.

3 Implementation of robotic system A based on M

Theoretical models set constraints on their material instantiations: functional modules described in the theoretical model should be implemented in the bio-robotic system. This process involves the identification of system variables mentioned in the theoretical model with some bio-robot measurable properties. In the bio-robotic investigation on spinal circuit properties [Chou and Hannaford, 1997], theoretical model variables concerning biological system S (such as activation value of α motoneurons, joint angular velocity, and electro-myographic activity) have counterparts in the bio-robotic system A. These correspondences are necessary to compare systems S and A with respect to the conjectured behavioral regularity R. For example, by establishing a common reference system to represent hand positions in human subjects and in a bio-robot, Sternad and Schaal are in the position to test whether the "2/3 power law", that is, a law-like connection between tangential velocity and radius of curvature of human end-effectors, is a common feature of every kind of arm control systems [Schaal and Sternad, 2001].

3.1 Bio-robotics and biologically inspired robotics

Bio-robotics and biologically inspired robotics adopt different attitudes towards the problem of implementing in robotic systems constraints imposed by theoretical models of biological system behaviors. In biologically inspired robotics, analyzes of biological solutions to sensorimotor control problems play heuristic roles in the design of efficient robots. However, fidelity to theoretical models of the relevant biological behaviors is not required, and the implemented robot is unlikely to be useful for the purpose of testing any theoretical model. This distinction is particularly evident in connection with the response delays that are typical of biological systems. Many theoretical models of sensorimotor coordination in biological systems account for significant delays of sensory transmission and processing in terms of biological neural processing. Current robotic technology allows for faster responses. Thus, if a close match with M is required, these delays should be simulated, thereby decreasing overall robot performance. Any bio-robotic implementation of the Smith Predictor [Miall *et al.*, 1993], for example, should generate "artificial delays". Another case in point is the bio-robotic investigation of primate oculo-motor systems [Horiuchi and Koch, 1996]. Two concurrent oculo-motor coordination mechanisms, smooth pursuit and saccade generation, are characterized by two different delays between stimulus and motor response. In particular, "visually triggered saccades [...] have latencies from 150 to 250 msec; the pursuit system has instead a shorter latency, from 80 to 130 msec. Consequently, in response to a stimulus, the pursuit system begins to move the eye in the direction of target motion before the saccade occurs". These conduction and processing delays are not naturally generated by the electromechanical circuitry of the bio-robotic system, which is modified to replicate this feature of the theoretical model: "because there is no explicit delay in the current saccadic triggering system, an artificial 100 msec delay was added in the saccadic trigger to mimic this behavior".

The above changes are introduced to achieve a closer match between robotic system and some theoretical model M. In the following, a bio-robot A is termed globally *correct* with respect to some theoretical model M if A meets every condition imposed by M, that is, if A is functionally organized as prescribed by M (in terms of its modular components, their mutual interconnections, and mappings performed). Understanding how global correctness is achieved and evaluated is a central epistemological and methodological issue in bio-robotics. Tentatively, correctness of a bio-robot with respect to some sharp theoretical model M can be evaluated by testing whether A divides into the interconnected functional parts corresponding to the black boxes of M, and the I/O mapping carried out by each functional part of A is a restriction of the I/O mapping that M associates to the corresponding black box [Tamburrini and Datteri, forthcoming].

In some cases, notably concerning sensory or motor modules, correctness is achieved by experimental trials. An example is found in [Chou and Hannaford, 1997] on the basis of a theoretical model specifying the I/O mappings carried out by some modular components. The "right" actuator to be used in the Anthroform arm is chosen by evaluating several kinematic, dynamic, and thermodynamic parameters of different artificial arms, against human arm properties specified in the theoretical model. This experimental procedure is applicable when information about I/O mappings of system components is available. We turn now to consider other experimental strategies that are needed to achieve correctness with respect to unsharp I/O models.

3.2   Calibration in bio-robotics

Calibration procedures are often performed to ensure that functional components of the material system behave as specified in the theoretical model. As an example, gain parameters in sensory modules of RoboLobster [Grasso *et al.*, 2000] were tuned on a daily basis, so as to keep sensory response linear in ordinary plume conditions, in view of possible oxidation or deformation of sensory elements.

Tuning of the I/O behavior of some modular component is also performed with the aim of having *the overall* system generate some reference behavior, irrespective of theoretical model specifications for the individual modular components. Parameters of the open-loop control system were tuned in RoboLobster, so as it walked at the typical American lobster speed. And Webb adjusts gains involved in the connection between sensors and motors of a bio-robotic cricket [Webb, 1998], so as to generate straight line travel when the same sensory data are present at both sensors.

Calibration procedures are needed to achieve some working implementation, when starting from an unsharp I/O model M as blueprint. However, if these calibration procedures make the robot behavior as similar as possible to the behavior of target biological system S, then one may object that the whole process of bio-robotic modeling and explanation is circular: in order to test whether M is an explanation for S's capacity, we use a robot whose behavior (assuming good calibration) cannot differ from that of S.

The circularity charge is neutralized by observing that calibration procedures do not involve exhaustive behavioral matches. In fact, one should require that calibration procedures enforce behavioral matches on a reasonably small sample of behaviors allowed by the theoretical model M. Once the bio-robot has been calibrated with known biological data, artificial and biological systems can be observed in different experimental situations. Clearly, a good calibration procedure does not entail that their behavior will continue to match as required by M. As an example, consider the robotic muscle spindle developed by Jaax and Hannaford [Jaax and Hannaford, 2002]. As recalled above, this system was tuned by means of known information about the biological spindle, but this reference or sample behavior did not exhaust the range of experimental possibilities:

> Once the robotic muscle spindle was tuned, we validated its performance by comparing its behavior to a different set of five experiments obtained from the muscle spindle literature.

Indeed, significant mismatches were detected between artificial and natural system behaviors in experiments performed on muscle spindle after calibration; the authors note that "no parameter values were adjusted while performing these studies".

Which theoretical model is actually tested in experiments performed *after* calibration? Indeed, the calibrated bio-robotic system may be conjecturally considered a *correct* implementation of some sharp I/O model M', obtained by sharpening some initial I/O model M on the basis of calibration procedures. The sharp I/O model is adopted as it accounts for the reference behavior used for calibration (that is, it supposedly explains other aspects of the target system's sensorimotor coordination capacities). And experimental results obtained after calibration bear naturally on the obtained sharp I/O model, to the extent that mismatches between artificial and biological behaviors might be ascribed to wrongly fixed parameters. More problematic inferences are involved when these experimental results are brought to bear on the starting unsharp I/O model. Indeed, various sharp models agree on the sample (reference) behaviors used for tuning the unspecified values in M, while differing from each other in the way of predictions about future, as yet unobserved behaviors. If the calibration procedure can produce different sharp I/O models, what is the "right" distribution of parameter values? The predicaments of arbitrary value adjustments in mechanism-based models are widely discussed in the theoretical biology literature [Hopkins and Leipold, 1996].

3.3 Mutual compatibility checks and boundary conditions for A

In the proper working of A, no module should disrupt the behavior of some other modules. Again, experimental procedures are often used to check the mutual compatibility of modular components of material models. As an example, a tuning process ensures that the robotic muscle developed by Jaax and Hannaford [Jaax and Hannaford, 2002] does not return force outputs that damage the sensory element included in the mechanic spindle. And, as far as the theoretical model is concerned, experimental procedures of this sort can be regarded as tuning procedures, that refine previous (un)sharp I/O models.

Similarly, the identification of boundary conditions associated to robotic systems is central for behavioral prediction purposes. Experimental trials, in which environmental or internal factors are changed, while the behavior of the robot is being observed, are useful to identify boundary conditions. A significant part of the experimental trials described in [Datteri *et al.*, 2003] is devoted to test the dependence of an implemented robotic system, performing a visuomotor coordination task, on varying background and lighting conditions. Notice that the set of boundary conditions BCA associated to a particular implementation A of M does not necessarily coincide with the set BCM associated to M itself. Some conditions in BCA may depend on implementation features that are unconstrained by the theoretical model; these features are mostly hidden into M's black boxes. And BCA does not necessarily coincide with BCS either, that is, the set of boundary conditions for the target biologic system; nevertheless, one has to check whether the boundary conditions explicitly set on S are needed to ensure normalcy for A as well, so that no negative analogy between A and S arises from limitations of S that do not affect A.

4   Experiments

The implemented bio-robot A may be used to perform experiments of different kinds. In this section we focus on experiments in which a theoretical model M is corroborated or falsified; then, we analyze experiments that bring to light aspects of the target theoretical model that were previously unheeded at, thus leading to the formulation of new empirical hypotheses.

4.1   Corroboration

Corroboration of M may be supported by similarity of artificial and biological system behaviors. Behavioral comparisons, in which the overall (motor) output of the two systems is compared, are often accompanied by "lower" level comparisons, whereby properties of modular components of the artificial systems are compared to neural recordings. A case in point is the bio-robotic investigation of hippocampus, involving a robotic system controlled by an artificial neural network [Burgess *et al.*, 1997]. The neural network is composed by four layers, roughly corresponding to the layers of sensory cells, enthorinal cells, place cells, and goal cells, that have been identified and recorded in the rat hippocampus. The proposed neural schema aims at explaining how rats represent and reach goal locations. Experimental results in simple environments show that the robotic system is actually capable of reaching goal locations (as biological rats do in the same circumstances). Moreover, the authors compare the receptive field of some simulated place cells, after learning, with the receptive fields of their biological counterparts; simulated and biological neurons show similar characteristic responses to geometrical changes in the environment boundaries. Analogous examples are reported in [Chou and Hannaford, 1997], where electromyographic recordings in humans are compared with αMN activation levels in the implemented system, and in [Horiuchi and Koch, 1996], where matches are detected between the number of spikes of the burst neuron in the VLSI oculomotor system and the short-lead burst neurons in the brain stem.

In lesion studies, a localization hypothesis – "the module m_1 of M is localized in the biological sub-system s_1 of S" – is corroborated or rejected by behavioral comparisons between biological systems with s_1 injured, and bio-robotic implementations of M with m_1 similarly injured. An example is the replication of the deteriorated saccadic behavior, observed in humans affected by muscle or nerve damages, by means of the above mentioned robotic oculomotor system [Horiuchi and Koch, 1996]. The phenomenon of "postsaccadic drift" consists in systematic saccadic under- or overshoots with respect to a target position; postsaccadic drifts are corrected in humans by adaptation processes. The same behavioral phenomena are detected in the VLSI oculomotor system, and ascribed to wrong gains in some burst signal generators. Adaptation processes are issued to restore the "right" gain, and to eliminate the postsaccadic drift in the artificial system.

4.2   Falsification

Behavioral mismatches between target system and bio-robot may lead one to falsify a theoretical model of target system behavior, provided that the bio-robot is an accurate implementation of that theoretical model. Additional conditions about boundary conditions have to be fulfilled too, before the behavioral mismatch is revisably attributed to the empirical inadequacy of the theoretical model, rather than to other concomitant factors.

In [Grasso et al., 2000] four different theoretical models of chemiotaxis in lobsters (differing from each other in control algorithm or sensorimotor connection) were tested and rejected alike by means of RoboLobster, a small mobile wheeled robot. RoboLobster was immersed in a stream of water to which a turbulent plume was added. The source of the plume was immersed as well, and the plume assumed a typical shape, easily replicated in various trials. The four theoretical models comprise two chemical sensors (antennae). These sensors can detect a gradient in plume concentration, and can independently control the steering angle of two motors. The mechanism described in two of the four theoretical models is similar to the mechanism of Braitenberg Vehicle #2, in which each sensor is connected to the ipsi-lateral motor. The mechanism described in the remaining models has a reversed configuration, – each antenna being connected to the contro-lateral motor; the two models within each group differ from each other in the way of control algorithm. The four theoretical models were implemented in RoboLobsters. In the experimental task one immerses RoboLobster in the plume, letting it reach the source. The 5 parameters that were adopted for measuring and comparing performances significantly include *closest approach* (the shortest observed distance between the robot and the source in a trial) and *path tortuosity* (the angular variance of turns measured over the entire path). The four theoretical models were tested in a variety of different conditions. First, the distance between starting point and source varied in different trials (50, 60 and 100 cm.) The initial steering angle was also changed, as well as the distance between the two antennae. Many of these combinations of theoretical models and boundary conditions were subjected to experimental tests. The two robots running Algorithm 1 (with forward or reverse connectivity) consistently failed to hit the source (the closest approach distance was very high). The better performance was obtained by algorithm 2 with forward connectivity, except when the robot started 100 cm away from the source. The authors labeled "distal patch field" (DPF) this region of the plume, in which both algorithms exhibited low performances. Before accepting these data as falsifiers of the theoretical models, the authors checked whether the selected distance between antennae in the various trials could affect RoboLobster efficiency, due to the fact that in the DPF region the gradient is not detectable between two points that are too close to each other. However, further changes of distance between antennae did not improve RoboLobster performance in DPF. It was concluded that the mismatch between target system and RoboLobster behavior does not depend on how far apart the antennae are placed. Having excluded distance between antennae as a relevant boundary condition, and assuming that no other sources of perturbation affected robotic system behavior without affecting target system behavior, experimental results were taken to show that in the DPF, no matter how initial conditions are changed, none of the four theoretical models accounts for target system behavior. The authors conclude: "Taken together the above results suggest that there is no concentration gradient information available to either algorithm in the DPF".

4.3 Experiments that bring to light unexpected facts

Heuristic experimental trials, in which a material instantiation of a theoretical model M is observed in varying environmental or internal conditions, may be conducted with the aim of identifying previously unheeded features of M. This class of experiments is included in Franklin's categorization of "good" experiments in physics [Franklin, 1981]:

Another class of "good" experiments are those which exhibit new phenomena, unexpected by existing theories, and call for the formulation of new theories.

Excitation and inhibition experiments described in [Bechtel and Richardson, 1993] fall in this category, in addition to many kinds of lesion studies. Three broad classes of experiments for exploring mechanism features (bottom-up inhibitory experiments; top-down excitatory experiments; and multilevel experiments) are discussed in [Craver and Darden, 2001]. Pioneers of Cybernetics pointed out that material instantiations of theoretical models might be helpful for observing results that "could not have been easily anticipated on the basis of the formal model alone" [Rosenblueth and Wiener, 1945].

If the set of system variables is reasonably small, one may search for new correlations in a systematic way. This is the case of the oft-quoted biorobotic study of spinal circuit [Chou and Hannaford, 1997]:

New experiments are performed in which responses to torque perturbation are measured when selected afferent pathways are blocked. A "covariance diagram" is introduced.

The covariance diagram describes if (and to what degree) system variables are uncorrelated, positively correlated, or negatively correlated. System variables include the state of activation of Ia and Ib feedback afferents, that are related to muscle length/velocity and muscle tension respectively, and the state of activation of α and γ motoneurons. In particular, the covariance of system variables is observed when modular components of the system are suppressed or injured. This systematic analysis of variable covariance in injury situations allowed experimenters to focus on data that suggest interesting, and previously unknown, features of the theoretical model in deteriorated conditions, resulting in a deeper understanding of the theoretical model itself:

It is interesting to note that Ia and Ib afferents become strongly co-varying when the γ dynamic excitation of the muscle spindle is absent [...]. This might imply their high redundancy. However, this covariance will decrease if variable descending command or different load pattern is given.

Hypotheses arise about the functional role of Ia and Ib afferents in deteriorated situations (with γ contribution absent), namely that the two neurons should not be given functionally different roles with respect to the posture maintenance capability to be explained.

Behavioral analysis of A in real-world situations may induce the experimenter to turn attention towards features of the environment that had not been previously detected. As an example, if A exhibits anomalous behavior in some environmental configuration, one can ask whether this configuration reveals significant facts about environmental input to M or about boundary conditions. In the bio-robotic investigation of lobster chemiotaxis [Grasso *et al.*, 2000], both tested algorithms perform poorly when RoboLobster starts at a distance of 100 cm from the plume source.

> On this basis we came to recognize two phenomenological regions of the plume which we termed the proximal jet (PJ) near the source and the distal patch field (DPF) further downstream.

In the DPF region, the plume concentration distribution is intermittent, contrary to the PJ where momentum of the jet gives the plume spatial continuity at the robot's sampling rate. "As the plume moves downstream the plume spreads out into numerous patches across the plume and loses its spatial continuity". This feature of the environment gives rise to behavioral mismatches between the robotic and the biological system:

> We conclude that the irregular paths in the DPF result from the intermittency of the plume concentration distribution.

Previously unattended, measurable features of the environment suggest are heuristically useful to proceed with model revision after falsification:

> Having excluded the most obvious concentration gradient hypothesis with these experiments the natural question is: what cues are these animals using? One obvious cue that is available to the lobster is the sense of mean flow [...]. By means of this cue the lobster or robot could cut possible directions to the source from any location in the plume at least in half.

5   Concluding remarks: bio-robotics and the art of model revision

In light of the above discussion, failure of A to behave as predicted by M in some experimental setting E may depend on various circumstances: A is not a correct implementation of M; M is not an adequate model of S's behavior; BCA, BCS, or BCM are not enforced in E; other mechanisms interfere with M in behavior generation; calibration led to a sharp I/O model that was not representative of the starting unsharp I/O model; there are internal inconsistencies in the theoretical model.

Compared to the diagnostic problem of selectively attributing responsibilities of unexpected observed behaviors in other fields of inquiry, evaluation of bio-robotic experiments distinctively involves possibilities depending on the experimental role of bio-robots. Only some (defeasible) methodological advices about the special diagnostic problems raised by bio-robotic experimental outcomes can be advanced at this level of generality. One is advised, *ceteris paribus*, to avoid revisions which disrupt the theoretical interest of further behavioral comparisons between biological system and machine. Suppose, for example, that temperature in E, unaffecting S's performance there, affects A's performance by deforming the robot's structure. One can respond to this finding either by adding a boundary condition, that is, by reducing temperature ranges allowed in E, or else by modifying A's structure, so as to make it insensitive to such temperature changes. In the former case, without modifying the material model, one introduces an additional restriction on the class of experimental environments that are suitable for comparing A and S; in the latter case, one modifies the material model, without tampering with the set of boundary conditions. One may reasonably opt for machine over experimental setting modification, if the introduction of additional boundary conditions on E turn A into an insufficiently representative material model of S's behaviors.

These are difficult model revision decisions, specifically emerging in bio-robotic approaches to the study of biological sensorimotor coordination. It is sensible to adopt a bio-robotic approach, and to address these special methodological problems if a real difference in empirical inquiry can be made by some bio-robotic experiments. Pioneers of Cybernetics Rosenblueth and Wiener were very careful to issue this warning about material models in general:

> If the formal model which suggests a material one is weak and trivial, the latter will be irrelevant and barren – i.e. a gross analogy is not scientifically fruitful. Again, if a material model does not suggest any experiments whose results could not have been easily anticipated on the basis of the formal model alone, then that material model is superfluous. Finally, if a model has a more elaborate structure and is less readily amenable to experiment than the original system, then it does not represent a progress. [Rosenblueth and Wiener, 1945]

The usefulness of a bio-robotic material models in empirical inquiry may depend on a variety of more specific factors, too. The adequacy of available hardware is a primary contingent factor. It is doubtful, for example, that one can presently build robotic hands that are comparable to human hands, – even in terms of sheer number of tactile sensors. Arguably, human visuo-motor coordination is a more suitable domain of investigation than human tactile-motor coordination, at least to the extent that one admits camera-based visual sensors as reasonable models of the retina. Again, the usefulness of testing models by means of robots equipped with "real" sensors and "real" actuators is to be properly assessed against theoretical and practical advantages of computer simulations. Consider again the presently unachievable human-like sensorized hand: it is definitely easier to simulate human hand behavior on a computer, strewing it with no-cost simulated Pacini cells. However, if one resorts to computer simulation of sensors and actuators, one must supply the simulated agent with appropriate sensory data, that is to say, one has to solve the non-trivial problem of computing sensory patterns for the simulated agent that are similar enough to those impinging on living organisms.

Let us finally note that epistemologically more basic issues concern the plausibility of modularity hypotheses underlying bio-robotic inquiries about mechanisms governing sensorimotor coordination. As illustrated above by reference to the Anthroform arm, in order to investigate the mechanisms that restore equilibrium in humans when forces are exerted on the body, one has to make the problematic assumption that human sensorimotor paths can be examined in isolation from other motivational concurrent mechanisms. Other human sensorimotor coordination mechanisms, where correlations between perceptions and motor actions seem to be more robust, like the vestibulo-ocular reflex or sudden withdrawals from pain, may lend themselves to more immediate, fruitful investigation by robotic systems, just like the study of sensorimotor systems in other animal species, as the initial example of *Cataglyphis* navigation capacity vividly illustrates.

BIBLIOGRAPHY

[Bechtel and Richardson, 1993] W. Bechtel and R.C. Richardson. *Discovering Complexity: Decomposition and Localization As Strategies in Scientific Research.* Princeton University Press, 1993.

[Beer, 1997] R.D. Beer.   The dynamics of adaptive behavior: A research program. *Robotics and Autonomous Systems*, 20:257–289, 1997.

[Burgess et al., 1997] N. Burgess, J.G. Donnett, K.J. Jeffrey, and J. O'Keefe. Robotic and neuronal simulation of the hippocampus and rat navigation. *Philosophical Transactions of the Royal Society B: Biological Sciences*, 352:1535–1543, 1997.

[Cartwright and Collett, 1987] B.A. Cartwright and T.S. Collett. Landmark maps for honeybees. *Biological Cybernetics*, 57:85–93, 1987.

[Chou and Hannaford, 1997] C.-P. Chou and B. Hannaford. Study of human forearm posture maintenance with a physiologically based robotic arm and spinal level neural controller. *Biological Cybernetics*, 76:285–298, 1997.

[Cordeschi, 2002] R. Cordeschi. *The Discovery of the Artificial. Behavior, Mind and Machines Before and Beyond Cybernetics.* Kluwer Academic Publishers, Dordrecht, The Netherlands, 2002.

[Craver and Darden, 2001] C.F. Craver and L. Darden. Discovering mechanisms in neu-
robiology: The case of spatial memory. In P.K. Machamer, R. Grush, and P. McLaugh-
lin, editors, *Theory and Method in Neuroscience*, pages 112–137, Pittsburgh, PA, 2001.
University of Pittsburgh Press.

[Craver, 2001] C.F. Craver. Role functions, mechanisms and hierarchy. *Philosophy of
Science*, 68:31–55, 2001.

[Cummins, 1975] R. Cummins. Functional analysis. *The Journal of Philosophy*,
72(20):741–765, 1975.

[Dario et al., 2002] P. Dario, C. Laschi, A. Menciassi, E. Guglielmelli, M.C. Carrozza,
and S. Micera. Design and development of a neurorobotic human-like 'guinea pig'. In
*Proceedings of Engineering in Medicine and Biology, 2002. 24th Annual Conference
and the Annual Fall Meeting of the Biomedical Engineering Society*, volume 3, pages
2345–2346, 2002.

[Datteri et al., 2003] E. Datteri, G. Teti, C. Laschi, G. Tamburrini, P. Dario, and
E. Guglielmelli. Expected perception: An anticipation-based perception-action scheme
in robots. In *IROS 2003, 2003 IEEE/RSJ International Conference on Intelligent
Robots and Systems*, pages 934–939, Las Vegas, Nevada, 2003.

[Franceschini et al., 1992] N. Franceschini, J.M. Pichon, and C. Blanes. From insect
vision to robot vision. *Philosophical Transactions: Biological Sciences*, 337(1281):283–
294, 1992.

[Franklin, 1981] A.D. Franklin. What makes a 'good' experiment? *The British Journal
for the Philosophy of Science*, 32(4):367–374, 1981.

[Glennan, 1996] S. Glennan. Mechanisms and the nature of causation. *Erkenntnis*,
44:49–71, 1996.

[Grasso et al., 2000] F.W. Grasso, T.R. Consi, D.C. Mountain, and J. Atema.
Biomimetic robot lobster performs chemo-orientation in turbulence using a pair of
spatially separated sensors: Progress and challenges. *Robotics and Autonomous Systems*, 30:115–131, 2000.

[Hannaford et al., 1995] B. Hannaford, J.M. Winters, C.-P. Chou, and P.-H. Marbot.
The anthroform biorobotic arm: A system for the study of spinal circuits. *Annals of
Biomedical Engineering*, 23:399–408, 1995.

[Hopkins and Leipold, 1996] J.C. Hopkins and R.J. Leipold. On the dangers of adjusting
the parameters values of mechanism-based mathematical models. *Journal of Theoretical Biology*, 183(4):417–427, 1996.

[Horiuchi and Koch, 1996] T. Horiuchi and C. Koch. Analog vlsi circuits for visual
motion-based adaptation of post-saccadic drift. In *Proceedings of the 5th International
Conference on Microelectronics for Neural Networks and Fuzzy Systems*, pages 60–66,
1996.

[Jaax and Hannaford, 2002] K.N. Jaax and B. Hannaford. A biorobotic structural model
of the mammalian muscle spindle primary afferent response. *Annals of Biomedical
Engineering*, 30(1):84–96, 2002.

[Lambrinos et al., 2000] D. Lambrinos, R. Möller, T. Labhart, R. Pfeifer, and
R. Wehner. A mobile robot employing insect strategies for navigation. *Robotics
and Autonomous Systems*, 30:39–64, 2000.

[Machamer et al., 2000] P. Machamer, L. Darden, and C.F. Craver. Thinking about
mechanisms. *Philosophy of Science*, 67:1–25, 2000.

[Miall et al., 1993] R.C. Miall, D.J. Weir, D.M. Wolpert, and J.F. Stein. Is the cerebellum a Smith predictor? *Journal of Motor Behaviour*, 25:203–216, 1993.

[O'Keefe and Dostrovsky, 1971] J. O'Keefe and J. Dostrovsky. The hippocampus as a
spatial map. Preliminary evidence from unit activity in the freely moving rat. *Brain
Research*, 34:171–175, 1971.

[Prescott et al., 2002] T.J. Prescott, K. Gurney, F. Montes-Gonzalez, M. Humphries,
and P. Redgrave. The robot basal ganglia: Action selection by an embedded model
of the basal ganglia. In L.F.B. Nicholson and R. Faulls, editors, *Basal Ganglia VII*,
New York, 2002. Plenum Press.

[Rosenblueth and Wiener, 1945] A. Rosenblueth and N. Wiener. The role of models in
    science. *Philosophy of Science*, 12:316–321, 1945.
[Schaal and Sternad, 2001] S. Schaal and D. Sternad. Origins and violations of the
    2/3 power law in rhythmic three-dimensional arm movements. *Experimental Brain
    Research*, 136:60–72, 2001.
[Tamburrini and Datteri,] G. Tamburrini and E. Datteri. Machine experiments and
    theoretical modelling: From cybernetic methodology to neuro-robotics. forthcoming
    in *Minds and Machines*.
[Webb, 1998] B. Webb. Robots, crickets and ants: Models of neural control of chemo-
    taxis and phonotaxis. *Neural Networks*, 11:1479–1496, 1998.
[Webb, 2001] B. Webb. Can robots make good models of biological behaviour? *Behav-
    ioral and Brain Sciences*, 24:1033–1050, 2001.
[Webb, 2002] B. Webb. Robots in invertebrate neuroscience. *Nature*, 417:359–363, 2002.
[Woodward, 2002] J. Woodward. What is a mechanism? A counterfactual account.
    Philosophy of Science, 69(S366–S377), 2002.

Edoardo Datteri
Dipartimento di Filosofia,
Università di Pisa, Pisa, Italy
Email: `datteri@na.infn.it`

Guglielmo Tamburrini
Dipartimento di Scienze Fisiche,
Università di Napoli "Federico II", Napoli, Italy
Email: `tamburrini@na.infn.it`

The Paradoxes of Rational Acceptance and the Logic of Belief

GREGORY R. WHEELER

ABSTRACT. This essay proposes to resolve the lottery paradox and the paradox of the preface within the framework of a non-monotonic logic called *Statistical Default Logic*, yielding a solution to the two paradoxes that falls within the tradition of restricting closure operations on rationally accepted propositions. The essay advances a structural view of the paradoxes, one that holds that a solution to the paradoxes must (*i*) offer a scheme for representing accepting less than certain propositions and (*ii*) provide a logic that preserves acceptance under entailment.

1

Henry Kyburg's lottery paradox [Kyburg, 1961; Kyburg (Jr.), 1997][1] is designed to demonstrate that three attractive principles governing rational acceptance lead to contradiction, namely that

1. It is rational to accept a proposition that is very likely true,

2. It is not rational to accept a proposition that you are aware is inconsistent, and

3. If it is rational to accept a proposition A and it is rational to accept another proposition A', then it is rational to accept A and A'

are jointly inconsistent.

One way to run the lottery paradox is to imagine a fair 1000 ticket lottery that has exactly one winning ticket. Suppose that this much is known about the lottery and that it is therefore rational to accept that one ticket will win. Suppose also that we regard an event very likely if the probability of

---

[1]Although the first published statement of the lottery paradox appears in *Probability and the Logic of Rational Belief* in 1961, the first formulation of the paradox appears in Kyburg's "Probability and Randomness," a paper delivered at the 1959 meeting of the Association for Symbolic Logic and the 1960 International Congress for the History and Philosophy of Science, but published in the journal *Theoria* (vol. 29, pp. 27–59) in 1963.

Lorenzo Magnani and Riccardo Dossena, editors, *Computing, Philosophy, and Cognition*, pp. 417–432 © 2005, G.R. Wheeler

its occurring is greater than 0.99, and so regard it rational to accept the proposition that ticket 1 of the lottery will not win. Since the lottery is fair, it is rational to accept that ticket 2 won't win either—indeed, it is rational to accept for any individual ticket i of the lottery that ticket i will not win. However, accepting that ticket 1 won't win, accepting that ticket 2 won't win, . . . , and accepting that ticket 1000 won't win entails that it is rational to accept that no ticket will win, which entails that it is rational to accept the contradictory proposition that one ticket will win and no ticket will win[2].

The lottery paradox, along with David Makinson's paradox of the preface[3] [Makinson, 1965] are correctly classified as *paradoxes of rational acceptance*: each aims to demonstrate the inherent tension found in adopting both a threshold measure less than unity for accepting a proposition and closing sets of so-accepted propositions under familiar (Boolean) logical operations.

The paradoxes of rational acceptance are interesting precisely because of the apparent price exacted for giving up either of the two aims that generate them. Restricting rational acceptance to only clearly true propositions severely restricts the range of topics to which we may apply logic to draw "sound" conclusions, thereby threatening to exclude the class of strongly supported but possibly false claims from use as non-vacuous premises in formal arguments. Whereas giving up logical closure operations for accepted propositions clouds our understanding of the logical form of arguments whose premises are rationally accepted but perhaps false, thereby

---

[2]It is not necessary that a lottery must yield a winning ticket in order to generate a contradiction. A lottery may be designed to entail only that it *very likely* will yield a winner. So long as this condition is above threshold for rational acceptance we may generate a contradiction in the same manner. For instance, when I book a flight from Philadelphia to Denver I judge it rational to accept that I will arrive without serious incident since I stand rough odds of $1 : 350,000$ of dying on a plane trip in the U.S. any given year (according to the *National Safety Council*), and stand considerably better odds of arriving without incident if I book passage on a regularly scheduled U.S. commercial flight. Nevertheless, I do not accept that there will not be a fatal airline accident on U.S. carriers in the coming year even though it is not necessary that there will be at least one accident each year. Indeed, 2002 marked such an exception: according to the 2002 *National Transportation Safety Board* there were 34 accidents on U.S. commercial airlines during 2002 but zero fatalities, a first in twenty years.

[3]The paradox of the preface arises from considering an earnest author who writes in a preface that though he believes all he has written in his book is true he nonetheless apologizes for errors that appear in the book, since surely there must appear some. So, for each page of the book the author believes that it is without an error and so he believes they all are without error, which is inconsistent with believing that there is at least one error.

threatening our ability to distinguish good argument forms from bad[4].

It is worth remarking that a satisfactory resolution to a paradox should not simply avoid inconsistency for this can be done merely by rejecting one of the conditions necessary for generating it. Rather, a satisfactory resolution should also address the motivations that generate the paradox in the first place. Satisfactory proposals typically take one of two forms. The first form rejects at least one of the conditions necessary for producing the paradox and then attempts to show independent grounds for denying that the rejected conditions are well motivated. The second form rejects at least one of the conditions necessary for producing the paradox but accepts the view that the original conditions are well motivated. A satisfactory proposal of this form must then offer alternative conditions that are jointly consistent but nevertheless satisfy the spirit of the original conditions. In the case of the paradoxes of rational acceptance a solution of the latter type is required. Namely, a satisfactory solution to the paradoxes of rational acceptance should provide a sufficiently expressive language for representing accepting less than certain propositions and also provide a sufficiently powerful logic to model entailments made in cogent arguments involving uncertain but rationally accepted premises[5].

2

In broad terms, the task of designing a logic is one of designing a system of rules that preserve some property or other by their application. Hence *soundness* (or its corollary in systems that don't preserve truth but preserve some other property under a consequence relation) is arguably a minimal condition that any system must satisfy to be called a logic. The paradoxes of rational acceptance teach us that rational acceptance (except in the limiting case where all premises are "certain") does not behave like truth in a model:

---

[4]It will not suffice to propose an *unstructured* closure operator on sets of accepted sentences, such as a closure condition defined exclusively in terms of consistency. An example of an unstructured closure operator would be Γ, defined over sets of accepted sentences X, such that a proposition A is in the image set of $\Gamma(X)$ if and only if $X \cup \{\neg A\}$ is not consistent. A suitable logical closure operation for accepted sentences should include applicable inference rules or conditions for how such rules may be constructed. This point is elaborated in section 4.

[5]Least we forget the option of denying the second principle, a short remark on paraconsistency. It should be noted that even the most radical approach to paraconsistent logic, *dialetheism*, does not (when seriously advanced) amount to a proposal to accept what one may. Hence, theorists tolerant of inconsistency still face the task of accounting for what consequences one may draw from uncertain premises, and so cannot avoid providing a means to sort out good argument forms from bad. Hence adopting a paraconsistent approach does not avoid the main task of reconciling the conflicting aims that motivate the first and third conditions.

we may apply truth-preserving rules to propositions accepted but not certain to yield propositions that fail to meet the threshold point for acceptance.

So what does a structured closure operation on sets of rationally accepted sentences look like? Let's consider an answer to that question in this section and the next. The two key ideas underlying my proposal are, first, that we may model acceptance rules as *default rules*, which are non-monotonic inference forms that appear in *classical default logic* [Reiter, 1980][6] and, second, that we may model the propagation of the essential content of rational acceptance under entailment within *statistical default logic* [Appendix B][7].

The account will be presented in the following manner. First, I will show that defaults are a natural framework for modeling the structure of rational acceptance, particularly when we expand the object language to include terms to explicitly represent measures of uncertainty for sentences of the language. Definition 1 addresses this expansion of the language, while Definition 3 and Definition 4 specify the general structure of acceptance rules. With this model of rational acceptance of sentences, we may turn to the task of defining closure operations, Definition 5 and Definition 7, that are sensitive to threshold values. From this we may define a fixed point operator in Definition 8 whose application yields only derivable conclusions that are above threshold.

In the next section we apply this machinery to the paradoxes of rational acceptance, showing that a consequence operator may be naturally defined that satisfies a weakened version of the third legislative condition for rational acceptance, namely

3^q. If it is rational to accept a proposition A and it is rational to accept another proposition A', then accept $(A$ and $A')$ if and only if the proposition $(A$ and $A')$ is above threshold for rational acceptance.

---

[6]For an introduction to default logic see [Reiter, 1980; Delgrande *et al.*, 1994; Marek and Truszczyński, 1991].

[7]A consequence relation R is non-monotonic if a sentence ϕ entailed by a set of sentences Γ under R is not necessarily entailed by R for every superset of Γ. Probability, *qua* mathematical function, is monotonic; however, the second place of the conditional probability function, $\Pr(\star|-)$, is non-monotonic in the sense that the probability of outcome $\star$ may increase, remain constant, or decrease when conditioned on smaller regions of the sample space: it is possible that $\Pr(\star|\phi) < \Pr(\star|\phi, \psi, \chi) < \Pr(\star|\phi, \psi)$. An interesting issue that is beyond the scope of this essay is whether the apparent non-monotonicity of certain kinds of reasoning signals the need for a logic with a non-monotonic consequence relation, or whether it may instead be represented by sequences of conditional probability functions, or whether the phenomenon of non-monotonicity is best regarded as essentially a non-logical property associated with making pragmatically useful but invalid inferences. In [Appendix B] and [omitted] it is argued that standard statistical inference may be viewed as a class of argument *forms* whose structure is essentially non-monotonic.

Before beginning, however, a word about notation. Since the account to be presented includes a proposal to enrich the object language, let us pause to make the notation and our conventions for its use more explicit. Let $I = \{1, 2, 3, \ldots\}$ be a set of indices and "A", "B", "A_1", "A_2", ... be sentences in a propositional language $\mathcal{L}$, hereafter called *sentences*. We will continue following the convention of letting context determine whether a sentence or other term is used or mentioned. Let $q \in [0, 1]$ be a threshold parameter for acceptance and let $\mathcal{F}$ be a countable set of sentences. We will add a stock of terms, $\epsilon, \epsilon_1, \epsilon_2, \ldots$, called *error bound parameters*, used to denote real numbers in the unit interval. Finally, a remark on the use of the terms "belief", "know" and their respective cognates. Their use in descriptions of formal definitions and results is shorthand for a sentence, negative or positive, or set of sentences that passes threshold; the complements of each term are likewise used informally to refer to a sentence or a set of sentences that does not pass threshold. Hence, no inference operations in this account are defined in terms of doxastic states of agents, ideal or otherwise.

Our first task is to build a general structure for rational acceptance in terms of *classical defaults*. A classical default rule is an inference rule of the form

$$(1) \quad \frac{A : B_1, \ldots, B_n}{C},$$

where the sentence A is called the *antecedent*, the sentences $B_1, \ldots, B_n$ are called *justifications*, and the sentence C is called the *consequent*. Expression (1) is interpreted to say, roughly, that when the sentence A is accepted and that no negations of any B_i's are accepted, conclude C by default [Reiter, 1980]. A default is a *normal* default if $C = B$; *semi-normal* if $\{C\} \subset \{B_1, \ldots, B_n\}$.

The first point to observe is that semi-normal default theories and normal default theories are sufficient to satisfy the second legislative condition for rational acceptance. We are not in a position to confirm this before seeing the logic, but we may nevertheless state the key reason that this observation is true: both semi-normal and normal default rules allow a consequent C to follow only if C is consistent. For example, the normal default $\frac{:C}{C}$ says that so long as C is consistent, C holds by default. What is missing is the assurance that sentences composed from consequents of applicable normal or semi-normal defaults are also consistent. But this guarantee, as we would expect, is a property of the logic.

The second point to observe is that more sophisticated acceptance rules may be represented by semi-normal defaults by filling the antecedent position with conditions that must explicitly hold before accepting the consequent and by filling the justification position with additional assumptions that must each be consistent to accept in order to accept the consequent[8]. A view introduced and defended in [omitted] and developed in [Appendix B] argues that this additional expressive capacity is necessary to adequately represent the structural form of standard statistical inference. Since the focus of this essay isn't the expressive power of s-defaults for representing various types of acceptance rules but rather the logical preservation of rational acceptance under entailment, we will not rehearse here the arguments for representing standard statistical inferences as s-defaults. Readers interested in the representational capacity of default logic and statistical default for these purposes are referred to [omitted] and [Appendix B], respectively.

To exploit default logic for my ends I must expand the object language to include explicit terms for a sentence's uncertainty measure, called that sentence's *error bound* parameter. We observed that a sentence may be entailed by premises that are rationally accepted without that sentence being rationally acceptable. To define "rational entailment," to speak loosely, we must be able to derive just those entailed conclusions that are also rational to accept. So, instead of defining closure operations directly on sentences we will define them on ordered pairs, where the first coordinate is a sentence and the second coordinate is an error bound parameter. This construction is called a *bounded sentence*.

Definition 1 *Bounded sentence*: The expression A *bounded by* ϵ is an ordered pair $\langle A, \epsilon \rangle$, also written A_{ϵ_A}, where $A \in \mathcal{L}$ and $\epsilon \in [0, 1]$. $A_{\epsilon_A} \equiv A$, if $\epsilon = 0$.

We will relax the notation for error bounds to allow names of sentences in $\mathcal{L}$ to serve as indices for error bound parameters. This convention is useful when we wish to speak of a particular sentence's error bound independently of the pair in which it occurs. A set of bounded sentences will be distinguished from a set of sentences by the superscript "b". It will be useful to have a function, *Crop*, that takes a set of bounded sentences $\mathcal{F}^b$ as an argument and returns the set composed of the first element of every pair in $\mathcal{F}^b$.

The relationship between sentences and error bound parameters requires some attention. We will work with sets of sentences where each sentence

---

[8]It should be noted that while semi-normal default theories are attractive from a knowledge representation perspective, the additional expressive capacity does not come for free. Normal default theories guarantee the existence of extensions, an important property if one's eye is on automation, and this property is a key reason that the proof procedures for normal default theories are relatively straightforward. However, there is no guarantee that an extension exists for every semi-normal default theory, which leads to a considerably more complicated set of issues when considering using the logic. See [Reiter and Criscuolo, 1981] for a discussion and example.

A may be associated with an error bound parameter $\epsilon \in [0, 1]$, such that $\Pr(A) \geq 1 - \epsilon$. We say error bounds are *associated* with sentences because the operations to be defined on bounded sentences yield conservative estimates of a sentence's error bound parameter and so, as a consequence, a conservative estimate of the probability that the sentence (expressing that an outcome occurs) is true. It is the conservation of this measure of error under entailment that underlies the structural solution to the paradoxes of rational acceptance. I will return to this point in my closing remarks.

Return now to the question of representing acceptance rules as defaults. We will use *statistical defaults* [Appendix B] to represent acceptance rules. A statistical default is an inference form that explicitly acknowledges the *upper limit* of its probability of error. Call a default in the form of

$$(2) \quad \frac{\langle A, \epsilon \rangle : \langle B_1, \epsilon \rangle, \ldots, \langle B_n, \epsilon \rangle}{\langle C, \epsilon \rangle} \epsilon_s,$$

an ϵ-*bounded statistical default* and the upper limit on the probability of error-parameter ϵ an ϵ-*bound* for short, where $\frac{\langle A, \epsilon \rangle : \langle B_1, \epsilon \rangle, \ldots, \langle B_n, \epsilon \rangle}{\langle C, \epsilon \rangle}$ is a classical default and $0 \leq \epsilon_s \leq 1$ is an error bound parameter. The formula (2) is interpreted, roughly, to say that, with respect to a threshold of acceptance of at least $1 - \epsilon$, provided A and no negated B_i's, the probability that C is false is no greater than ϵ_s. It turns out that a classical default is a special case of a statistical default, namely when all error bounds are zero.

With the basic elements of our language in place – that is, *bounded sentences* and *s-defaults* – we may now define the structure, called a *statistical default theory*, on which we will eventually define a bounded consequence relation.

Definition 2. A *statistical default theory* Δ_s is an ordered pair $\langle W, S \rangle$, where W is a set of bounded sentences, and S a set of statistical defaults.

The next series of definitions defines operations that preserve a sentence's upper bound on the probability of error under s-default closure.

Definition 3. *S-default ϵ-bounded conclusion*: A bounded sentence C_{ϵ_C} is an ϵ-bounded conclusion from a set of bounded sentences, $\mathcal{F}^b$, under a statistical default rule $\frac{\langle A, \epsilon \rangle : \langle B_1, \epsilon \rangle, \ldots, \langle B_n, \epsilon \rangle}{\langle C, \epsilon \rangle} \epsilon_s$ if and only if $(A)_{\epsilon_A} \in \mathcal{F}^b$, $\neg B_1, \ldots, \neg B_n \notin Crop(\mathcal{F}^b)$, $\epsilon_A + \epsilon_s = \epsilon_C$ and $\epsilon_C \leq \epsilon$.

Notice that ϵ-bounds are summed. Summing error bounds is a conservative measure for the depletion of confidence that accompanies the sequencing of bounded sentences by inference operations. A theorem of probability states the probability that outcome ϕ_1 occurs or that outcome ϕ_2

occurs is equal to the probability that ϕ_1 plus the probability that ϕ_2 occurs, minus the probability that both ϕ_1 and ϕ_2 occur. *Boole's inequality*, $\Pr(\phi_1) + \ldots + \Pr(\phi_n) \geq \Pr(\phi_1 \cup \ldots \cup \phi_n)$, follows trivially. (See Proposition 1, Appendix A.)

Applying this result to the preservation of error bounds, observe that we are interested in preserving an upper bound on the probability of accepting C when C is false. Assume that C is introduced to a default theory only by some rule s'. If the bounded sentence appearing in the antecedent position of s' is empty, this is equivalent to filling that position with $\top$ and the error bound of C is simply the error bound of s'. However, if the antecedent position is filled with a bounded sentence, then what must be considered is the probability of either the antecedent or the consequent being falsely accepted.

Set aside for the moment the question of why settle for an estimation of a consequent's error bound rather than an exact calculation. The question will be addressed in the next section. For now, let us continue building the logic. The next two definitions define a s-default closure and a closure operation on sets of s-defaults, respectively.

Definition 4. A set $\mathcal{F}^b$ of bounded sentences is closed under a particular s-default $s = \frac{\langle A,\epsilon\rangle : \langle B_1,\epsilon\rangle,\ldots,\langle B_n,\epsilon\rangle}{\langle C,\epsilon\rangle}\epsilon_s$ within ϵ if and only if every bounded sentence $\langle C,\epsilon\rangle$ that is an q-bounded default conclusion from $\mathcal{F}^b$ under s is a member of $\mathcal{F}^b$.

Definition 5. *S-default ϵ-bounded closure*: A set $\mathcal{F}^b$ of bounded sentences is closed under a set S of s-defaults within ϵ if and only if, for every $s \in S$, $\mathcal{F}^b$ is closed under s within ϵ. Let $Sn_\epsilon(S,\mathcal{F}^b)$, called the *$\epsilon$-bounded s-default closure of $\mathcal{F}^b$ with respect to S*, name an operator on S and $\mathcal{F}^b$ that produces a set $\mathcal{F}^{b'}$ of bounded sentences closed under S within ϵ. When S is fixed by context I will simply write $Sn_\epsilon(\mathcal{F}^b)$.

What this last series of definitions allow us to show is that if a bounded sentence is in the image set of the operator Sn_ϵ on a set of s-defaults S and a set of bounded sentences $\mathcal{F}^b$, then there is a sequence of s-defaults from S applied on $\mathcal{F}^b$ that yields that sentence as an ϵ-bounded conclusion (Theorem 2, Appendix A).

We are now in a position to define bounded logical consequence and bounded logical closure, Definition 6 and Definition 7, respectively.

Definition 6 Given a set of bounded sentences $\mathcal{F}^b$ and a threshold parameter $q = 1 - \epsilon$, a bounded sentence B_{ϵ_B} is an *ϵ-bounded consequence* of $\mathcal{F}^b$, written $\mathcal{F}^b \Rightarrow_\epsilon B_{\epsilon_B}$ if and only if:

- $(A_1)_{\epsilon_1},\ldots,(A_n)_{\epsilon_n} \in \mathcal{F}^b$,

- $A_1 \ldots A_n \vdash B$, and

- $\epsilon_B = \sum_{i=0}^{n} \epsilon_i < \epsilon$.

Definition 6 says that a sentence B bounded in error by ϵ_B is an ϵ-bounded logical consequence of a set of bounded sentences $\mathcal{F}^b$ when there is a derivation of B from a *list* formed from a "Cropped" subset of $\mathcal{F}^b$, the sum of whose corresponding error bounds is strictly less than the accepted error bound of the threshold for belief q, or $1 - \epsilon$.

It is important to notice two points about Definition 6. First, note that syntactic provability is used in the definition rather than its semantic counterpart. We stress this point by calling attention to $A_1 \ldots A_n$ being a list rather than a set, since an element may appear more than once in a list, just as a sentence may be applied more than once in a derivation.

Second, there is no step incorporated into Definition 6 to find the derivation for B with the least error bound. Hence, it is possible to have two sequences of inferences that yield different error bounds for a conclusion B corresponding to two distinct derivations for B under $\Rightarrow_\epsilon$. In Definition 7 below we define a closure operation Cn_ϵ in $\mathcal{F}^b$ that yields all bounded sentences that are ϵ-bounded consequences of $\mathcal{F}^b$. It is true that we are interested in the least bound derivation for B, but only indirectly so: a derivation of B that is minimal with respect to ϵ allows B to serve as a sub-derivation for another sentence C that may otherwise be out of bounds. However, the reason that a minimalization step is not incorporated directly into Definition 5 is that we may wish to include additional ϵ-bounded closure operations in our logic. Allowing strings of inference chains composed of derivations of mixed type, it is possible that, for some C, there is only a derivation of C within bounds that is of mixed type and that the least bound on error of a derivation of C is not composed of the least bounded derivations of each type. We will consider an example (Example 2) featuring this behavior in the next section.

Definition 7 *ϵ-bounded logical closure:* For any set $\mathcal{F}^b$ of bounded sentences, the operation Cn_ϵ in $\mathcal{F}^b$ is the *q-bounded logical closure* of $\mathcal{F}^b$ if and only if $\{B_{\epsilon_B} : \mathcal{F}^b \Rightarrow_\epsilon B_{\epsilon_B}\} \subseteq \mathcal{F}^b$.

What remains is to define a statistical default extension in terms of a set of bounded sentences $\mathcal{F}^b$, an error parameter ϵ, and the pair of ϵ-bounded closure conditions Sn_ϵ and Cn_ϵ for statistical defaults and bounded consequence.

A statistical default extension is constructed sequentially, much like a classical default extension. A default extension on a default theory $\langle W, D \rangle$ is built sequentially by first closing W under consequence, applying all applicable defaults in D to the set of consequences of W, closing that set (extension) under consequence, and so on. While a classical default is built sequentially by alternatingly closing an extension under consequence and the set of defaults until no more defaults can be applied, statistical default extensions are built by alternatingly closing an extension under bounded logical consequence (with respect to a specified threshold parameter ϵ) and closing the set of statistical defaults by bounded s-default closure (also bounded by the specified threshold parameter ϵ) until no more deductive or default inferences can be made at or below ϵ.

Given a statistical default theory Δ_s we may define a statistical default extension $\mathcal{F}^b$ on Δ_s at ϵ.

Definition 8. Where $\Delta_s = \langle W, S \rangle$ at ϵ is a statistical default theory and $\mathcal{F}^b$ is some set of bounded sentences, let $\mathcal{F}^b \in \mathsf{E}_{\Delta_S}(\mathcal{F}^b)$ be a minimal set satisfying three conditions:

SD1. $W \subseteq \mathsf{E}_{\Delta_S}(\mathcal{F}^b)$.

SD2. $Cn_\epsilon(\mathsf{E}_{\Delta_S}(\mathcal{F}^b)) = \mathsf{E}_{\Delta_S}(\mathcal{F}^b)$.

SD3. $\mathsf{E}_{\Delta_S}(\mathcal{F}^b)$ is closed under S within ϵ.

A set of bounded sentences $\mathcal{F}^b$ is a *statistical extension* for Δ_s at ϵ iff $\mathsf{E}_{\Delta_S}(\mathcal{F}^b) = \mathcal{F}^b$.

With this definition, we may prove that a statistical default extension constructed by applying, exhaustively, the fixed point operator defined in Definition 8 to statistical default theories when $Crop(W) \equiv W$ yields extensions composed of bounded sentences all of which are below the preassigned threshold parameter ϵ (Theorem 5, Appendix A).

A consequence operation may then be defined on extensions by taking the intersection of the Cropped extensions, yielding a unique, consistent set of non-monotonically derivable sentences from a statistical default theory at the specified error parameter value.

Definition 9. *Skeptical Statistical Consequence*: Let $\Delta_s = \langle W, S \rangle$ be a statistical default theory at ϵ and A a sentence. Then A is a skeptical consequence of Δ_s at ϵ – written, $\Delta \mathrel{|\!\sim}_\epsilon A$ – just in case $A \in Crop(\mathcal{F}^b)$ for each extension $\mathcal{F}^b$ on Δ_s at ϵ.

This is the logic. Now let's apply it to the paradoxes of rational acceptance.

3

In this section we will take up two items. First, we'll show how the structured closure operations from statistical default logic satisfy the weakened legislative closure condition for rationally accepted sentences, 3^q. Last, we return to the issue of estimating a conclusion's probability of error by way of considering two possible objections to the proposal.

To see how statistical default logic works, consider the following examples.

Example 1 Let $\Delta_s^1 = \langle W, S \rangle$ be a statistical default theory, where $W = \emptyset$ and S contains four s-defaults:

$$S = \left\{ \frac{:A}{A} 0.01, \frac{:B}{B} 0.01, \frac{A:B,C}{C} 0.01, \frac{A \wedge B : \neg C}{\neg C} 0.01 \right\}$$

For an error bound parameter $\epsilon_1 = 0.02$, there is one statistical default extension $\mathcal{F}_1^b$ where $Crop(\mathcal{F}_1^b)$ contains

$$A, B, A \wedge B, C.$$

The bounded sentence A at ϵ_A is included in extension $\mathcal{F}_1^b$ by applying the default $\frac{:A}{A}$ and bounded sentence B at ϵ_B is included by applying the default $\frac{:B}{B}$, where each inference has an error bound of 0.01, so $(A)_{0.01}$ and $(B)_{0.01}$. $(A \wedge B)_{\epsilon_{A \wedge B}}$ is included in the extension, since the sum of the error bounds of conjoining A and B is 0.02, that is $(A \wedge B)_{0.02}$. The bounded sentence C at ϵ_C is included by using A, whose error bound is 0.01, to apply the default $\frac{A:B,C}{C}$, whose error bound is also 0.01. Hence $(C)_{0.02}$. The default $\frac{A \wedge B : \neg C}{\neg C}$ cannot be applied because the resulting conclusion $\neg C$ would have an error bound of 0.03, $(\neg C)_{0.03}$ which is above the designated threshold $\epsilon_1 = 0.02$.

For a threshold parameter $\epsilon_2 = 0.03$, there are two statistical default extensions $\mathcal{F}_1^b$, which is the same as described above, and $\mathcal{F}_2^b$, where $Crop(\mathcal{F}_2^b)$ contains

$$A, B, A \wedge B, \neg C.$$

The default rule that could not be applied before is now applicable with respect to ϵ_2, giving rise to the second (partial) extension $\mathcal{F}_2^b$.[9]
□

Example 2 Let $\Delta_s^2 = \langle W_2, S_2 \rangle$ be a statistical default theory, where $W_2 = \emptyset$ and S_2 contains six s-defaults:

---

[9]The complete cropped extensions: when $\epsilon = 0.02$, $\mathcal{F}_1^b = \{A, B, A \wedge B, C\}$; when $\epsilon = 0.03$, $\mathcal{F}_1^b = \{A, B, A \wedge B, C, A \wedge C, B \wedge C\}$ and $\mathcal{F}_2^b = \{A, B, A \wedge B, \neg C\}$.

$$S_2 = \left\{ \frac{: \neg B, C}{C} 0.00, \frac{: C}{C} 0.02, \frac{C : B}{B} 0.01, \frac{: \neg B}{\neg B} 0.03, \frac{: \neg B, A}{A} 0.01, \frac{: \neg A}{\neg A} 0.01 \right\}$$

For an error-bound parameter $\epsilon = 0.02$, there is no statistical default extension, since while both $\frac{: \neg B, C}{C} 0.00$, $\frac{: C}{C} 0.02$ yield C only the bounded sentence $\langle C, 0.00 \rangle$ from $\frac{: \neg B, C}{C} 0.00$ may be substituted for the antecedent of $\frac{C:B}{B} 0.01$ which in turn is applicable in extensions consistent with B. But $\frac{: \neg B, C}{C} 0.00$ is applicable only in extensions consistent with $\neg B$.

For an error-bound parameter $\epsilon = 0.03$, there are three extensions. Because this example highlights the role that error bounds play in constructing extensions we display the partial extensions first in uncropped form, then in cropped form.

$$\mathcal{F}_1^b \supset \{ \langle C, 0.00 \rangle, \langle C, 0.02 \rangle, \langle \neg B, 0.01 \rangle, \langle A, 0.01 \rangle \}$$
$$\mathcal{F}_2^b \supset \{ \langle C, 0.00 \rangle, \langle C, 0.02 \rangle, \langle \neg B, 0.01 \rangle, \langle \neg A, 0.01 \rangle \}$$
$$\mathcal{F}_3^b \supset \{ \langle C, 0.02 \rangle, \langle B, 0.01 \rangle, \langle \neg A, 0.01 \rangle \}$$

And the three corresponding cropped partial extensions at $\epsilon = 0.03$ are:

$$Crop(\mathcal{F}_1^b) \supset \{ C, \neg B, A \}$$
$$Crop(\mathcal{F}_2^b) \supset \{ C, \neg B, \neg A \}$$
$$Crop(\mathcal{F}_3^b) \supset \{ C, B, \neg A \}$$

$\square$

Example 3 The Lottery. Let $\Delta_s^3 = \langle W_3, S_3 \rangle$ be a statistical default theory, where W_3 contains one sentence expressing the certainty that one and only one ticket will win, and where S_3 contains 1000 s-defaults expressing that the probability that each ticket will win is 0.001:

$$
\begin{aligned}
W_3 \quad = \quad & \{ O \equiv ((T_1 \wedge (\neg T_2 \wedge \neg T_3 \wedge \cdots \wedge \neg T_{1000})) \vee \\
& (T_2 \wedge (\neg T_1 \wedge \neg T_3 \wedge \cdots \wedge \neg T_{1000})) \vee \ldots \vee \\
& (T_{1000} \wedge (\neg T_1 \wedge \neg T_2 \wedge \cdots \wedge \neg T_{999}))) \}
\end{aligned}
$$

$$S_3 = \left\{ \frac{: \neg T_1}{\neg T_1} 0.001, \frac{: \neg T_2}{\neg T_2} 0.001, \ldots, \frac{: \neg T_{1000}}{\neg T_{1000}} 0.001 \right\}$$

There is *one* extension $\mathcal{F}^b$ on Δ_s^3 at $\epsilon = 0.01$, but its size is staggering. Since at $\epsilon = 0.01$ we may only build conjunctions up to length 9 among all of the consequents of S_2, this entails that there are $\binom{1000}{9}$ permutations of 9 losing-ticket conjunctions to include in the extension. Also, notice that

ϵ-bounded logical closure restricts the decomposition of O. Let j be an index such that $1 \leq j \leq 1000$ and S^b be the set of s-default consequents, $\{\langle \neg T_1, 0, 001 \rangle, \langle \neg T_2, 0.01 \rangle, \dots, \langle \neg T_{1000}, 0.001 \rangle\}$. Observe then that

$$Crop(\mathcal{F}^b) \quad \supset \quad \{O, \neg T_1, \neg T_2, \dots, \neg T_{1000}, \} \cup$$

$$Crop \left(\left\{ \bigwedge_{1 \leq j \leq 9} \langle \neg T_i, 0.001 \rangle_j : \langle \neg T_i, 0.001 \rangle \in S^b \right\} \right)$$

which yields the expected results: given a threshold for acceptance of 0.01, (i.) it is rational to accept that each ticket i loses, (ii.) it is rational to accept O that there is exactly one winner and (iii.) it is rational to accept that a conjunction of j tickets of one's choice will lose when j is no greater than 9. Observe that (i.) and (iii.) follow even if W is empty.
□

Example 4 The Preface. Let $\Delta_s^4 = \langle W_4, S_4 \rangle$ be a statistical default theory, where W_4 contains one sentence expressing that at least one page contains an error, and S_4 contains n s-defaults expressing that, for each i of n, it is very likely, q, that page i does not contain an error:

$$W_4 \quad = \quad \{P \equiv (E_1 \vee E_2 \vee \cdots \vee E_n)\}$$

$$S_4 = \left\{ \frac{: \neg E_1}{\neg E_1}(1-q)_1, \dots, \frac{: \neg E_n}{\neg E_n}(1-q)_n \right\}$$

Observe that there are *no* extensions on Δ_s^4 at ϵ if $\epsilon > n(1-q)$, where n is the number of disjuncts in P.

Proof. There are $n-1$ applications of the rule of disjunctive syllogism necessary to yield a positive atomic sentence E_i with a corresponding error bound of $(n-1)(1-q)$. Hence, if $n(1-q)$ is less than ϵ, then it is possible to derive (within ϵ) a contradictory sentence. This holds for all fixpoints on $\Delta_s^4 = \langle W_4, S_4 \rangle$ at $\epsilon > n(1-q)$ so there is no extension at ϵ if $\epsilon > n(1-q)$.
■

When $\epsilon \leq n(1-q)$, there is one extension on Δ_s^4 at ϵ that c ontains P, each $\neg E_i$, and $(\bigwedge_{1 \leq j \leq m} \neg E_j)$, where $m \leq n$ and the sum of error bounds $(1-q)_j$ from 1 to m is less than ϵ. Observe that Example 3 is an instance of this generalization. This observation is the justification for classifying the lottery paradox and the paradox of the preface as *paradoxes of rational acceptance.*

□

We close with a conjecture regarding the potential scope of s-default logic. One reason s-default logic is an interesting formalism to model rational acceptance is that it appears that there is a possibility of introducing a fragment of first-order logic into the theory. The idea, intuitively, is that a statistical default allowing for *decidable* first-order formulae (e.g., those in which no universal quantifier appears within the scope of any existential quantifier) to appear in the antecedent position of s-default forms would allow an error bound to be assigned to a *class* of inference forms, allowing one to speak of the probability of error for experimental protocols rather than particular experiments. Satisfying the applicability conditions for a type of acceptance rule would allow one to introduce an atomic sentence with a specific error bound probability into a theory when generalized conditions are satisfied. There is a tangle of issues to address here—soon, hopefully.

Appendix A

The first proposition shows that the summation of an error bound parameter forms an upper bound on the frequency of error. The proofs for the remaining theorems are in [Appendix B].

PROPOSITION 1 (Boole's inequality) $\Pr(\bigcup_{i=1}^{n})\phi_i \leq \sum_{i=1}^{n} \Pr(\phi_i)$

Proof. $\Pr(\phi_1 \cup \phi_2) = \Pr(\phi_1) + \Pr(\phi_2) - \Pr(\phi_1 \cap \phi_2) \leq \Pr(\phi_1) + \Pr(\phi_2)$ is easily extended to $\Pr(\bigcup_{i=1}^{n})\phi_i \leq \sum_{i=1}^{n} \Pr(\phi_i)$ by induction. ∎

THEOREM 2 (Wheeler 2004) *Let S be a set of statistical defaults, $\mathcal{F}^b$ a set of bounded sentences, $(C)_{\epsilon_m}$ a bounded sentence and the function $Sn_\epsilon(\mathcal{F}^b)$ be the s-default closure of $\mathcal{F}^b$ under S within ϵ. Define a statistical default inference chain on $\mathcal{F}^b$ within ϵ as a sequence of ϵ-bounded s-default conclusions from $\mathcal{F}^b$, $\langle (B_1)_{\epsilon_1}, \ldots, (B_n)_{\epsilon_n} \rangle$. If $(C)_{\epsilon_m} \in Sn_\epsilon(\mathcal{F}^b)$, then there is an s-default inference chain $\langle (B_1)_{\epsilon_1}, \ldots, (B_n)_{\epsilon_n}, (C)_{\epsilon_m} \rangle$ of s-defaults on $\mathcal{F}^b$ that yields $(C)_{\epsilon_m}$ as an ϵ-bounded conclusion.*

THEOREM 3 (Wheeler 2004) *Let $\mathcal{F}^b$ be a set of bounded sentences, C_{ϵ_m} a bounded sentence and the function $Cn_\epsilon(\mathcal{F}^b)$ be the ϵ-bound closure of $\mathcal{F}^b$. Define a deductive inference chain as a sequence of ϵ-bounded consequences,*

$\langle (B_1)_{\epsilon_1}, \ldots, (B_n)_{\epsilon_n}, (C)_{\epsilon_m} \rangle$ of $\mathcal{F}^b$. If $(C)_{\epsilon_m} \in Cn_\epsilon(\mathcal{F}^b)$, then there is an inference chain $(B_1)_{\epsilon_1}, \ldots, (B_n)_{\epsilon_n}, (C)_{\epsilon_m} \rangle$ of deductions on $\mathcal{F}^b$ that yields $(C)_{\epsilon_m}$ as an ϵ-bounded conclusion.

THEOREM 4 (Wheeler 2004) *If $\mathcal{F}^b$ is a set of 0-bounded sentences, $\mathcal{F}$ is set of sentences such that $Crop(\mathcal{F}^b) = \mathcal{F}$, then $Cn_\epsilon(\mathcal{F}^b) = Cn(\mathcal{F})$.*

THEOREM 5 (Wheeler 2004) *Let $\mathcal{F}^b$ be a set of bounded sentences, let $(A)_{\epsilon_1}, (B)_{\epsilon_2}, (C)_{\epsilon_3}$ and $(A_i)_{\epsilon_4}$ be ϵ-bounded counterparts to sentences $A, B, C, A_i \in \mathcal{L}$, and let $\Delta_S = \langle W, S \rangle$ at ϵ be a closed statistical default theory. Define*

- *For all $(A_i)_{\epsilon_{A_i}} \in W, \epsilon_{A_i} = 0$.*

- *$\mathcal{F}_0^b = W$, and for $i \geq 0$,*

- *$\mathcal{F}_{i+1}^b = Cn_\epsilon(\mathcal{F}_i^b) \cup \{(C)_{\epsilon_C} | \frac{(A)_{\epsilon_A}:(B_1)_{\epsilon_1},\ldots,(B_n)_{\epsilon_n}}{(C)_{\epsilon_C}} \epsilon_s) \in S$, where $(A)_{\epsilon_A} \in \mathcal{F}_i^b$ and $\neg B_1, \ldots, \neg B_n \notin Crop(\mathcal{F}^b)$ and $\epsilon_A + \epsilon_s \leq \epsilon\}$.*

Then $\mathcal{F}^b$ is a statistical extension for Δ_S at ϵ iff $\mathcal{F}^b = \bigcup_{0 \leq i \leq \infty} \mathcal{F}_i^b$.

BIBLIOGRAPHY

[Conee, 1992] E. Conee. Preface paradox. In J. Dancy and E. Sosa, editors, *A Companion to Epistemology*, Oxford, 1992. Blackwell Publishers.

[Delgrande et al., 1994] J.P. Delgrande, T. Schaub, and W.K. Jackson. Alternative approaches to default logic. *Artificial Intelligence*, 70:167–237, 1994.

[Douven, 2002] I. Douven. A new solution to the paradoxes of rational acceptability. *The British Journal for the Philosophy of Science*, 53(3):391–410, 2002.

[Foley, 1992] R. Foley. The epistemology of belief and the epistemology of degrees of belief. *American Philosophical Quarterly*, 29:111–121, 1992.

[Gabbay and Smets, 1998] D. Gabbay and P. Smets, editors. *Handbook on Defeasible Reasoning and Uncertainty Management Systems*. Kluwer Academic Press, Dordrecht, 1998.

[Hawthorne and Bovens, 1999] J. Hawthorne and L. Bovens. The preface, the lottery, and the logic of belief. *Mind*, 108:241–264, 1999.

[Kyburg (Jr.), 1997] H.E. Kyburg (Jr.). The rule of adjunction and rational inference. *Journal of Philosophy*, 94:109–25, 1997.

[Kyburg, 1961] H.E. Kyburg. *Probability and the Logic of Rational Belief*. Wesleyan University Press, Middletown, 1961.

[Makinson, 1965] D.C. Makinson. The paradox of the preface. *Analysis*, 25:205–207, 1965.

[Marek and Truszczyński, 1991] V.W. Marek and M. Truszczyński. *Nonmonotonic Logic*. Springer-Verlag, Berlin, 1991.

[Nilsson, 1986] N.J. Nilsson. Probabilistic logic. *Artificial Intelligence*, 28(1):71–87, 1986.

[Pollock, 1993] J.L. Pollock. Justification and defeat. *Artificial Intelligence*, 67:377–407, 1993.

[Ramsey, 1931] F.P. Ramsey. *The foundations of mathematics and other essays*, volume 1. Humanities Press, New York, 1931.

[Reiter and Criscuolo, 1981] R. Reiter and G. Criscuolo. On interacting defaults. In *Proceedings of IJCAI-81*, pages 270–276, Vancouver, BC, 1981.

[Reiter, 1980] R. Reiter. A logic for default reasoning. *Artificial Intelligence*, 13(1):81–132, 1980.

[Savage, 1972] L. Savage. *Foundations of Statistics*. Dover, New York, 1972.

[Wheeler and Pereira, 2004] G.R. Wheeler and L.M. Pereira. Epistemology and artificial intelligence. *Journal of Applied Logic*, 2(4):469–493, 2004.

[Wheeler, 2004] G.R. Wheeler. A resource bounded default logic. In J. Delgrande and T. Schaub, editors, *Proceedings of the 10th International Workshop on Non-Monotonic Reasoning (NMR 2004)*, pages 416–422, Whistler, British Columbia, Canada, 2004.

Gregory R. Wheeler
Centro de Inteligência Artificial (CENTRIA)
Departamento de Informática, Universidade Nova de Lisboa
Caparica, Portugal
Email: greg@di.fct.unl.pt

www.ingramcontent.com/pod-product-compliance
Lightning Source LLC
LaVergne TN
LVHW042331060326
832902LV00006B/96